DAILY GUIDEPOSTS

2018

New York

ZONDERVAN

Daily Guideposts 2018
Copyright © 2017 by Guideposts. All rights reserved.

Requests for information should be addressed to:
Zondervan, 3900 Sparks Dr. SE, Grand Rapids, Michigan 49546

ISBN 978-0-310-34647-0 (hardcover); ISBN 978-0-310-34652-4 (leather edition); ISBN 978-0-310-34648-7 (large print); ISBN 978-0-310-62925-2 (special edition); ISBN 978-0-310-35028-6 (ebook)

Acknowledgments: Every attempt has been made to credit the sources of copyrighted material used in this book. If any such acknowledgment has been inadvertently omitted or miscredited, receipt of such information would be appreciated.

Scripture quotations marked CEB are taken from the Common English Bible. Copyright © 2011 Common English Bible. Scripture quotations marked CEV are taken from the Contemporary English Version. Copyright © 1991, 1992, 1995 by American Bible Society. Used by permission. Scripture quotations marked ESV are taken from the ESV® Bible (The Holy Bible, English Standard Version®). Copyright © 2001 by Crossway, a publishing ministry of Good News Publishers. Used by permission. All rights reserved. Scripture quotations marked GNT are taken from the Good News Translation in Today's English Version—Second Edition. Copyright 1992 by American Bible Society. Used by permission. Scripture quotations marked ISV are taken from the *Holy Bible, International Standard Version*. Copyright © 1995-2014 by ISV Foundation. All rights reserved internationally. Scripture quotations marked JPS are taken from *Tanakh: A New Translation of the Holy Scriptures according to the Traditional Hebrew Text*. Copyright © 1985 by the Jewish Publication Society. All rights reserved. Scripture quotations marked KJV are taken from the King James Version. Public domain. Scripture quotations marked MSG are taken from *The Message*. Copyright © by Eugene H. Peterson 1993, 1994, 1995, 1996, 2000, 2001, 2002. Used by permission of NavPress. All rights reserved. Represented by Tyndale House Publishers, Inc. Scripture quotations marked NAS are taken from the New American Standard Bible®. Copyright © 1960, 1962, 1963, 1968, 1971, 1972, 1973, 1975, 1977, 1995 by The Lockman Foundation. Used by permission. (www.Lockman.org). Scripture quotations marked NCV are taken from the New Century Version®. © 2005 by Thomas Nelson. Used by permission. All rights reserved. Scripture quotations marked NIrV are taken from the Holy Bible, New International Reader's Version®, NIrV®. Copyright © 1995, 1996, 1998 by Biblica, Inc.® Used by permission of Zondervan. All rights reserved worldwide. www.Zondervan.com. The "NIrV" and "New International Reader's Version" are trademarks registered in the United States Patent and Trademark Office by Biblica, Inc.® Scripture quotations marked NIV are taken from The Holy Bible, New International Version®, NIV®. Copyright © 1973, 1978, 1984, 2011 by Biblica, Inc.® Used by permission of Zondervan. All rights reserved worldwide. www.Zondervan.com. The "NIV" and "New International Version" are trademarks registered in the United States Patent and Trademark Office by Biblica, Inc.® Scripture quotations marked NKJV are taken from the New King James Version®. © 1982 by Thomas Nelson. Used by permission. All rights reserved. Scripture quotations marked NLT are taken from the Holy Bible, New Living Translation. © 1996, 2004, 2007, 2013, 2015 by Tyndale House Foundation. Used by permission of Tyndale House Publishers, Inc., Carol Stream, Illinois 60188. All rights reserved. The Scripture quotations marked NRSV are taken from the New Revised Standard Version Bible. Copyright © 1989 National Council of the Churches of Christ in the United States of America. Used by permission. All rights reserved. Scripture quotations marked RSV are taken from the Revised Standard Version of the Bible. Copyright © 1946, 1952, and 1971 National Council of the Churches of Christ in the United States of America. Used by permission. All rights reserved. Scripture quotations marked TLB are taken from The Living Bible. Copyright © 1971 by Tyndale House Publishers, Inc., Carol Stream, Illinois 60188. All rights reserved.

Fellowship Corner photos: Lisa Bogart photo by Lisa Vosper; Mark Collins photo by Kathryn Hyslop; Brian Doyle photo by Jerry Hart; Julie Garmon photo by Brad Newton; Edward Grinnan photo by Amy Etra; Rick Hamlin photo by Julie Brown; Jim Hinch photo by Martin Klimek; Debbie Macomber photo by Deborah Feingold; Erin MacPherson photo by Bloom Austin; Roberta Messner photo by Craig Cunningham; Rebecca Ondov photo by Deborah K. Hamilton; Natalie Perkins photo by Kris Rogers Photography; GingerRue photo by Patrick Jacks; Daniel Schantz photo by Sherry Wallis; Gail Thorell Schilling photo by Doug Schwarz; Melody Bonnette Swang photo by Crystal Logiudice; Jon Sweeney photo by Pamela Jordan; Marilyn Turk photo by Sarah Clauson; Marion Bond West photo by Michael Schwarz.

Cover and interior design by Müllerhaus
Cover photos by Shutterstock and iStock
Monthly page opener photos by Shutterstock
Indexed by Patricia Woodruff
Typeset by Aptara

First printing July 2017 / Printed in the United States of America

Hello, friends.

Welcome to *Daily Guideposts 2018*. We're so pleased that you are joining us this year on a journey of inspiration and connection, as our writers share from the heart and reflect on all the ways—big and small—that God is at work in their lives.

This was a year when many of our contributors felt God's unfailing love: they felt it in joyous moments, such as when they were reunited with family, or when a beloved friend bestowed forgiveness, or in the closeness of a spouse, the companionship of a furry friend, a rising sun enjoyed on a back porch. God has been present for our community in bleaker times too: when a good friend passed away, when a family crisis could not be solved easily, when brokenness remained. In all times, God's love was steadfast.

This year's theme is "Unfailing Love": "May your unfailing love be with us, Lord, even as we put our hope in you" (Psalm 33:22, NIV). As we read this Psalm, we see how hope in God is closely linked to belief in His love. We pray that you will experience God's love in new ways as you spend daily time with Him. And we are very happy to welcome two new writers: Amy Eddings from Ada, Ohio, and Vicki Kuyper from Phoenix, Arizona. We also said farewell to some friends this year: Sam Adriance, Karen Barber, Katie Ganshert, and Jeff Japinga. Also, this is the last *Daily Guideposts* that Brian Doyle will appear in; he passed away on May 28, 2017, when we were going to press. We will miss his humor, wit, and ability to point us back to God's mercy and love with such grace and beauty.

Our *Daily Guideposts* writers welcomed God into all the details of their lives—from trusting His timing, to delighting in His gifts, to believing in His unfailing love in all circumstances. You'll hear how Rhoda Blecker continues to heal and grow after the death of her husband, Keith; how Logan Eliasen transitions to the demands of full-time law school; how Marion Bond West loves her two sons, even from afar, and welcomes someone new into her church community; how Ashley Kappel exults in the joy of her two young children.

We have five special series to bring to you this year. Julia Attaway tells us how she kept her family together and her faith in God in "Confidence in Difficulty." Julie Garmon shares how she came out of her depression and anxiety and started to see "The Beauty of Simplicity." Marci Alborghetti recounts the story of God growing her in grace and hope by using a serious accident and subsequent recovery for "Falling into Grace." During Holy Week, walk with Carol Kuykendall and her friend in "Preparing for the Resurrection." Jim Hinch reflects upon the coming of Christ in "Light in Our Darkness."

Get ready to greet God each morning, watching and praying for His unfailing love to show up in your life and your heart.

Faithfully yours,
Editors of Guideposts

P.S. We love hearing from you! Let us know what *Daily Guideposts* means to you by e-mailing DailyGPEditors@guideposts.org or writing to Guideposts Books & Inspirational Media, 110 William Street, New York, New York 10038. You can also keep up with your *Daily Guideposts* friends on Facebook.com/dailyguideposts.

Especially for You!
Get one-year instant access to the digital edition of *Daily Guideposts* delivered straight to your e-mail. You'll be able to enjoy its daily inspiration and Scripture anytime, anywhere, on your computer, phone, or tablet. Visit DailyGuideposts.org/DG2018 and enter this code: peace.

JANUARY

Your love, Lord, reaches to the heavens,
your faithfulness to the skies.

—Psalm 36:5 (NIV)

Monday, January 1

A wise son makes a glad father.... —Proverbs 10:1 (NKJV)

The Tournament of Roses Parade! Here I was, wedged into the Pasadena bleachers with my husband, taking in a New Year's celebration I had seen previously only on TV. Fantastic floats covered with millions of flowers rolled along Colorado Boulevard, rose fragrance wafting in their wake. High-stepping palominos bore their riders on flashing silver saddles. One marching band had scarcely passed our stand before another band's brassy march drifted through the sun-drenched morning.

This New Year's celebration capped our first Christmas holiday with Thad's California family. Now we would drive back to our home in Wyoming. Frankly, I was ready for quiet time after a week in the exuberant chaos of a household overstuffed with Thad's six madcap siblings, spouses, and erratic comings and goings. So when Thad's dad asked us to stay another day or two, I resisted, to no avail. We had no pressing obligations back home, so my husband insisted we stay to humor his father.

Dad sensed my frustration and cajoled, "In a year or two, you'll never remember staying here an extra day."

Ah, but I do remember, even though that was thirty-eight years ago. Mercifully, during those intervening years, I evolved from a self-absorbed bride to the tuned-in mother of four adult children. Only now do I understand the pang of parting with them after even the briefest visit. Though both my husband and his father have passed on, they awakened me to the precious gift of presence. *My* presence. Once a year, a beautiful parade reminds me.

*Loving God, in this coming year, may I better discern where
You need me to be—and to be there gladly.*
—Gail Thorell Schilling

Digging Deeper: Exodus 20:12; Proverbs 22:6

Now faith is the substance of things hoped for, the evidence of things not seen. —Hebrews 11:1 (NKJV)

I keep a favorite necklace hanging from the mirror of the vanity in my bedroom. The long chain holds a glass dome pendant that contains a single mustard seed. On the back is Matthew 17:20 (ESV): *"If you have faith like a grain of mustard seed... nothing will be impossible for you."*

I wear the necklace when I'm worried about the outcome of things.

Last night, in the midst of a dream, I heard the necklace fall. I didn't think much of it, but this morning when I went to pick it up, I noticed it had broken. That glass dome snapped right off the backing, and the mustard seed was gone.

I searched the surface of the vanity behind my jewelry box and then got down on my hands and knees, thinking it'd be easy to find and fix. I ran my hands on the floorboards and got back up to search the top of the vanity. No luck; it was gone. I tried to shrug it off, but for some reason I couldn't get the broken necklace out of my mind.

I could replace the mustard seed, but somehow that didn't seem right. I went back to the vanity and searched one more time, and just as I was getting up I thought, *Faith is believing in what is unseen. Fasten the glass dome back in place to help you have faith, even with the seed gone.*

Heavenly Father, because of You, broken things aren't truly broken at all. Even when the mustard seed is missing, it's all the more reason to have faith.
—Sabra Ciancanelli

Digging Deeper: John 20:29; Hebrews 11:1

RELYING ON GOD'S UNFAILING LOVE
Peace in Your Presence

On the day I called, you answered me; my strength of soul you increased.
—Psalm 138:3 (ESV)

Just a little lump.

It's amazing how quickly life can shift out of orbit, how a mundane day can suddenly become anything but. All it takes is one fragment of a second when something just doesn't feel right.

Lord, why? How? my soul screams. I never imagined this for my dear friend Sarah.

Suddenly a whir of doctor's appointments and biopsies, of friends calling to give advice, of doctors calling to give results, of treatment calendars and care calendars and a chicken-poppy-seed casserole in the oven from the next-door neighbor as you hold hands and pray on the couch.

Big words like *cancer* and *chemotherapy* and *radiation* being tossed around like pinballs, big feelings creeping in and overtaking what was simply joy and peace only days ago. Yet You are here, Lord.

In those crazy, mixed-up moments when I don't know what to say or what to do or how to act other than to look my friend in her eyes and pull her close and hold on tight. You are here.

When she doesn't respond, when words can't be found, when the gap between us is bigger than it has ever been. You are here.

In sickness and in hope and tears and sweat and pain. In every moment. You are here. And in Your presence, peace flows.

> *Father God, thank You for comfort even in the midst of the hardest days. You are the strength I need when I have no strength to walk forward. Amen.*
> —Erin MacPherson

Digging Deeper: Romans 8:16–17, 38–39

Wait for the Lord; be strong, and let your heart take courage; wait for the Lord! —Psalm 27:14 (ESV)

I waste a lot of time waiting. Waiting for Micah to get ready so I can drive my daughter to school. Waiting in car pool to retrieve her each afternoon. Waiting in line at the grocery store. Waiting to talk to my husband after his workday. Today, I'm waiting at the tire store while they rotate my tires.

I grab my smartphone to search how many hours the average person spends waiting, when another customer walks in. The cadence of a cane makes me look up from my time-wasting research. A young, slender man in fatigue pants limps across the linoleum. His cropped haircut makes me wonder if he's military. I go back to my search.

Moments later, he's at the computer in front of me.

"All four tires need to be replaced," says the salesman. He shows the customer a quote on the computer.

"I can't spend that much," I hear him mutter.

The salesman suggests a less expensive brand. The customer shakes his head. I'm curious why their business is taking place at the register directly in front of me. There are three other checkout desks.

"Just two," says the customer and hands over his debit card.

"Replace the others as soon as possible," warns the salesman.

The man takes a seat across the room. I scroll an article to discover how much time Americans waste waiting. I hear a voice inside my mind: *Pay for the other two tires.*

Holy chills run down my back. I'm not wasting time waiting. I'm waiting for a divine opportunity such as this one.

> *Lord, let me remember that I'm not just waiting;*
> *I'm waiting to hear from You.*
> —Stephanie Thompson

Digging Deeper: Psalm 145:15–16; 1 Corinthians 1:7

Friday, January 5

FALLING INTO GRACE: Holding On to Faith

"The Lord is my strength and my might, and he has become my salvation; this is my God, and I will praise him...." —Exodus 15:2 (NRSV)

I had a pretty spectacular fall. Late and rushing, as always, I'd run up the two cement steps to our apartment building and, preparing to wrench open the heavy door, braced all my weight against it...and then missed the handle. I catapulted backward over the steps, landing on the sidewalk. Only slightly less searing than the pain was the realization that everything in my life had changed because of one stupid mishap. Waiting for my husband, Charlie, and the ambulance, I felt agony, humiliation, terror.

Please, God, was all I could think, *change this! Take away this pain, this frightening helplessness!*

And now two strong women were manipulating my body for the imaging machine. With each X-ray they grew gentler, and I grew more afraid. One of them snatched up a phone on the wall and said a few quiet, terse words: "We need more pictures."

As dread threatened to overwhelm me, the thought came that this fear and pain were just fractions of what Jesus must have felt in those hours between the Last Supper and His death. Yet He put all His trust in the Father.

Please, God, help me to do the same.

As one X-ray tech, now very careful, moved me for more images, she noticed the cross around my neck.

"Do you need to take it off?" I asked.

Her eyes met and held mine. "We're not taking that off."

Lord, thank You for reminders of how much
I need You and need to trust You.
—Marci Alborghetti

Digging Deeper: Genesis 50:19–20

"I hereby command you: Be strong and courageous; do not be frightened or dismayed, for the Lord your God is with you wherever you go."
—Joshua 1:9 (NRSV)

The forecast called for a blizzard. *What should we do?* Kate was away at a conference, and the kids and I had made plans to see the new Star Wars movie. Snow began falling the night before. It was pretty thick by Saturday morning.

"What do you say? Do we go for it?" I asked Frances and Benji. Inwardly, I had misgivings. *Was this a fun adventure or Dad being reckless?*

"Yes!" they said excitedly.

I thought about how long we'd waited to see this movie, how much we'd looked forward to it. Surely God was present in our collective yearning.

We donned snow gear and plunged outside. Wind blew pellets in our faces. We trudged along powdery-white sidewalks, practically alone on streets usually packed on a weekend. Subways were still running. We took a train downtown and emerged into even more snow. The theater was hard to see through the horizontal veil, and we were practically alone in it. The Star Wars music struck up. The kids grabbed my arms. The moment at last!

We loved every minute of it. We emerged breathless and made it home in time to find out that the subways would be shutting down soon. We'd timed it perfectly.

Actually, God had timed it perfectly. I'd worried I was being foolish. But, really, it was just snow. And the looks on the kids' faces—well, deep yearnings like that don't come from nowhere. We had trusted our hearts, and in doing so we'd trusted God to guide us well.

*Help me to know when to wait, Lord, and
when to venture out in obedience to Your call.*
—Jim Hinch

Digging Deeper: Psalm 25:4–5; Revelation 14:12

Let them praise his name with dancing and make music to him with timbrel and harp. —Psalm 149:3 (NIV)

I have a song for you," said one of the women from church.

"Great!" I said, assuming she meant I should sing it. "Let me hear it and see if it's in my vocal range."

"I don't want you to sing it," she clarified. "I want you to dance to it."

I looked at her, confused. While I used to do gymnastics in my youth and love to dance for fun, I'd never performed in front of an audience.

"I'm not a dancer like you," I said, laughing.

"That doesn't matter," she said. "This song is for you."

I took a moment but just shrugged my shoulders and said, "Sure. Why not!"

We arranged our first rehearsal.

Putting the dance together, connecting the moves and emotions with the words to the song, was therapeutic. I was translating pain, suffering, prayer, healing, and joy through movement.

The day of the dance, I stood waiting in my long leotard and flowing skirt. For a moment I wondered what I was doing. Here I was, a woman in my forties who had never performed a dance before, standing in front of an audience.

I walked onto the stage, and the music began. I no longer felt self-conscious. The dance was simply a prayer I needed to express. And as my mother, in tears, hugged me afterward, I knew more than ever it was something I needed to share.

Lord, I praise You for all You have done. Thank You
for letting me express that in many ways.
—Karen Valentin

Digging Deeper: Psalm 30:11

"Yet turn, O Lord my God, to the prayer and supplication of Your servant...." —1 Kings 8:28 (JPS)

When my husband, Keith, and I moved from Los Angeles to Bellingham, Washington, we brought with us some well-loved knickknacks and pieces of art. However, I wanted something for the new house that had never been in the old one. In a museum gift shop, I found a framed paper cut, edged in lace and painted with what seemed like a perfect prayer: "May this home be a place of happiness and health, generosity and hope."

I bought it at once, and one of the first things we did when we moved in was to hang it in a prominent place by the front door.

Until Keith got sick, it seemed that prayer was working very well. Suddenly the "health" part was struggling. So were my "happiness" and, ultimately, my "hope." As I withdrew into myself, the "generosity" part just went away by itself. After Keith died, it got so I averted my eyes when I passed the paper cut—it just wasn't my prayer any longer.

Then a friend called me because she needed help, and I began to spend time with her, trying to cheer her up, opening my home to her when she needed anything, giving her things she could use, sharing as much time with her as I could.

One day I happened to look at the paper cut, and now that I was able to be generous again, God was showing me that the other parts of the prayer were possible too.

> *Let me be an instrument of Your generosity, God,*
> *just as You are the source of all generosity to me.*
> —Rhoda Blecker

Digging Deeper: 2 Samuel 7:27

Tuesday, January 9

A soft answer turns away wrath, but a harsh word stirs up anger.
—Proverbs 15:1 (ESV)

After a long week that included several conflicts where I might have pushed people too hard when I should have backed off, it was a relief to take our young golden retriever, Gracie, to her favorite dog run.

Today she picked out a big yellow Lab to play with. It took her a minute or so to get Elijah interested, but that's Gracie for you. She's persistent when it comes to making friends. Soon she and her new pal chased a ball and ran after each other. Then they started to wrestle. Gracie was getting the better of Elijah when he snapped. Elijah lunged and snarled. Immediately both his owner and I were on our feet, separating the dogs before any damage could be done.

I assumed that the friendship with Elijah was over before it began. But eventually Gracie tried to get Elijah to play again, woofing at him and nibbling on his ear. As before, he couldn't resist. This time, just as Elijah was starting to get aggressive, Gracie backed off. She let Elijah calm down and then went back for more play. Again, just as he was reaching his boiling point, Gracie broke it off, galloping all the way around the perimeter of the run and barking happily. *How amazing*, I thought. *She figured out exactly Elijah's tipping point and then respected it so that he wouldn't get upset and they could remain friends.*

When Elijah's owner finally leashed him up to go, the big Lab strained to stay and play some more with Gracie. She gave him a playful swat as he was led away, and I gave my golden girl a big hug for teaching me a little something about how to play better with humans.

> *Lord, teach me how to back off when things grow heated,*
> *to be guided by You instead of by my anger and frustration.*
> —Edward Grinnan

Digging Deeper: Romans 12:18; Ephesians 4:31–32; Colossians 4:6

For You are with me; Your rod and Your staff, they comfort me.
—Psalm 23:4 (NKJV)

I winced when the chiropractor put his finger on my spine. "I can't fix this. The vertebrae are fine. This is a disk issue. You need surgery."

No, God! Not again! I limped to my pickup. I was never going to have another surgery, not after the first operation for a ruptured disk four years ago had failed. I'd given up the life I loved as a cattle rancher. *I have nothing left, God. You have taken everything away from me.*

I texted my brother: "Pray 4 me. I need strength."

He replied immediately. "Will do."

I called my husband. "Maybe this is a blessing in disguise," he said. "Your back hasn't been right for years. Maybe this time you'll be healed."

I didn't share his optimism. I'd already tried Western medicine, Eastern medicine, and everything in between. I tried different doctors, no doctors, and doctors I wasn't too sure about. I did natural cures, yoga, vitamins, joint solutions, tilt tables, back exercises, brain exercises, and meditation.

Some things helped a little, but nothing really worked. I had long ago accepted my limitations. I'd even found joy here. But this new explosion of pain left me without hope.

Suddenly, unexpected peace stopped my tears. Confused, I glanced at my phone, which I'd silenced. "You're on the prayer chain at church," my brother texted.

I could feel the prayers. The one thing that had gotten me through these painful years was my faith that God was behind this and was guiding me to a new place of His choosing. He was with me. I wasn't alone. I prayed out loud:

> *Lord, I'm closer to You now than ever before. Even if I never heal,*
> *I would rather be crippled with You than stand tall without You.*
> —Erika Bentsen

Digging Deeper: Genesis 26:24; Deuteronomy 31:6; 2 Kings 6:16–17;
1 Chronicles 28:20; Psalm 27

Thursday, January 11

Therefore encourage one another and build up one another....
—1 Thessalonians 5:11 (NAS)

Talk about a late bloomer. I still type on an IBM Selectric from 1984. Progress ran off and left me while I thought maybe the computer thing wouldn't catch on.

My daughter Julie has gently begged me to get a computer. I was sure it was too late. I'd never learn.

Julie began coaxing me to at least get a tablet. I grew weary of saying no. One day, I agreed to just walk into an electronics store. It's a scary place for me. Not Julie. She goes there often and asks complicated questions and nods confidently at the answers. "I've prayed for the right salesperson for you, Mother."

She spotted a fella way across the store and dragged me behind her. "This is my mother," she told the young man like I was Mother of the Year.

"I'm Jeremy." He smiled.

Julie beamed at me as though his name, being my son's name, was a sure sign from God. When I became too tired to argue, I sighed. "I'll take it."

They both lit up like neon signs, and he asked simply, "What color?"

Oh, how I perked up. I'm all about color. "Gold," I told him knowledgeably.

"Mine's gold too." He grinned. "Something else I need to tell you, ma'am. You have a good attitude."

"Whatever do you mean?"

"Well, I could tell from way across the store when y'all came in that you are teachable."

Suddenly energized, I thanked Jeremy and asked Julie to take my picture with him—on my new tablet, of course!

Oh, Father, thank You for salespeople who encourage fragile beginners.
—Marion Bond West

Digging Deeper: Romans 15:5; Hebrews 10:25

Teach them to your children, talking about them when you sit at home and when you walk along the road.... —Deuteronomy 11:19 (NIV)

A colleague called to ask my advice. "I have to give my daughter some bad news, but I don't know how to approach it."

"Well," I replied, "don't make a production out of it, which might scare her. Just go for a walk together and then say, 'By the way, I need to tell you...'"

Later I thought about my own parents, who had such naturalness about their parenting. Oh, they were vigilant, with high standards for me, but they were never artificial or overbearing.

My father would come to my Little League games, just to enjoy the game. He cheered me if I got a hit, but he never scolded me when I flubbed. We were there to have fun, and we did, win or lose.

He didn't "take" me fishing. He "went" fishing, and I tagged along. When I saw how much he enjoyed it, I was hooked.

I was an introvert, but my father, a minister, never forced me into the public eye. He just took me with him on his rounds and introduced me to everyone. "This is my boy, Danny. He's a fine fisherman." I felt safe with Dad beside me.

My first report cards were terrible, but my mother never shamed me. She helped me with the hard subjects. "Just do your best," she said. "That's all we ask of you." Eventually, I made the honor roll and went on to become a college professor.

When I saw my colleague a week later, she said, "I took your advice, and it went really well!"

I smiled, feeling a deep sense of gratitude for good parents who gave me a happy childhood, a legacy of enchanting memories.

Lord, bless all the good parents who look to You for guidance.
—Daniel Schantz

Digging Deeper: Proverbs 13:21; Colossians 3:4

And let us consider how we may spur one another on toward love and good deeds. —Hebrews 10:24 (NIV)

What do you think?"

Our oldest son, Logan, is home for the weekend. His first year of law school is demanding, and homecomings are rare. On this day, he's bought an overcoat for upcoming internship interviews and dons it.

Before I answer, ten-year-old Gabriel rounds the corner. "I like it! May I try?"

Logan removes the black wool coat and holds it for his little brother. Gabriel sticks in one arm. Then the other. His hands are lost in fabric, and the hem skims the floor. Gabriel looks down, blond bangs falling forward. He wants to grow up to be like his big brother.

I think back to the days when my boys clomped around in their daddy's work boots. They'd be knee-high in steel-toed leather, each step an effort. But they persisted. There can be a desire, in one's center, to grow to be like those whom we hold in high esteem.

It's quite like my relationships with my spiritual sisters. There's the friend who reminds me to pray in all circumstances and another who speaks powerful hope into my plaguing worries because she knows that we belong to the One Who overcomes.

I want to be like these women, to stretch into similar spiritual skin, walking with the Lord being the heartbeat of who I am.

"I don't think it fits," Gabriel says. He bolts to the bedroom to look in the mirror.

Logan smiles and I do too. Gabriel doesn't fit into his brother's coat today. But one day he will.

Thank You, Father, for those who encourage us
to grow in relationship with You. Amen.
—Shawnelle Eliasen

Digging Deeper: Proverbs 27:17; Acts 2:46; 1 Thessalonians 5:11

"Come to me, all you who are weary and burdened, and I will give you rest." —Matthew 11:28 (NIV)

It's the second Sunday of the month, and I have nursery duty at church. I always sign up for the babies! It's a great opportunity to get lots of good cuddles while the parents enjoy a quiet worship service.

Today, I have only one baby. He's "fat and fine," as my grandmother would have said. Thirteen months old and lots to love. I can hardly wait to get my hands on him and tickle those adorable piggy toes! "He woke up at five thirty this morning, so he could really use a nap," his mother tells me before she leaves.

It's not long after she's out the door that the baby experiences separation anxiety. "Now, now. I understand, sweet doll," I say, holding him close. He's wailing at this point, and his eyes are beyond tired. I hold him close, but he fights me, resisting the sleep he doesn't realize he so desperately needs. My rocking chair keeps a steady pace, and I hum along with the hymn I can hear from the auditorium. The baby keeps on crying, but as I continue to rock him, he puts up less and less of a fight until finally he is limp in my arms, his tired little eyes closed and his face a relaxed picture of contentment.

For the next hour, I rock this precious gift on loan to me. When worship is over and his mother returns, we almost hate to transfer him to her arms and disturb his deep slumber.

Lord, how many times have I been stubborn and not heeded Your wisdom! Thank You for holding me close. Thank You for the perfect peace You offer when I trust in You.
—Ginger Rue

Digging Deeper: Psalm 46:10; Isaiah 26:4

Monday, January 15

I beseech you therefore, brethren, by the mercies of God, that ye present your bodies a living sacrifice, holy, acceptable unto God, which is your reasonable service. —Romans 12:1 (KJV)

During a visit to my parents' home in Maryland, I ran out to a local grocery store for a few items. As I pushed my cart, stopping periodically to grab things off the shelves, I noticed several stately young African American women who appeared to be near my own age. They laughed with each other, but there was something very dignified and, at the same time, familiar about them.

When I finished my shopping, I found myself in line behind them. Still mulling over how I knew them, I began to place my items on the checkout counter. As I did so, one of the women leaned over and placed her checkbook on the counter near my items. When she began to write, I noticed the last name printed on the check: Evers. I realized immediately who the women were: they were the daughters of slain civil rights leaders Medgar Evers and Dr. Martin Luther King Jr.

Not wanting to disturb their privacy, I did not introduce myself to them. I knew how much their fathers had sacrificed fighting for the rights of others. Both men knew the price of their efforts would likely be death. But until that moment, I had not thought about how much their spouses and children had surely sacrificed.

That extra something I noticed about the women, I think, was courage and determination. They had overcome heartbreak and carried on the legacies of their fathers.

Lord, bless the lives of pastors, leaders, and their families who serve to make life better for everyone. Shower them with goodness and mercy.
—Sharon Foster

Digging Deeper: Psalm 51:17; Ephesians 5:2; 1 Peter 2:5

"Behold, the virgin shall be with child, and bear a Son, and they shall call His name Immanuel," which is translated, "God with us."
—Matthew 1:23 (NKJV)

Every Tuesday morning several colleagues and I push chairs into the breakroom for prayer. It's brief: a snippet of Scripture and then we go around the circle praying about our teaching and any larger issues affecting it—trends, politics, world events. I'm guessing each of us is also secretly praying for whatever big bad things are going on in our lives and families.

That's, in any case, what I do. And it doesn't stop there. As I leave the breakroom, secret prayers overwhelm me. You know the ones I mean: prayers concerning suffering that no one knows about, troubles you can't list among your church's prayer requests, seemingly unsolvable worries.

Whenever I pray this way, I pray the same, almost hopeless prayer: "Heavenly Father, heal it, fix it, make it go away!"

Today, it occurred to me that the Father had already answered such prayers with His plan to banish all suffering and make everything right in the end. In the meantime, He's sent His Son—not to cure this world's ills just now but to be with us in our anguish. Jesus is not the fix-all dad I'm envisioning when I pray for help but a brother who's suffered similar miseries: the terrifyingly small faiths of loved ones, betrayals, looming anxiety about the future, and feeling forsaken by the only One Who can solve His problems.

Recognizing God as my co-sufferer doesn't magically heal or repair my hidden problems or even banish them from my consciousness, but it does make me feel less alone. I know that, like the best of siblings, Jesus commiserates. He's *with* me in my misery, lamenting with, and for, me.

Brother Jesus, be with us in our most secret prayers!
—Patty Kirk

Digging Deeper: Isaiah 7:4–14; Revelation 21:1–5

Wednesday, January 17

THE BEAUTY OF SIMPLICITY
Trust Always Outshines Worry

Let the morning bring me word of your unfailing love, for I have put my trust in you.... —Psalm 143:8 (NIV)

During forty years of marriage, my husband, Rick, and I have argued about one thing in particular: I love being prepared and doing things ahead of schedule; Rick is laid-back and never worries.

One night, during the 11:00 p.m. news, the weatherman forecast the possibility of snow. "We better run to the grocery store," I said.

"Nah, it's not going to snow."

"What if it does? What if we lose power? The freezer's full of meat."

"Relax," he said.

"How? We could be homebound if a blizzard strikes."

Sure enough, the next morning the house was cold and dark. No power. No heat. I peered into our snow-covered backyard. "The weatherman and I were right," I said, annoyance creeping into my tone.

"I'll set up the generator," he replied, getting out of bed.

"What generator?"

"The one I bought a few years ago." Minutes later, Rick restored enough power to save the meat, keep his outdoor parakeets warm, and make coffee.

I'd doubted my husband would take care of me, the same way I'd doubted God could handle my fears and worries. Filled with admiration and gratitude, I crunched my way through our snowy yard, the air smelling woodsy, like home and wintertime and safety.

"I worried for nothing. Your survival skills are quite impressive."

Rick winked at me. "Just doing my job, ma'am."

Plenty of times, I've assumed You weren't doing Your job, Lord.
I'm sorry. You always have everything under control.
—Julie Garmon

Digging Deeper: Isaiah 45:6–7; Jeremiah 29:11

If I take the wings of the morning, and dwell in the uttermost parts of the sea; even there shall thy hand lead me.... —Psalm 139:9–10 (KJV)

I landed in the hospital for two weeks with a mysterious lung infection. The doctors were baffled. My room was filled with specialists, rheumatologists, cardiologists, internists, pulmonologists, asking me a roster of questions, checking the machine that monitored my dangerously low level of oxygen. I did my best to answer—in between gasps of air from a tank of oxygen. Family members sat with me; nurses and techs scurried in and out.

That first day my hopes plummeted. Despair seemed a bigger enemy than anything going on with my body. But the one thing I remembered, as I drifted in and out of a fitful sleep, was my twenty-five-year-old son, Timothy, reading the words of a psalm by my bedside.

Timothy left the second week, heading to South Africa for ten months of mission work. Fortunately, I came home at the end of that week, my fever gone, my lungs able to function again on their own, my energy returning. The doctors still couldn't give me a diagnosis, but that was all right. "They kept me alive," I told friends. "Prayers healed me."

I still wondered, though, about that prayer by my bedside… had it even happened? I e-mailed Tim, "Did you read a psalm to me in the hospital?"

"Yes, Dad," he e-mailed right back. He couldn't remember which psalm it was and I certainly couldn't, but one of his favorites is Psalm 139, with this wonderful passage about God's power: "Even the darkness is not dark to thee, the night is bright as the day; for darkness is as light with thee" (verse 12, RSV). In my time of despair my son had given me words of light.

> *Lord, give me the words I need—Your words—*
> *to offer comfort to those in despair.*
> —Rick Hamlin

Digging Deeper: Psalm 71:5–6; 2 Corinthians 4:8–9

Friday, January 19

Do everything in love. —1 Corinthians 16:14 (NIV)

A barista at my local café is truly love made visible. I take such delight watching Kristi interact with folks at the drive-through. She'll be hanging out the window, all smiles, as she inquires about the pets and children in the back of a truck or the camping gear strapped to the top of a station wagon.

One morning I could stand it no more. "You must really enjoy what you do," I said. "You never fail to make every person in your path feel cared for."

"I'll let you in on a little secret," Kristi told me. "When I'm working that intercom, I ask all the customers, 'How are you?' and if they don't answer or just say, 'a chai tea latte,' then I'm extra nice to them when they pull up to get their drinks. That's what keeps me happy all day long."

Kristi's response got me to thinking about others in my own path who leave the world better than they find it. Joe at the shoe-repair shop who stretches my flats to accommodate the tumors on my feet. Because of Joe's genuine caring, my feet don't hurt as much as they used to. Nor my heart.

Then there's the welcoming homeowner on the street where I shopped at an estate sale today. When everyone else placed "No Parking—Towing Enforced" messages in their yards, this person took a different approach. A colorful sign was positioned in a geranium-filled flowerpot that read, "Okay to park in my driveway. Enjoy the sale."

Just everyday people doing their best to make the world a better place. Simple as it sounds, I want to be one of them. Don't you?

> *In an oft-unfriendly world, Lord, help me*
> *to represent You with a heart full of love.*
> —Roberta Messner

Digging Deeper: Ephesians 6:7; Colossians 3:23

Behold, you are beautiful. . . . —Song of Solomon 4:1 (RSV)

I was expecting our first child—and feeling wretchedly unprepared. I knew nothing about babies! My husband and I had been living in Europe, writing travel stories. Now we were back in the United States, in a tiny New York apartment, learning words like *bassinet.* I could change a typewriter ribbon in a flash but change a diaper? How did you fold the thing? What if the safety pin sprang open?

In stark contrast to my ignorance, I knew that my mother-in-law was an authority on infant care, an author and lecturer on the subject. What would she think of my floundering efforts?

Little Scotty was three weeks old when Mother Sherrill came up to New York to see him. I'd tried to breastfeed, but doctors in 1950 labeled this practice "unsanitary" and prescribed formula with Scotty's first sneeze. This meant sterilizing bottles and measuring powder exactly. In my nervousness, preparing for the visit, I got the measurements wrong and then spilled most of the second batch on the hot stove while trying to fill the bottles. Scotty was screaming, and the apartment reeked of scorched milk when the doorbell rang.

Mother Sherrill took the crying baby in her arms where he quieted at once. "He's beautiful!" "How healthy he looks!" "How neat and clean you keep him!"

It was like this with each visit afterward. No criticism, not even the ordinary advice an experienced mother might give a new one. Only compliments on my exceptional mothering skills. I've wondered if her tongue didn't bleed from biting it at the many mistakes I'm sure she saw me make. And certainly I could have used her wisdom! My mother-in-law gave me a bigger gift though. She gave me confidence in myself.

> *If I have some expertise of my own now, Father,*
> *remind me that people need my caring most.*
> —Elizabeth Sherrill

Digging Deeper: Proverbs 15:1; 1 Thessalonians 5:11

Sunday, January 21

The angels are only spirit-messengers sent out to help and care for those who are to receive his salvation. —Hebrews 1:14 (TLB)

When I looked at Norma's condo for sale in Florida, she warned me that she intended to find just the right person who would love it as much as she had. When she agreed to sell it to me, I was thrilled and told her she was my guardian angel because she sold me the perfect place to thrive in my newly adopted state.

Our friendship flourished. Even though she was twenty years my senior, my husband, Jack, and I socialized with Norma and her husband over the years, dining, dancing, and enjoying parties together.

One night Norma slipped on the dance floor during a dinner-dance at the clubhouse. I stayed with her in the emergency room while the doctor stitched up her head. During the procedure, Norma whispered, "You are now *my* guardian angel."

I took my role very seriously. When Norma's husband died, I mourned with her. When she moved into assisted living, I took her out to lunch and visited her.

Soon after Norma died, I was disappointed that during the time I was out of town, her place was cleaned out. I was hoping I'd have something to remember her by.

Weeks later I saw something in my jewelry box: a note pinned to the only thing Norma had ever given me years earlier. "Pat, thank you for being my guardian angel. Wear this butterfly and think of me. Love you! Norma." As I touched the small, delicate piece of jewelry, it hit me. It wasn't the pin or anything else that Norma had possessed that was important. She had already left me with the best gift of all: the honor of being her guardian angel.

Lord, help me cherish gifts from the heart, knowing
they come with multiple blessings from You.
—Patricia Lorenz

Digging Deeper: Psalm 91:7–13; Hebrews 1:1–12

Better is a handful of quietness than two hands full of toil and a striving after wind. —Ecclesiastes 4:6 (ESV)

Feeling encumbered by possessions, I've been in a discard-it state of mind. Sorting items in a file cabinet, linen closet, food pantry. *Will I use it? Do I value it?* If not, I've been gifting, donating, trashing. Then I turned to a kitchen cupboard. *Do I need all these old food containers, stockpiled for leftovers?* Half of them were dropped into a bag for recycling.

But the removals themselves didn't make me feel less burdened. Yesterday the urge remained strong, as if my spirit itself were crying, "Purge." Setting my sights on an office bookcase, I went at it. "Out! Out!" I said, exhaling and tossing books in a box that I strained to lift. Before I reached for a cup of coffee, I pulled another book off the shelf. *Vitamins for the Soul: 200 Ways to Nurture Your Spiritual Life.* I'd occasionally perused it when looking for an inspirational quotation. Should I keep or toss the book that had collected dust for decades?

I found the answer, and more, on page one in an epigraph by Henri Frédéric Amiel: "The man who has no inner life is the slave of his surroundings." I read the pithy statement a second and third time, inhaling deeply.

To counterbalance my household obsession—*get it out!*—today I enjoyed a nourishing spiritual feast. After worshipping at church, I visited a museum, taking in the exciting offerings. Before dinner I read chapter one of the *Vitamins* book, which, by the way, I've decided to keep.

> *Dear Lord, help me to learn that tending my spirit is*
> *at least as important as tidying my surroundings.*
> —Evelyn Bence

Digging Deeper: Matthew 6:19–21, 25–33

Tuesday, January 23

We may think we are doing the right thing, but the Lord always knows what is in our hearts. —Proverbs 21:2 (CEV)

I arrived early to New York City for a meeting, but I went to the wrong building... or so I thought. A concierge directed me to the building across the street.

When I arrived, I asked the receptionist where my meeting was taking place. "Do you know what her name is?" she asked. "I do not," I said.

This is when things took a turn for the worse. The woman snapped, "You don't know your name?"

I was taken aback and replied, "I know *my* name! I thought you asked if I knew the name of the person coordinating the meeting."

Instead of accepting that I misunderstood her, she acted as if I was wrong and finally directed me back to the building I had just come from. As I was leaving, I said, "Wow, what an attitude!"

"*You* have an attitude!" she responded.

During the meeting I couldn't stop thinking about my reaction to the woman. There had been no need for my comment, but I had let my emotions get the better of me.

Afterward, I went back and explained that I had misheard her and apologized for my remark. She looked at me and said, "It's okay." As I walked toward the exit, I looked back. She smiled and said again, "It's okay."

As Dr. Martin Luther King Jr. said, "The time is always right to do the right thing."

Lord, asking for forgiveness is not easy, but with
Your guidance it's the right thing.
—Pablo Diaz

Digging Deeper: Isaiah 51:7; James 4:17

"For now You number my steps...." —Job 14:16 (NKJV)

In an effort to stay fit, Wayne and I both got one of those devices that attach to our wrists and count our steps. It's been fun for us to compete with each other on who has the higher count at the end of the day. Because I'm a morning person and up and about before Wayne stirs, I walk our dog, Bogie. This gives me an advantage of four to five thousand steps before my husband is even out of bed. As a result he's playing catch-up for the rest of the day. Recently, I found him cheating by trying to put his device on Bogie.

It's good to want to be physically fit. I want to be spiritually fit also. That means taking time to read my Bible. And you know what? It's a great read. Our pastor commented one Sunday that there's good stuff in there, and he's right. Being spiritually fit also means making time for prayer and for service to others. Because of my heavy travel schedule, much of my service is reaching out with cards and personal notes to those hurting, both physically and mentally, loving others as Jesus loves them.

Counting my steps is important, but making my spiritual steps count is even more so. My goal is to follow in the steps of Jesus, Who I'm sure didn't have a problem getting to ten thousand a day.

Father, may my steps count for You.
—Debbie Macomber

Digging Deeper: Psalm 119:133; Hebrews 12:1–2

Thursday, January 25

Live joyfully with the wife whom thou lovest....
—Ecclesiastes 9:9 (KJV)

It was Thursday morning and the week was almost over. It had been a particularly productive period at work, and I had found time to volunteer at a local center for children in need. Now I was wondering if all my busyness had come at a cost.

"So how is Corinne doing?" one of my clients asked. I answered the way I usually do: "She's great...loves being a mom...there's never a dull moment at our house."

After I hung up, though, I realized I didn't *really* know how my wife was doing. Sure, we saw each other every morning and every evening, but with her mothering, volunteering, spending time with friends, taking care of the house, as well as all the rest of life's commitments, we had become like two ships passing in the night...well, at least passing in the morning and at night.

It had been a long time since I had said thank you to Corinne for making our dinners and washing our clothes, for helping to raise our girls.

I remembered noticing a card that she had propped up on the kitchen windowsill. It was several months old and was splashed and stained by kitchen work.

It was a note that came with flowers I had sent her on her birthday earlier in the year. The flowers were long gone, but the "I love you" on the card was still there. It obviously had meant a lot to her.

I picked up the phone and called the florist, but my resolve didn't stop there. The next time someone asked, "How's Corinne?" I was going to be sure to have an up-to-date answer.

Father, in my busyness, help me hold those
I love the most close in my heart.
—Brock Kidd

Digging Deeper: Proverbs 21:2; Jeremiah 17:10; Hebrews 10:24

Forgive as the Lord forgave you. —Colossians 3:13 (NIV)

Sunrise, my golden retriever, bounded by my side as I reined SkySong, my white horse with a black mane, across the parking lot at the trailhead and toward my horse trailer. Parked next to mine, a brand-new truck and horse trailer gleamed in the sunlight. I nodded hello to two gals who looked to be in their twenties and were saddling their horses with silver-studded saddles. One of them held her chin in the air as she glared with disdain at the dirt and sweat that covered us from our morning ride. She commanded, "Don't tie your horse to *this side* of your trailer."

I felt flushed with anger. *There's room for all of us. Besides, you don't own the trailhead.... Are you the Queen of the Universe?* But I rode to the other side of my trailer. Quickly, I unsaddled SkySong and loaded him. I breathed a sigh of relief when I drove away.

The whole way home, Sunrise licked her paws and my mind whirled with ominous thoughts about the Queen of the Universe.

At home, Sunrise loped to the back porch and licked her paws. I curled on the deck next to her. "What's up with your paws?" I scooped one into my lap and spread apart her pads. They brimmed with cheat grass, an arrow-shaped and barbed grass seed that burrows through the skin. "Oh, I've got to pull those out before they create an abscess inside of you." When I said that, I heard inside of my spirit, *And how about pulling out those dark thoughts about Miss Universe before they create a spiritual abscess?*

Lord, help me to choose forgiveness as my first response. Amen.
—Rebecca Ondov

Digging Deeper: Matthew 18:21; Luke 6:37

Saturday, January 27

For You formed my inward parts; You wove me in my mother's womb.
I will give thanks to You, for I am fearfully and wonderfully made....
—Psalm 139:13–14 (NAS)

My friend Mary Kay introduced me to the poetry of e. e. cummings forty-three years ago. Ever since, Cummings's often simple but cryptic voice has spoken to me in important moments.

Recently, I was thumbing through a beautiful children's book. To my surprise, I read a quotation from Cummings that resounded in my senior adult mind: "It takes courage to grow up and be who you really are." I may be nearing the age where I finally understand this.

All of my life I have attempted to be a lot of things I am not. As a child mesmerized by Hardy Boys mystery books, I wanted to be a detective. In high school, I longed to be an outstanding athlete. In college, I knew I would be a doctor until chemistry made a fool of me. As a young adult, I attempted to be the perfect parent until a three-year-old revealed the truth to me. In middle age, I longed to write the great book, preach the profound sermon, present a stellar lecture, but seldom felt "good enough." Now, on the fourth lap of a mile-long race, I think I am finally understanding that all God ever wanted me to be was just myself. This is both humbling and unfathomable; good news but hard to accept. God created me to *just be my best self*! And when this happens, God begins to really smile.

Father, may I have the courage to love myself. To be myself.
To believe that You made me just as I am for a purpose. Amen.
—Scott Walker

Digging Deeper: Psalms 23-24, 139:13-16

Two are better than one, because they have a good reward for their toil.
For if they fall, one will lift up the other; but woe to one who is alone and
falls and does not have another to help. —Ecclesiastes 4:9–10 (NRSV)

We were heading into the momentous opening night performance in a few short hours. The conversation took a turn, as it often will in a circle of actors, to "the business" and how it can be very exhausting as our careers literally live and die on our work ethic. One veteran actor noted how hard the downtime can be.

We all fell silent. The dreaded downtime is the period in between gigs when the phone has stopped ringing, the callbacks are few and far between, you don't know where your next paycheck is coming from—when doubt creeps in. We all knew it well. Another actor admitted to a voice in the back of her mind that says her agent will call any day now to tell her she should just give up.

And yet we don't. We keep pushing every day, living into our call. We find comfort in a community of people who will cheer when we are up and hold us when we are down, who know exactly what it feels like, and who aren't afraid to name depression or fear.

> *God, I am so eternally grateful for a community willing to*
> *open the doors to the dark places, let a little light in,*
> *and help me notice that we are not*
> *standing here alone.*
> —Natalie Perkins

Digging Deeper: 1 Thessalonians 5:14; Hebrews 10:24–25

Monday, January 29

I pray that you...grasp how wide and long and high and deep is the love of Christ. —Ephesians 3:17–18 (NIV)

My husband and I boarded a tram to Lian, a tiny Norwegian village six miles up a mountainside from Trondheim. As the tram made its way up the incline, we gazed at the neighborhoods nestled in the hillsides and the river snaking below.

At a stop midway, a group of backpack-laden schoolchildren waited to board. I noticed one boy charging toward another. "He must be the school bully," I said to my husband.

I was wrong.

One by one the children stepped into the tram, flashing their passes to the driver. The last to get on was the "bully." The front of his jacket was mud-plastered. His eyes were tear-filled and red-rimmed. The other kids walked to the back; he sat by himself in the front. I pretended to be absorbed in the scenery outside but watched him from the corner of my eye. The young boy's face was set with near-fierce anger and determination, but his eyes betrayed hurt. He wiped them quickly with the back of his hand.

I wanted to help him, hug him, tell him it would be okay. But I didn't speak Norwegian and, as my husband gently pointed out, comfort from an unknown woman would only humiliate him more. Yet I feared that whatever had happened would become a memory that would haunt him for years.

A few stops later the boy got off. As he hoisted his backpack and trudged up a hill, I prayed for him. Maybe, just maybe, that was exactly the help he needed most that day.

> *Lord Jesus, may that young boy learn to find*
> *strength and comfort in You.*
> —Kim Henry

Digging Deeper: Psalm 35:1; Isaiah 49:25; Ephesians 3:14–19

He gathers the lambs in his arms and carries them close to his heart;
he gently leads those that have young. —Isaiah 40:11 (NIV)

It wasn't even a real painting. It was a photograph of a watercolor in a cheap, chipped frame at a secondhand shop on Maui. Not your typical vacation souvenir. But something about the image connected with me in a deeply personal way. A large, dark-skinned woman, shading herself from the sun with a frilly parasol, held a sleeping baby to her chest while a long line of children played joyfully at her feet.

Though it had been a tough year, I felt like that child, cradled intimately next to God's own heart. When I returned home to Arizona, I hung *Tutu Fantasy* by James Warren in a prominent place on my living room wall, a reminder to thank God for His tender love and care.

When my daughter announced she was pregnant a few weeks later, those prayers changed. Now, I prayed for my grandbaby-to-be who was preparing to meet the world. When little Xander (Alexander the Greatest, to me!) was born, the fact that the baby in the painting was dressed all in pink didn't stop me from continuing to use it as a touchstone to remind me to pray for him every day.

Then, those prayers changed again when my son and his wife brought two foster children into their home. In three months, these two beautiful African-American sisters will officially become my granddaughters through adoption. Now, when I look at my painting, I see Lula and Shea, cradled in God's arms through the last several years of their lives, waiting for our family to join in the group hug.

Dear Lord, thank You for holding me and my family
close to Your heart today and always.
—Vicki Kuyper

Digging Deeper: Psalms 27:10, 98:6

Wednesday, January 31

Blessed be the name of God for ever and ever: for wisdom and might are his. —Daniel 2:20 (KJV)

When our first child was born, I vowed that I would try to read to her or tell her a story every night. I kept that vow, mostly, even as we had twin sons soon after and things got a little chaotic.

One night I remember she asked me that classic little-kid question: *Will you always love me?* I gave the correct and right and holy answer: *Yup, no matter what.*

As she thrashed through her teenage years and the tumultuous twenties, as she struggled with darkness and terrible decisions and illness, I struggled to love her. I say this with shame. Many times I was so angry at her, frightened for her, scared at what she might do or what might be done to her, that saying "I love you" felt thin, shallow, empty, dishonest.

But again and again some deep wise gentle thing reminded me that I do love her, and always will, and would happily give my life for hers, if necessary. This mysterious, wise thing came to me through my wife, whose love does not fade or ebb. Sometimes it came to me through other people speaking with admiration of our daughter's courage against her travails. Sometimes it was the disgruntled mercy and affection and generosity of her brothers that steered me true again. But always I was steered back to love, pained and confused and muddled though it can be.

I think that God is always there, even when we are not.

Dear Lord, I should say this every eight seconds and I don't, but maybe I will today. Thank You for my children. Bless them and hold them close and save them from the greed and idiocy of me.
—Brian Doyle

Digging Deeper: 1 Corinthians 13:8; 1 John 4:7

GOD'S UNFAILING LOVE

1 _____

2 _____

3 _____

4 _____

5 _____

6 _____

7 _____

8 _____

9 _____

10 _____

11 _____

12 _____

13 _____

14 _____

15 _____

January

16 _____

17 _____

18 _____

19 _____

20 _____

21 _____

22 _____

23 _____

24 _____

25 _____

26 _____

27 _____

28 _____

29 _____

30 _____

31 _____

FEBRUARY

But God showed his great love for us by sending
Christ to die for us while we were still sinners.

—Romans 5:8 (TLB)

Thursday, February 1

RELYING ON GOD'S UNFAILING LOVE: Your Will Be Done

Whatever you ask in my name, this I will do, that the Father may be glorified in the Son. If you ask me anything in my name, I will do it.
—John 14:13–14 (ESV)

We planned to meet under the big oak tree to pray for Sarah. It was still early after her diagnosis, and only a few of us knew the battle she was facing. We knew that within the week, letters would be sent, a port would scar her chest, her hair would begin to fall out.

We knew that without God, none of us would survive the coming months.

And so we met under that tree, leaves blowing down from waving branches, our hands clasping each other's, our faces streaming with tears. And we prayed that God would take this burden from Sarah, that she would be miraculously healed, that He would get all of the glory.

There was a moment when the hand grasping mine clenched a bit tighter and I looked up to see tears, eyes full of desperation. Every woman in that circle paused. Considered. Swallowed hard.

And then the terrifying, hopeful words were said: Not our wills but His alone.

And so our prayers changed. We prayed that God would fill us with peace and hope regardless of the circumstances; that He would surround Sarah, her husband, her children, and us with His unfailing, undying, undiminishing love; that our wills would align with His; that we would be able to rely unwaveringly on Him.

Lord, Your love is revealed to us every day, both in joyful moments and in painful situations. Thank You. Amen.
—Erin MacPherson

Digging Deeper: Psalm 145:18

Praise him with trumpet sound.... —Psalm 150:3 (ESV)

I'm watching the news when a segment about a trumpet player begins. "Solomon, come here!"

My son sighs and comes in from the dining room. Hearing the sound trumpeting from the TV, he eases beside me on the couch.

"He's good," he says. The only things I know about the trumpet are that Solomon has been playing with the school band for almost five years now and he is proof that practice makes better. And that trumpets are among the loudest, if not the loudest, instruments on the planet.

Solomon's eyes are fixed on the screen. He mumbles a bunch of music terms that don't stick with me because I don't have the vocabulary and then he says, "He's really good. Wait. Here. See what he's doing now. The way he can change the note. Wait. Listen. Right there. That's really hard to do."

Solomon surprises me with his skilled ear, telling me things I had no idea of, things I'd never thought about, things that most likely only brass players know. Of all the moments of being a parent so far, this one, this moment, right here, is up there among my favorites.

The segment changes to the weather, and Solomon gets up. I turn off the TV and take in the silence, loving my little boy who isn't so little anymore.

Heavenly Father, I praise You for the blessings of my children—
for the countless lessons they teach me and
the endless love I feel for them.
—Sabra Ciancanelli

Digging Deeper: Deuteronomy 6:6–7; Proverbs 22:6

Saturday, February 3

For my thoughts are not your thoughts, nor are your ways my ways, says the Lord. —Isaiah 55:8 (NAB)

It was my first visit home from college since I got sober a few months earlier, and I was a jumble of emotions. It was comforting to be back in my old room, among the posters, books, and stuffed animals of my childhood. But this familiar landscape brought back painful memories as well, like the time I was too hung over and queasy to enjoy the Thanksgiving meal my mom had cooked. Or the time I got drunk at a high school football game and ran onto the field during halftime.

In finding the strength to stay sober, I had found a new relationship with God. My faith deepened every time I met the challenges of the day without needing to have a drink. But this newfound trust in God still seemed like a narrow, rickety bridge over the deep chasm of my difficulties. It was prone to rock and groan with the slightest breeze.

The light breeze of sadness that I felt upon my return home was quickly turning into a gale of self-pity and anger.

I lay on my back, alone, on the top bunk of the bed I shared with my sister, and burned with envy for normal folks.

God, how come I had to be an alcoholic? No one else in my family has this problem! Why do I have to be the one to have this terrible, lifelong affliction?

The answer came. It boomed in my head and whispered in my heart at the same time. *Because it brought you here*, it said. And the voice vanished, quick as a clap.

I lay there in bed for a long time, eyes wide, heart open and racing. Here I was in my childhood bedroom, three months sober, lying on my old bed and talking to God. Seeking Him, like I hadn't in years. And He came.

> *God, Your Way is always the right way.*
> *Help me to see my problems through Your eyes.*
> —Amy Eddings

Digging Deeper: Genesis 50:20; Jeremiah 29:11–14; Mark 4:38–40

You, God, are my God, earnestly I seek you; I thirst for you, my whole being longs for you, in a dry and parched land where there is no water.
—Psalm 63:1 (NIV)

The boys were finally in bed, and I raced excitedly to the refrigerator door. I poured myself a tall glass of cold milk, found my stash of chocolate cookies, and sat on the couch watching my favorite show. For a few months this was the highlight of my day, reality television and anything chocolate.

"What am I doing to myself?" I mumbled, looking at the empty tin of cookies, feeling bloated and guilty.

The next evening I decided not to eat any sweets as I decompressed. It proved to be more of a challenge than I'd imagined. I could feel the void in my chest growing, gnawing to be filled. This was beyond hunger. This was loneliness.

Long mornings of writing my memoir brought up emotions I didn't realize were still there. Afternoons were spent in the throes of responsibilities at home, and being a single mother doubled the load.

"Chocolate is all I have." I chuckled pathetically, wanting to open the freezer, where fudge ice cream waited to be devoured. I longed for family, but they were too far away; I desired close friendships, but I had little time to nurture them. And as content as I felt in being single and free from the stress of relationships, I felt alone.

"I'm choosing chocolate over Jesus," I said to myself after my binge. During the next weeks I faced my emptiness by allowing myself to feel it instead of feeding it.

Father, fill in the areas of my life that need Your healing love.
Let me depend only on You to make me whole again.
—Karen Valentin

Digging Deeper: 1 Peter 5:7

Monday, February 5

FALLING INTO GRACE: In God's Hands

I know, O Lord, that the way of human beings is not in their control, that mortals as they walk cannot direct their steps. —Jeremiah 10:23 (NRSV)

In the mirror, my husband's eyes were red-rimmed, his brow creased. And to say that about Charlie is indeed saying something distressing. He is the most optimistic, affable, easygoing person in any room.

In the emergency room after my fall, I'd watched Charlie beg an orderly to give me pain medication, only to be told that we'd have to wait for the doctor. He dashed back and forth, as near to panic as I'd ever seen him.

"Well," the doctor began grimly, when he came in holding the X-rays, "you really did a job." Broken collarbone. Cracked rib. Deep tissue bruising. I was warned against puncturing a lung.

Now, twenty-four hours later, a good part of me was purple with lines of red and yellow. Charlie and I surveyed the damage in the mirror. He clasped my right hand. I began to cry. A week ago we'd renewed our vows and planned daily workout walks, activities with our godsons, and travel.

"Nothing will ever be the same," I said choked up. Even sobbing hurt.

"That's not true. Don't say that," Charlie pleaded, and then his face crumpled.

Charlie's unique combination of charm, intelligence, and kindness has accustomed him to easily getting and maintaining control. While I constantly battle myself to acknowledge that God is in charge, Charlie quite contentedly assumes that God wants him to take control.

But now *neither* of us had it.

When I saw Charlie's face fall, God gave me new words: "We're in God's hands now. We've always been, but now we know it." Charlie's fingers tightened on mine.

Lord, let me release my pain and sin to You and not burden others.
—Marci Alborghetti

Digging Deeper: Matthew 4:15–16

Let love be genuine; hate what is evil, hold fast to what is good; love one another with mutual affection; outdo one another in showing honor.
—Romans 12:9–10 (NRSV)

Suddenly, my sister-in-law was shouting at me. Our discussion had quickly dissolved into an argument, with both of us trapped on our sides. I fought to make sure I was being understood and she, a self-proclaimed stubborn redhead, dug her heels into the ground.

We're getting nowhere, I thought.

A few more rounds we went, trying to figure out if we stood on any common ground. The conversation was stressful.

Finally, we reached a compromise of sorts: our eyes softened toward each other, and we really saw each other. That day we did not come to a place of agreement, and we may never. But I'm grateful that we both fought just as hard to continue to love each other, even in unlovable moments.

It's still a little awkward between us; I suppose it will be for a while, but I'm glad to have her in my life and look forward to continuing to work at loving each other.

God, as I build relationships with in-laws,
thank You for familial love, even when it gets messy.
—Natalie Perkins

Digging Deeper: Isaiah 12:1; John 13:35

Wednesday, February 7

*Now He who supplies seed to the sower...will supply and multiply
your seed for sowing and increase the harvest of your righteousness.*
—2 Corinthians 9:10 (NAS)

I'll bring my own books," I told our local elementary school staff
person when she invited me to read to fifth- and sixth-graders on
Dr. Seuss Day. One book I selected, *One Grain of Rice* by Demi, reveals
a raja in India who will not share his plentiful storehouse of rice when
famine hits the land. A clever girl gets him to agree to give her one
grain of rice doubled each day for thirty days. That one grain increases
to over one billion!

Handing out ziplock bags containing a half-cup measure of rice to
the students I said, "Think about how choices—foolish or wise—grow
from one to two to four to eight. Take these bags to your desks and
multiply the rice, making a separate pile for each day."

The kids were completely engaged, counting fast and furiously. We
ran out of time by day ten at 512 grains. On their desks was a visual
display of how making good decisions in their lives could increase
mightily.

I needed this lesson myself. I should have stopped at times and
counted rice before making hurtful choices. But I've also seen how
one giving or forgiving act leads to another and another. The apostle
Paul puts it this way: "Do you not know that a little leaven leavens the
whole lump of dough?" (1 Corinthians 5:6, NAS).

*Jesus—Master of good decisions—strengthen my heart to choose
what is right in Your eyes.*
—Carol Knapp

Digging Deeper: Deuteronomy 30:19; 2 Timothy 2:21; Hebrews 13:16

You hem me in, behind and before, and lay your hand upon me.
—Psalm 139:5 (ESV)

This morning a fellow professor arrived smiling radiantly. She's young, with two children, and not around much when I'm on campus. When she's here, she holes up in her office, looking preoccupied. "What's up?" I asked.

"I'm overwhelmed by the reach of God's hand!" she reveled.

Not the sort of answer one generally gets to a passing question, so of course I asked her why.

"Well, my husband and I are worried about childcare, and today this woman at the kids' nursery school comes running up, asking if we have a nanny. 'No,' I tell her. 'Ours is leaving at the end of the semester.' So she says, 'I know this nanny, and she's really good and looking for work,' and I was suddenly so glad there's someone out there, seeing the whole picture, looking out for us." Her face glowed with joy, momentarily unadulterated by stress or worry.

I needed that reminder: that the story my mind tells of her was incorrect, not to mention insufficiently compassionate.

I thought back to when my own daughters were toddlers and cattle prices suddenly sank and I was scrambling to rebuild my career. How impossibly stressed I was, trying to be a good teacher, a good farmer, a good mom. Lulu sometimes held my face in her hands, hoping to capture my full attention, and both daughters complained, as they got a little older, "You love your students more than us!"

How hard it is to prioritize—moment by moment—our most important concern and to be present to it. How blessed we are to have Someone out there making things right.

Help me to remember and trust in Your large view, Father!
—Patty Kirk

Digging Deeper: Colossians 1:27–29

Friday, February 9

If we are faithless, He remains faithful.... —2 Timothy 2:13 (NKJV)

Our local library is a temple of wisdom to me, and I revere the librarians who minister to us. So when Nola, everybody's favorite librarian, abruptly died in midlife of a rare disease, my wife and I were heartbroken.

The aging process is a series of losses. Nola was the seventh good friend we have lost this year, and it was the last straw for me. I was angry with God. "What possible purpose can her death serve?" I argued with Him. "She was supposed to be helping us find wisdom for the rest of our lives and cheering us on with her musical laugh."

For days we couldn't go to the library. It was like an empty warehouse without Nola's presence at the circulation desk.

I don't like feeling at odds with God. After all, the greatest commandment is to "love God with all your heart," but grief has a way of blocking all sense of God's loveliness.

A turning point came one evening when we were watching the old musical *Carousel* and I heard that beautiful tune "If I Loved You": "If I loved you, time and again I would try to say...how I loved you, if I loved you."

I found myself praying, "Lord, I do want to love You, but right now I can't find the strength."

Months later, when the fog of grief had lifted, I could see that Nola was, herself, a profound expression of God's love. Her life was not long, but it was a masterpiece. As her friend Carol said at the funeral, "Lucky Nola, lucky us."

Father, thank You for loving us faithfully,
even when our love for You falters.
—Daniel Schantz

Digging Deeper: Isaiah 60:20; Matthew 5:4

From his abundance we have all received one gracious blessing after another. —John 1:16 (NLT)

I put the car in Park, but I don't turn off the engine. I'm a few minutes early to pick up my date. The wipers squeal as they clean my windshield.

I should be excited. Amy is a nice girl, and I've been looking forward to tonight. But now, sitting outside her apartment, old feelings for somebody else creep up. This is the first time I've gone out since we parted ways.

At first, the hurt had come in frequent pangs. Now it's just a dull ache. I wish that she was in the passenger seat. She would talk, and I would know her expressions without taking my eyes off the road. Her mouth would shift to a straight line just before she said something serious. She would lift two fingers to her forehead when she was embarrassed. I miss the playful banter, the familiarity. I had known her for ten years, and I met Amy only a few weeks ago. So I sit in my car with a ghost while a real girl waits for me.

I know that the Lord brings one blessing after another, but I'm so full of the past that there's no room for the future. I have to let go of what's already gone.

I turn off the car, and the squeaky wipers stop in midswing. I take one last glance at the empty passenger seat and step outside. I don't know what the Lord's next blessing will be. Maybe I'll find it tonight, maybe not. But I'm ready.

Lord, thank You for the good things You've given me
and for those yet to come.
—Logan Eliasen

Digging Deeper: Philippians 4:19; James 1:17

Sunday, February 11

God's chariots are twice ten thousand—countless thousands!
—Psalm 68:17 (CEB)

My wife, Carol, grew up in Connecticut and her family came from the Midwest. I grew up in Southern California and two of my grandparents were born there, back when there wasn't much around but orange groves. But I like to think we have chariot races in common.

Chariot races? Bear with me.

Turns out that Carol's great-great-grandfather Lew Wallace wrote the novel *Ben-Hur*. In fact, Carol, who writes under her maiden name Carol Wallace, has gone back and rewritten that great nineteenth-century classic with its magnificent chariot race scene, memorable to all movie-goers whether it was Charlton Heston or more recently Jack Huston holding the reins. "I've got chariot races in my heritage too," I tell her, eliciting a raised eyebrow or two.

So on a visit to Pasadena, where my mom still lives, I took her to see Tournament Park. "Here is where the chariot races were held," I said, "back in my grandparents' day. In fact, my family probably watched right here where those eucalyptus trees grow."

Pasadena is famous for its Rose Bowl and Tournament of Roses Parade, but early in the twentieth century, chariot races were staged on New Year's Day. "No doubt inspired by Lew Wallace's book," I said.

In a novel that was subtitled *A Tale of the Christ*, Lew Wallace created a spectacle that has been re-created on stage and cinema. Behind all the drama of that epic there is a very simple message: no matter where we're from, we are all brothers and sisters in Christ.

Or in our case...husband and wife with chariots rumbling in our background.

> *Lord, I give thanks for all my ancestors and*
> *for Your guiding hand on their lives.*
> —Rick Hamlin

Digging Deeper: Leviticus 26:45; Psalm 20:7

*I will give you a new heart and place a new spirit within you, taking
from your bodies your stony hearts and giving you natural hearts.*
—Ezekiel 36:26 (NAB)

"H i, Mom. What's up?" I said, answering my cell phone with an
exasperated sigh.

"Hi, honey. We haven't talked in a while, and I just wanted to hear
your voice! You sound distracted. Did I catch you in the middle of
something?"

"Mom, I'm always in the middle of something," I snapped.

Something in me opened, and I noticed the meanness of my tone.
"Mom, I'm sorry," I blurted.

Lent was about to begin, and I had been thinking about a spiritual
discipline to take on. I found it in that phone call.

"Tell you what, Mom," I said. "For Lent, I'm going to call you every day.
It can just be for five minutes. But I'm going to call you. Every day."

And I did. I called Mom in the evening as I drove home after work.
We talked, as such daily contact leads you to do, about what she and
Dad had for dinner, how loud my husband snored the night before,
the funny snippet of conversation she heard in the grocery store. I
appreciated her insights and her wit. I relaxed into our talks and shared
more deeply.

A few weeks into this practice, my husband and I visited my parents.
My dad pulled me aside. "Those calls to your mother," he said, "keep
them up. She really enjoys them. They make her day!"

I smiled. They had already started to make mine too.

> *God, help me to see where I'm acting from a heart of stone
> and replace it with a heart of flesh.*
> —Amy Eddings

Digging Deeper: Proverbs 11:25; Galatians 5:22–23

Tuesday, February 13

"Yea, I have loved thee with an everlasting love...." —Jeremiah 31:3 (KJV)

One of my favorite delights is sending valentines. Come February, I carefully address my missives, affix the required postage, and mail them all to Loveland, Colorado. Volunteers in the Sweetheart City hand-stamp these envelopes with a special postmark and forward them to the recipients.

Many of my friends tell me they save both my valentines *and* the envelopes as the postmark changes each year. So I was really surprised when I visited my friend Catherine and my card wasn't displayed on her antique breakfront. Instead, she had used it for a scratch pad.

I was annoyed, to say the least. *Is that all she thinks of our friendship?* I seethed. Once I calmed down, I studied Catherine's scribblings. "Scan normal." Catherine had been battling cancer. Now, I learned, her follow-up test was A-OK.

As my eyes traveled to the bottom of the exquisite hearts-and-cupids card, I read: "Made of 80% recycled paper." It was then that God whispered to my heart. *Eighty percent, Roberta. Isn't your friendship with Catherine just about perfect 80 percent of the time? Aren't you thrilled to pieces about her test results?* After giving the incident a lot of thought, I made a decision that affects all of my friendships. If someone does something that annoys me, I consciously cut them a break. "Eighty percent," I tell myself. "That's what most relationships are."

Everyone is a disappointment *some* of the time, including me. By Divine design, only One meets all of our expectations. Rejoicing in my rediscovery, I hummed the old hymn and thanked my oh-so-perfect Lord.

There's not a friend like the lowly Jesus, no, not one! No, not one!
—Roberta Messner

Digging Deeper: Proverbs 17:17; John 15:12–15

*Get rid of the old yeast, so that you may be a new unleavened batch—
as you really are. For Christ, our Passover lamb, has been sacrificed.*
—1 Corinthians 5:7 (NIV)

On Ash Wednesday, I'd headed to the chapel. I'd come for answers.
I was feeling distant from God and wasn't sure why. I knelt down
and prayed. *Lord, what do I need to do to feel close to You again?*

I looked over at a daddy and his young daughter seated across the
aisle. The daddy reached over and picked up the child's doll and storybook. "Why don't we move your stuff out of the way, so you can get
closer to me," he whispered.

Is that it? I wondered. *Do I have stuff that's gotten in between God and
me?* I thought about my busy life full of commitments—career, family,
church, and community work. And as a member of a carnival krewe,
I'd spent all my spare time recently gluing sequins on costumes and
shopping for beads and trinkets to throw from my float during our
parade.

Yes, I thought, *I've placed a lot between God and me.* And to make
matters worse, they were things that took up so much time that I'd
become too exhausted to read my Bible in the mornings, too tired to
journal, and too sleepy for nighttime prayers. As a result, I'd lost my
closeness to God.

I knew what to do. I'd get rid of everything that was getting in the way
and I'd add back my most important commitments: prayer time, Bible
study, and reflection. After all, nothing in my life was more important
than my relationship with God.

Forgive me, Father, when my earthly activities separate me from You.
—Melody Bonnette Swang

Digging Deeper: Isaiah 55:6; James 4:8

Thursday, February 15

"Your attitude must be like my own, for I, the Messiah, did not come to be served, but to serve, and to give my life as a ransom for many."
—Matthew 20:28 (TLB)

As the Lenten season began, our church filled a large basket with black antique-looking, two-sided, two-inch-long nails with flat heads. We were asked to take one or two to remind us of the sacrifice that Jesus made for us on the Cross. I took five nails, with no clue what I'd do with them.

They sat on my dining room table for a week until I finally gave one to my husband, kept two to slip into my pocket each day, left one on the dining room table, and the other I put in the coin purse that holds my credit cards and cash.

Every time I was out shopping or eating out or buying anything, I saw that nail in my coin purse and was reminded what Jesus endured for us.

Every week I'd find those nails in the most unexpected places. Sometimes they fell out of my pocket and I'd find one on the recliner. I found one in a jacket I hadn't worn for two weeks. But no matter where they popped up, every time I'd think about the nails that were pounded into the flesh of Jesus. My nails were doing exactly what they were meant to do.

At the end of Lent, I didn't have the heart to toss the nails. I kept the one in my coin purse as a reminder not to purchase extravagant, unneeded items. The others I scattered around my condo just to keep me aware of God's infinite, unfailing love and the painful sacrifice that Jesus made on that Cross.

Heavenly Father, thank You for sending Your only Child to teach us how to get along in this world and that all good things come with a price.
—Patricia Lorenz

Digging Deeper: Luke 18:31–34; John 19:28–37; Romans 5:6–11

"I will fully satisfy the needs of those who are weary and fully refresh the souls of those who are faint." —Jeremiah 31:25 (NET)

My wife and I are raising a daughter now. Two older kids have left home—years ago. Both of them are done with college. Occasionally, our daughter asks for a sibling. *No way!* I usually think whenever the subject comes up. My wife and I are already fifty years old; and here we are still attending kindergarten parent meetings!

At a recent parent-teacher conference I couldn't help but wonder, *How do elementary school teachers do it?* I watch my daughter's classroom for five minutes and I'm dizzy. I need an aspirin.

"There are ways to take a break during the day," her kindergarten teacher explained to me. "At my desk, when the kids are quiet and working on something for just a few minutes I will collect my thoughts."

I've seen other people do this too. There was a cab driver once, at a stoplight, who closed his eyes and crossed himself, mouthing something, while I sat watching from the backseat. Then there is my friend Jill who tends incredible gardens for a living: she tells me that her spade reminds her to be grateful. "The symbolism of it is private," she said, so I didn't ask for details. But I've seen her pause when she picks up that spade. I know that she's praying.

I, too, pause throughout the day. I pray, and I walk, and sometimes I pray and walk at the same time.

I am tired, God. But when I pause to be with You, as I will today,
I find my rest. You are my daily fresh air.
—Jon Sweeney

Digging Deeper: Psalm 127:1–2

Saturday, February 17

CONFIDENCE IN DIFFICULTY: God's Protective Love

Is not the cup of thanksgiving for which we give thanks a participation in the blood of Christ? —1 Corinthians 10:16 (NIV)

I was in the psychiatric clinic waiting for my daughter Maggie to be evaluated for suicide risk when another daughter, Elizabeth, called. She was at an appointment with her eating disorders specialist. Her doctor came on speakerphone and said that while Elizabeth's weight was dangerously low, her vitals were okay. So they were not going to admit her to the hospital that day.

My stomach heaved. A large portion of the deaths related to anorexia come from cardiac failure, often during sleep, and I had a keen sense that my daughter was in danger. I'd been praying fiercely for Elizabeth's safety and was counting on the doctor to mandate hospitalization. It is a hard, hard thing when a child is legally an adult, and parents can't coerce her into medical care. The idea that my very ill twenty-one-year-old would be going back to her apartment, alone, was terrifying.

Maggie was declared safe as well, so I broke the news about Elizabeth to the family over supper. The mood was tense and distraught. Everyone was worried.

My cell phone rang. I answered, listened, let out a whoop.

"What is it, Mom? What is it?" Stephen, my youngest, begged.

"Elizabeth's lab tests just came back, and *thank God* the doctor paused to look at them before heading home for the day. Her phosphorus and potassium levels are way below normal, and Elizabeth has been told to go straight to the emergency room!"

Stephen pumped his fist and shouted, "*Yessss!*" The house erupted in cheers. I did a thank-You-Jesus dance, singing for joy. For sometimes God's unfailing love shows up in unusual ways, like getting a young adult admitted to the hospital to keep her safe.

Father, help me see Your love even in what might seem like bad news.
—Julia Attaway

Digging Deeper: 1 Chronicles 16:34; 1 Thessalonians 5:18

Thy word was unto me the joy. . . . —Jeremiah 15:16 (KJV)

Memories of my mother's little leather suitcase had followed me through my life. There on a top shelf, or in the recesses of her closet, it remained a mystery. "What's inside?" I would ask.

"Just some papers," she would reply, moving it to another location.

And now the little suitcase was mine. My mother had taken me into the bedroom and handed it to me. "These are for you," she said. "They are letters from your daddy. After you read them, I want you to promise that you will burn them."

She knew her time on earth was nearing its end. This was, I would soon discover, one of her final gifts to me. They were a stunning history of my parents' courtship and early marriage. They chronicled the struggles of separation as my father was forced to leave home to work at the "Secret City" and other sites during World War II. They were full of love and longing and hope for the future.

A few days later, I called my mother. "I'm breaking my promise," I said. "I can never burn the letters. They are my treasure."

"Okay," she answered. I think she was pleased.

There is something about that suitcase of letters that makes me feel safe and helps me understand that my life is built upon a rock of love. I wish everyone could have a similar legacy tucked away somewhere. And maybe we do.

Remember that old red letter edition of the Bible, stuck back on a shelf like my mother's suitcase? Pull it out. Open it. You'll find love letters there. Words of wisdom, beauty, and truth. Words written for you and me.

> *Father, we have it in writing. All is well.*
> —Pam Kidd

Digging Deeper: Isaiah 34:16; John 5:39

Monday, February 19

I urge, then, first of all, that petitions, prayers, intercession and
thanksgiving be made for all people—for kings and all those in authority,
that we may live peaceful and quiet lives in all godliness and holiness.
This is good, and pleases God our Savior. —1 Timothy 2:1–3 (NIV)

A friend of mine told me she was looking for an up-to-date list of all the Supreme Court justices. "Why do you need that? Do your kids have a social studies report due?"

She laughed. "No. I'm going to see my mom and she wanted to update her prayer cards."

"What?"

"My mom prays for all the Supreme Court justices by name. She prays for the president, the cabinet, the Senate, and the House of Representatives as well. She also prays for her local mayor, police chief, fire chief, and so on. Once her life became so limited in the nursing home she decided to use her time in prayer. It's her ministry."

This was taking prayer to a whole new level! I never thought to pray on a regular basis by name for my elected officials. Half the time I didn't even agree with what they were doing. And I told my friend as much.

"Oh, Mom doesn't agree with all of them either, but she knows their jobs need the covering of prayer."

This gave me pause. If I get overwhelmed with the concerns of running my home and family life, how much harder is it to run a country, a superpower at that? I take my concerns to the Lord in prayer. I can't run my life without His help. The least I can do is offer the same compassion and help to the president of the United States. His job is one of the most difficult there is.

Please cover our president with wisdom and humility, Lord. Give us
the compassion to work with our elected officials to bring about
peaceful solutions to the problems we face. Amen.
—Lisa Bogart

Digging Deeper: Romans 13:1; 1 Peter 2:13–17

"For whoever has despised the day of small things shall rejoice...."
—Zechariah 4:10 (NRSV)

After being out of the corporate world for more than a decade, I felt God calling me to go back to work. Micah was in middle school and stayed late for sports practice after classes. My husband's workday was flexible, so he could pick her up. We needed more money and had to be saving for our daughter's college expenses. It just made sense.

In the 1990s I'd organized employee awards banquets for hundreds of people, but my most recent event planning was twelve years of birthday party celebrations. I'd once created fund-raising annual campaigns, auctions, and golf tournaments that grossed tens of thousands of dollars. These days, my expertise was used to persuade PTA parents to help their students sell enough cookie dough to purchase playground equipment.

My current skill set consisted of motivating my husband to help with chores, carpooling for my daughter, and arranging to have all of us land at the dinner table at the same time. The only group I'd recently managed was seventeen four-year-olds at Bible Study Fellowship once a week—and I needed an afternoon nap once that was over!

Who would want to hire me? If I snagged an interview, would they laugh me out of the door once they realized who I was now?

Still, God's stirring in my heart was unmistakable. I didn't doubt I was on the verge of a new beginning. Regardless of how I saw my small self, God was big. His plan for my life would prevail despite my insignificance.

When all I see are minor, unimportant acts, God, help me to trust
that You use what seems trivial to create my future.
—Stephanie Thompson

Digging Deeper: Proverbs 16:9; Jeremiah 29:11; 1 Corinthians 2:9

Wednesday, February 21

Let us not become weary in doing good, for at the proper time we will reap a harvest if we do not give up. —Galatians 6:9 (NIV)

My friend John led the job skills program at a nearby juvenile correctional facility. He asked me to take on the ministry when medical tests showed no slowing of the cancer he was fighting.

Last night I wondered, as I drove to the detention center, if the program was making a difference. It had been two years since John died. Questions kept cycling through my mind: *Are we working on the right things? Are we connecting in relevant ways to help the youth live crime-free? Will we ever know?*

Before the session started, Tim, one of the incarcerated youth, handed me a letter: "Thanks for finding James." James, who is a valuable member of our ministry team, spent eighteen years in prison and is now living a successful life on the outside. James is "helping motivate kids in trouble to get jobs and not hang on the streets. I never wanted to make it to prison. The question is, do I want to change?" And then, answering his own question, Tim added, "My answer is yes because it's time to let my light shine."

By the way, I didn't find James. Nudged by a light on his own path, James found my friend John, who gave me James's name before he died.

Dear God, thank You for encouraging me to keep on planting seeds and for reminding me that You are at work bringing about the harvest. Amen.
—John Dilworth

Digging Deeper: Psalm 94:19; 2 Corinthians 9:12; Ephesians 4:28

THE BEAUTY OF SIMPLICITY
An Impromptu, Stress-free Wedding

A pretentious, showy life is an empty life; a plain and simple life is a full life. —Proverbs 13:7 (MSG)

One afternoon my daughter Katie shared plans for her upcoming wedding. "Nothing fancy, Mom. A judge is marrying us."

"What about guests? Cake? A reception?"

"No. I want everything simple this time."

Nine years earlier, Katie and I had coordinated every detail for her first wedding, including apricot-colored bridesmaids' dresses with matching roses and candles; a storybook ceremony. The marriage ended in divorce.

On the morning of her second wedding, my husband and I headed to the courthouse. "What about flowers? Every bride needs flowers!" I texted Katie. "Can I bring you a bouquet?"

"Okay, but no stressing."

I ran to the grocery store. Katie's dress was ivory, but I had no idea what color her three-year-old stepdaughter, Rilynn, would be wearing, so I grabbed a dozen white roses. Before I could choose the perfect ribbon, the florist tied one around the stems, the kind meant for birthday presents.

At the courthouse, we spotted Katie and Rilynn who had spilled juice all over her blue chiffon dress. "No worries," Katie said. I couldn't believe it.

We walked down a messy hallway filled with cardboard boxes and found the judge inside his office. He greeted us warmly and Katie and Chris were married. Joy filled the room, despite only three attendees, a grocery-store bouquet, a juice-stained dress, and me serving as the photographer.

> *Father, Your ways are unpretentious, simple, gracious.*
> —Julie Garmon

Digging Deeper: Matthew 6:21

Friday, February 23

Be not overeager to go to the House of God.... —Ecclesiastes 4:17 (JPS)

For the first six months after my husband died, I don't remember dreaming. Then, over the next few months, I could remember having dreams but not what had happened in them.

One year later, once the memory of a dream began to linger in the morning, I knew I was dreaming that I told people Keith was dead. I would wake up sad and depressed and couldn't understand why I was making myself feel worse. Things I had been doing with some routine satisfaction—like teaching, shopping, and exercising—began to pall and it felt like just going through the motions.

Then I had a dream in which I was reunited with Keith. I awoke feeling happy and wanted to remember as much of the dream as I could, to recapture all those emotions I had not been able to experience in such a long time. I remembered what I had said to him in the dream: "Am I dead now?"

"Ask yourself that after you wake up," he answered.

God was speaking to me through my husband, as God had so often before. As long as I was alive, I had to go on living.

Please keep reminding me that You still have a purpose for me, Lord: that You want me to be present to every moment with a full heart.
—Rhoda Blecker

Digging Deeper: Deuteronomy 30:15

Your word is a lamp to my feet and a light to my path.
—Psalm 119:105 (NKJV)

I stared at the ceiling through waves of pain. Even after the first surgery on my back had failed four years prior, the doctors were in the dark as to what was wrong. No one could fix me. Now that I'd ruptured the disk a second time, it seemed all I had left was God.

"Let the worst happen, Lord," I said. "I still choose You."

Something changed in the moment I surrendered everything. It felt like God had been waiting for me to say that.

My husband came home. "Call Nancy," he said. "She's a dairy farmer who hurt her back just like you did, but she's already returned to doing what she loves and it's only been seven weeks since her surgery."

I called. Nancy not only calmed my fears, but she made me excited to try again. Step by step she outlined what she did in order to find the best surgeon in Oregon.

Doors that had long been closed began opening. This was my miracle. The way had been laid out; I had only to follow.

The MRI showed the rupture clearly. The surgeon gave me confidence. I was in the right place with the right doctor. I didn't count the days until my operation; I counted the days until my miracle.

This was God's path for me. If I had been healed before, I would have returned to life as usual and missed the faith-building lessons. I had to be broken in order to be restored.

You ask me to trust You, Lord, and to believe the impossible.
I bury my doubts and follow You.
—Erika Bentsen

Digging Deeper: 1 Samuel 12:20–22; Psalm 36:9;
Luke 1:37; John 10:27

Sunday, February 25

She is clothed with strength and dignity. —Proverbs 31:25 (NLT)

Recently my wife, Julee, was asked to give an unusual performance: to sing at a big fashion show in New York City during the annual hoopla of Fashion Week.

The collection was shown in Mason Hall, a gorgeous old theater. Shane and Chris, the young designers behind the hip "Creatures of the Wind" label, designed a dress and shoes for Julee to wear onstage. Julee's voice, both strong and ethereal, wafted above the crowd.

I hung out after the show while Chris, Shane, and Julee did interviews and posed for photographs. Later, I took some of my own. Both Shane and Chris wanted to make sure I got their mothers in the pictures. They'd traveled from the Midwest to New York to experience success with their sons. They were two proud moms all right!

In the car on the way home Julee started crying a bit.

"Glad the show is over?" I asked. "It was a lot of pressure, that's for sure."

"No, I just miss my mom is all."

I thought of Shane's and Chris's moms, beaming with pride.

"Mom used to come to every one of my performances when I was a kid."

Julee's mom, Wilma, had died ten years before. Julee always was a mama's girl. She'd finish a show in Paris or London and all she'd want to do was run back to the hotel and call her mom in Creston, Iowa.

"I still try to make her proud every time I sing. Sometimes it's the one thing that keeps me going."

I held her hand tightly. Isn't it wonderful, a little sad but still so wonderful, that we always try to make our moms proud?

> *Lord, thank You for the blessing of loving mothers.*
> *May I never stop making mine proud.*
> —Edward Grinnan

Digging Deeper: Exodus 20:12; Proverbs 1:8–9; 2 Timothy 1:5

The desert and the parched land will be glad.... Like the crocus, it will burst into bloom.... —Isaiah 35:1–2 (NIV)

My son Jeremy had hit rock bottom. Again. His punishment for reckless driving while under the influence would be harsh. As it should be. Part of the judge's ruling was that Jeremy wear an ankle monitor and be under house arrest for six months. His driver's license was revoked and his vehicle wrecked.

He had been off his bipolar medications for who knew how long. He'd also been in a treatment facility, and now it was time to return to his house. He'd asked me to pick up a few things from his home. I dreaded going inside. As I suspected it reflected months of desperation. His sister Jennifer and her daughter Libby insisted on giving it a thorough cleaning. I gathered up mountains of dirty clothes and took them to a self-service laundry.

Finally, his home was organized. Clean. We even put a bowl of fresh fruit on the kitchen table and prayed over each room. I'd decided not to drive Jeremy home. I didn't want to continue enabling. So I sat in his driveway and simply stared at the small house he so loved. Jeremy has the green thumb in our family, but his yard looked bleak now. Abandoned. Hopeless.

Suddenly I saw it differently. Not exactly a vision, but on the front porch I imagined a big, red hanging geranium.

That afternoon my son phoned. "Mom!" A happy voice, like the real Jeremy. "The geranium is beautiful. I know you left it and I know what it means. Thanks for believing in me—again."

> *Father, only You could have created something so beautiful*
> *that it conveys what words sometimes stumble over.*
> —Marion Bond West

Digging Deeper: Job 14:7; Psalm 19:1; Matthew 6:28

Tuesday, February 27

I love you, O Lord, my strength. The Lord is my rock, my fortress, and my deliverer, my God, my rock in whom I take refuge, my shield, and the horn of my salvation, my stronghold. I call upon the Lord, who is worthy to be praised.... —Psalm 18:1–3 (NRSV)

I arrived at the intersection moments after the crash. Two cars were sliding to a rest, only a split second after they had collided head-on. That awful metallic scream was still ringing in the air as I jumped out of my car and headed toward them.

Nothing was crumpled. It could have been worse.

I saw one person alone in each car. Both were conscious. Another nearby driver arrived on the scene, too, and we each headed for a car. My driver was a man about my father's age. I opened the driver's side door and I will never forget what happened next.

"Whoa!" he exclaimed, peeling his hands off the steering wheel like it was a hot iron.

"Are you okay?" I asked. He began to get out of the car and stand up.

"Careful now," I said. But his feet were already on the pavement. Then he grabbed both of my hands in his and looked me full in the face.

"In every thing give thanks," he said, "for this is the will of God in Christ Jesus concerning you."

"King James," I said, smiling, acknowledging that he was quoting a famous verse (18) from 1 Thessalonians 5.

"A rule of life," he responded.

Whoa.

There are so many reasons why life is precious, Lord.
May I see them everywhere I go today.
—Jon Sweeney

Digging Deeper: Ezra 9:9

A new commandment I give to you, that you love one another: just as I have loved you, you also are to love one another. —John 13:34 (ESV)

As the movie credits scrolled, I sighed, pondering the film's message. For two hours I'd stepped back into history, to a time when women had fought for their right to vote. The courage of these women inspired me. Their sacrificial resolve challenged me. Their perseverance empowered me.

This story also made me think of my mother, whom I had lost a year before. On Election Day several years ago, my mom asked if I'd voted. I swallowed and answered honestly: I had not. Having recently moved, I was barely acquainted with the state public officials and I knew nothing about the current candidates. I'd figured that voting would have been useless.

"Daughter," my mother responded with conviction, "there's no excuse for not voting. Don't you know people lost their lives fighting for the right to vote? They died, so you and I could have that right."

Her words struck a nerve deep inside. As a woman of color, I knew that many African Americans had lost jobs, homes, and even their lives while fighting for the right to vote. I knew that women also had sacrificed much for this very same right.

Since my mother spoke those words to me, I have never missed an opportunity to cast my vote. Her words remind me of other courageous souls who sacrificed much, so I could enjoy the blessing of rights and freedoms: the right to choose any seat in a movie theater; the right to send my children to schools with students of all races, cultures, and backgrounds; the right to vote. These freedoms were bought with a price, and I must live my life in honor of so many sacrifices.

Lord, may I never take for granted the sacrifices of others on my behalf.
—Carla Hendricks

Digging Deeper: Luke 12:4; 1 John 3:16

GOD'S UNFAILING LOVE

1 _____

2 _____

3 _____

4 _____

5 _____

6 _____

7 _____

8 _____

9 _____

10 _____

11 _____

12 _____

13 _____

14 _____

15 _____

16 _____

17 _____

18 _____

19 _____

20 _____

21 _____

22 _____

23 _____

24 _____

25 _____

26 _____

27 _____

28 _____

MARCH

And I pray that you . . . may have power, together
with all the Lord's holy people, to grasp how wide
and long and high and deep is the love of Christ,
and to know this love that surpasses knowledge. . . .

—Ephesians 3:17–19 (NIV)

You will hurl all our sins into the depths of the sea. —Micah 7:19 (CEB)

It's interesting what we can remember and what we may regret. When I think about the kind of dad I was when my kids were younger, I hate to recall the times when the two of them tested my patience. Two boys, three years apart, roughhousing indoors, the playful tussling that turned into wrestling matches, threatening to destroy furniture if not send antique pottery falling from living room shelves, smashing on the floor.

I can hear myself say between gritted teeth, "That's enough, boys," and then raising my voice to ear-splitting volume when my seemingly mild-mannered request was totally ignored. "If you don't stop it right now," I would holler, "you're going to both be sorry. Somebody's going to get hurt." My demand for a time-out was a request for myself. I needed a time-out. All that shouting...I hated to think what the neighbors made of it. What kind of dad was I?

Not long ago I said to our now twentysomething, ever-patient son Timothy, "You boys would make me so angry when you were younger. Oh, how I would yell at you."

Tim looked at me quizzically. "You never yelled at us, Dad."

I smiled at this bit of grace being delivered firsthand. "Just so you know, I *did* raise my voice, really loud. But I'm glad you've forgotten it." It was as though I was being given forgiveness without even asking for it. Note to self: God can do some amazing, ex post facto rewriting of the most cringe-worthy scenes of our lives, at least as they are remembered by our loved ones.

Thank You for being a God Who forgives and forgets...
and helps us to do the same.
—Rick Hamlin

Digging Deeper: Psalm 103:12; Hebrews 10:17

Friday, March 2

We love because he first loved us. —1 John 4:19 (NIV)

It's time to put up the Easter decorations!" I proclaimed to Chuck and my grandson Logan.

"I'll get them out of the attic," Chuck said.

Logan bounced on his toes and clapped his hands. "Can I help decorate too?"

"Sure," I said.

I love to decorate our home for the seasons, and Easter runs a close second to Christmas for me with its signs of spring's arrival—warmer days and new life abounding.

As Logan and I survey the collection of baskets, bunnies, and ornaments I've kept through the years, I feel the love of generations passed down. Some of the special baskets were given to my children by their dear-departed grandmothers. We fill the baskets with plastic eggs and arrange them around the house.

Logan finds the carton of plastic Resurrection eggs and exclaims, "This is mine!" The eggs are a tradition we started when Logan first moved in with us at age three. Now that he is seven, he can read the Easter story himself before opening an egg containing an object that symbolizes part of Christ's sacrifice and Resurrection.

Some of my favorite decorations are fold-out paper bunnies in their baskets. One of them was a gift from my mother to me when I was ten years old. But even more unique is the one given to her by her father when she was ten, the year written on it: 1924.

As I survey our assortment of Easter decorations, I am overwhelmed with love. Love from parents and grandparents, love to children, and, especially, love from our Savior to us.

> *Thank You, Lord, for Your love and the love*
> *that has been shared by our family.*
> —Marilyn Turk

Digging Deeper: Psalm 26:3, 6–7; John 3:16

See what great love the Father has lavished on us, that we should be called children of God! And that is what we are! —1 John 3:1 (NIV)

Y ou should try it," my husband said.
"I don't know."

We were on a date in our favorite small town where Main Street means old-fashioned candy shops, antiques stores, and boutiques filled with lovely, unusual things. We walked hand in hand, sipping coffee and window-shopping, until I saw the blouse. It was a delicate floral print of deep blue and white. Tiny vintage buttons trickled down the front.

"I'm sure it's expensive," I said.

"Let's see," Lonny said. He held the door and grinned wide.

A few moments later, I admired the blouse in the dressing room mirror. It was perfect.

"Beautiful," Lonny said when I pulled back the curtain.

Then fast as the fondness came a barrage of thoughts. Two boys needed soccer shoes. One needed a jacket. Another grew overnight and had high-water jeans. The blouse was an extravagance.

I shut the curtain, worked the tiny buttons, and returned the blouse to the hanger. But as I slipped back into my own top, Lonny's smile and the love in his eyes came to mind. It made me think of God's love for me. It's extravagant. It's rich and lovely and beyond what I can ever deserve. He knows my heart and loves me anyway.

I opened the curtain once more. "I'm going to insist," Lonny said.

"I adore it," I replied. "Thank you."

Besides a sweater that my boys bought me years ago, the blouse is my favorite thing to wear.

Lord, Your extravagant love covers me. Thank You.
—Shawnelle Eliasen

Digging Deeper: Zephaniah 3:17; Romans 8:28

Sunday, March 4

Kindness makes a man attractive. —Proverbs 19:22 (TLB)

I drive "one of the ugliest cars on the road," as an automotive reviewer described it.

I'll admit, it's no head-turner. It's a small, olive, drab rhinoceros on wheels, with a hatchback that resembles the stern of a bulldog.

"I think it's kinda cute," my wife consoles me.

"Yeah, like a baby warthog, maybe."

Then I remembered a line from Chaucer: "Handsome is as handsome does," and this car "does" handsomely. On the road it's as smooth as a swan, and the cabin is as quiet as an evergreen forest. It has a tiger for an engine, but it sips gas like a butterfly on a petunia. It steers like a hummingbird and stops on a dime, giving me nine cents change. Inside, my ugly car is surprisingly roomy, with fold-down seats, so I can haul lumber or nursery plants. And the dashboard controls are as easy to operate as our kitchen stove.

"Handsome is as handsome does" is a phrase that gives me hope. At my age, there's not much I can do about my looks, short of plastic surgery, but I can control my attitudes and my behavior. I can be friendly and kind. I can be clean and well dressed. I can smile and be upbeat. Above all, I can be morally clean so that people will see not an ugly old man but Christ in me.

I will never make the cover of *GQ*, but, by living well, I might at least be "kinda cute."

I am thankful, Lord, that even when nature slights us, we can
still be presentable by practicing a godly way of living.
—Daniel Schantz

Digging Deeper: Psalm 90:17; 1 Peter 3:3–4

FALLING INTO GRACE: Unlikely Blessings

They shall console you, when you see their ways and their deeds; and you shall know that it was not without cause that I did all that I have done....
—Ezekiel 14:23 (NRSV)

Almost pleading, I asked the orthopedic doctor when I could resume some of my exercise routine. I knew I wouldn't be doing planks or sit-ups for a while, but I desperately hoped to get back to walking. Preferably, yesterday. Believing that my sanity depended upon maintaining something of my before-fall life, I was willing to work through the pain, but I needed the doctor's okay.

Turning from the X-rays of my broken bones, he smiled at me. "The only activity you'll be doing is lifting a coffee cup."

Seeing he was ready to dismiss me, I quickly asked another question. I wanted him to show me where the breaks were on my body, so I would know where to expect the pain to be concentrated. He pointed to a small bump between my neck and shoulder and then to an area on my side near my back. I got ready to leave.

"You know," he began, and I turned to see him looking at me with compassion, "the pain will radiate. It won't just be concentrated in those spots. You'll have pain like you can't believe in places that will surprise you, at times that don't make sense."

And I did. But it was easier because he'd prepared me. I didn't panic when a movement took my breath away; I knew to expect it.

I've had too many doctors in my life. But I've learned that God works through them. Every time I flinched with pain, I knew that through that doctor, God had given me a bit of certainty, even if it was about how uncertain my life could be. Oddly enough, that felt like grace.

Lord, thank You for unlikely blessings and unexpected consolations.
—Marci Alborghetti

Digging Deeper: Luke 12:25–28; 1 John 4:11–12

Tuesday, March 6

For I consider that the sufferings of this present time are not worth comparing with the glory that is to be revealed to us.
—Romans 8:18 (ESV)

About three-quarters of the way through the semester, after midterm grades but before final papers were due, I started hearing from students.

"My computer crashed, so I'm not going to get it in on time."

"I have a biology paper due the same day, and I don't know how I can get both done!"

"I've got a migraine and feel nauseated all the time. I went to the nurse, but apparently I just have to wait it out. I can't work."

With each confession, I sank further into end-of-semester anguish. "I'm the worst teacher in the world," I told myself. "Too picky. Too demanding. I'm stressing them to the point of making them sick."

That week, at an instructional seminar, the invited speaker denounced just such teaching. "Learning should be play!" she concluded brightly. I sank deeper into self-reproach with every word of her spunky message.

A week later, though, I read my students' work. Their writing exceeded anything they'd done all semester.

"Wow!" I said as I handed back their papers. "I'm so impressed! You've really learned!" Their faces glowed.

Every semester reteaches me that progress—whether physical, academic, or spiritual—typically involves struggle. There are fun moments but also hard ones, and God promises to use every bit of effort for His ends.

> *Father, help me remember Your purpose in my struggles.*
> *Help me to not give up.*
> —Patty Kirk

Digging Deeper: 2 Corinthians 4:8–9; James 1:1–5

Whether you turn to the right or to the left, your ears will hear a voice behind you, saying, "This is the way; walk in it. —Isaiah 30:21 (NIV)

Tell the group who you are," the facilitator instructed us at a business workshop. Responses were "I am the manager…I am the director…I am the vice president…" Afterward, she observed, "You all told us what you do, not who you are."

To help us better understand, she introduced herself saying, "I am a follower of Jesus. My husband and I live on our ranch. I enjoy writing, teaching, and speaking. Now, who are you?" The answers were different the second time around as we struggled to publicly redefine ourselves.

At lunch, the discussion centered on why the instructor made an issue of the introductions. Some questioned why she revealed her faith. A few thought she was trying to establish a reverent tone. Others saw it as an icebreaker. Most of us thought it was a lesson in not confusing who you are with what you do.

I believe it was more. We were there to develop our leadership skills. Our teacher began by leading us to rethink our identities. Intended or not, she pointed us to her source: Jesus.

Whether you're the leader of an organization, a church committee, a community project, or a family, what greater expert to seek direction from than the Source of wisdom, guidance, and strength?

Thank You, Lord, for experiences that cause us to ponder
who we are. Keep them alive in our minds until
we find the treasures they hold. Amen.
—John Dilworth

Digging Deeper: Proverbs 3:6, 16:9, 28:26

Thursday, March 8

"I will refresh the weary and satisfy the faint." —Jeremiah 31:25 (NIV)

I feel like I just had the wind knocked out of me," my friend Krista confided over the phone. She'd applied for a job recently and thought the interview had gone well. But they didn't hire her. She'd been job hunting for more than six months and was discouraged. Before I could offer any words of encouragement, she mumbled that she needed to go and hung up.

I called her later and invited her to lunch the following day. The minute she sat down, she looked over at me. "I don't know what to do," she blurted out. "It's harder and harder to keep on looking when I keep on getting knocked down."

I reached over and took her hand. "I know this is hard," I said. "Let's pray about it." I prayed quietly. "Lord, give Krista the courage and tenacity to keep looking for the job that will fulfill Your perfect will for her. Amen."

We finished our meal, talking about possible jobs she could apply for when a message alert sounded on my phone. I glanced at it. It was from my friend Jessica. She'd posted a story online about her son at school that day. I read through it quickly, then looked up at Krista and smiled. "I think you'll like this story," I said.

I read Jessica's post out loud: "Here's a great lesson from my five-year-old son, Sam. He just told me that someone pushed him down at recess today. So I asked him, 'What did you do?' He replied, 'Well, I just bounced right back up!'"

Krista and I both laughed. She said, smiling, "Well, if Sam can do it, then I guess I can too!"

When it feels like life has knocked me over, Lord,
give me the strength to get right back up.
—Melody Bonnette Swang

Digging Deeper: Ephesians 6:10–18; 1 John 4:4

"Honor your father and your mother, that your days may be long in the land that the Lord your God is giving you." —Exodus 20:12 (ESV)

Both of my parents fell ill this year at the same time. This was the first time either of them had been hospitalized for a serious condition. It seemed as if the moment that one of them was released from the hospital, the other would have to go back in the very next day. It was overwhelming to experience the entire thing from more than seven hundred miles away.

I had planned a trip home to celebrate the birth of my nephew, but by the time the trip arrived, my parents needed help; the trip was filled with doctors' appointments, calls to different health care professionals and providers, monitoring medicine intake, fluid bags, and sleep.

I felt sad not to have special time to bond with my new nephew, but I also couldn't help feeling grateful for opportunities to give back, in any profound way, to those who nurtured me and helped me grow.

The week was in no way glamorous, nor were there grandiose gestures made. However, I do not underestimate the power of showing love and I didn't take for granted that one emotion-filled week where love was not just a word but an action.

Lord, help me to be fully present in the time I spend with my parents and to honor them by simply practicing love.
—Natalie Perkins

Digging Deeper: John 13:34–35

Saturday, March 10

"Blessed are the peacemakers, for they will be called children of God."
—Matthew 5:9 (NIV)

Scarcely older than I am, cousin Nancy had touched us all with her loving-kindnesses: Christmas ornaments for the children; lavish meals for family holidays; weekly visits and treats for my declining mother. She remembered birthdays and kept in touch with the Swedish relatives. Her motherly ways nurtured and connected our family.

Suddenly, a fast-moving illness had taken her from us, and I felt that the keeper of the family flame had been snuffed out. Now I dreaded her funeral visitation, not just because of the aching loss but because two family members no longer on speaking terms would undoubtedly be present. I loved them both, yet prayers for their reconciliation had gone unanswered. The spat had started, as spats often do, with both parties under stress. An emotional e-mail. An unkind retort. A standoff nearly four years long. Neither seemed willing to offer an olive branch.

The jammed parking lot at the funeral home attested to Nancy's network of relatives and hundreds of friends here in her lifelong hometown. Not surprisingly, the queue for the receiving line ran out the door. I merged into the end—right behind one of the feuding relatives. No sooner had I offered a hug, than the other estranged relative arrived behind me. These two eyed each other briefly, shook hands, and began to talk about the upcoming Fourth of July. The spell was broken. I sniffled into my tissue, not because I missed my cousin but because I could feel her goodwill still holding our family together.

*Loving God, thank You for the gifts of grace and
a loving cousin. May she rest in peace.*
—Gail Thorell Schilling

Digging Deeper: Matthew 5:23–24, 44; Romans 12:18–21;
Ephesians 2:14–22

"He says to the snow, 'Fall on the earth,' and to the rain shower, 'Be a mighty downpour.'" —Job 37:6 (NIV)

Just when I am sure we will go the whole year without one snowstorm, I wake up to half a foot of white on the ground. Grabbing a cup of coffee, I put on my coat and boots to take our small dog, Soda, out for his morning walk. Every tree sparkles in the rising sun. I stop in the doorway, taking in the beauty.

"Did you order this?" my neighbor yells out.

"I did," I say. And I mean it, because I was just telling the boys we didn't even get to sleigh ride once this winter. Now there's more than enough to glide down our big hill or build a snowman, and I feel like God has answered a prayer I'd kept secret.

The daffodils are bent over from the weight of their new snow jackets and Soda is up to his collar in drifts. He jumps around and then rolls on his back, frolicking, and I realize there's one more thing to add to my absolute favorite things: my boys' laughter, the scent of line-dried sheets, and now Soda dancing in the snow.

My legs are frozen between the tops of my boots and pajama bottoms, but I can't hurry Soda because he's just too cute and I asked for this—deep in my heart, I asked.

Heavenly Father, thank You for surprises like this,
for unexpected beauty and dogs that dance.
—Sabra Ciancanelli

Digging Deeper: Matthew 6:8; Luke 12:30–31

Monday, March 12

As we have received mercy, we do not lose heart. —2 Corinthians 4:1 (NKJV)

I awoke from anesthesia surrounded by the warm, loving presence of God. I didn't want to leave that place of utter peace so near to Him. Reluctantly, I regained my senses.

God had answered my prayers for healing. By rupturing the same disk a second time, I discovered that doctors were able to perform the surgery needed to fix problems that had been plaguing me for four years.

Over the next few weeks, my strength returned and the pain from surgery faded. Every day I could do a little more. I'd received my very own miracle.

Then I heard news about a family member who had been battling cancer since childhood. The bone marrow transplant surgery he'd just undergone hadn't worked. The cancer was back. His last hope was a trial drug.

I felt the wind drop from my sails. Who was I to ask God for healing? There was a twenty-three-year-old man who needed this miracle more than I did. I'd been dealing with crippling pain for a few years, but it wasn't threatening to take away my life.

Dear Lord, why me and not him?

I know I cannot answer that question, but what I can do is share some of my miracle with my family member and tell him about the complete warmth I experienced when God was protecting me during surgery. The end isn't something to fear but to celebrate.

Lord, Your mercies are more than I deserve.
Please don't let the miracles You work in me be squandered.
Help me to show others Your everlasting goodness.
—Erika Bentsen

Digging Deeper: Luke 18:1; 2 Corinthians 4:15–16;
Ephesians 3:8–13

"Simon, are you asleep? Could you not watch one hour?" —Mark 14:37 (RSV)

I am a lifelong churchgoer, so you'd think by now I'd have the rigors of Holy Week figured out. Yet I continue to model myself after Saint Peter in the Garden of Gethsemane: fast asleep.

I was supposed to meet my wife, Sandee, at Maundy Thursday services, but I was (as usual) late. The church was mysteriously empty, save for some stragglers. Had I missed everything?

As I sat in the dark church in an even darker mood, I heard voices somewhere, then the vague but unmistakable smell of incense. The service, I realized, was in the small chapel below, as it always is. I simply wasn't paying attention.

Welcome to my own Lenten metaphor. I am often too distracted to find out where I should really be, too preoccupied to focus on what I should really do. Instead, I flit from place to place, a driverless car hauling my inattentiveness to its next missed appointment, ignoring the distant voices calling me to my real purpose.

Today, more than ever, I am feeling my Peter-like humanity. Try as I might, I am struggling to stay awake to watch, to witness, to pray. "Could you not watch one hour?" My heart says yes, but my actions show the real answer: well, no, probably not.

One day I'll have to answer for that answer.

Lord, the spirit is willing, but the rest of me sleeps.
Wake me to the possibilities of this world and the next.
—Mark Collins

Digging Deeper: Psalm 121:2–4

Wednesday, March 14

He entrusted himself to him who judges justly. —1 Peter 2:23 (NIV)

I am hopping mad.

I wish I were angry with someone who's treated me badly, but it's worse than that. Someone has humiliated one of my children. It's not another kid; it's an adult, a Christian. That makes it so much harder to take. The callousness, the downright meanness...I can hardly stand to think about it! The mama bear inside me wants to attack.

I've already tried talking things over with him, but he refused to consider the possibility that he was in the wrong, so now all I can do is to remove my child from his influence and walk away. I can't fix him. Only God can do that.

As I decide to pray for my child and leave the rest to God, I think of Jesus's warning against causing a little one to stumble. I imagine this man giving a reckoning before the Lord, answering for this offense. I think of the wrath he will face. Then I realize I'm kind of excited about it. *Vindication! Justice! Let him have it, Lord!*

And then I remember the gift of forgiveness that God has given me, and I'm filled with shame. Maybe while I'm praying for my child, I should also pray for the wrongdoer. *Oh, Lord, that's too hard! How can You expect that of me? How can I possibly do it?*

I can't. Not on my own. But God promised me that I can do all things through Him Who strengthens me (Philippians 4:13).

Lord, help me share the gift of forgiveness.
I know You can do anything...even tame a wild mama bear.
—Ginger Rue

Digging Deeper: Matthew 25:40; Luke 17:2

Then he began to wash the disciples' feet, drying them with the towel he had around him. —John 13:5 (NLT)

I'll admit, I don't keep the neatest office. My bookshelves sag under the burden of more volumes than they were intended to hold. My desk is piled with the detritus of a harried editor—manuscripts, books, letters, magazines, an accordion of sticky notes. It is the area underneath my desk, however, that is the most unsightly.

Not to point fingers but my wife monopolizes most of the closet space where a man would store his modest shoe collection. So I keep my workplace shoes in my office and wear something comfortable to commute. The shoes under my desk are in complete disarray.

One morning recently I ducked under my desk to locate the shoes I wanted to wear only to find everything was mysteriously matched up, the shoes neatly lined up in pairs. I knew I hadn't done it. But who? Who would have known about this hidden mess? It was my dirty little secret.

José, who comes evenings to clean our offices, was the culprit. Or angel. He empties the trash can under my desk, which made him privy to my shoe situation. Usually I'm still working when José appears so I just hand him my trash can. But I'd been out for a few days and José had seen the state of affairs.

"José," I said, "you really don't have to do that."

"It's a little thing. Don't worry."

Since then, I try to keep my shoes neat...with improving results. Still, whenever things get out of control under my desk, José steps in. Maybe it is a little thing, but it's made a big impression on me.

Father, help me to see all the little opportunities
You give me to help others.
—Edward Grinnan

Digging Deeper: Proverbs 11:25; Galatians 5:13–14; 1 Peter 4:10

Friday, March 16

"Everything is possible for one who believes." —Mark 9:23 (NIV)

When I moved to Massachusetts, I discovered that in Boston, March 17 is not only Saint Patrick's Day but also Evacuation Day, with military drills by Revolutionary War enactors. It's all to honor a young Boston bookseller who took on an "impossible" task.

British troops had occupied Boston. Thousands of redcoats were billeted in the city; a fleet of warships blockaded the harbor. In July 1775, George Washington arrived to take charge of the ragtag Continental army. If only he could place cannons on Dorchester Heights overlooking the harbor, he saw at once that he could force the British to withdraw. But, as everyone knew, the Americans had no cannons.

True, word had traveled east that the Green Mountain Boys had captured Fort Ticonderoga with its plentiful artillery. But that was three hundred miles and a mountain range away, in upstate New York. This is when twenty-six-year-old Henry Knox appeared at Washington's headquarters: "I can bring you those cannons."

So began the most astonishing logistics feat of the Revolutionary War. Commandeering oxen from farms along his route, Knox's expedition arrived at Ticonderoga in December. There they constructed huge reinforced sleds, loaded them with sixty tons of cannons and equipment, hitched them to teams of oxen, and began the laborious trek across the frozen Hudson River and the snow-covered Berkshire Mountains.

One spring morning the British looked up to see what could not possibly be: a ring of cannons lining the hill above them. There was a hasty assembling of redcoat ranks, a swift raising of a thousand sails, and on March 17, 1776, the British evacuated Boston, never to return. It was the Continental army's first victory, an all-important morale booster for the difficult years ahead.

Teach me, Father, that the word impossible *has no place in the life of faith.*
—Elizabeth Sherrill

Digging Deeper: 2 Kings 6:15–17

"The Lord searches every mind, and understands every plan and thought. If you seek him, he will be found by you...." —1 Chronicles 28:9 (NRSV)

My friend Mike wears green on Saint Patrick's Day, and he wears a red, white, and blue pin on the Fourth of July. He's known around town for his holiday spirit throughout the year. Mike is present at every parade and festivity. He's a cheerful, joyful man. But what no one knows is that every day Mike also carries a set of prayer beads, attached to a cross, in his pocket. I've known Mike for twenty years, and I found this out one day only by accident.

We were sitting at breakfast and our server, Sarah, playfully asked for a bigger tip.

"I don't have it," I said, and, standing up, pulled both of my pants pockets inside out as if to demonstrate that I had nothing left to give.

"What about you, Mike?" she said with a grin. "What's in your pockets?"

He stood up, too. And then Mike pulled out his car keys, the cross and beads, and two quarters, which he promptly placed in Sarah's palm. She chuckled and walked away. She had other tables to tend to.

"I didn't know you carried that," I said to Mike.

"Well, why would you?" he said. "I use it when I pray." I knew that Mike prayed. We've sat near each other in church for years. But I didn't know, as Mike explained that day, that he carried a "prayer reminder" every day. That was four years ago.

Since that day, I have also carried a prayer reminder in my pocket. I touch it sometimes by accident, and sometimes my hand goes quickly to it with special intention, and I pray.

Forgive me, Lord, when I don't remember You as I should.
—Jon Sweeney

Digging Deeper: Romans 12:1–2

Sunday, March 18

CONFIDENCE IN DIFFICULTY: Mercy to Carry My Cross

"Whoever wants to be my disciple must deny themselves and take up their cross daily and follow me." —Luke 9:23 (NIV)

Our daughter Maggie was being admitted to a psychiatric hospital. It wasn't a surprise. Her mood hadn't budged past "I'd rather not be alive" for months, and now she was flying into rages several times a day. My husband, Andrew, called from New York City with the news while I was trudging through snow in the Midwest from our daughter Elizabeth's apartment to the hospital where she had been admitted.

After visiting with our seventy-nine-pound daughter, who was on an IV and a heart monitor, I stopped in at Elizabeth's church to pray. I'd gone there the year before, during her first battle with anorexia. At that time I'd pleaded desperately, "What do You want me to do, Lord?"

The answer came back clearly: "Love her. Pray for her. Draw her close to Me." It wasn't what I expected, but it made sense.

This time I knelt without words, without thoughts, without tears. My whole being consisted of heartache encased in skin. I waited, but no sudden lightening of my load occurred and there were no messages of encouragement or hope. I didn't feel stronger or wiser or comforted. I knew my children were hurting, knew they were God's, knew things might not be okay in the end. That was it.

Yet in that nothingness I grew curiously certain I was doing all that I could, all that God expected of me. That was an enormous mercy. For to accept my limits and accept my tasks gave me freedom. It meant I could tap into the energy I might have spent railing against my sense of helplessness.

Lord, keep me from fighting the cross You have given me and help me to use that energy to carry it instead.
—Julia Attaway

Digging Deeper: John 19:17; 2 Corinthians 1:5

These commandments that I give you today are to be on your hearts.
Impress them on your children. Talk about them when you sit at home
and when you walk along the road, when you lie down and when
you get up. —Deuteronomy 6:6–7 (NIV)

I grabbed my wallet off the counter, pulled on my coat, and headed toward the sunporch, where my mom was waiting to go shopping.

"Sorry," I said as I plunked myself into a wicker chair. I fished underneath for my shoes. "I hate making you wait for me."

"Don't worry about it," she said. "Ready to go?"

She sat across from me, her hands wrapped around a Bible. She had propped it open on her lap. It was the same one that she had used since I was a baby. She was taking this brief moment to read a few verses.

I knew that her Bible was well loved. It had only half a cover. The margins overflowed with her looping handwriting. The text was highlighted and underlined and highlighted again. She took it almost everywhere with her—to the doctor's office, to my brothers' soccer practices, to the swimming pool. She didn't want to waste a second.

I wanted that drive. To read a Psalm between classes instead of checking Facebook. To carry God's Word with me until the pages were all dog-eared and the binding was held together by tape. To seek out my heavenly Father every moment I could. Just like this wise woman who tucked her Bible under her arm.

Lord, help me to seek You diligently.
—Logan Eliasen

Digging Deeper: Deuteronomy 11:18; Joshua 1:8

Tuesday, March 20

It happened in the spring of the year.... —2 Samuel 11:1 (NKJV)

I stood over the remains of what would have been tulips. They'd been nearly ready to bloom, but a hard freeze following the snowstorm was too much for them.

Most people hear "Oregon" and think "rain." While that's often true along the coast, it doesn't apply to the east side of the Cascade Range. Where I live, there are more sunny days than not, but our weather is more wild than mild. We have a limited growing season because of late frosts. Snow is common in June. Temperature swings are more like roller-coaster rides.

While half of the state celebrates the gentle coming of spring with a glorious array of daffodils, rhododendrons, and cherry blossoms, I've learned to see past the lingering snowdrifts for more subtle signs of winter's retreat. Here, spring is marked with birds, not flowers.

Mid-February I begin searching for the greater sandhill cranes. Looking like a pterodactyl with feathers, these giant birds typically arrive ahead of the worst blizzard of the year. Robins appear soon after the first thaw, no matter how briefly it lasts. Red-winged blackbirds, nuthatches, Stellar's jays, killdeer, and swallows materialize without fanfare. More vocally, Canadian geese begin pairing up and bickering with their neighbors. Often they are fighting to claim trophy nesting sites, which look more like ice sculptures.

God has made each place beautiful and each climate unique. How wondrous!

Light of this life, thank You for spring!
—Erika Bentsen

Digging Deeper: Isaiah 52:7; Matthew 5:14–16; Mark 4:21–22; Luke 11:33–36; Acts 13:47

God... giveth grace unto the humble. —James 4:6 (KJV)

The streets of Colombo, Sri Lanka, where my husband and I were visiting, were dirty. Here and there, sewer smells permeated the air. Yet, as we walked along, the faces of the people were open and friendly. Haunting music could be heard somewhere in the distance and the sounds of prayer drifted out from a nearby mosque.

The outdoor market offered bins of bright spices and mysterious vegetables, while children laughed and played between the stalls.

I was feeling proud of my adventurous spirit and openness to exotic cultures as we made a turn down an alley and found ourselves standing in from of a beautiful, colorful Hindu temple. The huge blue door was flung open in welcome, and a series of bells invited all inside.

Shoes lined the entrance. David stooped to remove his.

"I'm not going barefoot in there," I announced in my best neurotic voice. "The streets are filthy and most of these people walk around without shoes. I can't even imagine the germs."

We agreed that I would wait, as David disappeared through the entryway. I stood outside the door and peered in. A shaft of sunlight from a high window created a path, urging me inside.

I didn't go; my fear won.

Over and over, I asked David what it was like. "Well...you really had to be there," he would answer. David came home completely free of foot fungus...and I with a heart heavy for what I had missed.

Father, when my haughty spirit holds me back, push me forward toward the wonders You spread out before me.
—Pam Kidd

Digging Deeper: Proverbs 11:2, 16:18

Thursday, March 22

THE BEAUTY OF SIMPLICITY: Everyday Hospitality

Not that I have already obtained this or am already perfect; but I press on to make it my own, because Christ Jesus has made me his own.
—Philippians 3:12 (RSV)

My husband, Rick, thought it would be a great idea to sign us up to be church group leaders, and I explained why his idea wouldn't work. "What about our driveway? Whenever we get heavy rain, it turns into a mudslide. Your roosters go nuts when people come over. Who wants to be licked to death by an overfriendly Lab?"

"You're worrying for nothing."

"We live way back in the woods. What if our home isn't what they're looking for?"

"What do you think they're looking for?"

One word came to me, too ugly to share: *perfection.*

Rick studied me, his brown eyes full of sincerity. "Julie, I've prayed about this."

I groaned. *Maybe he's right. We had to try, but would it work?*

The night of our first meeting, I lit candles and set the table. The roosters were behaving. No sign of rain. So far, so good. I put the dog upstairs, made a pot of coffee, and surveyed the kitchen. I didn't have enough matching china. Paper plates and cups lined the counter, and an antique pitcher holding silverware was tied with a red bow.

At 7:15 p.m., fourteen men and women held hands and Rick said the blessing. While we ate tacos, beans, and rice, I sensed sweet warmth moving among us—laughter, honesty, the beginning of friendships.

The remedy for my fear and doubt was simple. When I focused on God and others, our home became a place of peace and healing.

Father, I know I'm not perfect, but I'm yours.
—Julie Garmon

Digging Deeper: Job 31:32; Acts 16:34; 1 Peter 4:9–10

"I have come that they may have life, and have it to the full."
—John 10:10 (NIV)

I joined the staff of a small school that is committed to serving the poor in our community. Every year we host Run for Hope, a marathon that functions as our largest fund-raiser. This past weekend I enjoyed my first Run for Hope, which united runners from all over the United States. As I talked with several participants, I discovered each had brought his or her own history of personal losses and triumphs: brain tumors, amputations, cancer. Many had jumped multiple hurdles before they'd stepped up to the starting line.

When the first runners began trickling into our finish-line party, we volunteers applauded. "Great job!" I yelled as the 5K runners entered, panting and wiping their brows. Later, I cheered for the half marathoners, rubbing their shins and soaking their feet in ice. Hours into the race, we were honored to welcome our full marathoners. I practically screamed my head off for this dedicated crew, many of them limping and hobbling after the long run.

Near the end of the race, my husband and I packed up to go home, assuming that all of the runners had joined the party. Then a volunteer announced, "There's one more runner on his way. He'll be our last to welcome."

Ten minutes later, we cheered for a seventy-year-old man! I thought I'd heard the most amazing stories of triumph, but this was the best of all. He had run a full marathon and even placed first in his age group.

As I belted out my loudest accolades, this man's perseverance spoke volumes. Each day is a gift to be treasured. Each year is an opportunity to reach new heights. Each decade is a call to share my talents, passions, and heart with others.

> *Lord, help me live each day with joy and service,*
> *until the very moment You call me home.*
> —Carla Hendricks

Digging Deeper: Psalms 16:11, 90:12

Saturday, March 24

PREPARING FOR THE RESURRECTION
Walking on Sacred Ground

He has also set eternity in the human heart. —Ecclesiastes 3:11 (NIV)

I vividly remember the day I went to visit my friend Leslie, shortly after hearing that she'd chosen to stop treatment for her advanced breast cancer.

Leslie's husband, Alan, welcomed me and led me into the living room where Leslie sat in a comfy chair wearing a soft, pale-blue knitted hat. "How are you?" I asked, hugging her and realizing how thoughtless that question sounded. But Leslie didn't miss a beat.

"I'm preparing for the Resurrection," she said with a smile.

Her blunt honesty both stunned and intrigued me. How does a person prepare for the Resurrection?

Our lives had crisscrossed through the years; I was more than ten years older and I'd gone ahead of her in our shared challenges. I'd survived Stage 4 ovarian cancer and was cancer-free when Leslie was diagnosed with breast cancer. We spent time together then and again when her cancer returned. I was now a healthy twelve-year survivor and she was in her fifties, planning her funeral.

This time Leslie was going ahead of me. And I wanted to watch. To listen. To walk with her on her journey.

I want to journey intentionally through Holy Week so that I, like Jesus, like Leslie, will reach Easter Sunday with a louder *Hallelujah!* because of what I discover along the way.

Lord, I, too, am preparing for the Resurrection.
Please help me discover Your truths along the way.
—Carol Kuykendall

Digging Deeper: Jeremiah 29:11; John 11:25–26

PREPARING FOR THE RESURRECTION
Following Jesus
"Come, follow me," Jesus said. —Mark 1:17 (NIV)

I stood in church on Palm Sunday watching the children parade through the aisles, waving their palm branches. I loved how the youngest ones held on to a rope tethered to their Sunday school teacher so they could follow her through the crowded sanctuary because they could hardly see where they were going. It reminded me of the way Leslie so faithfully followed Jesus on her journey.

How could I be that intentional?

Leslie pictured herself following Jesus ever since she gave her life to Him at church camp when she was thirteen. Since then she lived within a word picture where she and Jesus were on a hike up a mountain together, maybe because she loved hiking.

By the time Leslie reached the last weeks of her life, when the climb got harder, her familiar habit of following Jesus comforted and strengthened her. She trusted Jesus to keep showing her the way and to welcome her with open arms when she reached her destination at the top of the mountain.

The memory of Leslie's consistent following challenges me. I've survived way beyond my two-year life expectancy, and I now see myself on a Divine Detour. I don't always know my way, but I can trust that Jesus does and He goes before me. Yet sometimes I forget to look for Him.

I want to forget less often. So I'm practicing a new habit. When I close my eyes to pray, I picture Jesus on the back of my eyelids, which reminds me that He is right there, between me and the circumstances of my day.

Jesus, whenever I want to see You, I can close my eyes and there You are,
because You promise to always go before me and lead me safely home.
—Carol Kuykendall

Digging Deeper: Matthew 16:24; John 8:12, 10:3–5

Monday of Holy Week, March 26

PREPARING FOR THE RESURRECTION
Choosing to Surrender

"Father, if you are willing, take this cup from me; yet not my will but yours be done." An angel from heaven appeared to him and strengthened him. —Luke 22:42–43 (NIV)

How did you make the decision to stop treatment?" I asked Leslie one morning, longing to know how she made that brave choice to put God in total control of numbering her days.

"It was hard," she admitted, suddenly tearing up. "I felt a conflicting tension, but I began to see this was about my willingness to surrender to God's will and trust Him to give me the strength to face my future. Like Jesus in Gethsemane."

During this Holy Week, I've been thinking about Leslie's courageous surrender and Jesus's agony in Gethsemane. Three times Jesus prayed, asking the Father to "take this cup from me" as He anticipated the Cross in His future. But He added His willingness to surrender to God's will. After His third prayer, He surrendered and walked out of the garden to face those who came to arrest Him—with the strength He needed to face His future.

Yesterday, I received a hurtful e-mail and immediately wrote a defensive response. It felt good and fair and justified...until I was ready to push Send and I paused. Was this one of those times where God gives me the opportunity to follow Jesus's example? Was this a small but important surrender opportunity? *"Not my will but yours be done."*

Instead of Send, I pressed Delete.

Later, when I reread the original e-mail, the words sounded different. More constructive. Less hurtful. I smiled.

Jesus, may I keep learning to pause and seek and surrender to God's will. Because that's the way to follow You. All the way to the Resurrection.
—Carol Kuykendall

Digging Deeper: 2 Samuel 22:33; Matthew 26:36–46

PREPARING FOR THE RESURRECTION
Dealing with Regrets

He who began a good work in you will carry it on to completion until the day of Christ Jesus. —Philippians 1:6 (NIV)

Leslie often talked about one of her greatest regrets: she was too much of a people-pleaser, which made her feel self-conscious and confined one of her greatest joys, her writing.

"In school, I wrote stories and my teachers told me I was a good writer. I didn't have great confidence but I knew I could write," she told me. "Yet my people-pleasing began to hold me back because I feared others might not like the stories. So I never shared my most creative writing and now I regret hiding so much of myself from others."

Her description reminded me of something I've heard: the number one regret of dying people is about living a life others expected rather than living true to themselves. That was reason enough for me to try to talk Leslie out of her regrets. But the more we talked, the more I realized that I'm something of a people-pleaser, too, and my talking was partly in my own defense.

"Even Jesus was a people-pleaser...sometimes," I offered, but I'm not sure I convinced her—or myself.

During Holy Week, I've been thinking about Jesus's last days in Jerusalem. He was not Who everyone wanted Him to be, but He had the courage to always be Who God created Him to be. He was a God-pleaser Who didn't fear what others might think. And in heaven He redeems our regrets and unfinished business. That's a blessing for Leslie now.

As for me, it's a wake-up call.

Lord, I pray for the courage to know and to be who You made me to be, on this side of heaven, and that You will redeem the regrets I might still be carrying when I reach the Resurrection.
—Carol Kuykendall

Digging Deeper: Psalm 139; 1 Corinthians 12:14–20

Wednesday of Holy Week, March 28

PREPARING FOR THE RESURRECTION
Learning in Loneliness

"Surely I am with you always, to the very end of the age."
—Matthew 28:20 (NIV)

I'm lonely," Leslie told me one morning. She sat in a new place, on the couch in the family room, wrapped in a blanket and propped up with pillows.

"Tell me about it," I urged.

"My world is growing smaller. I need people but I don't really want them to stop by because I don't have enough energy. And they don't know what to say. Most people don't want to talk about dying.

"Heaven is mysterious," Leslie went on, "and there's so much we don't know. But I know that something holy is happening within me. I just can't find the words to describe it. Jesus says heaven will be better than earth. Still, it's a little scary because it's unknown."

I didn't stay long that day. Leslie was tired and needed to sleep.

As I headed home, I thought about how many times I'm physically alone in a single day. Driving my car. Walking my dog. Writing at my computer. Early morning conversations with God. Maybe God intends us to get used to being physically alone at times.

Did He intend that for Jesus in Gethsemane? Jesus knew His time was drawing near and wanted His disciples to circle up and pray with Him, but they fell asleep instead and left Him alone—with the Father. Maybe there was a purpose in that. Maybe God wants us to get used to knowing He is with us always, even when we think we are alone. Because there are places we must go alone. Like heaven.

Father, may I spend my earthly days learning how safe and
secure I am alone with You. Always.
—Carol Kuykendall

Digging Deeper: 1 Kings 19:1–8

PREPARING FOR THE RESURRECTION
Practicing Laughter

She laughs without fear of the future. —Proverbs 31:25 (NLT)

The time came when Leslie spent most of her days in bed. The first time I found her there, I pulled up a chair and held her hand. We laughed together that day, mostly as I reminded her of things she'd already told me.

Like the Thanksgiving when her eccentric grandmother dropped the cooked turkey on the kitchen floor and immediately started kicking that slippery old bird around the room in frustration. Leslie saw it as a hilarious example of her grandmother's unpredictable personality.

I loved that in the midst of the hardest things, Leslie still liked to laugh.

"Do you think there will be laughter in heaven?" I asked her.

"For sure," she said with confidence. "So we have to practice."

During Holy Week, I attended a funeral for Ray, our church's beloved custodian who died suddenly of a heart attack at age forty-nine. I walked into church with a heavy heart. His death stunned everyone who filled our sanctuary that day. But what I appreciated most during that service was the blessing of laughter.

Ray had come to know and love Jesus during his years of service to our church, and woven into the reflections about his life were many humorous reminders of his fierce protection of all things "church." Nobody messed with Ray. Or the church building. Laughter filled the sanctuary in the midst of sadness, and I thought about Leslie practicing laughter, which is the sound of hope and joy—at funerals and surely in heaven.

> *Lord, the sound of laughter here gives me a taste of the joy*
> *I will experience there. Remind me to keep practicing.*
> —Carol Kuykendall

Digging Deeper: Ecclesiastes 3:4; Luke 6:21

Good Friday, March 30

PREPARING FOR THE RESURRECTION
Enduring Suffering

I want to know Christ—yes, to know the power of his resurrection and participation in his sufferings, becoming like him in his death, and so, somehow attaining to the resurrection from the dead. —Philippians 3:10–11 (NIV)

After saying good-bye to Leslie during our weekly visits, I always stopped to talk with her husband, Alan.

"Why has God allowed Leslie to endure all this suffering?" he asked one morning, shaking his head. "I know some answers but I'm having a hard time believing them." I nodded in agreement because he voiced a question I've often asked in watching another person suffer. It doesn't make sense in the way I try to make sense of God's love.

When I left their house that day, I felt sad that I didn't have a better answer for Alan. Or for me. But I remembered that early on, Leslie talked about suffering.

"In my stronger moments, I see suffering as something I share with Jesus. He had to go through the temporary pain of dying on the Cross to get to the Resurrection, which brings us the eternal gift of new life in heaven. And I have to endure suffering and die to get there too."

As I sat in the darkness of our Good Friday service at church, I tried to comprehend the unimaginable suffering that Jesus endured. I could think of only one place where I came close to experiencing something similar. As a pregnant mother, going through intense labor pains in order to receive the joy of bringing new life into the world. Enduring the temporary pain was the only way to get to something beautifully better.

Jesus, I'm humbled by the suffering You endured to fulfill Your life purpose and to give us the hope-filled promise of eternal life.
—Carol Kuykendall

Digging Deeper: Isaiah 53:5; Romans 8:16–18; 1 Peter 5:10

PREPARING FOR THE RESURRECTION: Embracing Silence

Precious in the sight of the Lord is the death of his saints.
—Psalm 116:15 (KJV)

I t is done."

Those three words in an e-mail from Alan told me that Leslie had completed her journey. I expected the news, so why did I suddenly feel unhinged to the faith that had carried us through this season?

If Leslie is finally home with You, God, why don't I feel like celebrating? I sensed an answer but didn't know if it came from God or my struggling heart: the death of someone you love forces you to face what you believe about the mystery of heaven.

The last time I saw her, I reminded her how she saw herself hiking up a mountain toward the summit where Jesus waited with arms open wide. Just a few more steps to Jesus and heaven. Then I repeated the words of the song we'd often shared in her last weeks:

Turn your eyes upon Jesus; look full in His wonderful face,
And the things of this world will grow strangely dim
In the light of His glory and grace.

Why couldn't I simply believe what I believed that day? My question remained unanswered.

Maybe that's why God gives us a day in Holy Week that I call "Silent Saturday," between Good Friday and Easter Sunday. A day of silence when grief can cloud our thinking about death and heaven. On this Silent Saturday, I remembered all that Leslie had said about heaven becoming more real, while admitting she didn't always understand.

Lord, much about heaven seems a mystery, but I trust You will
give me the same increasing faith You gave Leslie.
—Carol Kuykendall

Digging Deeper: Mark 16:9–11; Luke 24:13–26

GOD'S UNFAILING LOVE

1 _____

2 _____

3 _____

4 _____

5 _____

6 _____

7 _____

8 _____

9 _____

10 _____

11 _____

12 _____

13 _____

14 _____

15 _____

16 _____

17 _____

18 _____

19 _____

20 _____

21 _____

22 _____

23 _____

24 _____

25 _____

26 _____

27 _____

28 _____

29 _____

30 _____

31 _____

APRIL

Do you think anyone is going to be able to drive a wedge

between us and Christ's love for us? There is no way!

—Romans 8:35 (MSG)

PREPARING FOR THE RESURRECTION: He Is Risen!

If we have been united with him in a death like his, we will certainly also be united with him in a resurrection like his. —Romans 6:5 (NIV)

The ringing bells in the tower sounded like a *Hallelujah!* as we joined throngs of people funneling toward the church on Easter morning. Birds were singing, crocuses blooming, and a blue sky promised plenty of sunshine. All of creation seemed prepared to celebrate. Me too.

With our daughters and their families, we filled a whole row in the sanctuary, six adults and six grandchildren, girls in colorful Easter dresses, boys with moussed hair.

I leaned back, absorbing the buzz of anticipation to celebrate the Resurrection. I thought of Leslie and how she kept seeing Jesus in her final journey, but I realized it wasn't just Jesus. She saw the *resurrected* Jesus because she believed in the Resurrection.

I looked around and saw many people whose stories reflected similar faithfulness and hope. And others I knew were hungry for the hope of the Easter message: a family raising other people's children; a widower learning to find a new way in a life alone; people in financial crisis, unemployment, and homelessness; folks in broken relationships. Here we were, all together, waiting to hear the Easter message that Jesus's death and Resurrection promises eternal life with Him in heaven, where there will be no more pain or stress or loneliness or death.

Soon the music started, and the pastor stepped forward and pronounced: "Jesus Christ is risen!"

Together, we all responded: "He is risen indeed!"

"Let the celebration begin."

Hallelujah, Jesus! Your Resurrection promises
that the best is yet to come. Amen!
—Carol Kuykendall

Digging Deeper: Acts 2:24; 1 Corinthians 15:12–19

Monday, April 2

May your unfailing love be my comfort according to your promises to your servant. —Psalm 119:76 (NIV)

During a vacation in Mexico, I went for a walk on the beach near a wall of huge sand-colored rocks that skirted the ocean. Suddenly, I stopped dead in my tracks. A three-foot-long iguana was sitting right in front of me as if to say, "This is my path. Back off."

I continued nonetheless, but slowly. I was on alert for the gray-tan reptiles. Soon I started seeing them everywhere on the rocks. They'd been right in front of me all along, only I hadn't seen them because they were so well camouflaged.

I began to wonder what else I hadn't seen clearly that was right in front of me. I thought about the more than one hundred workers who made things run smoothly at the immense resort where we were staying. I hadn't gone out of my way to show much appreciation to any of them.

When I returned to the resort, I decided to pay closer attention to those helping to make my vacation so pleasant. I smiled more and started using my high-school Spanish to say "Good morning" and "How are you?" to each waiter, housekeeper, and pool and beach attendant. I put dollars in my beach bag to share with the workers, even though tips were included in our stay. I started cleaning up after myself after each meal to make it easier for the staff.

When I returned home from Mexico, I made an effort to talk to and appreciate the people who help me in so many ways, such as grocery-store clerks, waitresses, even my pastor. Thanks to those well-camouflaged iguanas, I'm now trying harder to show my gratitude for every person who makes my life richer.

Heavenly Father, help me to keep my head out of the sand and to show kindness to everyone who crosses my path.
—Patricia Lorenz

Digging Deeper: 2 Corinthians 6:3–10; 1 John 1:5–7

I consider that our present sufferings are not worth comparing with the glory that will be revealed in us. —Romans 8:18 (NIV)

L onny, the three youngest boys, and I rode on the bike path that stretches alongside the river. It was finally spring. The trees held tender buds. A family of turtles sunned on driftwood. The valley was rich with endless shades of green. Everything was waking, changing. There were changes in my boys too.

Seven-year-old Isaiah steered his three-speed close to my rusty green Schwinn.

"Did you notice, Mom," he said, "the difference in me?"

"What do you mean?"

"Last year I could only make it to the bench. This year I'm going to make it to the bridge."

He was right. Just last fall his legs gave out. He'd pushed all he could, but the bridge was too far.

"You've grown, Isaiah," I said. "You're one winter stronger."

My son smiled, pedaled, and kept his bike even with mine.

One winter stronger. I could relate.

For a long time now, a young-adult son has struggled. Watching him hurt brought deep heartache, and seeing him walk away from the things I taught him took me to a place of panic. I tried to help, but worry and fear settled strong. Recently, though, I've begun to pray to grow in understanding—not in the circumstance but in knowledge of the Lord.

And as I one-day-at-a-time let go of fear and control and choose to claim God's powerful presence in my son's life, my faith-muscles firm.

"What do you think, Mom?" Isaiah asked from under his helmet. "Race me to the dock?"

"You're on," I said. And off we went, both of us stronger.

Father, thank You for the growth that can happen during tough times. Amen.
    —Shawnelle Eliasen

Digging Deeper: Psalm 9:9–10; James 1:2–4; 1 John 4:4

Wednesday, April 4

Neglect not the gift that is in thee. —1 Timothy 4:14 (KJV)

As a little kid, I would swing on my swing over the garden and belt out songs from "Jambalaya" to "Jingle Bells." We lived far out in the country, so no one heard me. I sang for pure joy. Over the years, I've sung hundreds of lullabies to my children and later learned to read music well enough to join choirs. My joy surged exponentially. By my forties, I had developed enough confidence to sing solos, mostly at church and for weddings and funerals.

Now a retiree, I had been back in New Hampshire from my month-long winter sojourn in Florida and still hadn't rejoined the church choir, opting to curl up with a book on my couch. Nor had I picked out, much less practiced, a song for the church musical fund-raiser. As for the invitation to sing with the faculty choir for commencement, well...

I might have contented myself with just singing in the shower until my friend Robin roused me from my lethargy. As we left church together, there in the stairwell I burst into the "Wishing Well" song from *Snow White*.

"How do you do that? You just open your mouth and that comes out! That's your gift, Gail. You need to sing more. If you didn't, you'd be selfish."

Selfish? My gift, it seems, isn't just for me. Guess who went to choir practice this week and signed up for faculty choir? Now I need only find a song for that musical.

> *Lord, thank You for friends who jerk the bushel away*
> *when I'm hiding my light.*
> —Gail Thorell Schilling

Digging Deeper: Psalm 126:2; Isaiah 44:23; Matthew 5:15

FALLING INTO GRACE: A New Way to Pray

"Hear my prayer, O Lord, and give ear to my cry; do not hold your peace at my tears. For I am your passing guest...." —Psalm 39:12 (NRSV)

I had a routine for my daily prayer hour. I stood for a time before a cross, prostrating myself in humility before God. I knelt, praying for forgiveness, my needs, and the needs of others. And I spent time hunched over my Bible, which also has devotions and readings.

After my accident, I couldn't move well or assume these positions for long, if at all. How would I pray? Technically, I knew I could pray in any place, any position, but this was my routine!

I had always worshipped God with body, mind, and spirit, but now my body was too broken to "pray right." I was determined to find a new routine for my prayer hour; I couldn't imagine going to God without a plan. It seemed almost disrespectful, like wasting His time.

I decided to sit in a comfortable chair and run through all my prayers in that position. But then my mind started blanking out during prayer; I had a hard time remembering all my prayers, and sometimes I even dozed! I was mortified. I wondered if God was as disappointed in me as I was in myself.

I poured all this out to a friend who shook his head, smiling in his gentle, wise way. "You are not sleeping on the job before God," Nick said. "God is giving you the rest that He knows you need. He's leading you to pray the way you need to pray now."

For the first time since I fell, I understood that God was using this time to mend more than my bones.

Lord, teach me the right way to pray, which is any way.
—Marci Alborghetti

Digging Deeper: Job 9:1–4; Matthew 6:7–8

Friday, April 6

"I will send you rain in its season, and the ground will yield its crops and the trees their fruit." —Leviticus 26:4 (NIV)

I was making the trek to pick up my son Kalin from college, exactly an hour away from our home in Tennessee. I had driven this route more times than I could remember, but on this spring day, I noticed cloudy skies as I embarked. Minutes later, the sky turned an ominous gray, and by the time I pulled on to the highway, a torrential rain had begun.

I struggled through the downpour, barely able to see the road. I contemplated pulling over, turning on my hazard lights, and waiting out the storm, but I decided to persevere and keep moving.

I complained to myself the entire time. *Man, why is it raining so hard? This is so annoying!*

When I arrived at my son's campus, I let out a huge sigh, grateful that I'd made it safely. My son ran to the car and quickly loaded up his overnight bag, and all I did was complain some more. "We've had such terrible rainstorms recently. It's been ridiculous. I hate the heavy rains this time of year, especially here in the South."

I had just finished stating the long list of reasons why the rain offended me when we approached our street. The sun was showing off now, shining brilliantly, and it served as a spotlight on my neighbors' fuchsia azaleas, white cherry blossoms, and red Knock Out roses.

"April showers bring May flowers," my son simply said.

Of course, I thought. It was a saying my late mother was fond of reciting. I smiled at the lesson in the words and at the sweet memory they brought. *How could I have forgotten?*

Lord, thank You for producing glorious beauty after storms.
—Carla Hendricks

Digging Deeper: Psalm 85:12; Joel 2:23

"The Lord is the one who goes ahead of you; He will be with you.
He will not fail you or forsake you. Do not fear or be dismayed."
—Deuteronomy 31:8 (NAS)

W hat do you think of our former Colombian exchange student, Andres, and his family joining us? Their dream is to create a signature line of handbags to market in New York City. They can live here inexpensively and quietly while they get up and going." That's how the owners of the home we share approached us. Being big believers in hospitality, we said, "Absolutely!"

A large desk in the upstairs living quarters is crammed with sketches for bag and fabric designs. Conversation wafts down the steps as Andres and his wife, Carolina, talk animatedly with their young sons and make numerous phone calls setting business plans in place.

At times one parent or another travels to line up production details and potential retail sites. It is strenuous, uphill work. Some days the outcome seems promising; other days it looks bleak. "It's up to God," Andres says.

Recently Carolina has been away for a lengthy time. My husband and I—sensing Andres missing his wife—take him to lunch. "Andres," I counsel, "I think you are in something I call the 'Saturday Place.' Between Jesus's Friday Crucifixion and His Sunday Resurrection, His followers waited in uncertainty. Saturday Places are difficult. They ask us to trust God when the answer has not yet materialized. But then came Sunday—and a risen Jesus appeared in their midst. A whole new story!"

"This really encourages me," Andres responds.

Silently I thank God for my own Saturday Places that allow me to build up the faith of another.

Lord, from Friday—to Saturday—to Sunday—You promise
never to leave us, never to fail us, never to forsake us.
—Carol Knapp

Digging Deeper: Job 42:2; Psalms 27:14, 145:14–16; Acts 1:4

Sunday, April 8

"For I know the plans I have for you," declares the Lord, "plans to prosper you and not to harm you, plans to give you hope and a future."
—Jeremiah 29:11 (NIV)

I posted a video of my son doing a front flip at a small open gym near my home.

"You should put him in gymnastics over here," my friend and former coworker said when he saw the video.

He still worked at the elite gym where I coached gymnastics for years before my kids were born. I had dreamed of sending my boys there. But my answer was the reason that had kept me away thus far.

"I could never afford that place," I said, wishing I could.

He encouraged me to apply for a scholarship and in the meantime send the boys in to be tested for Pre-Team. I did it.

The boys made the Pre-Team, but I had to pay full price until the scholarship committee gave me an answer. I didn't have the heart to pull them out, but I barely had the funds to keep them in. And what if I didn't get the scholarship?

I watched from the mezzanine as the boys listened to their coaches and excitedly displayed their strength and agility.

"Help me, Lord," I prayed. "If you want them here, help me find a way."

I started a GoFundMe page for my little athletes. Friends and family responded and covered three months of classes, and the scholarship committee came back with a decision to grant us 50 percent off the tuition for six months.

The boys have been training for five months and are already being moved up to the competitive team. They are fearless! And I'm learning how to be fearless right along with them.

Lord, remind me that You are the maker of my future
and the provider of all that I have.
—Karen Valentin

Digging Deeper: Isaiah 41:10

Do you not know that your bodies are temples of the Holy Spirit, who is in you, whom you have received from God?... —1 Corinthians 6:19 (NIV)

I couldn't understand it. Recently my legs felt leaden, dead, like they had weights on them or the muscles were all gummed up. And they were a little achy too. I noticed I wasn't walking at my usual clip, and my stride had shortened. What was wrong with me?

Perhaps most alarming, my numbers on the bike were down slightly. I've been doing competitive indoor cycling for more than twenty years. I don't rack up as many miles annually as I used to, but I still keep a pretty grueling pace. Something was wrong, something serious.

I went to see my doctor. He had me do some balance and strength exercises while he took notes. Then he flipped through my chart. Finally I demanded, "So what's wrong with me?"

"Nothing," he said, "except that you're getting older."

"How can that be?" I asked. I detected a note of absurd disbelief in my voice.

"You have birthdays, you get older. Pretty straightforward," he said. "Look, you do things that people age forty-two can't do. But you can't do things that you could do back when *you* were forty-two, right? You're normal. The body slows down. It's perfectly natural. Accept it and stop worrying."

I left feeling both depressed and reassured. Nothing wrong with me except I was getting old. Yet why did that seem wrong? I looked down at my legs. I'd put more than one hundred thousand miles on them in the past twenty years because I always wanted to come in first. Maybe it was time to shed my baby-boomer sense of immortality and thank God for the years and the legs He had given me.

> *Father in heaven, let me never lose sight of the blessings of health,*
> *even if I'm slowing down—just a bit.*
> —Edward Grinnan

Digging Deeper: 1 Corinthians 9:24–27; 3 John 1:2

Tuesday, April 10

I will counsel thee with mine eye upon thee. —Psalm 32:8 (ASV)

Early on a delicious spring morning, I discovered what I'd feared. A small bird had somehow managed to build her nest in our garage. She selected a shoebox and, in an empty corner, fashioned a delicate funnel-shaped nest in it. No eggs yet! Even though we'd tried to be careful to keep the garage door down, she somehow still got in.

Finally, I was able to get her out into the open. She perched on our flagpole and screamed so loudly, it startled me. I hurried back into the garage and grabbed the box, which was within easy reach.

Back outside, I searched for a safe place to reposition her nest.

Still in my nightgown, I ran from one spot to another. Nothing was right. Then I caught sight of our reproduction of a well. Other birds use this area annually. I wedged the shoebox tightly near the roof.

The mother bird still screamed at me. I rushed back inside, praying she'd agree with the change. I knew best. Slightly out of breath, I sat down in my prayer chair and continued writing in my prayer journal, "Please, God, let her understand that the garage isn't safe and to settle down underneath the well roof. Guide her..."

God seemed to interrupt my prayer so that my pen stopped midair.

Marion, you're like the little bird. You select paths that seem perfect to you and confidently follow them. I have My plans for you daily. Let Me guide you, Child.

I laid down my pen and shut my eyes. "You're right, Father. So often I run around making choices for myself and others—only to discover I've been oh so wrong."

Forgive me, Lord, for being headstrong.
Help me submit to Your guidance today.
—Marion Bond West

Digging Deeper: Psalm 25:5; Isaiah 55:8–9

I am with you always.... —Matthew 28:20 (KJV)

When my husband, John, and I were students in Paris, we rented an apartment in the village of Saint-Rémy-lès-Chevreuse, the last stop on the metro. We purchased our very first set of dishes from Emil, the local potter.

"I'm going to Paris myself some day!" Emil told us proudly.

We stared at him. Was it possible that this man, maybe forty-five years old, had never visited his capital city, an hour's train ride away? Emil must have taken our astonishment for doubt. No, he insisted, he really was going to ride the train all the way there.

"Why not go with us someday?" said John. Yes, Emil would do just that! But week after week he had a reason for staying home. Then one day when we arrived at the station, Emil was there, wearing his Sunday suit and carrying a leather bag in which his wife had packed a lunch that could have fed six. All the way in, he sat on the very front of his seat, staring out the window with little cries of what sounded like pain.

At Cluny station, he walked up the subway stairs so close to us that he jostled the textbooks out of my arms. The cars and buses, the noise, the crowded sidewalks, seemed to fill him with terror. I cut class that day: no way could we leave our friend alone! I sat with him on a bench in quiet Luxembourg Garden, sharing his bountiful lunch. I longed for a cup of coffee, but Emil refused absolutely to venture into a café.

He never saw Paris! I thought as the three of us boarded the train for Saint-Rémy. But now, for all of the ride home, he bubbled over with excitement, impressions, delight! Clearly, he'd live on this trip for years to come.

What had helped him dare the unfamiliar? Simply knowing that someone would be with him.

> *Where I am afraid to go, Lord Jesus, remind me that*
> *Someone will be with me too.*
> —Elizabeth Sherrill

Digging Deeper: Deuteronomy 31:8; Hebrews 13:5

Thursday, April 12

For the godly who die shall rest in peace. —Isaiah 57:2 (TLB)

Jack and I decided to give our ten children (his six, my four) the gift of not having to make decisions on one of the most stressful days of their lives... the day one, or both of us, takes our last breath. So we prepaid for our transportation, refrigeration, cremation, and funeral services. Then I sent my children a letter telling them that I hoped to live to be 110, but if it didn't happen, enclosed were my final arrangements, plus the names of my financial adviser and bank accounts and where I'd like my ashes to be placed.

At the end of the letter I said, "So there you have it. Easy peasy. When I die, you just have to come to Florida to wrap things up, attend my memorial service, give away my things, collect your inheritance, and go on enjoying your lives. I love you very much and thank you for appreciating this gift I've given to all of you. Thank you for being such a blessing to me and for helping make my life so happy and fulfilled. With all my love, Mom."

When I mailed the letters, I put "Celebrate!" stamps on them as a gentle reminder that the death of a parent should come with joy, not sorrow... the joy of celebrating a wonderful, happy life filled with love and adventure. I, for one, am looking forward to the rest of the ride, and to find out what's waiting for me!

Father, thank You for everything You've given me on earth and
for the greatest gift of all: looking forward to being
with You in heaven for all eternity.
—Patricia Lorenz

Digging Deeper: Genesis 3:19; John 11:11–27

And the servant of the Lord must not strive; but be gentle unto all men, apt to teach, patient. —2 Timothy 2:24 (KJV)

I detest male stereotypes, especially when I prove them true.

I always fancied myself as an equal partner in housework ("equal" meaning that my wife does 70 percent). So when Sandee's job took her abroad for a month, the three of us left at home—Faith, Grace, and Mr. 30 Percent—were confident in our abilities to run the household.

That lasted roughly 17.3 hours.

The first casualty was laundry, followed by dishes and then groceries. We set a skillet aflame. Dust bunnies grew into dust rabbits and built their own hutch. Toilet paper rolls, prescriptions, and promises all went unfilled. There I was, on day five, standing in the kitchen, wearing mismatched socks, eating peanut butter with a fork for dinner. *Mr. Mom* meets *Lord of the Flies.*

Finally, we regrouped. It took all three of us to do what Sandee does in one day *when she's not at work.* It was humbling, and it made us all feel dumb. Did it really take her absence to show us what she did? Were we that clueless? (Rhetorical—don't answer that.)

Such troubling, dawning awareness spills into larger questions. How much of other people's efforts do I take for granted every day? How solid is my bedrock commitment to "love my neighbor as myself" if I don't even notice my neighbor?

I don't know the answers. I do know this: somewhere between the flaming skillet and the peanut butter supper, things changed. I realized that I'm not master of my fate; I cannot even master my kitchen. I need guidance, both divine and otherwise.

Lord, Your peace passeth all understanding.
Let me understand the many contributions of those around me—
and please passeth the fire extinguisher.
—Mark Collins

Digging Deeper: 2 Corinthians 5:7; Hebrews 12:1–2

*"Do you hear what these children are saying?" they asked him. "Yes,"
replied Jesus, "have you never read, 'From the lips of children and infants
you, Lord, have called forth your praise'?"* —Matthew 21:16 (NIV)

In celebration of my brother's mother-in-law's ninety-fourth birthday, we gathered at his house for a party. It was an intimate family event, but significant given her recent health challenges. Madeline had fallen and suffered a hairline fracture on her hip, which took a while to heal, and soon after she was hospitalized with heart-related problems.

Later in the day, Madeline's daughter invited everyone around the table for an Italian feast filled with wonderful food and pastries. She then asked me to say grace. Just as I was about to say a prayer, Madeline's three-year-old great-granddaughter, Isabella, exclaimed, "I want to say grace! I want to say grace!"

Tom, her grandfather, said, "Pablo is going to say grace." Nonetheless Isabella insisted that she say grace. I knew that she said grace for her family meals at home and looked forward to doing so.

I thought Isabella's enthusiasm was wonderful, so I suggested that she say the prayer. I wasn't sure what to expect, but Isabella straightened up in her chair and recited, "Bless us, O Lord, for these thy gifts, which we are about to receive from thy bounty, through Christ our Lord. Amen." There was no need for me to add anything. God heard her heartfelt words and blessed our family. It was the best gift Madeline could have received.

*Lord, thanks for the prayers of children and all others
as they lead us back to You.*
—Pablo Diaz

Digging Deeper: Deuteronomy 11:19; Matthew 19:14

This hope we have as an anchor of the soul, a hope both sure and steadfast.... —Hebrews 6:19 (NAS)

I ambled down a beach boardwalk today and wandered into a deep-sea-fishing supply store. The store sold bait, rods and reels, saltwater fishing attire, and almost anything else a fisherman might need. I was looking for sunglasses, and as my eyes gazed at the incredible array of merchandise, I glanced at the back wall and saw a large nautical mural with these words prominently written beneath: "To know the strength of your anchor, you've got to feel the fury of the storm."

I nodded in agreement. I am learning that when you cast off from the safety of the familiar and sail the seas of the vast unknown, you will inevitably confront difficult and turbulent storms. It takes enduring the fury of human experience to trust that God will not desert you or let go of your hand.

As I left the store, I hummed the tune of a folk hymn that I have not heard since childhood. I could even hear the clinking of an old piano and simple country voices singing. The hymn is "In Times Like These" by Ruth Caye Jones, and I quietly sang the lyrics: "In times like these you need a Savior, In times like these you need an anchor; Be very sure, be very sure, your anchor holds and grips the Solid Rock."

Lord, may I be anchored to Your presence this day. Amen.
—Scott Walker

Digging Deeper: Psalm 89:8–9; Isaiah 25:4

Monday, April 16

Through the Lord's mercies we are not consumed, because His compassions fail not. They are new every morning; great is Your faithfulness.
—Lamentations 3:22–23 (NKJV)

It's only a little puddle, I told myself. It probably just splashed out of the sink. I used paper towels to wipe it up and went on to other stuff.

The next day I saw the same puddle again. I also saw warped hardwood floors and floating dollar signs.

It's a lesson I've learned before but have to keep learning again: don't give little problems an opportunity to become big problems.

The plumbing under my kitchen faucet had sprung a slow leak. Who knows how long it had been like that? All I know is that I noticed it, ignored it, and paid a price.

I turned off the water and bought the parts I needed to repair the leak.

But how to repair the hardwood floors? The damage was done. A dozen boards were swollen and twisted. It would be an expensive repair. I felt discouraged and blamed myself. If only I had taken care of the problem the first time.

A few days later, I went into the kitchen for morning coffee and devotions. I was reading that day of a God Whose mercies "are new every morning." The floorboards were barely warped. A little bit of time had allowed them to dry out. They returned to their original shape, they undid their own damage—mercies new every morning.

Precious Father, how I praise You for the grace that fixes the mess
I made and the mercies that are new every morning.
Give me eyes to see Your never-ceasing love. Amen.
—Bill Giovannetti

Digging Deeper: Psalm 36:5

O Jerusalem, I have posted watchmen on your walls: they will pray day and night, continually.... —Isaiah 62:6 (NLT)

I filed and tossed my way through the stack of papers on my desk. A corner of a plastic sandwich bag peeked out from the bottom. I pulled it out. Warmth filled my heart when I saw my favorite necklace carefully tucked inside, a dainty silver cross overlaying the Star of David, which hung from the silver chain with a broken clasp.

I'd purchased it many years before because I felt that God was asking me to pray for all those involved in the Israeli-Palestinian conflict. After a few years, the clasp broke. I'd taken it into the jewelry store to ask what they'd charge to fix it. I huffed out of the store. *They want nearly as much to repair it as I'd originally paid. It's not worth that!* I'd tucked the cross and star into the plastic bag, and it'd been there ever since.

Gently I cradled the cross in my hands. Without wearing it, I'd forgotten to pray for Israel and the Jews on a regular basis. The cross with the Star of David wasn't just a piece of jewelry I wore around my neck. It was a key reminder to following my assignment from God. My heart sank as I realized that I'd let my wallet speak louder than God.

Lord, I'm sorry. The warmth of His love washed over me, and I felt led to tuck the necklace into my purse. On my next trip to town I would be stopping by the jewelry store.

Lord, I'm so grateful to know that when I fail to pray for Your people, You will forgive me and give me the opportunity to start over. Amen.
—Rebecca Ondov

Digging Deeper: 2 Chronicles 7:14; Psalm 122:6–8

Wednesday, April 18

Then she will call in her friends and neighbors and say,
"Let's celebrate!..." —Luke 15:9 (CEV)

After visiting a friend who was hospitalized about thirty miles from my house, I stopped at a dollar store to buy sympathy and get-well cards. "It seems like I'm buying cards every week!" I complained to the clerk.

"When you get older, your contemporaries tend to get sick and die," she said, ringing up the sale. She hesitated and then added, "You're fortunate to know people whom you care about. I've moved so often, I never made friends. I don't have anyone to send a card to or who would send a card to me."

"Maybe you'll stay here long enough," I said.

She shrugged. "I'll probably move again before long."

As I drove home I thought of things I could have done, like offering to introduce her to a local pastor or asking if we could pray together instead of my praying silently for her. I didn't do either one of them, and the next time I visited that store she was gone.

Even though I didn't help her, she helped me by reminding me how much I appreciate those who enrich my life through their friendship. I'm grateful for a friend with a fading memory who sends birthday cards, just never close to my birthday. I'm privileged to enjoy another friend's young grandchildren; mine are nearly grown. My friends and I have supported one another through sorrow and heartbreak and loss. We've also laughed ourselves silly over corny jokes and rejoiced wildly at successes and joys. Most of all, I am loved and treasured by the best friend of all, Jesus the Christ.

Most Precious Friend, forgive me when I neglect to befriend
someone in need. Thank You for the wonderful friends
who mourn and celebrate with me. Amen.
—Penney Schwab

Digging Deeper: Proverbs 27:9; John 15:15

RELYING ON GOD'S UNFAILING LOVE: Just Be

Fear not, for I am with you; be not dismayed, for I am your God; I will strengthen you, I will help you, I will uphold you with my righteous right hand. —Isaiah 41:10 (ESV)

I was desperate to do something for my friend Sarah who had cancer. I pulled up Google and searched "gifts for cancer patients," sorting through a plethora of pink scarves and T-shirts before realizing that none of them would work. Sarah didn't even like pink. She's more of a magenta-rock-star type of gal.

So maybe dinner? I could whip up some cheesy comfort food, something to fill her belly and show her she was loved. But she was feeling awful. The mere smell would likely make her throw up.

I could write letters or cards, send text messages, make phone calls. Or maybe I could watch her kids, help with her laundry, scrub her floors, do her dishes.

My mind whirred as it sorted through all of the ways Sarah would need help, the ways I could contribute. I began writing a list, throwing down ideas, searching for something—anything—I could do.

"Lord, please, I want to help her," my soul cried.

And His answer came clearly, immediately: Just be. Be there. Be in prayer. Be a listener. Be hope.

My suffering friend doesn't just need a maid or a chef or someone to buy her pink trinkets and slip them into her already jammed-full mailbox. Instead, she needs someone who will hold her hand, pray out loud, sit with her when things get stormy.

That's who I want to be for my friend right now, when she needs it more than ever.

Lord, I want to show Your perfect love to those in need. Help me to exude Your mercy and grace everywhere I go. Amen.
—Erin MacPherson

Digging Deeper: Zechariah 7:9; John 16:33; Romans 8:10

Friday, April 20

THE BEAUTY OF SIMPLICITY: Love from a Child
It's a good thing to quietly hope.... —Lamentations 3:26 (MSG)

God answered my secret prayer. I became a grandmother, although not in the typical way. My daughter Katie married Chris, who had a three-year-old named Rilynn. Together, they chose the most wonderful name for me: Grandma Jewels.

Rilynn already had two grandmothers. Did she have room in her heart for one more?

A few months after the wedding, Katie asked me to keep Rilynn overnight. I'd pick her up from preschool and spend the night at their house. But she barely knew me. Would she feel uneasy around me? Should I dare to let myself hope for a special relationship?

When I pulled into the preschool parking lot, excitement and fear bubbled up. *Lord, can this possibly work? We're brand-new to each other.* After signing in, I went outside to where the children were playing.

There she is. My granddaughter. Laughing with friends.

Rilynn's long blonde hair blew in the breeze. She glanced my way. Careful not to invade her space, I stood still and waved. "Grandma Jewels!" she yelled across the playground and raced toward me with her arms wide open. "You came to get me!" I bent down. She hugged me, sure and strong.

She chattered about her day, the same way Katie used to. She showed me where they kept crackers and juice boxes, and we had an afternoon snack and played dolls. Later, I went to fix supper.

"Grandma Jewels"—she tapped my leg—"could you play with me, please? For just one more minute?"

"Of course, Rilynn. I'll play with you for lots more minutes."

Father, You're full of good surprises!
Help me not to be afraid to hope in every situation.
—Julie Garmon

Digging Deeper: Psalm 147:11; Romans 5:5

Share with the Lord's people who are in need. Practice hospitality.
—Romans 12:13 (NIV)

I attended a wedding recently for Eric and Nana. They'd planned a ceremony in one town and a reception in another. Heavy rain and flooding was predicted throughout the week.

Wedding guests arrived, laden with raincoats and umbrellas. At the end of the service, we stood as the beaming newlyweds walked down the aisle. The couple disappeared into a private room while we prepared to leave. Patti, a church member, materialized in the doorway. "We just got word that the reception is canceled. The road to the venue is flooded."

Sighs of dismay were heard. She went on: "We've broken the news to Eric and Nana. As you can imagine, they are very disappointed. However, they want to greet everyone. Please wait in our fellowship room across the hall."

I walked over, looking around the stark room with its harsh fluorescent lights and metal chairs. A beautiful reception with carefully selected music, food, and wedding cake would not be part of their memories. *How sad,* I thought. Patti, however, had a different plan.

Boxes of pizzas arrived, along with paper plates, cups, and soft drinks. Patti's son came with his laptop and speakers to play music. The bright lights were turned off. Church candles became table centerpieces. Altar flowers were placed alongside a two-layer cake from a local deli.

When Eric and Nana appeared in the doorway, they looked around, stunned. The fellowship hall had been transformed. On their faces was gratitude for those who had seen to it that their love and commitment would still be celebrated.

Lord, thank You for people who are willing and eager to extend hospitality. They become a testament to Your generosity.
—Melody Bonnette Swang

Digging Deeper: Genesis 18:7–8; John 14:2; 1 Peter 4:8–10

Sunday, April 22

Be kind to one another, tenderhearted, forgiving one another, as God in Christ forgave you. —Ephesians 4:32 (ESV)

Gracie's first few puppy forays on to the noisy, crowded, busy streets of Manhattan were fraught with anxiety. But then she found something that made it all okay: other dogs. She made friends with every dog she encountered.

Along came a rescued greyhound named Morticia—a tall, stately, magnificent athlete of a dog with the sweetest eyes. She would stand stock-still while Gracie pranced in circles around her. "These racing dogs aren't treated very well," her owner explained. "They're kept mostly isolated."

Every time we saw Morticia, Gracie would greet her like an old friend while Morticia froze like a statue. Then one day Morticia wagged her long, thin tail just a little. A few encounters later she wagged it a lot. Next time she hopped, her front paws coming off the ground. Slowly but surely my gregarious golden retriever was drawing this poor abused dog out of her shell.

Now when Morticia sees Gracie coming down the street, she pulls her owner in our direction so she can play with her new friend. "Every morning when we come out the door she looks for Gracie," her owner says. "I never thought she would loosen up like this. She was so scared."

So what about me? Am I always as friendly as I can be, like my golden retriever? Some people who might seem cold or standoffish or rude are really just scared. It's up to me to reach out and try harder instead of writing them off or walking away.

Lord, it is so easy for me to simply tunnel through life, doing too little for those who are hurting and who need so much but don't know how to ask. Help me show love to all who come my way, especially the hurting.

—Edward Grinnan

Digging Deeper: Ecclesiastes 4:9–12; Mark 12:29–31; Colossians 3:12–13

This is the day the Lord has made; We will rejoice and be glad in it.
—Psalm 118:24 (NKJV)

Considering that Scotland's Shetland Islands are swaddled in a blanket of clouds or fog about 75 percent of the year, my sister and I were delighted to wake up to skies as blue as the water beneath our cruise ship. Almost giddy with the prospect of exploring Mousa Island off the coast of Lerwick, Cindy and I quickly dressed in layers. We were prepared for anything.

Well, almost anything. Apparently the clear skies were due to the howling wind. This meant the waves were too high for the ship's tenders to ferry passengers to shore. So we sat, anchored right off the coast, and we waited. I felt like Moses seeing the Promised Land from a mountaintop, but not being able to actually set foot on it. Of course, he traveled for forty years to reach his destination. I'd been traveling less than a week.

I had a choice. I could either spend my time cursing the wind or I could enjoy the day right where I was. So my sister and I walked laps around the deck, burning calories with the goal of eating more dessert. We took pictures of ourselves in every reflective surface we could find, just for fun. We used the telephoto lenses on our cameras as binoculars to survey the beauty of the landscape just out of our reach. We had a marvelous, memorable day—even though we never made it to shore.

What I want is not always what I get in life. I may not have chosen my current circumstances, but I can choose whether I'll live in a state of disappointment and discontent or search out the treasures hidden in the unexpected and imperfect.

Dear Lord, help me to see today as a gift, even if it's a gift
I never wanted to receive. Help me to embrace the beauty and
the possibilities of whatever You allow to come my way.
—Vicki Kuyper

Digging Deeper: Philippians 4:11–13

Tuesday, April 24

"In my father's house are many mansions: if it were not so, I would have told you. I go to prepare a place for you." —John 14:2 (KJV)

One of my dearest friends had died unexpectedly, and I couldn't shake the feeling I might never see her again. Oh, I knew Dixie had trusted Christ as her Savior and had a promised home in heaven, but would I really be reunited with her one day? As much as I believed the Bible's truths, it all seemed so unreal.

Then I had to travel by plane to a distant city for a workshop. Because of health issues, I never fly alone. But this time my sister couldn't accompany me. I didn't say anything to anyone, but inwardly I panicked.

Out of the blue, a fellow workshop participant e-mailed me. Peggy lived close to the facility where the workshop was taking place. "Why don't I meet you at the airport and drive you to the workshop, Roberta?" she wrote. Peggy assured me it wouldn't be the least bit of trouble.

I'd attended other events with Peggy, but I didn't know her well. I assumed that meeting me at the workshop meant she'd be waiting outside near Ground Transportation. But when I stepped into the airport, Peggy and her husband were the very first people I spotted. There they were smiling and waving like I was the most important person in the world.

My thoughts turned to Dixie, and at once I knew. On the day of my arrival in heaven, God would whisper the news of my coming to my dear friend and she would, most assuredly, be waiting just for me.

Thank You for friends, Lord, who help us over life's hurdles.
—Roberta Messner

Digging Deeper: 1 Corinthians 2:9; Revelation 21:1

Behold, thou desirest truth in the inward parts; make me, therefore, to know wisdom in mine inmost heart. —Psalm 51:8 (JPS)

After keeping the house closed up through the winter, I'm always relieved when there's a warm enough day to open the windows. I enjoyed the breeze that wafted across my office on that first nearly balmy morning. The squirrels were especially active, obviously having decided that my fence top was the safe road around my yard.

I was working at my computer when I heard such loud birdsong that I was certain the bird had to be on the fence directly outside my window. The chirping was beautiful—three notes that sounded the same and then a full-throated liquid crescendo of joyous singing. The whole song repeated every few seconds.

I looked out, expecting to see the pretty singer, but the fence was empty except for some stray tendrils of blackberry vines. I would have thought the bird had flown away, but I could still hear its lyrical chirping. I got my binoculars to scan my neighbor's roof and some nearby trees but saw only robins or jays, neither of which has such a melodious song.

I resolved to find the songbird, so I trained the binoculars on the blackberries. In the shadow of a curving stem was the tiniest brown bird, throat feathers ruffling as it gave out its huge, lovely song.

It seemed a wondrous reminder that the way we look on the outside really has no bearing on what may be within—and how blessed we are when we encounter what's hidden there.

> *Turn me inside out, Lord, so that*
> *what I show the world is the song inside me.*
> —Rhoda Blecker

Digging Deeper: Psalm 28:7

Thursday, April 26

A soothing tongue is a tree of life, But perversion in it crushes the spirit.
—Proverbs 15:4 (NAS)

Our teen grandsons came over for a visit last week. Those boys argued over *everything*. Twice the fourteen-year-old erupted in frustration—launching into a tirade against his younger brother before stomping outside. When he returned, the twelve-year-old mumbled, "What's *he* doing here?"

That did it. They got "alpha" grandma. Not condemnation or anger, but a firm teaching.

I broke down the nasty sound bite. "'What's *he* doing here?' says 'You are not welcome, you don't belong, I don't like you, go away.'" I went on, "Boys, these things you are saying are careless words. They go down inside a person and create hurt. Arguing and running each other down has become such a habit that you don't hear what you are saying. I'm going to step in when I hear this happening, and we're going to look at what is *really* being said. If you can just start to see careless words, then I'm hoping you can choose better ones."

My grandsons made more peaceable attempts toward each other for the remainder of their visit. Later I looked up Bible teachings about careless words—a reminder for myself about speaking without thinking—or intentionally letting go an unnecessary volley.

The real awakener for me was Matthew 12:36. Jesus states, "Every careless word that people speak, they shall give an accounting for." I decided right then that I want to make this a very short list.

You, Lord, are the living Word. Fill me with pleasant words—
as a honeycomb, "Sweet to the soul and healing
to the bones" (Proverbs 16:24).
—Carol Knapp

Digging Deeper: Psalm 141:3; Proverbs 12:14;
Jeremiah 15:19; Matthew 15:15–20

"Build houses and settle down; plant gardens and eat what they produce."
—Jeremiah 29:5 (NIV)

To get a head start on our garden, we sprout our tomatoes from seeds indoors. We plant them in a cute little germination station that we move around the house, from window to window, finding the best sunlight.

My favorite part of tending to the tomato plants—the part that touches my heart—happens when the glorious little green stems surface from the dirt. Each seedling receives a soft touch, from left to right, up and down, a few times a day, to encourage strong stems.

When I first learned about the brushing technique, I wondered if it was related to stress. Was a little pressure the same as "what doesn't kill you makes you stronger"? For a long time I believed that was the case (stress was behind the strength), but this morning I changed my theory.

Today as my hands grazed each plant, I thought that maybe the brushing is more about caring enough to take a moment to reach out and be a part of its growth. Afterward, the herbal fragrance of the plants, the smell of spring, was left on my hands, reminding me of the beautiful exchange that happens when we care for another. The benefit of our effort changes us as well.

*Heavenly Father, thank You for the gift of caring, for
the fulfillment I receive from planting seeds and watching them grow,
and for creating fruit that nurtures my mind, body, and spirit.*
—Sabra Ciancanelli

Digging Deeper: Galatians 5:22; Ephesians 4:32

Saturday, April 28

She openeth her mouth with wisdom; and in her tongue is the law of kindness. —Proverbs 31:26 (KJV)

A friend of mine has been talking about all the women she knows and how so very many have silent scars and hidden pains and secret sins—things they only reveal to their deepest friends. And then we get to talking about how tough and sinewy women are, how they look so slender and gentle and empathetic, but they are tougher than the toughest men, quite often.

My friend says, "A woman I know gave away her first child. She was only eighteen. She never told a soul. Not her parents, not the father, not her husband, not her best friends, not either of her sons.

"But she never forgot her daughter. Not a day went by that she didn't yearn for the child and worry over her and wish to make it right again somehow, sometime, somewhere.

"Years later, matters conspired so that she did meet her daughter at a farmers' market in the city. The daughter said, 'I will be by the blueberries.' The mother was terrified. Would the daughter hate her? Could the daughter ever forgive her? Could she ever forgive herself? What if the daughter was a cold, wordless, grim, glaring accusation?

"But when they met, the daughter flung her arms open and said, 'I have been waiting for you all my life! I love you, Mom!' The mother was so overcome she couldn't speak. The daughter took her by the hand and led her to a bench, and they sat for a while holding hands.

"Anyone who says confidently what love can and cannot do is a fool. Anyone who sells love short is blind as a bat. Anyone who doesn't get that love is why we are here is missing the crucial memo."

> *Dear Lord, whenever I get pompous and arrogant, or cocky and snide, or weary and dark, remind me of those last three sentences, okay? Burn them right into my cortex again.*
> —Brian Doyle

Digging Deeper: Proverbs 1:7, 3:5

He who finds a wife finds what is good, gaining favor from the Lord.
—Proverbs 18:22 (CEB)

A husband knows that he should never, ever forget his wedding anniversary. The date should be enshrined in his memory, etched in gold, marked with an exclamation point on his Google calendar: "Your anniversary!"

The one that was coming up for me wasn't a particularly noteworthy number, but I did remember to get a card and a smallish present—a couple of days early, mind you—that I wrapped and hid in a bureau drawer for Saturday, April 30.

Imagine my surprise, then, on Friday morning, when Carol appeared at the breakfast table with a present and a card for *me*. "Happy anniversary!" she said.

"This is so nice," I said, wondering for a moment if *I* had made the mistake. I glanced at the newspaper with some relief. April 29, it said, not 30th. "Thank you so much, honey, but it's tomorrow."

The headline in the paper could have read: "Wife Shows Rare Memory Lapse."

Carol's eyes widened in surprise, then she laughed. We both laughed. "It's your only mistake in thirty-two years," I said.

"Thirty-three," she corrected.

"Thirty-three," I concurred, after doing some quick math. "Should I get your present?"

"No. I can wait." And we did, celebrating with a wonderful dinner. What neither of us will ever forget about that first April 30th is that we took a leap of faith, trusting God with our love, and every year since has been filled with wonder, including atypical moments when we discover that neither of us is perfect—except in each other's eyes.

As I am forgiven, Lord, may I always remember to forgive.
—Rick Hamlin

Digging Deeper: Matthew 19:4–6; 1 Corinthians 13:4–8

Monday, April 30

For whoever keeps the whole law and yet stumbles at just one point is guilty of breaking all of it. —James 2:10 (NIV)

I write chapter books for young readers. It's the only job I ever dreamed of having. As a little girl, I'd look at authors' names on books I loved and wonder if, someday, my name might be on a book a child loved too. I take my work seriously and try to get everything right, always remembering what an honor it is to have my words read by children.

Recently, after I'd sent final edits to my publisher for a novel, I realized I'd missed a mistake in the manuscript. Even though we'd been through multiple edits, the fault was mine—the blame rested solely with me. Sheepishly, I e-mailed my editor and told her my error. All the major kinks should have already been worked out. Now I would waste the copy editor's time and create a hassle. My one blunder made all the hard work I'd done on the book seem to fade into the background. *How could I have been so stupid?* I felt sick to my stomach. I couldn't eat; I couldn't concentrate on anything except the guilt.

After I beat myself up most of the day, my editor called and assured me it was no big deal. "Stop worrying," she said. "We'll take care of it."

Just like that!

How strange it felt to have my burden taken away so quickly, so completely. Especially when I didn't deserve it. I hardly knew how to respond.

But why should it have felt strange? Isn't this what God does for me every day?

Lord, thank You for Your amazing grace!
Thank You for the endless edits You allow.
—Ginger Rue

Digging Deeper: Galatians 5:4–5; Jude 1:24

GOD'S UNFAILING LOVE

1 _____

2 _____

3 _____

4 _____

5 _____

6 _____

7 _____

8 _____

9 _____

10 _____

11 _____

12 _____

13 _____

14 _____

15 _____

April

16 _____

17 _____

18 _____

19 _____

20 _____

21 _____

22 _____

23 _____

24 _____

25 _____

26 _____

27 _____

28 _____

29 _____

30 _____

MAY

*Love is patient, love is kind. . . . It always protects,
always trusts, always hopes, always perseveres.
Love never fails. . . .*

—1 Corinthians 13:4, 7–8 (NIV)

Tuesday, May 1

"Ho! Every one who thirsts, come to the waters...." —Isaiah 55:1 (NAS)

Oh, can we stop?" came the urgent request from the backseat. I almost didn't. The underground spring water flowing from the open pipe was on the opposite side of the two-lane highway. Just then the dirt pull-out was vacant, so I quickly maneuvered to the wide spot along the wooded bank. People from all around brought jugs and filled them up with that good pure water. Soon another car arrived. I visited with the couple while my granddaughter Ruby and her friend Liz cupped their hands and drank the refreshing water.

The man informed me, "This water has been flowing for decades. It's checked often for purity. Always passes the test. It runs six gallons a minute."

"Girls, did you hear that—six gallons a minute! I wonder how much that'd be in a day." Before I knew it, Liz and Ruby were scrambling for sticks and crouching on the ground along the road, doing the math in the dirt. After an erasure or two on their "tablet," they announced, "Eight thousand six hundred forty gallons."

Here was an opportunity to water their young hearts with the Word of God. "Jesus says He gives living water—the kind that satisfies our hearts—to all who come to Him. Water that never runs out no matter how long—or how many—people drink from it" (John 4:10, 14).

What we would have missed if Liz hadn't made her impromptu request, if I hadn't stopped. God had a flow going—drinking of Him through His Word even as we drank from the spring. And we girls will tell anyone who wants to know: His water is the best!

I love the image, Lord, of You spilling from me
in life-enhancing living water.
—Carol Knapp

Digging Deeper: Isaiah 12:3; John 7:37–39

If we live by the Spirit, let us also walk by the Spirit.
—Galatians 5:25 (NAS)

I recently read a story about John Knox, the founder of the Presbyterian Church of Scotland. He was a valiant prayer warrior. As he lay on his deathbed, he asked his wife, Margaret Stewart, to read him Scripture. While reading to him, she noticed that John Knox had started to pray aloud, his voice growing slower and dimmer. Then, as he prayed for those he loved, his spirit slipped from his body and joined Jesus in heaven. What a wonderful testament to this mighty man of God.

Over the years I've struggled with prayer. I've made long lists and prayed through them. I've written my prayers down, which I continue to do to this day, and I've tried my best to be continually in prayer by having an ongoing conversation with the Lord as I go about my day.

John Knox was a man who lived by prayer, so when it came time for him to leave this earth, prayer was a natural part of his life…and death.

This is what I want for my relationship with God, a life of prayer that is so engrained that communication with Him is simply part of my every thought and deed. And when it comes time for me to leave this earth, I want it to be with a prayer on my lips.

Father God, thank You for the beautiful example of John Knox's life,
this saintly man of prayer. May I live a praying life.
—Debbie Macomber

Digging Deeper: Jeremiah 33:3; Colossians 4:2

Thursday, May 3

This is the day that the Lord has made. —Psalm 118:24 (NRSV)

Anyone who knows me well knows that I don't always have the most loving relationship with my dog, Max. He frustrates me as often as he delights me. And I suspect that he feels the same way about me, the guy holding his leash.

I want to run more! I want to eat more! I want to play more! If dogs think these things, and I imagine they do, then Max thinks them when he looks at me throughout the day, most every day.

But the other day I woke up after sleeping very little. I was worrying about some project that was still undone when Max stuck his muzzle in my hand as if to say, "Take me outside." So I did. It was just after dawn, and the sun was coming up. There I stood, watching Max in the morning light, but my mind was still at my computer. *Do your business and let's get back inside* was all I was thinking.

Max wanted to linger. He walked over to the hedge and smelled it. Then he paused to look up at the bird feeder as if to acknowledge the chickadees that were already chattering away there. Then he sat down in the grass and just looked around, seemingly taking it all in for the first time.

"Come on," I said. *It isn't as if we don't do this every single morning.* And, instead of following me inside, Max, who is usually obedient, as dogs are, turned his head and looked at me. It was like a tap on the shoulder.

Stop, look, smell, listen.

> *May I live for You in the present today, Lord.*
> *Oh, and I look forward to tomorrow too!*
> —Jon Sweeney

Digging Deeper: Psalm 66:5–6

Trust in the Lord with all your heart and lean not on your own understanding. —Proverbs 3:5 (NIV)

Bent over the soil, I cleared off leaves and began to wake up my garden by sweeping away winter's mess. My thoughts turned to an upcoming business trip. I had volunteered for the project and was looking forward to it, but now as it grew near, all my excitement turned to dread. Would the flight be delayed? Would my presentation go over well? In a flash, a garter snake slithered right in front of my knees! My heart jumped, and I let out a squeal.

I caught my breath, and my mind traveled back to elementary school. In fourth grade, we had garter snakes in the classroom. The first day of school, the teacher picked one up out of the tank and strolled the aisles between our desks. The snake slinked up his left arm, and kids backed up their chairs.

"We're afraid of things we don't understand," he said. "I'm going to teach you all about these amazing creatures. You don't have to touch them or go near them if you don't want to. But I'll bet by Thanksgiving each one of you will have held one. Anyone want to touch one now?"

I folded my arms and shook my head. I wasn't about to touch a snake, let alone hold one.

It started out simply. For a few minutes in the morning our teacher would go to the tank and pick one up. He showed us how snakes weren't slimy but strong. He offered facts and asked us to look closely, so we could see the beauty of their scales.

It didn't even take until Thanksgiving. Before the end of September there wasn't one of us who hadn't grown to care for what we once feared. My business trip was going to be just fine.

Heavenly Father, when worry enters my heart, help me remember that what is beyond my understanding is in Your hands. I have nothing to fear.
—Sabra Ciancanelli

Digging Deeper: John 14:27; Philippians 4:6–7; 2 Thessalonians 3:16

Saturday, May 5

I shall not die, but live, and declare the word of the Lord.
—Psalm 118:17 (KJV)

Bargain hunters had already begun ambling across my lawn, browsing my old sewing patterns, holding glassware to the light. One of the shoppers headed toward me with the portable TV when my daughter Trina, then five years old, planted herself firmly in my path. As the youngest of four children, she knew how to hold her ground.

"Mummy," Trina demanded, "is it true I'm going to die?"

Where did that come from? Oh, sweetheart, not now with strangers everywhere! What can she understand? Dying flowers? That little gold-fish... Before I could respond, Trina thumped her hands on her hips and shouted, "Well, I don't want to!" Off she stomped as only a defiant five-year-old can do.

Later that evening, Trina snuggled in my lap on the rocker. "Honey, do you remember how this morning you said you didn't want to die? Well, I don't want to either. No one does. Life is pretty nice, don't you think?" She sucked her thumb and nodded.

"But one day, probably a long, long time from now, everyone dies... even Kitty and me. But it's okay because when we die, we go to heaven. All together. By then, we won't need this life anymore. You know, it's a little like our yard sale. We sold your peppermint-striped pajamas because you didn't need them anymore. Do you miss them?" She shook her head.

"We'll live in a new and beautiful way."

"Okay." Trina suddenly hopped off my lap to trail the cat.

I don't know how much talk of eternal life comforted her that day, but the promise reassured me. It always does.

Eternal Father, our lives are in Your hands.
—Gail Thorell Schilling

Digging Deeper: 1 Peter 1:3; 1 John 2:25

The sacrifices of God are a broken spirit; a broken and a contrite heart, O God, You will not despise. —Psalm 51:17 (NIV)

There are only about thirty-five of us in our little congregation. We're more like a family than a church. We used to be larger. I sometimes wonder what visitors think when they stop by.

One early spring morning a new couple came in to our service. Newcomers are easy to spot. Before the sermon, Pastor Tom asks us to share anything we'd like—what God has done for us that week or what we might need prayer for.

One of the recovering addicts stood to say in a broken voice that he'd gotten a job. Finally. He was clean. Applause.

Another shared what life had been like in prison and then when he became homeless, but now things were good. More applause.

The visiting young man stood. He spoke openly about deep family problems with no answers or hope. His wife looked down. That he sobbed didn't keep him from saying what he needed to get out. "We didn't mean to come to this church, but we got lost and time was running out." Before he could sit down, most of us rushed to embrace him. Her too. He practically fell into our arms.

During the altar prayer, they came quickly, hand in hand, and stood in line. They were family now. After church, many of us stayed to visit with them, exchange telephone numbers, and bask in God's sweet, sweet Spirit, which lingered.

"We'll be back next week," they said in unison. "We love your church."

> *Could it be, Father, that brokenness is so precious to You because Your very own Son was broken?*
> —Marion Bond West

Digging Deeper: Psalms 34:18, 147:3; Isaiah 66:2

Monday, May 7

FALLING INTO GRACE: Embracing a New Role

"The kingdom of God... is like a mustard seed, which, when sown...
is the smallest of all seeds on earth; yet... it grows up and becomes the
greatest of all shrubs...." —Mark 4:30–32 (NRSV)

I sat in the car outside of the homeless shelter where I'd been volunteering for years. My arm was safely encased in its sling—"to keep people from jostling you," the doctor said—but I wasn't moving.

"Too soon to come back?" my husband, Charlie, asked. "Should we wait another week?"

I'd always come here to help others. I'd always come from a place of strength. No one here had ever seen me weak, broken. I couldn't even carry the bag of fruit we'd brought or the Scrabble game I occasionally engaged in. I missed the residents and staff, but I was nervous about how they would react.

I pushed open the door and heaved myself out. We hadn't even reached the shelter before people asked, "What happened?" "You okay, Marci?" "Let me get the door for you." "You need help with anything?" "Want to say a prayer?"

Celida, who runs the shelter and had been praying for me for weeks, embraced me gently. I tried to pass out the fruit, but someone took over that job. I was told to sit; they would do the work this time.

I felt strange. This was not my role, but this is exactly where God wanted me to be: The helper had become the helped.

> *Lord, let me accept Your love and help*
> *through the love and help of others.*
> —Marci Alborghetti

Digging Deeper: Isaiah 50:4–5; Mark 1:30–31

"I have come that they may have life, and have it to the full."
—John 10:10 (NIV)

In celebration of National Nurses' Week, the staff in my hospital department were filming a video of something called "Uptown Funk." "You know, Bruno Mars and Mark Ronson made it popular," Stephanie told me. "They're the new Michael Jackson."

No, I didn't know. When it came to moving to music, I didn't know much these days. The new tumor in my foot had taken care of that. I could barely walk, let alone dance.

"Just count me out," I announced to my colleagues dressed in hoodies and dark glasses and laughing up a storm. "I'll cheer everybody else on."

But I wasn't prepared for how sitting on the sidelines would make me feel. Suddenly, I was fifteen years old again and watching my peers from the bleachers in my junior high gym class. "Epileptic," someone hurled at me in reference to a seizure I'd had in front of my classmates several days before.

Today, my hospital peers were having a terrific time. How I longed to be one of them.

Then my boss, Paula, spoke up. "Get a big sheet of paper and a marker, Roberta," she said. "Make a sign that says, 'I'm not a part of this!' You can appear at the end and you won't have to dance. Trust me. It'll be great."

After the video was filmed, I heard someone in another department remark: "This is hilarious. I think Roberta had the best part of all."

So did I. Thanks to my sensitive coworkers, I was really a part of things. Now *that* was something to celebrate!

> *Because of You, Lord, I don't have to live*
> *in the past anymore. Thank You.*
> —Roberta Messner

Digging Deeper: Isaiah 43:18–19; Matthew 6:31–34

Wednesday, May 9

So faith comes from what is heard, and what is heard comes through the word of Christ. —Romans 10:17 (NRSV)

This year I officially decided to stop saying that I run twenty-one miles a week—because, increasingly, I don't.

The truth is I mostly jog. Ever more slowly. With sometimes long moments of walking in between. Not infrequently, I stop altogether—to examine a bird through binoculars I carry or tally a count for eBird.org or record on my phone a writing idea to work on later that day.

The older I get, the slower I get—and the quieter and more alert.

I didn't realize this was happening until recently. I was running—no, jogging—along, and suddenly, without planning to, I was differentiating the birds' voices around me, one from the other, and acknowledging their presence before I even saw them. Without meaning to, I was listening for which birds were there with me: out-of-season or newly arrived voices, voices I'd forgotten from previous years, voices I didn't know at all.

I was aware that the flock of meadowlarks surrounding me were Westerns, not Easterns, though the two species look identical. And I heard before seeing a little towhee, a rare sighting in these parts, squawking forth its funny name. When the cardinal's *chip-chip* of winter changed to its fluting summer cry, I sensed the approach of spring.

And it's not just birds. Today, without even realizing I was listening, I knew the train approaching invisibly from the distance had three locomotives and was not pulling cars. I heard it, knew it, without even thinking about it, and when I turned to look, I found I was right.

That's my hope for the coming seasons: as my life slows down, as it inevitably will, and gets quieter, I'll hear and become ever more aware of God's voice speaking His presence into my days.

Help me slow down and hear You, Lord.
—Patty Kirk

Digging Deeper: Ecclesiastes 3:1–8

"Give us this day our daily bread." —Matthew 6:11 (KJV)

I was a newly married, pregnant student at Western Illinois University before I learned about hunger. It's a time I rarely speak of. My former husband, a college athlete, was unable to find work, and no one would hire me with my baby bump.

Our first few weeks in graduate student housing went well; we had food that relatives had sent with us. But soon it was gone. With just shortening, flour, salt, and water, I made Navajo fried bread my mother had taught me to make. First, we ate the hot salty bread with butter and jelly. Then there was only the bread. Finally, nothing.

My husband practiced with the basketball team and was able to get a meal with them, but there was nothing for me.

"Lord, please don't let me faint," I prayed. One class required that I walk through the student union where the smell of hamburgers and fries was overwhelming. I hoped other students would leave leftovers on their tables or that I could glean food from trash cans.

My stomach was empty, but I was filled with too much shame to ask for help. That's what people seldom talk about—the shame that rides along with poverty and hunger. I ended up losing two teeth, but my beautiful daughter, Lanea, survived.

As my family and I sit down to dinner now, I give thanks for the food we eat and for my time without food, a temporary affliction that helped teach me compassion for others.

Thank You, Lord, for blessing my family.
Help us to consider the poor and to share what we have.
—Sharon Foster

Digging Deeper: Psalm 41:1

Friday, May 11

At daybreak, he called together his disciples. He chose twelve of them whom he called apostles.... —Luke 6:13 (CEB)

*W*hy do we have to meet so early in the morning? I wondered. Friday morning, men's breakfast at church, and I was the one in charge of coffee. Which meant rolling out of bed at 5:30 to get out of the house by 6:30 to get to Dunkin' Donuts in time for a Box O' Joe to get to the church to get everything ready for our 7:30 gathering.

I stumbled through the motions. The train was early—thank God—the rain held off for a few moments, the line for coffee wasn't too long, the front door at church was already unlocked. "Hey, John," I said to our perennial early bird. We both poured ourselves cups from the Box O' Joe. Mark stumbled in, shaking out his raincoat, then Robert with his umbrella. C.J. brought his dog. Ron passed out a print on "original sin." Jim plopped down at the table. Milton sat next to me. Michael showed up with his well-thumbed Greek New Testament—our linguist, he was always helpful when we got into any arguments about Scripture.

"Let's pray," I said. A quick prayer and then we were off into one of our usual discussions, people raising questions, offering second and third takes on the topic at hand. What did Jesus say about it? How did it apply to our workaday lives?

At meeting's end we went around the room and shared concerns. It was only then as each one spoke that I noticed we were twelve, like the Twelve described in Scripture. We closed with the Lord's Prayer and I dashed out to work, not without checking to see if there was any coffee left in the Box O' Joe. Yes, a cupful.

Where two or three are gathered, Lord, together we seek You.
—Rick Hamlin

Digging Deeper: Matthew 16:24–26; Mark 1:16–18

Many waters cannot quench love, neither can the floods drown it....
—Song of Solomon 8:7 (KJV)

My mama is about four inches shorter than she used to be, and a bit shorter still now that she's bent over her walker when on the move. But when she is sitting at the head of the table, she is once again the wry, wise, regal, witty, quippish soul I have admired for fifty years.

Today she sips her eternal tea and says, "Yes, of course I worry about you all every day. That's part of loving you. Not a day goes by when I do not think of you all and say a prayer. Your love for your children is full-flow all the time with your heart in your mouth. Like a river in flood.

"Your father and I had to learn to let you all go. Parents never admit how hard that is. Even now we imagine your days and nights, we worry, we want you to make the best decisions, to bring the gift of yourselves to bear.

"Don't you think that's how the Creator works? The Chief Musician, as the Psalms say? You're a song God sings, but you are also free to make your own music, either sweet or sour. Your kids are teenagers—now you know what I am talking about. You never don't love them, but you always worry about them. Even as you know there's nothing you can do to help most of the time. You have to let them go, but you hope like crazy they'll go with grace and sense and tenderness. You pray for that every day. Every hour, sometimes.

"The fact is I have worn out three rosaries on you alone over the years. That's what you can get me—a new rosary to pray for you."

Dear Chief Musician, I confess, mortified and abashed, that
I have not knelt down every day and thanked You for the astounding
gift of my wry, wise, brave mother. I'll start now. Thank You.
—Brian Doyle

Digging Deeper: Proverbs 31:26–27; Ephesians 6:2

Sunday, May 13

But Mary treasured up all these things and pondered them in her heart.
—Luke 2:19 (NIV)

Going to church is supposed to be a homecoming, a breath of fresh air, and a chance to learn something. But sometimes on Mother's Day, it's more than that: it's a sinking pit in a stomach, a hidden tear behind a program, or a skipped sermon blamed on a little bug.

I grew up smiling as the pastor asked the mothers in the congregation to stand, recognizing them on their special day. It wasn't until I struggled to have our first child, losing two precious children along the way, that I realized those experiencing infertility often dread Mother's Day sermons.

I mentioned to my mom that I wasn't sure I could sit through another service about motherhood. Christmas Eve had gutted me as I sat contemplating Mary's moments before motherhood. Easter left me hopeful but still forlorn, longing for the child I didn't have. And now I had to face Mother's Day with empty arms and an aching heart.

I went anyway. I sat and breathed deeply, desperate to hear and feel the song of Mary's heart as she learned about her pregnancy. How confused, how panicked she would have been, even as her faith bolstered her for the journey.

I got my happy ending. My beautiful baby was born the next year and another the year after. Mary had her joyful moment too.

No mother has it easy. No mother's journey is perfect, smooth, or remotely the same. No matter what your path to motherhood, or if you are still on that journey, or have relinquished that dream altogether, I'd like to celebrate *you* this Mother's Day. You are loved. You are seen. You are valued.

Lord, help me to show love to those around me today, as they may
be experiencing this day differently than I am.
—Ashley Kappel

Digging Deeper: Deuteronomy 7:14; Psalm 113:9; Matthew 18:1–5

He will yet fill your mouth with laughter.... —Job 8:21 (JPS)

My graduate school roommate, Judy, and I have been close friends for fifty years, even though we haven't lived in the same place since we left school. My only stint as a bridesmaid had been at her wedding; she and Rod vacationed with my husband, Keith, and me a number of times, and every year on our birthdays we called each other to catch up.

After Keith died, the birthday calls were more subdued. News from Judy's side was much more interesting. Rod and Judy were traveling, working with a local theater company, and adopting dogs from the animal shelter where she volunteered. And they were together, two of them to my one.

I didn't think my updates measured up. I was putting one foot in front of the other, trying not to slip back into the pit of grief I'd struggled so hard to climb out of. I certainly didn't want to subject Judy to my problems, so I tried hard to sound cheerful.

"You know," I said, "I keep that picture of Rod and you on my bureau, so I see it every day."

"The church directory shot I sent you years ago?" She sounded startled.

When I said yes, she said, "But that picture is so old!"

I was about to ask her for a new one when she sighed and added, "Oh well, we're old, too, so I guess it's appropriate."

I started laughing, and after that I was able to tell her about my down times as well.

> *You really blessed us when You gave us*
> *a sense of humor, Lord of laughter.*
> —Rhoda Blecker

Digging Deeper: Psalm 126:2

Tuesday, May 15

For when I am weak, then I am strong. —2 Corinthians 12:10 (RSV)

I didn't plan to sign up for Boston's annual Lupus Walk this year. "Who wants a ninety-year-old slowing everyone up!" I said to my friend Suzy.

That's when she told me this story.

I'd known that Suzy suffered with asthma from birth. In her sixties, with her condition worsening, someone suggested that swimming could increase lung capacity. "I started kind of dog paddling around my neighbor's pool every morning."

Eventually she was able to swim nonstop for almost twenty minutes. Elated, she decided to try out for New Mexico's Senior Olympics. When she entered Albuquerque's vast echoing arena, though, and saw the size of the pool, her courage failed. She was about to flee when she noticed an elderly man being carried to the starting platform. With only the use of his upper body, the old man came in third among eight contenders. "It made my asthma problems look pretty small."

So when Suzy's race was called, she took her place alongside the others. "Swimmers up. Take your mark." *Bang!* Her dive was an inelegant belly flop, her stroke a frantic splashing. "I kept getting tangled in the lane dividers. I reached the far end and clung there like a barnacle."

The other swimmers were already on the return lap. Aching limbs flailing, Suzy finally followed. On and on she swam. Surely someone had moved the end of the pool! At last, she touched the wall.

As she hung there, gasping, she heard cheers. The next race must have started. Only slowly did Suzy grasp that the cheering was for her. Not because she won: "I was four minutes behind the next slowest swimmer. They cheered," Suzy said, "because I did it."

"I think," I told her, "that I'll sign up for that Lupus Walk after all."

Remind me, Father, that I don't have to be first to be a winner.
—Elizabeth Sherrill

Digging Deeper: Matthew 20:16; 1 Corinthians 9:26

The Lord's lovingkindnesses indeed never cease, for his compassions never fail. They are new every morning.... —Lamentations 3:22–23 (NAS)

Hibiscus is my favorite flower. In the Philippines, where I spent my childhood, these plants grow to be tall shrubs and even small trees. Hardy green hibiscus produce large trumpet-shaped flowers that vary in color from white to pink, red, orange, peach, yellow, or purple. My wife, Beth, and I now raise potted hibiscus plants on our porch in Georgia.

A unique trait of hibiscus flowers is that they live for only one day. At the end of the day the flowers wilt, drop off the plant, and are replaced by a whole new crop of blooms. Each morning, as I walk out our front door, I pause to look at each fresh bloom that has emerged overnight. I greet them all with "Good morning!" and welcome them into their new world.

Recently, I reflected on how God expects the same of me. Each day is a new gift. The good that I might have done yesterday needs to be recreated today. I cannot be content with yesterday's achievements or tomorrow's hopes. Today is the one day I have to live, and I must live it with purpose and creativity. I need to tell someone that I love her. I must set out on a new endeavor to help someone, encourage my students, give a fresh compliment, utter a special prayer for my neighbor, and teach an old thought in a different and compelling way. With each sunrise, the world awakens anew and I have the privilege of stepping into a morning filled with promise.

Father, help me to live today as if it were my first day of life and my last day of opportunity. Amen.
—Scott Walker

Digging Deeper: Matthew 6:25–34; John 15:1–11

Thursday, May 17

CONFIDENCE IN DIFFICULTY: Faith in All Circumstances

What is gained if I am silenced, if I go down to the pit? Will the
dust praise you?... —Psalm 30:9 (NIV)

I went in search of the nurse. "My daughter is very sensitive to chaos," I reminded him, for the hospital already knew of Maggie's post-traumatic stress disorder. "She needs help in finding ways to feel safe when the others become aggressive."

The boy two rooms down punched walls and shouted, and the kid across the hall screeched endlessly. Around the corner was a teen who cried loudly much of the day. The nurse wrote down my concerns, but no accommodations were made.

Every day my daughter pleaded, "Get me out of here! I can't take this. I'll kill myself!"

Staff heard the threat but not the distress. They removed all of the furniture from Maggie's room, leaving only a mattress and blanket, and parked someone in an armchair in the doorway to watch her twenty-four hours a day. The noise of others cursing, punching, crying, and howling continued.

"There's not much we can do," said the psychiatrist. "We only have the staff and space we have."

"Surely there's a quiet area where Maggie can go when others blow up," I insisted. "Or you can give her earplugs. Or someone to coach her through the trouble spots." The psychiatrist didn't see modifying the environment to help my daughter as an option. It was up to Maggie to figure out how to cope.

I prayed through despair as I went home. I prayed for ideas, alternatives, my daughter, the doctor, and help. Mostly, I asked for perspective.

Father, I don't understand what good is coming out of this. Yet even if
I never understand, even if it hurts, I will still be Your servant.
—Julia Attaway

Digging Deeper: Joshua 24:15; 2 Corinthians 6:4

As it is, there are many parts, but one body. —1 Corinthians 12:20 (NIV)

A friend of mine told me about her trip to Papua New Guinea. She and her husband had a marvelous time. But she described seeing stray dogs everywhere. Because none of the animals are spayed or neutered, they have pups over and over. It's a problem that touched her deeply.

She wanted to investigate ways to address the stray dog problem and make a difference. But she bemoaned her efforts as such a small thing to do.

We do that, don't we? We want to make a difference in the world in a big way. Maybe even in a way others will see or admire. I pointed out, "You should help where your passions are strongest. Then you will make a difference."

Like my friend, I want to make a difference. But my passion seems small: encouraging others. For me, that means sending cards to friends facing tough times. I often wonder if it helps. In this digital age, sending a card in the mail means I don't get an immediate response. It's very different from someone clicking "Like" on Facebook in response to something I just posted.

But the other day I found out what those cards can mean. I'd sent my friend going through chemotherapy a Superman card. It was just to remind him: "Your cape is showing! You are amazing!" Turns out the card arrived on the very day he was facing a new diagnosis and needed some extra encouragement. Yes, my card was silly, but sometimes that's the point.

We all don't see the same problems in the world, but we all have a passion for something. Take the one thing you care most about and see how much good will come from your response. When we take on the concerns closest to our hearts we certainly make a difference.

Take my passionate heart and use it for Your service, Lord. Amen.

—Lisa Bogart

Digging Deeper: Mark 12:41–44; 1
Corinthians 9:24–27; Ephesians 4:11–12

Saturday, May 19

Serve wholeheartedly, as if you were serving the Lord, not people.
—Ephesians 6:7 (NIV)

"Honey, I can't take the pain in my throat. Please find a doctor that I can see today."

It had been a long week with multiple visits to the hospital, but no progress had been made. "God, help me find someone who can diagnose the symptoms and heal me." Elba called back to let me know she had scheduled an appointment for noon, the only available slot.

As I waited in the doctor's office, the military commendations on the wall caught my attention. After quick introductions were made, I mentioned the awards. The physician told me that he had served twelve years in the navy, with a tour in Iraq, and was now serving in the reserves. I shared about Guideposts' long history with the military and my travels to bases to meet with chaplains.

He then examined my throat and expressed concern about my vocal cords because of the wear and tear from my years of speaking. "I know that you are a preacher and need your voice," he said. "My goal is to get you back to one hundred percent." God had answered my prayer and ordained my steps. Out of all the doctors in the area, he was the only one available.

Lord, thank You for the medical professionals
who serve us and our country.
—Pablo Diaz

Digging Deeper: Ezekiel 27:10; 1 Peter 4:10–11

"But seek first his kingdom and his righteousness, and all these things will be given to you as well." —Matthew 6:33 (NIV)

I sat down at church, waiting to hear the guest speaker. It was the annual Women's Night at my church, and I always looked forward to coming. This year the speaker talked about facing difficult situations where she had to "give up and give it to God." And each time she'd pray, "Lord, I don't know what to do, but my eyes are on You."

What a perfect prayer, I thought.

The next day I was sitting in the office of my dermatologist. With a concerned look on her face, she'd just referred me to a specialist. I immediately felt alarm. I prayed, *Lord, I don't know what to do, but my eyes are on You.*

A few days later, a colleague called and asked me to join the board of an organization. I wanted to, but I knew it would take up a great deal of my time. I prayed, *Lord, I don't know what to do, but my eyes are on You.*

At the end of the week, a friend called. She was overwhelmed with a difficult financial situation and asked for advice. I prayed, "Lord, we don't know what to do, but our eyes are on You."

The following Sunday in church, Pastor Dave spoke about living a discerning life that always is centered on asking for God's guidance. He said, "Sometimes we have situations where we don't need to try harder, we just need to give up and turn to God."

What a different week it would have been had I not been reminded to look to God first, I thought.

> *Lord, it's not up to me; it's up to You.*
> *Help me to first seek Your will.*
> —Melody Bonnette Swang

Digging Deeper: Deuteronomy 4:29; 1 John 4:6

Monday, May 21

Do not boast about tomorrow, for you do not know what a day may bring. —Proverbs 27:1 (NIV)

Hi. My name is Marilyn, and I'm a procrastinator. People think I get a lot of things done. But they don't know how much time I waste and how much more I could accomplish if I was more disciplined.

Take exercising, for example. Every day, I plan to go for a walk. But each day, I find reasons to postpone the exercise. I tell myself I'll do it after I drink my coffee, read my devotion, check my e-mail, or do the laundry. Then it's lunchtime, and I'm hungry. Besides, it's too hot, too cold, too something or other now. Tomorrow I'll start out earlier, but the scenario repeats itself.

When I heard about Carol, though, my attitude changed. She's been in our church choir for years, even directing it at times. But since her surgery, she hasn't returned. She hasn't been able to regain her strength, and the medications she's on only make her weaker. Before the surgery, she power walked the trails in the woods near her house, but now she can barely get from one room to another.

The next time I had the urge to walk, the old excuses started to pop up again. But I decided to walk for Carol, praying for her healing as I did, no matter the temperature outside or what else I could be doing. Today I have the strength to walk, and I can show my gratitude by taking those extra steps.

> *Thank You, God, for giving me good health today.*
> *Help me to take advantage of it while I can.*
> —Marilyn Turk

Digging Deeper: James 4:13–16

THE BEAUTY OF SIMPLICITY: Spiritual Glue for Marriage

And what does the Lord require of you but to do justice, to love kindness, and to walk humbly with your God. —Micah 6:8 (NAS)

Every morning my husband, Rick, and I sit on the front porch. Nothing fancy. We drink coffee, talk, and pray. One bitter-cold day, we were in our rocking chairs at dawn. In the quiet stillness, my man of few words asked me a startling question. "Would you still love me if I couldn't fix things?"

We'd been married for almost forty years—the same length of time he'd owned an auto repair business—and it sounded like he needed reassurance. But he'd always appeared confident. He was my rock.

What I had to say felt so intimate that my heart grew full. "I'm sorry. I should've told you this a long time ago. I admire you. You serve people behind the scenes without caring if you receive recognition. Yesterday, you were at church at 5:00 a.m. to help set up. After the service, you helped tear down. After you finished, you fixed Jamie's leaky roof."

He sipped his coffee and looked out into the darkness. "It's no big deal."

"Yes, it is. You have the gift of service. You're a mechanical genius. And you're generous. What you do matters. The other day you stopped to help an elderly woman having car trouble. Last night at Mother's house, you put her broken lamp back together."

"I'm just doing the right thing," he said.

I knelt in front of him. "When you fix broken things, you're helping to mend broken people." Putting my arms inside his warm coat, I hugged him. "And, yes, even if you couldn't fix things, I'd still love you."

> *Father, no matter how long we're married,*
> *simple kindness holds us together.*
> —Julie Garmon

Digging Deeper: Proverbs 3:3; Galatians 5:22

Wednesday, May 23

"Peace I leave with you; my peace I give to you, not as the world gives do I give to you." —John 14:27 (NAS)

Wayne and I had several meetings set up with our attorney for estate planning. We wanted to protect our assets as much as possible for our heirs' sakes. I lost count of the hours we spent reviewing every detail in order to properly take care of our children and grandchildren.

After one lengthy session we returned home, mentally and physically exhausted. Wayne commented that he wished it wasn't so complicated.

That got me to thinking. *Did Jesus leave a will?* Then I read the fourteenth chapter of John and realized that He did. He willed His body to Joseph of Arimathea. He willed His mother to John and from the Cross He willed His Spirit back to His Father. But to His disciples and His followers, He said, "My peace I give to you."

His peace. As He was nailed to that Cross His thoughts were on those He loved. While dying He took care of all that was necessary to pave the way to eternal life for me and for you. Amazing, isn't it? What a legacy. He laid down His life for us and then rose from the dead to execute His own will.

The next time Wayne and I met with our attorney, I felt calmed by the gift of peace that Jesus has left with me.

> *Lord, how fortunate we are to have a Savior Whose thoughts were on us as You went to the Cross. May my thoughts turn to You in every aspect of my life.*
> —Debbie Macomber

Digging Deeper: Isaiah 26:3; Philippians 4:6–7

The birds brought Elijah bread and meat every morning and every evening. And he drank water from the brook. —1 Kings 17:6 (ICB)

It was still early in the day, but I was sprawled on my couch in the dark, every drape drawn, curtain closed, and eyelid securely shut. Mentally, I was blowing up balloons for my pity party....

"There's a tear in your cornea," the nurse at the Minute Clinic had explained. "Your contact lens was probably too dry and scratched your eye."

My eye throbbed as tears streamed from beneath my closed lid. To top it off, I now had a migraine. But despite being nauseated and in pain, all I could think of was a Five Guys burger. The more I thought about it, the hungrier I felt. The restaurant was only a seven-minute walk from my apartment. But in my vampirish state, that was seven minutes too long.

That's when my phone buzzed. The text read, "Want to join me and Lila's friends for lunch?" Now I was even more upset! I'd have to miss out on food and fun with my friend Tami and her daughter. I texted back, explaining I was homebound. I started to text, "Could you please pick me up a burger..." but I felt too needy, like too much of an inconvenience. I deleted it.

"Can I pick up something for you?" Tami texted right back. That's how I wound up popping all of my pity party balloons and enjoying a burger with a smile on my face—in the dark. I don't know why I continue to be surprised when God uses my friends to meet my needs in delightful ways.

> *Dear Lord, I wouldn't hesitate to help a friend in need,*
> *but so often I'm hesitant to ask friends to help me.*
> *Teach me how to receive as well as to give.*
> —Vicki Kuyper

Digging Deeper: 1 Kings 17:7–16

"In the same way, let your light shine before others, that they may see your good deeds and glorify your Father in heaven." —Matthew 5:16 (NIV)

I sat with the birthday boy and his friends on the grass in Central Park, singing songs with my guitar. I'd begun a small entertainment business, singing and face painting at children's parties.

I connected with my group of kids, talking with them, looking at them with a smile as I sang each song. One little girl, however, was particularly fixated on me. Her dark curls framed big brown eyes. I responded with lots of eye contact for each song.

"Okay, guys," I said after my last one, "I'm going to set up my face paints now, so start thinking about what you'd like me to paint."

I prepared my brushes and paints, and one by one the children came to be transformed into pirates, tigers, princesses, and puppy dogs. The little girl sat down last. Her parents stood by her, looking a bit hesitant.

"What do you want me to paint?" I asked her.

"A butterfly," she said shyly.

I dabbed my brush in light green paint, and began to create her butterfly.

"I can't believe she's letting you do this," her mom said in surprise.

"She's on the autism spectrum and has sensory issues," her father clarified. "She never lets anyone touch her face."

My heart swelled as I continued to paint; each tiny stroke felt enormous. When she looked in the mirror, her big eyes sparkled with delight.

> *Lord, I love how You use small things to show Your greatness.*
> *Thank You for the privilege of being Your hands and feet*
> *as You work in the lives of others.*
> —Karen Valentin

Digging Deeper: Matthew 25:40

"Whoever receives one of these little children in My name receives Me...."
—Mark 9:37 (NKJV)

If I were a millionaire, I would still go to rummage sales on Saturday mornings. There is more to these sales than bargains.

I pride myself on my fiscal discipline at such sales, but I have one weakness: the children. At the sight of two little girls in matching dresses, selling pink lemonade, all my strict business savvy crumbles.

"I would like to buy a glass of your lemonade," I say.

The excitement on their faces is unforgettable. No Wall Street transaction ever came close to this in importance! They take their business seriously, carefully stirring the icy liquid, then helping each other lift the heavy glass pitcher. They pour me an oversize serving, then count out my change meticulously, and I am reminded of the old-fashioned business principles of generosity and honesty.

"Thank you, girls. This is just what I need on a hot day."

I buy from the children partly as a payback to all the adults who bought from me when I was a boy selling magazines door-to-door. I remember how exultant I felt when I made a sale and how crestfallen I was when I was rejected.

But I am also buying hope. This is the children's first business venture. If it fails, they might lose heart. If it succeeds, it might inspire a future career. I think of a boy named Jimmy from nearby Hamilton, Missouri, who started out with a lemonade stand, then later founded a business called the J. C. Penney Company.

By noon on Saturday I am pretty much intoxicated on lemonade, but the hangover is sweet. Where else in life can you buy hope and happiness for just twenty-five cents a glass?

Thank You, God, for the inspiration I receive from Your smallest teachers.
                    —Daniel Schantz

Digging Deeper: Matthew 18:10; Mark 10:14

Sunday, May 27

Happy is the man... that getteth understanding. —Proverbs 3:13 (KJV)

I send my favorite fly sailing across the surface of the water. Plop. It lands in the exact spot that I had targeted. The pure joy I felt as a small child, sitting on the pier beside my dad, surrounds me. The pressures of work and the anxiety of the world fall away. Here, at the water's edge, I am content.

The ways to catch a fish are just as varied as the people who pursue the sport. There are bait fisherman who use live bait like minnows and worms. They take a bare hook tied under a float or bobber, bait the hook, and then throw it out into the water and sit patiently until it bobs up and down. Then, there are lure fisherman who use different types of buzz baits, plugs, and spinners—and there are hundreds of colors, types, and styles. Finally, my favorite, fly fishing. From studying the local habitat to choosing a fly that most represents the insects currently hatching on the river, it's like becoming one with the spot where I've chosen to fish.

Fishing is all about "catching the big one." Catching happiness is much the same.

We all cast about in our own ways to find peace, happiness, and, ultimately, God. Like fishing, each person has his or her own style. Some of us crave action; others want the quiet satisfaction that comes with sitting on the shore. But aren't we all looking for that perfect spot where we become one with our Father God?

Successful fishing takes a lot of effort. I'm resolved to try even harder to search for and find the peace that God offers. On a grassy bank, by a quiet stream, in a boat on a calm lake, by the mighty ocean's edge, I know He's there, waiting for each of us, hoping we catch the happiness that He offers.

Father, Your presence is my finest catch.
—Brock Kidd

Digging Deeper: Psalm 35:9; Proverbs 19:8; Ecclesiastes 2:26

But God demonstrates his own love for us in this: While we were still sinners, Christ died for us. —Romans 5:8 (NIV)

I t was the weekend we'd been waiting for: open-the-pool day. Lonny and the boys worked various chores involving hoses and chemicals and a two-man struggle with the thick winter tarp. Our pool was small, just enough for a good game of volleyball or Shark, but the excitement was big. The morning pulsed with summer.

But before the fun, we gathered, as we do each Memorial Day, and walked toward the Mississippi River. We went down two blocks, past a barge, along the road until the bank was thick with spring-green grass. We walked until we reached neat rows of knee-high white crosses, slender and shining in the sun—a memorial to fallen soldiers.

Our village is small, but it's lost quite a few sons. Some served in World War I. Several were buried at sea. One was a POW. There are also crosses representing soldiers who served in World War II, Korea, and Vietnam. We stood silent and read each name.

The river flowed in solemn cadence. I thought of parents and spouses and their children and those who fought but didn't come home. I didn't know these families, but I know love. My heart ached for their giving that offered everything.

After a few moments, we headed home. Seven-year-old Isaiah's hand slipped into mine as we climbed the hill toward the first day of summer, toward the pool and a picnic and family and friends, and toward our long-awaited day.

Thank You, Lord, for sacrifice that saved us. Amen.
—Shawnelle Eliasen

Digging Deeper: John 15:13

Tuesday, May 29

Let us rejoice today and be glad. —Psalm 118:24 (NIV)

It's unseasonably cool this week. The heat's turned off in my building, and I'm wearing a hoodie that's hiding several long-sleeve layers. Even my thoughts are chilled—focused on discomforts of my childhood in the northern climes, like walking a wintry mile to school, or sleeping in a bedroom upstairs with no heat. From the window, I scope the overcast morning sky for a glint of hope.

The phone rings, interrupting my negative thoughts. It's my friend Sandra. "If you want to come over, the rhubarb is ready to pick. And I want you to have the first batch."

"Oh, great! Thank you! I'll be there within the hour." Just hearing the word *rhubarb* pushes my mind off its icy block. Driving a few miles north, I fondly remember my dad and me as a teen walking into a nearby field to harvest an abandoned rhubarb patch, every spring producing all our family could ever eat and more. Rhubarb pies, cakes, sauces galore!

Now back home, I wash and cut the stalks and then reach for a well-worn cookbook. How much sugar do I add to sweeten the sour gift, so full of promise?

With anticipation, I turn on the oven. Its supplemental heat warms my apartment. I bake a rhubarb pie. Its memorable tang turns my heart's weather around.

Lord, when negative memories complicate difficult days,
help me to reach further, dig deeper, to find a positive grace.
—Evelyn Bence

Digging Deeper: Psalm 85:4, 6–13

"Son," Abraham answered, "God himself will provide the sheep for the holocaust." Then the two continued going forward. —Genesis 22:8 (NAB)

I sat on my bed, cradling the telephone in my lap. I had until 5:00 p.m. to call New York University and accept their offer to enter a graduate degree program in the fall. I was hoping to have the twenty-five-thousand-dollar annual tuition waived by working as a graduate assistant to one of the professors there, but that job went to another student. I needed to decide whether I wanted this master's degree enough to pay for it myself, through loans.

I called my parents. My dad answered. I asked him what he thought.

He paused. I knew, on the other end, he was thinking, breathing, praying, maybe, weighing his words.

"That's an awful lot of debt for you to be having to pay off, sweetie," he told me gently. He didn't say anything more.

"I know, Dad," I said. Now it was my turn to be silent.

When I found my words, I told him, "I'm going to turn them down."

I hung up the telephone and cried. A cherished dream was coming to an end. But behind the deep disappointment was a strange lightness in my heart. It was like glimpsing a patch of blue sky behind the dark clouds of a fast-moving thunderstorm. I felt a freedom in obedience, in conforming myself to the reality of my life as it was.

Resolved in my decision, I reached purposefully for the telephone. It rang before I could pick up the receiver.

It was a university secretary, calling to offer me the graduate-assistant position and a tuition-free education at NYU. The other student had decided not to return to school and had declined the job offer.

"Yes," I said. "Yes!" My heart nearly burst, so surprised was I by the movement from anxiety to despair to acceptance, and then, miraculously, to joy.

God, I offer You my will today. I trust You to help me to continue moving forward. —Amy Eddings

Digging Deeper: Genesis 22:16–18; Psalm 40:8; Romans 12:1–2

Thursday, May 31

"Aren't two sparrows sold for a small coin? But not one of them will fall to the ground without your Father knowing about it already."
—Matthew 10:29 (CEB)

Several years ago my husband, Don, and grandson Caleb built a rock fountain in our yard. The water flows down slabs of rock into a small pool surrounded by a low, horseshoe-shaped wall. Don put a bird feeder nearby, and we keep a couple of bird books and binoculars handy to identify the many types of birds who come to eat, drink, and bathe.

The birds behave in very different ways. This spring we have six fat robins who take turns splashing in the pool. The redwing blackbirds, grackles, and cowbirds drink but aren't fond of being wet. Our pair of house wrens perches on a rock and takes dainty sips. A fat chucker, no doubt an escapee from a local gamebird farm, spent three days walking around the yard, occasionally hunkering down to rest inside the brick wall. An injured cardinal sheltered in the small space between the wall and the running water. We have juncos, messy and raucous doves, and an occasional squawking blue jay.

The birds I love most, though, are the house sparrows. There are dozens of them; small and plain, indistinguishable from one another in their drab gray and brown dress. They come many times a day for food and water, flocking in and flying out in seemingly random patterns. Their lifespan is short; we often find their bodies under the trees.

But these sparrows have value in God's sight and in mine. Daily, they remind me of a God Whose love and care for the tiniest of creatures encompasses life and death, and Whose love and care for me is infinite, compassionate, and far beyond my understanding.

*Loving God, let me learn from the birds
to rest and to trust in You. Amen.*
—Penney Schwab

Digging Deeper: Matthew 6:25–27, 10:30–31

GOD'S UNFAILING LOVE

1 _____

2 _____

3 _____

4 _____

5 _____

6 _____

7 _____

8 _____

9 _____

10 _____

11 _____

12 _____

13 _____

14 _____

15 _____

May

16 _____

17 _____

18 _____

19 _____

20 _____

21 _____

22 _____

23 _____

24 _____

25 _____

26 _____

27 _____

28 _____

29 _____

30 _____

31 _____

JUNE

*But I am like an olive tree flourishing
in the house of God; I trust in God's
unfailing love for ever and ever.*

—Psalm 52:8 (NIV)

Friday, June 1

How precious to me are your thoughts, O God! How vast is the sum of them! If I would count them, they are more than the sand. I awake, and I am still with you. —Psalm 139:17–18 (esv)

A water bottle filled with sand sits on the windowsill beside my desk. I've never been one to collect sand from the beach. That was my sister, Maria, and the bottle is filled with sand from our last vacation together in Wellfleet, Massachusetts.

A few weeks after Maria died in her sleep, I was helping my brother-in-law clean up their yard and there it was, under a tarp in a pile of things from the vacation—a bottle of sand from my sister's favorite beach; her way of bringing paradise home.

I held the bottle in my hands, picturing Maria sitting comfortably on her towel with a big straw beach hat on, funneling the sand, handful by handful, into the bottle. "Okay if I have this?" I asked. Maria's daughter nodded.

The bottle of sand has been on my windowsill ever since. Sometimes it reminds me of the soap opera my mom has watched almost every day since I was a kid—"Like sands through the hourglass" begins the show.

After Maria died, Mom stopped watching TV for a while. The day I went onto Mom's porch to borrow something and the show's theme song echoed out of the open window, it made me feel better. Maybe the grief over Maria's unexpected death had shifted just enough that Mom wanted to feel back to normal, whatever normal had become.

But, mostly, the sand in the bottle is a message from heaven, a reminder for me to take the time to take it all in. Everything—the green grass, the sound of birds singing, even the grief. Take in every amazing moment of life.

> *Heavenly Father, help me be mindful. Guide me to see*
> *Your infinite blessings in sand and stone.*
> —Sabra Ciancanelli

Digging Deeper: Deuteronomy 2:7; Romans 15:29

"The Lord himself goes before you and will be with you; he will never leave you nor forsake you. Do not be afraid; do not be discouraged."
—Deuteronomy 31:8 (NIV)

Saturday afternoons at the local pool are a particular kind of crazy. Every neighborhood kid over thirteen is here alone, being cool at the snack bar and diving off the high board. Young families abound, burning the hours between naptime and dinner.

Often I brave the bedlam by myself with the kids, Brian coming to meet us later. That means I've got a little guy, only six months old, who needs me to hold him (and hates to be splashed) and a two-year-old who moves so quickly she often produces her own wake.

It doesn't take long for Olivia to get a decent distance from me, and thanks to her swimmies, I don't worry. As long as I can see her, I know she's okay.

But Olivia doesn't know that. One afternoon it hit her that I wasn't right beside her anymore. From her vantage point, all torsos and floats, she was completely surrounded and yet all alone.

I could see the panic spreading across her face as she grew more tearful and fearful by the minute. Though I was just a few feet away, to Olivia, I might as well have packed my bags and headed home. I called out to her, but in her fear she couldn't hear me. "I'm here! Just look at me! Find my face!" I called as I moved toward her.

But I know something Olivia doesn't. I can see the bigger picture. I know her mommy is there, that she is safe, that her swimmies are keeping her afloat, that she's about four feet from a lifeguard. All Olivia knows is that she is alone, scared, and lost.

How often do I find myself lost, alone, and adrift? How often is God just inches away whispering, "I'm here. Just look to Me. Find My face"?

Lord, help me, always, to see Your face.
—Ashley Kappel

Digging Deeper: Deuteronomy 31:6; Psalms 34:17–18, 121:1–8

Sunday, June 3

Having then gifts differing according to the grace that is given to us....
—Romans 12:6 (KJV)

Clare "buzzes" the bumblebee puppet into the middle of a model flower as large as a cabbage. She's demonstrating pollination by insects to our volunteer workshop here at Bok Tower Gardens in central Florida.

First, we learn that flowers must attract pollinators like Buzzy to help the plant produce seeds to ensure the next generation. To draw the bees, bugs, birds, or bats to the vital pollen, some flowers flaunt alluring designs "like marks on a landing strip," says Clare. Other flowers glow in eye-popping colors irresistible to the pollinators. Many flowers, however, are plain white. We volunteers learn that these less showy blossoms attract essential pollinators with their strong fragrances, not by appearances.

Though I'm familiar with the heavy scent of white orange blossoms that pervades my car, even with the windows up, I later roam the garden to test Clare's theory, sniffing all the white flowers I can find: gardenia, jasmine, camellia. Sure enough, the most inconspicuous blooms have knockout scents.

And I consider the visible and not-so-visible ways that church members perpetuate the faith for the next generation. Some dynamic believers, clearly visible, take charge: clergy, leaders, managers, financial consultants. More introverted souls may gravitate toward maintenance and hospitality: arranging flowers, making coffee, and cooking for potlucks. Few who feed, console, or teach make headlines, but they do make folks feel comfortable and welcomed enough to stick around and become helpers themselves.

No, one doesn't need to be the center of attention to perpetuate a beautiful legacy of love.

God of Wonder, may we discern our unique gifts and use them for Your glory.
—Gail Thorell Schilling

Digging Deeper: Matthew 6:5–6; 1 Corinthians 12:4–6

Then they sat upon the ground with him silently for seven days and nights, no one speaking a word; for they saw that his suffering was too great for words. —Job 2:13 (TLB)

The storm was unusually severe, even for southwest Kansas. As bolts of lightning hit near the house and thunder boomed, my dog Tarby whined and pawed at the door until I let her in. She is supposed to stay on the back porch, but she followed me into the living room and tried to crawl onto the sofa and into my lap. She was terrified, so I ended up sitting on the porch floor with her head on my legs, stroking her back until the storm passed.

A week later my daughter Rebecca called to say how grateful she was for her pastor. "When Olivia was in the emergency room getting treatment for a severe migraine, he sat with us for over an hour," she said. "We hardly talked, but his presence meant the world to me."

I remembered the time a friend held my hand silently while I mourned my mother's death; the dear ones who stayed with me during my husband's cancer surgery; the stranger who handed me a cup of water and a tissue as I choked back tears after I was criticized for remarks I'd made.

There are times when the right words are important and helpful. There are times when spoken prayer is essential. But there are also times, I'm learning, when simply being fully present with a hurting person—or a frightened dog—is enough.

Merciful Savior, help me to know when to speak and when to be silent. Keep me willing to offer the same comforting solace to others as Your presence gives to me.
—Penney Schwab

Digging Deeper: Isaiah 66:12–13; 2 Corinthians 1:3–4

Tuesday, June 5

"And do not be grieved, for the joy of the Lord is your strength."
—Nehemiah 8:10 (ESV)

My four-year-old son, Will, plays on a soccer team with his three cousins.

The YMCA Screaming Eagles, with daring feats of goal-scoring aptitude and magnificent ball-handling skills, lead their team to sure victory each week as only preschoolers can do.

Okay, that's not entirely accurate. There is a whole lot more ladybug catching and grass picking going on than there is soccer playing.

Last week, in a moment of sheer energy (read: craziness), Will noticed that his cousin Isaac was sitting in the grass at the edge of the field looking at a tiny daisy. And so, instead of heading to the goal and shooting, he picked up the ball and took it to his cousin and set it in front of him. "Here, Isaac. You score this time."

Isaac stood up and kicked the ball toward the goal. The crowd went wild. The parents cheered. The ref blew the whistle.

"Hand ball!" The ref bent down next to Will and kindly explained that in soccer you can't touch the ball with your hands. The other team got the ball and quickly scored (another) goal.

And as I stood on the sidelines, shaking my head, wondering if the effort of finding soccer socks in laundry baskets and shin guards under the seat of the car was really worth it, the whistle blew. And eight bright-eyed kids ran to the sidelines, laughing and high-fiving and talking about how that was the best game ever.

And I remembered that it didn't matter who scored or who found a ladybug, but that our kids were holding hands, playing together, and loving every minute of the game.

> *Lord, show me how to find joy in life even when*
> *things don't go exactly as I think they should. Amen.*
> —Erin MacPherson

Digging Deeper: Psalm 5:11–12; Ecclesiastes 9:7

For even the Son of Man did not come to be served, but to serve, and to give his life as a ransom for many. —Mark 10:45 (NIV)

Row upon row of white crosses stand in military precision. The stillness of ten thousand graves reverberates in my heart. I made this visit to the American Cemetery in Normandy, France, reluctantly, not wanting to feel the emotion of a place where so many died. Now, in this voiceless sanctuary of remembrance, I pay homage to those soldiers and all the others who've come after.

Perhaps my emotion is deepened because I understand. My son and son-in-law, in multiple deployments, have risked their lives. I've experienced the angst, yet been blessed by their return. The parents of those who died here were not so fortunate. I owe them, as well as their children, acknowledgment and honor for their gift of unshackled life.

I walk in silence to where thousands of young lives were extinguished in a single day. The beach is stark, windswept, empty. It's easy to forget, important to remember. Being where it happened overwhelms me. I can't ignore the immensity of the sacrifice. These people gave all; their lives stopped or forever changed, so mine could go on.

I climb steep banks, peer into scooped-out shelters, imagine the thundering battle. Water gently licks the well-worn sand where hundreds of thousands of boots carried their owners into the unknown. The sea is calm now. I am filled with gratitude and awe.

Thank You, God, for all the soldiers who sacrificed their lives.
—Kim Henry

Digging Deeper: Psalms 7:9, 33:12, 60:12

Thursday, June 7

If anyone, then, knows the good they ought to do and doesn't do it, it is sin for them. —James 4:17 (NIV)

I rounded the corner and headed for home after my morning walk. I could see my new neighbor out in her yard, pulling weeds. Another neighbor had told me this new gal was a walker like me. "She would love to walk with you in the mornings, I'll bet."

I thought about all this as I kept walking by. *I should stop and say hi, but there's not really time.* I continued walking. *I should ask if she wants to walk some morning.* Still I kept walking. I got to my driveway. I hesitated. I walked to my front door. I turned around and walked back down the driveway. *I'm going to do it! I'm going to ask her to walk with me.* But instead I pretended to pick up a nonexistent newspaper and turned back toward the house. Then the argument in my head really started:

I just don't have time for this right now.

Really? What are you going to do?

I have things to do.

Things?

Yes, things. Besides, I am a sweaty mess.

She's out in her yard working. She's a sweaty mess too.

I unlocked my front door. I went inside, took a shower, and started my busy day.

Now I am too much of a chicken to go knock on her door. *Hi, I'm the neighbor who walked right by you. I'm the neighbor who ignored you.*

I am very aware of this missed opportunity. I hope when it comes again I will step out in love and faith.

Forgive me, Lord, for passing by opportunities to know
my neighbors and to build community. Amen.
—Lisa Bogart

Digging Deeper: Jeremiah 15:5; Romans 7:15–16

And he said: "Truly I tell you, unless you change and become like little children, you will never enter the kingdom of heaven."
—Matthew 18:3 (NIV)

My daughters Charlotte and Lulu are becoming independent. We no longer support them (much). With both of them in grad school in faraway California, we don't see them very often. When they're home for holidays, they talk about friends we haven't met, foods we've never eaten, exciting places we'll probably never visit. Lulu reads the news nowadays and votes. Charlotte belongs to a knitting and crocheting club, by far the youngest member, and goes to yarn shows with women twice her age. Their lives are very different from and not very connected to ours.

I used to long for this day: when they'd be mature women of their own shaping. I knew I'd never lament my empty nest, and I don't. Still, I miss being the wise one in their lives, their go-to person for advice, large and small.

Increasingly, I find myself being advised by them.

Charlotte recently sent me a purse with birds on it. A purse! Who chooses a purse for another woman? But she's right: it's "me."

And today Lulu spoke sternly about my usual end-of-semester woes: "Mom, you didn't cause your students' stress. They did. If they'd started their papers sooner, they wouldn't be stressed! They have to learn that."

Contrary to my expectations, I feel I'm getting younger—the one needing care—as they mature.

The same callowing is happening with God. It used to be that I thought I orchestrated my life. Now I find myself simply accepting God's plans for me. His parental will, I find, is my unquestioned destiny and my hope.

Help me grow more childlike, Father, and depend on You.
—Patty Kirk

Digging Deeper: Psalm 127; Luke 12:13–21

Saturday, June 9

Here is my servant, whom I uphold, my chosen, in whom my soul delights.
—Isaiah 42:1 (NRSV)

Sometimes everything is just right. Now it was the rain that was right.

We were on our way home from a trip to Maine, where friends from church had invited us to stay at their small cabin on a lake. It had been a glorious few days. Kayaking. Canoeing. Bike rides. A day trip to the coast to see a lighthouse. Dinners outside and s'mores around a small campfire. The haunting calls of loons at night.

We were sad to go home, not looking forward to the gritty city. But then it began to rain. It rained harder and harder, pelting our car. Our spirits had been flagging, but we all grinned as the rain drummed on the roof and sent up fountains of spray from the highway.

"Let's keep reading," I said to the kids. I'd been reading to them while Kate drove. Suddenly, the car became cozy and warm as the story unfolded with the rain hammering outside. It was almost as if we were on our own screened porch, safe and dry, listening contentedly to the sound of falling water.

"Look!" cried Benji. We turned and saw, through a distant parting of the storm, not one but two rainbows. They stood out starkly against the dark clouds nearer to us.

Every last trace of sadness was gone now. What could be more perfect than a good story on a rainy day, graced by a double rainbow? What an unexpected gift. We should have expected it from the Giver Who never tires of delighting those who seek Him.

Lord, help me always to be open to the unexpected ways in which
You show me how much You love me.
—Jim Hinch

Digging Deeper: Ephesians 3:17–19; 1 John 4:16

Then you will experience God's peace, which exceeds anything we can understand. His peace will guard your hearts and minds as you live in Christ Jesus. —Philippians 4:7 (NLT)

We have a trampoline in the yard. Countless kids have jumped on it over the years—friends of our lineup of boys. But on days like today, when the sun is warm and the air is cool, we sit on the trampoline and read.

I read out loud, and my two younger boys stretch out on their backs, arms folded under heads, smiles to the sun. Suddenly, it's too good to pass up. I dog-ear our book and stretch out too. The blue of the sky is rich and deep. There's not a single cloud. I close my eyes and let my face grow warm. Radiance presses past the physical into my soul.

I begin to think about how this golden rest is like "the peace of God, which surpasses all understanding." The Bible tells us that when we commit to prayer rather than worry, when we present our needs with an offering of thanksgiving, we'll experience God's brand of peace. It's consuming, completing, pure, and like nothing else.

This isn't always easy for me. Often I struggle and scrap for control. It's then that I cower in the darkness. When I let go, when I open my heart to God, the light comes in.

My boys settle beside me, and my arms cradle their necks. Our breath becomes a rhythm. "We should get back to lessons," I say eventually.

"Five more minutes?" a boy asks.

I kiss their blond heads. They smell of soap and skin that's warmed by the sun. I can't resist. "Okay," I say, "we'll stay." I want to rest in this peace.

> *Father, sweet, true peace is found only in You. Amen.*
> —Shawnelle Eliasen

> *Digging Deeper:* Psalm 29:11; Isaiah 26:12

Monday, June 11

"I will put a new spirit within them...." —Ezekiel 11:19 (NKJV)

I was exhausted from gardening in the blistering heat and praying for relief when I heard the neighbor's radio promoting the Missouri State Fair.

At lunch I said to my wife, "Let's go to the state fair."

Sharon stared at me blankly. "The fair? We don't do fairs. Think of the parking problems, the crowds, the heat, and all that walking..."

"Okay," I yielded, "but they do have a quilt show."

Her eyes widened. "Quilts? Well, I suppose it wouldn't hurt to try it once."

We arrived at the fairgrounds early in the morning. Parking was easy, on the grass, by the entrance. The morning crowds were light. Pretty, high clouds moved in, bringing cooler air. Instead of walking, we rode the farm wagons pulled by strong green tractors, and we hopped off to see interesting sights, like the clever product demonstrations and the free samples of home-baked goodies. Most charming were the people: wide-eyed children petting the goats; weathered master gardeners surrounded by their hybrid creations; handsome highway patrolmen guarding a cage of beautiful tigers; real, live artists sitting beside their masterpieces; lively seniors learning to square dance; sidewalk musicians performing bluegrass magic. And, yes, a barnful of quilters with their colorful creations—to die for.

When we finally left the fair, I was not tired but exhilarated, my heart beating musically.

That night I thought of Sharon's words: "We don't do fairs," and I decided that what "we don't do" is just what we need to be doing. Before dozing off, I made a list of new things to try. Just making the list made me feel good about the future.

Lord, give me the energy that comes only from new experiences.
—Daniel Schantz

Digging Deeper: Romans 7:6; Revelation 21:5

Sing to God; sing praises to the Lord; dwell on all his wondrous works!
—Psalm 105:2 (CEB)

Wesley Henderson was a distinguished member of our church. Not only was he a superb singer, working with some of the great studio musicians in New York back in the 1940s and 1950s, but he also was a Tuskegee Airman, part of that cadre of African American pilots and ground crew who fought in World War II.

Toward the end of his long life he was homebound, and on Sunday afternoons I liked to go visit him. The pleasure was always mine, listening to his stories of growing up in New York, hearing about the war. We usually sang together, Wesley from his hospital bed, making harmony on whatever hymn I came up with. The last time I saw him his voice was weak but his musicianship was impeccable as always. What a gift.

When I was away on vacation I'd heard that he'd been in the hospital. He'd come home on hospice care. In midweek I got a call from a church member that he was fading. "I'll come to sing to him this weekend," I said. That was the soonest I could get there. I hung up. *Sing to him now*, the thought came. *Do it on the phone.* I called back and while Wesley's caregiver held the phone up to his ear, I sang "Amazing Grace." Later, as I was heading home, I called again with another song in mind.

"He passed," his caregiver told me. "Just this afternoon." He'd died right after I'd called the first time. I was stunned, sad, wishing I could do something but so glad I *had* sung earlier. There on the sidewalk I sang to myself the last verse of another hymn, "High King of Heaven, thy victory won/May I reach heaven's joys, bright heaven's sun..."

Lord, thank You for my dear friend Wesley and the gift of music we shared.
—Rick Hamlin

Digging Deeper: Ephesians 5:19; Hebrews 2:12

Wednesday, June 13

"Be perfect, therefore, as your heavenly Father is perfect."
—Matthew 5:48 (NRSV)

I'm always thinking up ways to make my students revise. "Revision—reseeing!—is how you improve," I preach. I let them revise any paper for a new grade, but few take me up on it.

This semester, after handing back their first papers, I dragged my whole class to a computer lab to revise during class time for ten more points. They sat dutifully at the computers and set to work. Upon grading the revisions, though, I found my students had made only cosmetic changes—removed the "decorative commas" I'd pointed out, fixed run-ons. No substantial improvement to the argument.

The next time I took them to the lab, one of my best writers asked if she could work on her next assignment instead of revising.

"I don't do extra credit," she told me flatly.

"This isn't extra credit," I said. "I'm *requiring* you to revise."

"Well, I don't revise," she said. "When I get something back, I think, 'Well, that's good' or 'I could've done better.' Either way, it's done. I want to start on the next thing."

I've been thinking about her remark all semester. Is this what all my students think? I started worrying that maybe I'm a sick perfectionist and should adopt my student's healthier attitude: just put it behind me.

Then I remembered God at the creation. There wasn't a mighty "Poof!" Rather, in a patient passage of days, He labored over each part of our amazing universe until He could hold it up and call it good. God's all about revision. He created us in His own perfect image, but when we fail He gives us second chances.

So I slog on, hoping to solve this teaching dilemma, determined someday to succeed!

Creator God, help me to resee, ever to resee, until I am like You.
—Patty Kirk

Digging Deeper: Genesis 1–2; Romans 12:2

Yet you do not know what tomorrow will bring. What is your life?
For you are a mist that appears for a little time and then vanishes.
—James 4:14 (ESV)

Stephanie." My mother's voice sounded strained when I answered the phone. "Tom's dead."

I collapsed onto the living room chair, too shocked to speak. My cousin hadn't been feeling well and left work early. Hours later, he wasn't home. The mobile carrier tracked the location of his cell phone. A police officer found his car still running, parked on the shoulder of the highway. Tom had died in the driver's seat.

I hung up the phone and cried.

Tom had four children. My heart broke for his young widow. I couldn't imagine the pain she was going through.

My tears weren't just for Tom and his family. I thought about my own life. This morning, my husband had gone to work early without waking us. On school days, I often was too hurried to say good-bye, let alone take time to stop and kiss him as I rushed out the door to drive our daughter to school. More often than I cared to admit, I'd left the house in a huff, mad about something that really didn't matter.

When my husband left for work the next morning, I hugged him tighter and kissed him a little longer. There was no way to combat the unpredictability of life, but the best way to honor my cousin was to live each moment like it might be my last.

No one knows what the future holds, Lord. Help me to share
love with others and embrace this life You've given me.
—Stephanie Thompson

Digging Deeper: Psalms 89:47, 90:12; John 10:10

Friday, June 15

You are precious in my sight, and honored, and I love you....
Do not fear, for I am with you.... —Isaiah 43:4–5 (NRSV)

The problem was not that one of the boys was bigger than the others or that he was swinging too high; the problem was that the swing set simply wasn't designed to hold five kids at once.

I have nightmares about these things. I'm one of those parents who imagines the worst. And when my wife or anyone else tells me not to worry or quotes the Bible telling me why I shouldn't worry, I feel like saying, "And how exactly do I do that?"

My son and four of his friends were playing outside, and I wasn't paying close enough attention. They were enjoying themselves, and everyone seemed to be getting along. But then the swing set quite literally tipped over.

Thank God—and I mean, I thank God—the kids were all okay.

You see, despite my worrying, bad things happen. I've learned that despite my worrying, God protects my kids. I have no doubt that God wants me to keep a watchful eye on them, and I have no doubt that God would be pleased if I trusted Him more than I do. But I also know that God cares for me and for them all the time, even though they make mistakes and I lack faith.

> *Thank You, God, for Your watchful eye and*
> *Your guiding hand today. I am so very thankful for both!*
> —Jon Sweeney

Digging Deeper: Colossians 3:15–16

The Lord will perfect that which concerns me; Your mercy, O Lord,
endures forever; Do not forsake the works of Your hands.
—Psalm 138:8 (NKJV)

I'm physically tired this morning, having maintained a regular work-week schedule with an additional challenge: each evening accompanying a neighbor girl to a high-energy Vacation Bible School.

The first night I smiled nostalgically as the youngsters learned an old-timey song: "Do Lord...oh, do remember me, way beyond the blue." Addressing potential confusion, the leader quickly explained that we were singing a prayer meaning "God, please remember me forever."

Throughout the week I noted new renditions of the classic song, and hand motions, like a smooth horizontal ride along a straight road, dropping off into an abyss, which reminded me of the longevity and depth of grace.

In last night's session, my young friend completed a page titled "I Pray For" by writing one word: *Jesus*. Was she thinking of a Bible story and praying for Jesus facing death? Maybe, but in her eyes I saw her more basic request, that Jesus remember her, hold on to her, make her enduringly strong. Today, tomorrow, forever.

The past few days I've turned the song into a baseline prayer: "Dear God, remember..." my neighbor and her family, a dying church friend, a floundering graduate, strangers who have no one to pray for them (a refugee mother, a street urchin, an overwhelmed caretaker), and, yes, even me, looking for strength and mercy as I embrace the challenges of this new day.

> *Dear Jesus, I pray that You will remember me and*
> *the concerns of my heart, as I claim Your steadfast promises.*
> —Evelyn Bence

Digging Deeper: Nehemiah 13:31; Psalm 29:11;
Isaiah 41:10; Luke 23:42–43

Sunday, June 17

The words of the mouth are deep waters.... —Proverbs 18:4 (NIV)

My father had a talent for expressing a lot with few words. He spoke and wrote succinctly, yet conveyed much. Rather than lecturing, he'd share sayings such as these: "Your friends don't need explanations and your enemies won't believe them." "Your first loss is your smallest." "There's nothing good to do after 11:00 p.m., and if there is, you shouldn't be doing it." "What's the first thing you'd do if you won a million dollars? Tell someone!" (He said that when I told him I was engaged.)

Daddy had a sharp and inquisitive mind but was an "I'll do it my way" kind of man. He believed in God but thought Jesus had been only a great person, not more. For years I prayed for Daddy and attempted to persuade him to put his faith in Christ as God's Son Who died for our sins. But Daddy remained stubborn and set in his unbelief.

Then, after decades of my waiting, Daddy's questions about God became more frequent, more pointed, more serious. Instead of dismissing my responses, he listened intently. Finally, on a day I will never forget, he spoke the words I'd been longing to hear: "Jesus Christ is my Lord and Savior."

He didn't discuss it further. Those seven words were all he said. But from that moment on, our family observed a softening, a gentleness in his nature that had never before been evident. He exhibited greater patience, tolerance, and love for others. Just months later, God took him home.

Lord, I'm so grateful I'll see Daddy again!
Thank You for loving us, even in our disbelief.
—Kim Henry

Digging Deeper: Proverbs 2:1–5, 16:23; John 3:16, 6:63–64, 68

CONFIDENCE IN DIFFICULTY: Move toward the Light
"I am the light of the world...." —John 8:12 (NIV)

Anorexia brings with it a torment of negative thoughts, and my daughter's malnourished brain had slid into depression. Elizabeth could see nothing good in her future and grieved the loss of her past. I reminded her that even if she couldn't see the light in herself, I could.

Every Saturday I took the bus from New York City to Boston, where Elizabeth was living in a residential treatment center. I stayed overnight at a friend's house, then on Sunday took Elizabeth to church and out for a cup of coffee. We chatted. She cried. I comforted. I brought her back to the center. I got on a bus for the four-and-a-half-hour trip back to New York City.

My phone rang throughout the weekend. Often it was my daughter Maggie in distress. Sometimes it was the staff at the hospital where Maggie was, which was never good news. I received a barrage of texts from twelve-year-old Stephen, anxious to know when I'd be home. My son John neither texted nor responded to mine, slipping back into his own depression. My husband, Andrew, was struggling as well.

"How do you do it?" a friend asked in wonder. It seemed like a curious question.

"Giving up isn't an option," I replied slowly, "because even if I fear I'm falling down a mine shaft, I have to act as if I'm in a very long tunnel or I'll get stuck in the dark."

Only later did it occur to me that my perspective is faith-based. For as people of faith, no matter what happens in this life, we will always emerge into the light.

> *Lord Jesus, in the midst of deep darkness,*
> *keep me ever-moving toward You.*
> —Julia Attaway

Digging Deeper: Luke 1:79; John 12:46

Tuesday, June 19

A faithful man shall abound with blessings.... —Proverbs 28:20 (KJV)

I was in Australia when I met a tiny, gnarled, cheerful man who had been in "The War." You could hear the opening capital letters on those words when he said them quietly. He was nineteen years old when he fought against the Japanese in New Guinea.

"My girl waited for me all through my two years in the belly of the beast. She never went out with another fella, though the other fellas sure chased after her. She was true blue, that girl.

"We were married ten days after I got home—sixty years and seventy days. The kids and I were with her when she went. We all kissed her, but she and I let our last kiss linger.

"'I'll wait for you,' she whispered. 'I'll be waiting for you.'

"I visit her grave every day just up the hill there. I take the dog and the paper, and we go sit a while with her under the gum trees.

"You're looking at the luckiest man who ever lived. She chose *me*, d'you see? All the lads she could have picked, and she picked me. We had our waxes and wanes, sure, but we never spent a night apart that we didn't have to.

"She was true blue, that girl. Still is. You can't kill that. That sort of thing doesn't die when the body does. All the religions argue about what happens after we die, but I don't worry about all of that. I know she is waiting for me and I will see her again and I know we will be together.

"I love this life, I do, but I won't mind when my time comes. It'll be just like when I was home from the war."

> *Dear Lord, give me the strength and peace and joy*
> *to love steadily and consistently and well and openly*
> *for all the days of my life.*
> —Brian Doyle

Digging Deeper: Romans 8:28; 1 Corinthians 13:1–13

For you have made the Lord, my refuge, even the Most High, your dwelling place. No evil will befall you, Nor will any plague come near your tent.
—Psalm 91:9–10 (NAS)

A couple of years ago there was a bombing in my neighborhood of Chelsea. No one was killed but dozens sustained minor injuries.

At the time I was coming up out of the subway at West 28th Street just a few blocks from the blast and just a minute or two before it went off. Walking west toward my apartment, I heard an explosion and felt the ground tremble. I didn't pay it much mind. There's a lot of construction in my neighborhood. As I turned onto my street I heard the wail of sirens coming up Eighth Avenue. That got my attention.

I flipped on the news when I got inside and learned about the mysterious blast just as my phone was lighting up with queries about my well-being.

That night I lay in bed thinking about close calls. I had almost gotten out of the subway at 23rd Street. The car was crowded and stuffy and I figured I'd just as soon walk a couple of extra blocks on a lovely summer's night, which would have put me exactly at the blast site just as the bomb went off. Instead, someone's bike was blocking my way off the car and I didn't make it before the doors slid closed.

How many other close calls have I had that I was never even aware of? What about the people who aren't so fortunate?

I don't think God picks and chooses who lives and who dies on any given day or how we meet our end. I think He loves us no matter what. He walks with us through life, through the good and the bad, through the painful and the joyous. And through it all I think He protects our souls above all else.

Father, no matter what good or ill befalls me,
no matter how well or badly my day or my life goes, You are there.
—Edward Grinnan

Digging Deeper: Deuteronomy 31:6; 2 Corinthians 4:8–9; Hebrews 13:6

Thursday, June 21

"She, poor as she is, has given everything she has." —Luke 21:4 (TLB)

Anytime I'm tempted to complain about the limitations that come with getting older, I think about a Frenchman named Jean-Dominique Bauby. In 1995, this popular journalist, at forty-three, suffered a stroke that left him totally paralyzed. Lying in a hospital bed, Jean-Dominique made a life-giving discovery: he could move his left eyelid!

Blinking it, he managed to communicate to the nurses that his mind was still awake. Jean-Dominique was the victim of "locked-in syndrome," an alert mind imprisoned in a motionless body. With someone saying the alphabet out loud, he would blink at the letter he wanted written down. A word would form. Then a sentence. Then messages to family and friends.

With one, a publisher friend, he arrived at a remarkable plan: he would write a book about his condition! During the long nights, Jean-Dominique would compose in his head, revising and memorizing a segment of his story, then blink it out the next day, letter by letter. The account was wrenching. "I'd be the happiest man in the world if I could just swallow the saliva swamping my mouth." Worst of all was when he could not speak to his young son and daughter when they climbed onto his bed.

But for all the suffering, the book is a shining testimony to the love of life—however limited—to a journalist's curiosity about everything, to his delight in communicating, contributing, loving. Jean-Dominique had other projects, other books in mind, when two days after *The Diving Bell and the Butterfly* was published, his damaged heart stopped beating.

So you can't do everything you once did, Jean-Dominique says to me. If you can move as much as a single eyelid, you have something to give.

Increase my gratitude, Father, as You increase my years.
—Elizabeth Sherrill

Digging Deeper: 2 Corinthians 8:12; Galatians 6:9–10

"If you, then, though you are evil, know how to give good gifts to your children, how much more will your Father in heaven give good gifts to those who ask him!" —Matthew 7:11 (NIV)

I am almost overcome with giddiness.

School let out recently. My daughters split the summer between their dad and me, and they've been gone for two weeks. As I write this, they will be home within a few hours.

I've made sure everything is ready: fresh linens on their beds, their favorite pajamas clean and folded in their drawers, a homemade pie chilling in the fridge. Best of all, this surprise awaits them: I redecorated their dressers with pretty flower arrangements, lovely little multicolored bottles from the hobby store, and an eclectic mix of knickknacks I picked up at tag sales and on clearance at trendy boutiques.

While I sit and admire my handiwork, I can hardly stand the anticipation. I imagine how thrilled they will be to see all that I've prepared for them. And I realize that few pleasures on this earth compare with the happiness I feel from delighting my children.

Yes, there is a time for discipline. No, we shouldn't give our children everything they want. But sometimes, when I can fulfill a little heart's desire, what a treat it is for me!

Surely this is how our heavenly Father adores us too. Surely He smiles when we experience joy at the good and perfect gifts He gives to us. Surely His heart is made glad when we say, "Oh, Father, thank You! Thank You for loving me and taking care of me. I love You so!"

> *Father, You are kind and generous to Your children.*
> *Thank You for loving me and for blessing me beyond measure.*
> —Ginger Rue

Digging Deeper: Psalms 35:27, 147:11; Luke 12:32

Saturday, June 23

But they that wait upon the Lord shall renew their strength; they shall mount up with wings as eagles; they shall run, and not be weary; and they shall walk, and not faint. —Isaiah 40:31 (KJV)

Rarely have I had opportunities to see eagles. While I attended Auburn University, an eagle sat perched on the sidelines during football games, symbolizing the Auburn spirit. On a trip to Alaska, I saw eagles sitting on tree stumps near Juneau. And once at the Daytona 500, an eagle made a short flight near me during "The Star-Spangled Banner." Although each of these encounters was majestic, none displayed the great power of an eagle's wings.

Imagine my joy to see eagles flying over the lake where we spend most weekends. The most thrilling performance came during a beautiful fall afternoon walk with my wife, Pat, and our dog, Tish. An eagle was circling high above us against the crystal-blue sky. An eaglet, developing its wings, was flying in smaller circles and focusing on its parent. The parent, soaring amazing distances with each flap of its large wings, widened the circle each time around, moving the aerial spectacle along with us for a while. The eaglet, always waiting for its parent to advance, gained confidence and discovered power within its own wings to soar.

I get to observe not only the eagle's powerful wing strength but also a live performance that brought to mind how God guided me out of a decade-long battle with fear and anxiety. They crumbled only as my trust in Him grew...waiting for His guidance and discovering His strength to confront each fear with the power of "wings as eagles."

Dear God, thank You for encounters with magnificent
creatures who share our world and who bring
new understanding to our own interactions with You. Amen.
—John Dilworth

Digging Deeper: Deuteronomy 32:11; 2 Samuel 22:33;
Philippians 4:13

THE BEAUTY OF SIMPLICITY: Just Being Myself

"If you're content to simply be yourself, your life will count for plenty."
—Matthew 23:12 (MSG)

I believed two lies: I didn't think I was good enough; and Christians should always be full of joy.

So a few years ago, in an attempt to prove my worth, I pushed myself to exhaustion. I stopped sleeping, lost my appetite, and my thoughts raced. Full of shame, I never planned to share my secret: I was clinically depressed.

To get better, I discovered that I had to keep life simple. Healing came slowly—through medication, counseling, and prayer. I wrote about my battle with depression for *Guideposts*. Sharing my story felt safe and therapeutic; there were reassuring miles between readers and me.

But before the photo shoot, I discovered that the photographer would also record me talking about my depression in order to post on Guideposts.org, where thousands of people would see it.

Dear Lord, what have I gotten myself into? How can I relate my most humiliating secret? What if I can't speak? How many people will see me?

Michael, the photographer, arrived early, and I met his assistant, Katie. Her dark eyes and hair reminded me of my daughter Katie. After the photo shoot, Michael set up lights for recording. "Julie, pretend I'm not here. Talk to Katie like she's your best friend."

Katie eased herself onto a stool in front of me, and I imagined we were friends having coffee together. I told her the truth. Before long she smiled at me through sparkly tears, and afterward we hugged the way good friends do.

It was simple. All I had to do was to be myself.

> *Lord, when I'm simply myself, with no pretenses, no shame,*
> *and no secrets, You make my life count for plenty.*
> —Julie Garmon

Digging Deeper: Romans 12:1–2; Hebrews 6:18–20

Monday, June 25

I don't mean to say that I have already achieved these things or that I have already reached perfection. But I press on to possess that perfection for which Christ Jesus first possessed me. —Philippians 3:12 (NLT)

Bill! Bill! Bill!" The little company of happy people chanted my name. They were cheering for me to cross a rickety footbridge strung over a deep canyon.

I detest heights. So when my teenage kids asked to go zip-lining, I planned to send them off at the beginning and pick them up at the end.

"No, sir," I was told. "They need an adult with them."

I reluctantly volunteered. They strapped me into the harness, drove us higher than I thought safe, and walked our group to a tiny wire and platform. When it was my turn, I bravely stepped up and zipped. To my surprise, I had fun. "Not too bad," I said. My kids were proud.

After the third zip, we came to the suspension bridge. It seemed designed to provoke panic. I started, stopped, backed up, and let others cross before me. Finally, I was the last one.

Now they all watched me, chanting my name for encouragement. My heart pounded like a rabbit's. I tried three times. Each time I froze up. Eventually, I told them I'd just walk to the next zip line and meet them there.

When we all got together, my son asked, "Dad, were you afraid?"

I thought for a moment and said, "Son, the number-one fear in this country is public speaking. I do that several times every weekend, even though it scares me. So, yes, I have some fears. Some I've conquered; some I haven't. It just means God isn't finished with me yet."

Lord, I haven't reached perfection. But please keep me going in the right direction to experience more and more of Your grace. Amen.
—Bill Giovannetti

Digging Deeper: Hebrews 12:1–2

Thank you for making me so wonderfully complex! It is amazing to think about. Your workmanship is marvelous—and how well I know it.
—Psalm 139:14 (TLB)

I want to sleep up *there*!" I said, pointing to the bunk perched high above the double bed in our hotel room.

"Go right ahead," my friend Cynthia replied. "Knock yourself out."

I don't think she meant it literally. But considering that I'm a card-carrying member of AARP (and have a nighttime bladder the size of a sesame seed), there's a distinct possibility it could happen. After all, shimmying down a child-size ladder in the dark isn't without its challenges.

So why risk it? Because the little kid I once was is still alive and well inside this increasingly wrinkled body—and she loves adventure as well as heights. I'm grateful for her curiosity, chutzpah, and enthusiasm. But I'm also grateful that after all of these years there's more to me than just her.

Maturity has offered gifts of its own, qualities like wisdom, faithfulness, courage, and grace. I've learned how to wholeheartedly celebrate a job well done as much as the chance to sleep in a bunk bed in Bavaria. And I know for certain that loving God and those He's put in my life has turned out to be a greater adventure than anything that red-haired, freckle-faced little girl could have come up with in her wildest dreams.

As I snuggled into my cozy upper bunk that night, I felt so relaxed and at peace. And I don't think it's because I was closer to heaven. I think it's because on that day I felt so comfortable with who I am, so at home with all of the complex little pieces that make up the big picture of me. Gratitude makes a comfortable pillow.

Dearest Father, thank You for all of the ways
You've helped me grow up, grow strong, and grow to love You
and all You have created—including me.
—Vicki Kuyper

Digging Deeper: Proverbs 19:8; Ephesians 2:10

Wednesday, June 27

If any one imagines that he knows something, he does not yet know as he ought to know. —1 Corinthians 8:2 (RSV)

Unsolicited advice: don't skimp on tires, brakes, or paint. Read the reviews. Buy the good stuff.

I know because I've gone cheap on all three. Then—while sliding around corners, squealing to a stop, or adding another coat—my thoughts are always the same: *I should've taken my time. I should've done the right thing.*

Should've is the word I use the most. To paraphrase Frank Sinatra: Regrets, I've had a few—in fact, far too many to mention. Experience is a great teacher. Regret? Not so much.

I recently put a new carburetor in my ancient truck. I made 10.5 million mistakes, including one that nearly cost me the top of my thumb. What should have taken one Saturday took much longer. Finally, I heard the engine catch, then start.

I recounted all of this to my brother. Halfway through my woeful saga, Kevin stopped me. "Give yourself some credit," he said. "I don't know how many people have ever seen a carburetor, let alone worked on one."

This took me aback. In my rush to explain my overweening ignorance, I forgot to be thankful for these small gifts of skill and experience.

"Our deepest fear is not that we are inadequate," says writer Marianne Williamson. "Our deepest fear is that we are powerful beyond measure.... We ask ourselves, 'Who am I to be brilliant, gorgeous, talented, and fabulous?' Actually, who are you not to be? You are a child of God. Your playing small does not serve the world."

She's right. And Kevin is too. I am a child of God, no matter how long it takes me to change a carburetor.

Lord, despite my multitude of shortcomings, allow me to remember that I am made in Your image, capable of things both great and small.
—Mark Collins

Digging Deeper: Matthew 7:1; 1 Corinthians 13:11–12

Offer yourselves to God.... —Romans 6:13 (NIV)

I stood in front of the bathroom mirror braiding my long hair. Quickly I listed my morning prayer needs from friends and finished by asking God to show me what He wanted me to do. I sighed as I thought about my whirlwind day coming up. Even though I was busy doing things for Him, I felt like I never did quite enough. After spritzing my bangs with a new brand of hairspray, I took one last glance in the mirror, then raced out the door to feed the horses before I headed to work.

SkySong met me at the gate with his usual nicker. I slipped open the latch. As I walked through, I noticed his nostrils quiver. His brows puckered, and he stuck his face in mine. "SkySong, what are you doing?" I brushed him aside.

When I came out of the barn with an armload of hay, he moved his head into my forehead, nearly bonking me. I growled. "Move!" He stepped back and blinked. A few strands of hay slipped to the ground. SkySong towered over me. It was as if he was asking for something.

I looked up at him quizzically as I stood still.

Gently with his lips, SkySong ruffled my bangs. His nostrils flared as he smelled my hair. I giggled. "Oh, you like my new hairspray." I turned to walk away, but once again he arched his neck over my head, then he rested his lips on my hair. He was asking me to stand still while he enjoyed smelling my hair and just being with me.

> *Lord, thank You for quiet—and funny!—moments,*
> *even during the busiest days.*
> —Rebecca Ondov

Digging Deeper: Psalm 35:9; Isaiah 58:14

Friday, June 29

Seventy years are given us! And some may even live to eighty....
—Psalm 90:10 (TLB)

How did you like the book?" Marcia, our librarian, asked when I returned a mystery.

"I enjoyed it," I told her, "but I wouldn't recommend it for your senior readers. It's a bit too violent."

Marcia got the funniest look on her face. It took me a second to figure out why: "Oh, I'm one of those seniors," I said, and we both laughed.

In fact, my next stop was the senior center for the monthly catered dinner. While we waited in line, my friend Sharon remarked that she sometimes wasted food since she only cooked for herself and her husband. "I've been thinking about getting containers and dishing up half of what I make to take to senior citizens," she said.

"Sharon, we *are* senior citizens!" I answered.

"So you think I ought to bring my extra food to you?" she shot back.

It's true that we are older, with the aches, declining strength, and occasional memory lapses that come with age. But deep within ourselves we are pretty much the same people we were decades ago, and many are still doing productive work.

There is one difference though. Years of living have taught us to be a little kinder, a bit quicker to forgive, and a lot more thankful to the gracious God Who continues to uphold us.

All the way my Savior leads me—what have I to ask beside?
Can I doubt His tender mercy, Who through life has been my Guide?
Heavenly peace, divinest comfort, Here by faith in Him to dwell!
For I know whate'er befall me, Jesus doeth all things well (Fanny J. Crosby).
—Penney Schwab

Digging Deeper: Deuteronomy 34:7; Psalm 92:14

Make me know Your ways, O Lord; Teach me Your paths.
—Psalm 25:4 (NAS)

There is an ancient Asian saying: *"When the student is ready, the teacher appears."* I have found this to be true in my life.

I remember decades ago when Beth and I were newlyweds. We had just moved to Louisville, Kentucky, where I was attending seminary. Neither of us had found a job. It was winter, and we were down to our last twenty-dollar bill when we took our first trip to the grocery store. As we placed food in our cart, I neglected to keep a running account of the prices. Then the moment came when the attendant rang up our groceries. I slipped into a quiet panic attack: *What if we don't have enough money? What am I going to say?*

Suddenly, "the student is ready and the teacher appears." I was learning hard lessons about economics and responsibility. Much to my relief, the teacher of the moment was gentle and returned to us twenty-six cents, which did not buy much gas on the way home!

This morning I wrote to a recent Mercer University graduate who just arrived in Thailand to teach English for a year through a program that I direct called Service First. He is experiencing culture shock and dislocation from home and college. Anxious and homesick, he wonders if he has made the right decision. He's reached the "teachable moment." He can choose to come home. Or he can allow Thailand to teach him valuable lessons about life and our global culture. I am confident that he will stay and learn much about himself.

> *Father, You are my Teacher.*
> *I am ready to follow You. Amen.*
> —Scott Walker

Digging Deeper: Matthew 14:22–33; Mark 6:33–44

GOD'S UNFAILING LOVE

1 _____

2 _____

3 _____

4 _____

5 _____

6 _____

7 _____

8 _____

9 _____

10 _____

11 _____

12 _____

13 _____

14 _____

15 _____

16 _____

17 _____

18 _____

19 _____

20 _____

21 _____

22 _____

23 _____

24 _____

25 _____

26 _____

27 _____

28 _____

29 _____

30 _____

JULY

*Behold what manner of love the Father
has bestowed on us, that we should be
called children of God! . . .*

—1 John 3:1 (NKJV)

Now faith is confidence in what we hope for and assurance about what we do not see. —Hebrews 11:1 (NIV)

After learning to make fondant from marshmallows and powdered sugar, my cake designs for special occasions became more elaborate. Soon I began to receive requests for my cakes from friends and family.

"I want a monster truck," one friend announced. This would be a paid commission, so it had to be perfect.

I had no idea how I would pull this off, yet I had complete confidence in myself to figure it out as I went along.

My unshakable confidence was a far cry from all I'd been panicking about in the other areas of my life. I had just quit my job in order to write and live as a freelance artist. Money wasn't coming in as steadily as I'd imagined.

With no plan for this truck, I worked one detail at a time, molding pieces of Rice Krispies treats, wrapping them in fondant, and fitting them together with skewers.

Little by little, my monster-truck cake was coming to life as I finished the sculpture and decorated the cake where it would sit. I loved it!

Karen, I thought to myself, looking at the finished product on my kitchen table, *you need to stop panicking about the future.* No, I didn't have a concrete plan or any guarantees for success, but I did know that I would figure it out as I went along and I could trust in the call God had on my life to be the mother and artist He made me to be.

> *Thank You, Lord, for leading me with each step.*
> *Help me to trust You along the way.*
> —Karen Valentin

> *Digging Deeper:* Matthew 6:25–34

Monday, July 2

Love suffers long… bears all things… endures all things.
—1 Corinthians 13:4, 7 (NKJV)

Here's a weird love story. My wife and I came horrifyingly close to losing our marriage. It was a dark, sad, confused, frightening time. We had children together; a shaggy, comfortable old house; a warm, hilarious past; big, friendly, generous families; a glorious tribe of mutual friends. For years we had walked together hand in hand through every sort of pain and joy, and I, for one, thought we would honor and love each other until the day we died.

But then dark times came, and we slid apart. I was angry, terrified, furious, lost, bitter. I felt myself growing colder daily. Do you know what I mean? I remember sitting by a river, my head in my hands, trying to resign myself to what was going to happen, trying to keep the children as priorities, trying not to think of divided assets and visiting rights and a lonely apartment.

And I remember the oddest epiphany, as the river burled and thrummed past me. Even if I never saw my wife again, even if we communicated only icily, businesslike, about the kids for the rest of our lives, I would always want to know that she was okay, that she was happy, that she had joy and peace in her life, that she was making the most of her extraordinary gifts as an artist, a mother, a teacher.

I would always hope that someone loved her for who she is, as complicated and alluring a human being as ever was. I suppose I realized that I would always love her, and deeply too—that my love wouldn't fail, even if our marriage did. Isn't that odd? But it's true.

Dear Lord, give me the eyes to see the hymn of her
every minute of every day. Please?
—Brian Doyle

Digging Deeper: Proverbs 18:22; Colossians 3:19

And God is able to provide you with every blessing in abundance, so that by always having enough of everything, you may share abundantly in every good work. —2 Corinthians 9:8 (NRSV)

In New York City, one of my favorite things to do in the summer is to go to Jamba Juice in Whole Foods at Columbus Circle and then for a walk through Central Park. I geared myself up to do just that on one particularly hot day off. As I stood in line with a number of others (because in this city there's always a line for everything), one of the employees put up a sign that said, "Out of Kale." Sighs and groans rippled through the line. I placed my order and waited for my smoothie. A few minutes later, the employee returned and removed the sign. He scribbled at the bottom of it and hung it back up. It now read, "Out of Kale and Carrots." There was more murmuring in the line, but I was unfazed by this news, as my order necessitated neither.

It wasn't until later during my walk that I realized how odd this was. The Jamba Juice I went to, housed inside of a Whole Foods supermarket, was quite literally right next to fresh produce. Kale and carrots galore! Yet they could not, probably because of supplier regulations, access the bounty surrounding them.

I found myself pondering if I was acknowledging the bounty surrounding me! Sometimes what we need is right there all along.

To the Creator of the universe, I trust that You will provide all I need. Help me to remember to open my eyes, to see Your gifts, and to use them to Your will and purpose.
—Natalie Perkins

Digging Deeper: 2 Corinthians 9:6–15

Wednesday, July 4

Make a joyful noise unto the Lord…make a loud noise, and rejoice….
—Psalm 98:4 (KJV)

I can hardly wait for Independence Day to be over. I have to get up at 4:00 a.m., so I am in bed by 8:00 p.m. But tonight neighborhood fireworks are raging, and I can't sleep.

I think I'll get up and call my daughter Teresa. This is her favorite holiday, and the only one she decorates for, with red-white-and-blue dinnerware, American flags, and a patriotic quilt her mother made her. She loves the outdoor celebrations and the simple foods, like burgers and chips, ice cream and watermelon. Above all, she loves her country.

"Tell me again, Tee, why you like this holiday so much?"

"Well, Dad, it's about freedom, you know? America is just a beautiful, wonderful gift. When I hear 'The Star-Spangled Banner,' I can hardly believe that God provided a free nation like this one. I mean, there's nothing like it anywhere else on earth. It may be tarnished, but it still has something good going on."

"Okay, but why does it have to be so noisy?"

"Dad, get with it! Buy some fireworks, make some noise, show some enthusiasm!"

"How about if I set them off at five a.m., my good time of day."

"Well, I hope your neighbors have a sense of humor."

"But you said this is a free country."

"It's also a civilized country, Dad. Go back to bed. You're hopeless."

On my way back to bed, I stop and peek out the front door. I can see "the rocket's red glare, the bombs bursting in air," and my neighbor's flag waving proudly, and I get a little lump in my throat.

*Thank You, God, for these noisy, irritating, but free
United States of America.*
—Daniel Schantz

Digging Deeper: 1 Corinthians 8:9; 1 Peter 2:13–17

FALLING INTO GRACE: A Welcoming Faith Community

He [Jesus] said, "Those who are well have no need of a physician, but those who are sick." —Matthew 9:12 (NRSV)

My arm nestled in its ever-present sling, I looked at the small group gathered for the evening service and realized something. We all had something wrong with us! Mary Ellen had punctured a lung. Carole was confronting cancer. Ken had chronic back pain. And Audrey, our oldest and wisest, had fallen like me.

To make matters worse, our beloved pastor, Michel, was retiring. My husband, Charlie, and I had chosen this church because of its pastor, and it would be hard to continue without him. Prior to my accident, we had discussed whether to stay at the church after he left because we were not particularly close to other parishioners and it would be hard to continue without Michel.

God had another plan, though, and He revealed it that Sunday. After the service, we all started talking. I had been in awe of Audrey, who was also legally blind, but when her daughter Ellen told her I'd been hurt, Audrey turned to me and shared her experience and slow recovery. I told her, "I'm sure you didn't throw tantrums and sob like a helpless child." Audrey laughed and nodded toward Ellen, who said, "Believe me, there have been tears."

Our conversation about pain and fear became a discussion about our church's future and choosing a new pastor. Charlie was nominated as the spokesperson for our group. People in our church had been as shy and uncertain of Charlie and me as we had been of them.

Had I not been broken, I'm not sure I would have been able to see what God was showing me: that this church was home.

> *Lord, open my spiritual eyes so that*
> *I can focus not on my plan but on Yours.*
> —Marci Alborghetti

Digging Deeper: Psalm 40:4–8

Friday, July 6

No one serving as a soldier gets entangled in civilian affairs, but rather tries to please his commanding officer. —2 Timothy 2:4 (NIV)

My husband, Gene, and I were in the fourth row of Hodgen Hall at the University of Georgia awaiting the start of the 1940s musical *In the Mood* with the String of Pearls Orchestra.

They traveled the United States and were now in Athens, Georgia. I'd be hearing the music I'd loved as a youngster. My mother had 78 rpm records, and I was allowed to play them if I was careful. I'd danced alone in our living room to songs like "Swinging on a Star," "Chattanooga Choo Choo," and "Begin the Beguine."

Glancing down at the program, I saw that act 2 included music from wartime: patriotic songs with sweetly familiar words: "When the Lights Go On Again," "The White Cliffs of Dover," and "Over There."

Just as the program was beginning, a man sat down directly in front of me—an unbelievably tall man. I leaned to the right and to the left to see around him. After a while, my neck ached and my resentment rose. I imagined whispering, "Could you slouch down, please?" Instead, I silently clung to my miffed emotions.

Toward the end, as the patriotic music filled the auditorium, each branch of military service seated in the audience was asked to stand. Thunderous applause followed.

When the orchestra played "Anchors Aweigh," the gentleman in front of me stood. Slowly. So tall. No longer young. Even from the back I sensed unmistakable courage, willing sacrifice.

And I blinked fast to keep tears of gratitude from sliding down my face.

God bless America, land that I love . . . and each veteran.
—Marion Bond West

Digging Deeper: Psalm 33:12; Isaiah 42:13

And people should eat and drink and enjoy the fruits of their labor, for these are gifts from God. —Ecclesiastes 3:13 (NLT)

"Eight sleepovers—that's my goal," announced Micah, after I'd shared my summer expectations of getting ourselves and our home in shape. I planned to clean closets, donate clothing, paint the spare room, organize the garage, and weed our flower beds. I also wanted my twelve-year-old daughter to exercise with me and keep her bedroom tidy. The way I saw it, we had ten weeks to improve ourselves and our living quarters. But as usual, Micah just wanted to "hang out."

At the beginning of the summer, my husband rented a carpet shampooer. The next day I mopped floors, cleaned shower stalls, and scrubbed bathrooms. It took me hours to weed the flower beds and put down fresh mulch. Micah joined me by riding her bike when I walked the dogs around the neighborhood.

Then sand volleyball practice started. Getting up early was a chore. Micah wanted to quit.

It seemed like I had to offer incentives to get Micah to do anything that was difficult or not fun.

One morning while organizing the garage, clutter overwhelmed me. It was humid and, to be honest, I just didn't want to do it. I opened the door to the house and lay on the cool tile floor. Summer was almost half over, and all I'd done was work. Maybe Micah had the right idea.

She was surprised to find me sprawled on the floor.

"Wanna hang out?" I asked sheepishly.

We played table tennis, watched movies, goofed off. That weekend we tackled the garage as a family, which actually made the chore fun.

> *Father, help me to remember that You created us*
> *for both work and play.*
> —Stephanie Thompson

Digging Deeper: Ecclesiastes 2:24–25; Matthew 11:28; Mark 6:31

Sunday, July 8

You are the body of Christ and parts of each other.
—1 Corinthians 12:27 (CEB)

Francis, Edgar, Margaret. Even though they're in their nineties, I still think of them as pillars of our church. They held it up when times were tough, when there were few members, when doors were locked and wire mesh covered the stained-glass windows.

They were there to welcome us when we were just kids, willing to take a risk on an old church in an edgy neighborhood. They showed up at our choir concerts and passed around baked goods at coffee hour, and when we launched a soup kitchen, they were ladling out the soup. They prayed for us and encouraged us to serve on committees as they had, but one thing they never said to any of our new ideas was "But we've always done it *this* way."

We missed not having extended family close by, especially when we brought our newborns to church, but Francis, Edgar, and Margaret jumped in as surrogate grandparents, putting on baby showers, remembering birthdays, cheering the younger ones in Christmas pageants and Sunday school skits. They ministered to us when the children grew up, reassuring us that the boys always had a church home.

We somehow became pillars, too, never knowing how it happened. They were our models, living out a life in Christ in big ways and little ways, and as we celebrate their megabirthdays, we remember what it is to be welcoming and how never to say, "But we always did it *this* way." It is God's way that the church keeps rebuilding itself and that pillars get renewed. God never changes, even when everything else feels brand-new.

Let me know, God, how I might serve You best this day.
—Rick Hamlin

Digging Deeper: Romans 12:12; Galatians 3:27

Let the heavens rejoice, let the earth be glad; let the sea resound,
and all that is in it. Let the fields be jubilant, and everything in them;
let all the trees of the forest sing for joy. —Psalm 96:11–12 (NIV)

It had been a day. You know the kind: Spouse out of town, kids wound up from school, dinner taking extralong to get on the table, and bedtime strung out with a few added requests for milk, water, books, and snuggles. The days with two little ones can be so long; I wouldn't trade it for the world, but I do value the few minutes of peace I get when everyone is safely tucked in.

Shutting their doors for (really) the last time, I made my way down the stairs feeling completely discouraged. Olivia's final, unprompted "I love you, Ma" after my terse denial to keep her milk cup in her bed had pretty much broken me.

Suddenly, I heard a huge gush of water. A thunderstorm unloaded gallons of rain on our neighborhood. I rushed to the window, in awe of this midsummer deluge, and that's when I saw it: the most beautiful sunset looming low in my kitchen window.

I have no doubt that God sent me that sunset to remind me that His mercies, like my patience, will be renewed in the morning.

Perhaps foolishly, I marched back upstairs, sneaked into the kids' rooms, and covered their dozing faces with kisses.

Now, when I see a beautiful sunset at that window, I'm reminded that God knows my heart and hears my prayers, even when I forget to say them out loud!

> *God, help me to remember that these precious children are Yours,*
> *only on loan to me for a little while, and that sleep*
> *always, eventually, comes.*
> —Ashley Kappel

Digging Deeper: Genesis 9:16; Psalm 19:1; Lamentations 3:22–23

Tuesday, July 10

The godly care for their animals, but the wicked are always cruel.
—Proverbs 12:10 (NLT)

My mother could never bear to hurt another living creature, even spiders. She'd scoop them up with a newspaper and set them outside over my father's protests. He favored using the newspaper to dispatch them by another method, but Mom insisted that God cherished all His creatures.

My first pet was a box turtle I found one summer meandering through our yard. Mom said I could keep him until school started. I christened him George and installed him in a basement window well where I would bring him water and food every day. He had beautiful geometric markings on his shell in brown and gold.

Then disaster struck. A neighbor's dog somehow got hold of George. I rescued him but not before his markings had been chewed off. All he had left was a plain yellow shell. I was sure he was going to die and prayed desperately for God to intervene.

As it happened, my uncle Eddie, a research biochemist, was visiting. He rushed George inside and gently washed his shell. "The dog's teeth scraped off George's keratin," he explained. "That's a little like our skin." Uncle Eddie then applied Bactine to George's poor shell. George protested by waving his legs. "It probably stings a little but it will prevent infection. He should be fine."

I put George back in his window well with fresh water and a piece of iceberg lettuce, which he crunched hungrily. And that night I added a covering over the well. When I released him into the woods a few weeks later, his markings had already started to grow back.

Father, Your love extends to all creatures great and small
and You have given us dominion over them. Loving the creatures
of this earth is another way for us to honor and love You.
—Edward Grinnan

Digging Deeper: Genesis 1:26; Psalm 50:10–11; Matthew 10:28–30

God has united you with Christ Jesus. For our benefit God made him to be wisdom itself. Christ made us right with God; he made us pure and holy, and he freed us from sin. —1 Corinthians 1:30 (NLT)

On a family vacation, I lost my credit card halfway through the trip. I tore apart the rental car to find it. No luck. Labels from my childhood immediately raised their ugly little heads: *Stupid, Dummy.*

Five days later, I lost my driver's license after making it through airport security, something I discovered only after boarding an aircraft and flying home. Where could it be? Did I leave it on the plane? At the airport? The old labels practically screamed: *Stupid! Dummy!*

I know I'm not, and on a deeper level I know that Jesus Christ became for me the wisdom from God (1 Corinthians 1:30). God says I share Christ's wisdom; He says I "have the mind of Christ" (1 Corinthians 2:16). The ugly labels don't apply, yet there they were, sticking to me like a gooey mess.

My wife, Margi, encouraged me. "You just have a lot on your plate. Don't worry about it." She was right. I knew those names from my past didn't apply. I am who God says I am, and He says I'm perfect in His sight. I just had to see myself that way.

I smiled, leaned over in the rental car, and gave her a kiss. "Thanks for the reminder."

*Heavenly Father, help me to see myself as You see me—
through Christ. Amen.*
—Bill Giovannetti

Digging Deeper: Ephesians 2:4–7

Thursday, July 12

For everything God created is good, and nothing is to be rejected if it is received with thanksgiving.... —1 Timothy 4:4 (NIV)

"Please, Logan, we don't need to save it," I plead with my seven-year-old grandson, who holds a flattened pinecone.

"But I want to keep it," he whines.

I give in because Logan is a collector. Our back porch is loaded with evidence to prove it.

On a recent trip to the beach, he returned with a bucket of seashells and sand dollars, many broken; a huge horseshoe crab shell (which is pretty cool, I must say); some seaweed; and something that looks like a bone.

He also has a bug collection, one I avoid and delegate to my husband, Chuck, to admire. Of course, some of those bugs were alive when he caught them, but they didn't do well as pets.

To Logan, these things are treasures; I bite my tongue to refrain from calling them "junk." They're important to him, and I appreciate his childhood fascination.

What I really value is that these treasures are all part of the natural world. He is captivated by the beauty and uniqueness in things I've long ignored. What's more, I've begun to notice things I had never seen: the design of a shell, the colors of a lizard, the spiky uniformity of a sweet gum tree ball—features I see as evidence of a creative God.

Having raised three sons already, I know how fleeting these little-boy years are. Logan will eventually lose interest in his collections, and I'll have a clean porch. But until then, I'm learning to cherish his treasures.

Thank You, God, for a child's perspective to open my eyes to the intricate details of Your creation. May I never take these wonders for granted.
—Marilyn Turk

Digging Deeper: Colossians 1:16; Revelation 4:8–12

A friend loves at all times. . . . —Proverbs 17:17 (NIV)

K nee-high weeds suffocated the carrot patch. The larger, quicker-growing vegetable plants like cucumbers and beans had been easier to protect with mulch. However, carrots with their wispy foliage disappeared under rampant weeds. Seven months' pregnant, I could no longer bend over to yank them. Even if I could, my toddler and infant demanded all my energy not already sapped by the ninety-degree heat. This year's carrots were a dead loss.

When my friend Sonya dropped by one sweltering afternoon, I was too wiped out to be embarrassed by my weed patch. Sonya's garden, by contrast, deserved a color spread in a glossy magazine.

"Looks like you could use some help," she murmured.

"Oh, Sonya, you do *not* have to pull my weeds. Just let them go."

So many times Sonya had come to my rescue. When we adopted our first child, she mentored me on feeding, fevers, and "normal." When I had the flu, she sent over dinner and collected my children for a play-date. She taught me how to hang wallpaper and stitch buttonholes by machine. Now these detestable weeds had brought her again to my aid.

"I'll be here early tomorrow morning, when it's cool. I know what it's like to be pregnant with a garden!"

At six thirty the next morning, I found Sonya smiling and tearing out my weeds. The more the trash sacks bulged with weeds, the more feathery carrot tops emerged in neat rows. Thus revived, my carrots continued to grow far into October and fed us until February. They tasted doubly sweet that season: thanks to good earth and a true friend who did a very dirty job out of love.

> *Lord, I find Your love everywhere—even in a weed patch.*
> —Gail Thorell Schilling

Digging Deeper: Job 6:14; Matthew 7:12

Saturday, July 14

A threefold cord is not quickly broken. —Ecclesiastes 4:12 (KJV)

Finally my son, Harrison, was old enough to join my father and me on our annual fly-fishing trip to Colorado. It was a decades-old tradition, which included our good friend Bob and his son, Brad.

Each year, we flew into Denver, then drove to Kremmling, where we stayed at a quaint cabin located near our favorite spot on the river. Staying at the cabin, called "Grandma's House," was half the fun of the adventure. There were always fresh cinnamon rolls baked when we arrived, the grill was clean, and there was a little pond next to the lodge where we could fish after dinner.

Over and over I had told Harrison about this place, and I couldn't wait to take him there. I was filled with anticipation as I called to book the trip with our friend Dean who ran the guide service.

"I'm sorry, Brock, Grandma's is booked," Dean said, suggesting a nearby hotel.

To say I was disappointed is an understatement. I said a prayer, inviting God into the mix, and booked the rooms in the hotel.

Soon we were on our way to Denver, excited for the fishing but still bummed over missing out on Grandma's.

Once we arrived, we went fishing, and that evening we huddled together, regaling the fish both caught and missed. I could tell Harrison enjoyed belonging, at last, to the community one finds on a fishing trip.

As I studied the faces of my buddies, laughing and sharing stories, it was no different than our many stays at Grandma's House. It turned out that it wasn't about where we stayed, but about being together and sharing life, as we welcomed Harrison into our grand tradition.

> *Father, the bonds of community are beyond measure,*
> *especially when You are there.*
> —Brock Kidd

Digging Deeper: Proverbs 27:17; Ecclesiastes 4:9

In his hand are the depths of the earth; the heights of the mountains are his also. The sea is his, for he made it, and the dry land, which his hands have formed. —Psalm 95:4–5 (NRSV)

We have waited all year for this—our West Coast trip, with visits to Kate's and my families, and leading a family camp.

We set aside a few days just for us in our favorite place, the Sierra Nevada Mountains. This year we're staying in Mammoth Lakes, a ski town on the steeper, more rugged eastern side of the range. Even in summer the topmost peaks are clad in snow. The air is clear and cool and smells of pine and sage.

Right now we're wending our way over the Sonora Pass, a narrow cleft in the range with a ribbon of highway. We're less than a mile from the pass when suddenly the kids point out a stunningly beautiful meadow, bisected by a tumbling creek and backed by a steep slope. "Can we get out here?" they cry.

Kate and I shrug. *Why not?* We pull over into a turnout, pile out of the car, and trudge across the meadow to the creek.

We find a way across the water and climb part of the slope. The kids bend down to examine sage stems, taking in their smell. We are inside God's handiwork.

We pile back into the car, elated and ready to finish the drive. We'd love to stay, but we know we are only visitors here. God is at work in us, too, taking us toward destinations we know and have yet to discover.

> *Today, Lord, I will revel in the mystery of Your creation.*
> —Jim Hinch

Digging Deeper: Job 12:7–10; Psalm 19:1; Romans 1:20

Monday, July 16

RELYING ON GOD'S UNFAILING LOVE
Joy and Peace Will Guard Our Hearts

For he will hide me in his shelter in the day of trouble; he will conceal me under the cover of his tent; he will lift me high upon a rock.
—Psalm 27:5 (ESV)

Sarah handed me a pair of scissors right as I walked in the front door. "Take a big piece off from wherever you want."

She turned around and showed me other places on her head where huge chunks of hair were missing.

I took a deep breath and closed my eyes. Sarah's smiling face urged me forward. I snipped a large chunk off the top, staring as tufts of brown hair floated to the floor and landed in a pile around her green flip-flops.

I blinked back tears and looked into her eyes, expecting to see anguish. Instead, I saw peace. Pure, God-given peace that seemed to hover in the air, making what would otherwise be a terrible evening one of laughter, of joy even.

She took the scissors out of my hand and gave them to my ten-year-old, who wavered between relishing the idea of being allowed to hack off a chunk of an adult's hair and fear that there would be repercussions. But there weren't. And his wide eyes turned to laughing eyes as he sheared off what was left of Sarah's bangs.

And so the night progressed, one snip after another, until Sarah's hair was a mottled mess of missing chunks and frazzled tufts. And then came the grand finale: her husband shaved her head.

We all watched and cheered. Sarah laughed. And the torment of what could have been terrible—chemo stealing away my beautiful friend's hair—was replaced by a peace that transcended understanding.

Lord, be our peace and joy in otherwise desperate situations. Amen.
—Erin MacPherson

Digging Deeper: Isaiah 41:10; 1 Peter 5:7

The wolf also shall dwell with the lamb, and the leopard shall lie down with the kid; and the calf and the young lion and the fatling together; and a little child shall lead them. —Isaiah 11:6 (KJV)

My friend Mary leads Bible Witness Camp for girls each summer, and there's always something new to learn.

"Do any of you hold grudges?" she asks the girls.

As a leader, I'm tempted to answer, but remain silent.

Several of the campers raise their hands. Mary chooses one of the campers and places a basketball in a girl's open palms. It's comical to watch as she balances the balls with her outstretched arms. "My arms are getting tired," the girl whines.

"But you have to hold on to the balls. Those are your grudges."

Then Mary picks up a bag of candies. The other girls sigh with delight. "Hold out your hands," Mary says and pours candies into their outstretched hands. "These are the blessings of the Lord." The blessings are beautiful to behold—showers of red, blue, yellow, green, and orange.

It is a lesson for the girls, but I look into my own heart. *What grudges am I holding on to?* The ones that come to mind first are childhood memories to protect me from those who hurt me, abused me.

Mary lifts the two balls from the camper's hands and replaces them with candy. I'm not a girl anymore. I'm safe, and I don't need grudges to protect me. I forgive and then feel a weight lift from my shoulders. My hands are open now, ready to receive blessings.

Lord, show us the weights that we carry, grudges that are invisible to us.
Give us the courage to forgive, then shower
Your beautiful blessings on us!
—Sharon Foster

Digging Deeper: Ezekiel 34:26–27; Matthew 6:14–15; Luke 18:17

Wednesday, July 18

Test me, Lord, and try me, examine my heart and my mind....
—Psalm 26:2 (NIV)

Gabriel and I sat under the shade of our old maple. I read, and my ten-year-old Cub Scout whittled.

"What are you making?" I asked.

He held up a stick that had a thick bottom and an upper part that split to a V.

"I don't know," he said. "Maybe a slingshot. Or a rabbit. The top could be ears."

His dimpled grin warmed me. He tipped his blond head and went back to whittling. His wrists flicked, and bits of bark flecked off and fell into the long, cool grass. I let my book rest on my lap and watched, and as I did I thought of the Psalm I had read earlier in the day: "Search me, O God, and know my heart; test me and know my anxious thoughts. Point out anything in me that offends you, and lead me along the path of everlasting life" (Psalm 139:23–24, NLT).

I adore the relationship between David and God. Because David is secure, standing in the safety of their love, he offers a bold prayer. His desire to be upright before the Lord is as powerful as his need for breath. He knows that God is just, and he also knows God's love. This must be the kind of prayer that the Lord delights in—an invitation to shape the human spirit with holy hands.

"Look at this, Mom!" Gabriel said, holding up a stripped stick. "I'm going with the rabbit. It's not finished, but it's a start."

I could see it! Undeniable beauty is revealed through the process of paring.

Search me, Lord. Remove what isn't pleasing and lead me. Amen.
—Shawnelle Eliasen

Digging Deeper: Job 13:23; 1 Corinthians 11:28

There are companions to keep one company, and there is a friend more devoted than a brother. —Proverbs 18:24 (JPS)

I had purchased an Alex Beattie needlepoint canvas of *The First Day of Creation,* starting it before my husband, Keith, became ill and picking it up again after I began to recover from his death. The beauty of the design helped to heal me, so as soon as I found out that this canvas was the first in a series covering six days of creation, I phoned to purchase the next five. Somehow the idea of re-creating all that splendor gave me a sense of peace.

The person taking my order told me that day six was sold out, and the artist didn't think he would return to the series. I bought days two, three, four, and five and asked to be put on a list so that if Beattie ever rereleased day six again, I could get it.

The canvases exceeded my expectations. As soon as I finished the first, I began work on the second, which surprised me by being even more beautiful, as if I had never realized that creation became lovelier as it went on. I was sad I would have to stop once I finished the fifth canvas, that I would never finish the series.

I mentioned it to my friend Dawn, who thought about it for a short time and then said, "It's appropriate, really."

"Why?" I asked.

She smiled. "Because creation is really never finished."

Thank You, God of Creation, for including friends
among Your gifts to us.
—Rhoda Blecker

Digging Deeper: Job 42:10

Friday, July 20

We also glory in tribulations, knowing that tribulation
produces perseverance.... —Romans 5:3 (NKJV)

"Adversity does not build character; it reveals it," American novelist James Lane Allen is credited with saying.

I wondered if that was true. Didn't adversity make us stretch beyond ourselves, so we would get to a better place?

My body strained. Muscles complained. Four weeks after disk-replacement surgery in my spine, I was okayed by the doctor to start exercising again. After several months of forced inactivity due to injuries, stretching was my number one priority for getting my mobility back. "Reach a little farther than you're comfortable with and then hold it for thirty seconds," the physical therapist instructed. "It's as simple as that."

My muscles trembled as I held on. Finally, time was up. I got up and walked around. Immediately, I felt freer. The stiffness that had locked up my movement had been reduced.

Maybe that's why God is always right there, just out of our reach. It's so we have to stretch beyond ourselves toward Him.

It's not only good for my muscle tone, but it's good for my spirit too.

Lord, please help me stay the course and remember I am gaining
strength in difficult times. Help me grow
as I stretch out to You.
—Erika Bentsen

Digging Deeper: 1 Chronicles 29:12; Romans 8:18–21;
2 Corinthians 12:9–10

"I was hungry and you gave me food...." —Matthew 25:35 (RSV)

Fred was assistant manager of our local bank in the New York suburbs and for years spent every Saturday volunteering at a soup kitchen in Manhattan. The time my husband and I went with him, there were two women and perhaps thirty men already waiting at 9:15 a.m. for the noon meal. By lunchtime there must have been two hundred people there. The "clients," as Fred called them, said little as they bolted for their food. The only comments I overheard, in fact, were gripes. The stew didn't have enough carrots. It had too many carrots. Yesterday's rolls had raisins.

"Why do you do it?" we asked Fred as we helped with the cleanup. Certainly it wasn't for the thanks!

"Do you really want to know?" Fred unbuttoned his left sleeve and pushed it up. A tattoo on a banker's arm?

"Albrecht Dürer's *Praying Hands!*" my husband said.

"Dürer's drawing," Fred agreed. "But to me, those are my grandmother's hands." He'd seen her hands pressed together just that way a thousand times.

His grandmother, he said, had suffered real hunger, growing up in Lithuania. Years later, in this country, when her husband was killed in a coal mine fire, she'd turned every square foot of their small yard in Wyoming into a vegetable garden from which she fed their five children and later three more "coal orphans." Fred's whole family lived with her during the Great Depression. "She fed all of us and half the neighborhood."

"Before she died she told me, 'Freddy, never, ever turn your back on a hungry person.'"

Fred smiled as he buttoned his sleeve. "If I'm ever tempted to skip a Saturday here at the soup kitchen, don't you know those hands yank me right back!"

Father, teach me to pray.
—Elizabeth Sherrill

Digging Deeper: Matthew 9:13; James 1:27

Sunday, July 22

THE BEAUTY OF SIMPLICITY: Letting God Be God

"I am the Lord; there is no other God...." —Isaiah 45:5 (NLT)

Twenty years ago, I told a close friend about some family members who had DUIs, court dates, and jail time. She insisted that *I* needed help and recommended Al-Anon. "I'm doing just fine," I said. "The rest of them are in trouble." However, I agreed to go.

By the end of my first meeting, my own addictions were undeniable: people pleasing, perfectionism, trying to play God. My temptation wasn't alcohol but the high that comes from control.

After all these years of working my program, I had a relapse. A brother was living in a homeless shelter, and I had the powerful urge to fix him.

After days of research, I located a hospital that treated the shelter's residents free of charge, including counseling and medications. If my brother would simply follow my plan, we could turn his life around. I vowed to do whatever it took—weekly visits, lunch dates, and driving him to his appointments. All I needed was a few minutes to explain it to him.

The shelter manager arranged a phone call. When the number appeared on my caller ID, I felt the familiar adrenaline rush, the high that comes with control.

I talked quickly, not sure how long my brother would listen. I offered to take him for an evaluation that very day. Holding my breath, I waited for his response.

"Julie, I appreciate it," he said, "but I'm doing fine. I don't need any help."

I couldn't believe it. I'd reverted to my addictive habits. Once more, I started all over again with step one: "I am powerless over..."

> *Lord, help me to remember there is no other God but You.*
> —Julie Garmon

Digging Deeper: Exodus 8:10; Deuteronomy 4:35

"Are not two sparrows sold for a cent? And yet not one of them will fall to the ground apart from your Father. But the very hairs of your head are all numbered. So do not fear; you are more valuable than many sparrows."
—Matthew 10:29–31 (NAS)

For the last eight months I have been the interim pastor at the First Baptist Church of Montezuma, Georgia. This week, one of the elderly men in the church had a massive heart attack. Jack was in the army during World War II and was part of the Greatest Generation. Now he lay in an intensive care unit, connected to tubes and depending on a respirator for life.

Last night I stayed up late with Jack's son in the hospital. I drove home and fell into a deep sleep. As dawn broke, I was jerked awake by the flutter of wings and a small object flying across our bedroom. Somehow a sparrow had entered our house and was now trapped inside. The bird was seeking the nearest light flooding through a bathroom window. Carefully, I entered the bathroom and closed the door. There was the poor sparrow, plastered against the closed window glass and trembling in fright. There was no escape.

Slowly I moved toward the bird, and it flew to the sink and mirror. I carefully opened the window and walked quietly out of the room, closing the door behind me. When I returned, I found the sparrow gone and was delighted that it was now free.

Several minutes later the phone rang and Jack's son told me that his father had taken his last breath. I instantly thought of the bird. Death is not a closed door but an open window, not the end of life but the beginning.

God, may I live my life confident that
the best is yet to be and that You are good!
—Scott Walker

Digging Deeper: Isaiah 31:5; John 5:24

Tuesday, July 24

Let us run with patience the race that is set before us. —Hebrews 12:1 (KJV)

I'm too old, too fat, and too out of shape! I should cancel now or I'll wind up holding everyone else back. I was scheduled to hike Havasupai Trail into the Grand Canyon in less than forty-eight hours, but my inner critic just wouldn't stop talking. The eight miles each way didn't scare me. I worried that I lacked the stamina to make it back up the final mile of switchbacks, which ascended two thousand feet.

I'm not a newbie to hiking. I've hiked the Inca Trail, Pikes Peak, and Great Britain's two-hundred-mile Coast to Coast Walk. But now I'm pushing sixty. My picture of someone that age is an elderly woman crocheting in a rocker, not someone trotting like a mule up a nearly vertical canyon wall.

Then God reminded me this was exactly the same dialogue that had been going through my head before I hiked the Inca Trail—twenty years earlier. So, in faith, I decided to do the very same thing I did then: practice the Walk of the Patient One.

"The Walk of the Patient One doesn't get its name from others having to be patient with you," my guide back in Peru had explained. "It's because you have to be patient enough with yourself to put one foot one inch in front of the other. Then repeat."

One small step at a time, I not only made it in and out of the canyon right in stride with my younger, fitter companions, but I also came away with the reassurance that I was stronger and tougher than I'd thought I was. It's perseverance, not speed, that gets me where God wants me to go.

> *Lord, please calm my anxious, critical heart and give me*
> *the courage to keep moving forward, one step at a time,*
> *regardless of how perilous the road ahead seems to be.*
> —Vicki Kuyper

Digging Deeper: Isaiah 40:28–31; Philippians 4:13

"Her own clothing is beautifully made—a purple gown of pure linen."
—Proverbs 31:22 (TLB)

I'm cleaning my closet and filling donation sacks with clothing in usable condition that I no longer wear. I've readily parted with sandals that are cute but a half size too small, green-gray slacks that don't match any of my shirts, four sleeveless blouses, and a suit that never really fit.

My sacks don't contain a single dress. Ah, my dresses! They are like friends; just looking at them brings happy memories. I almost wore the lace-trimmed silk from my son Patrick's wedding to his son Ryan's wedding. It's still lovely but too short. I bought the stunning royal-blue party dress for an ultrafancy Hindu wedding last year, but I'll probably never attend an event like that again. The button-front red coatdress and the brown suede two-piece are classics, but at least a full size too large.

My mind knows I'll never wear these dresses again and that letting them hang in my closet is selfish. My mind is willing to part with them; my heart is not ready.

Then I spot the black rayon print with buttons bordered in antique gold that originally belonged to my sister Amanda. She loved it, but she gave it to me one Christmas. It still fits, and I receive compliments every time I wear it.

I carefully fold the other dresses and put them into a sack. It's past time to give other women the same joy of a loved and lovely dress that my sister gave me.

> *Lord, forgive me for holding on to earthly treasures too long.*
> *Bless the women who wear those dresses with the*
> *sense of beauty that was mine each time I put one on. Amen.*
> —Penney Schwab

Digging Deeper: Matthew 6:19–21, 25:34–40; Acts 9:36–39

Thursday, July 26

Jesus said, "Father, forgive them; for they know not what they do."
—Luke 23:34 (RSV)

In 1991, Vukovar, Croatia, was the center of a devastating war. Ninety percent of its homes were destroyed. Thousands of soldiers and civilians were killed. At war's end, a writer for the *Washington Post* observed, "Not one roof, door, or wall in all of Vukovar seems to have escaped jagged gouges or gaping holes left by shrapnel, bullets, bombs, or artillery shells—all delivered as part of a three-month effort by Serb insurgents and the Serb-led Yugoslav army to wrest the city from its Croatian defenders. Not one building appears habitable or even repairable. Nearly every tree has been chopped to bits by firepower."

More than a quarter century has passed since that brutal conflict. Yet the town still reflects a transition between war and peace. I saw many new and lovely homes and buildings, yet scores remain scarred and bullet-ridden, testimony to the ravages of a humanity that cannot get along. As I walked Vukovar's now tranquil streets, I was intensely aware that battles had once raged there. Though sunshine and birdsong surrounded me, I could not shake an aura of sadness and oppression.

But then I came upon a scene that arrested my footsteps and left me transfixed. Against a backdrop of bombed-out, pockmarked ruins stood a majestic white stone cross. It towered from a pedestal encircled by a wrought-iron fence. On the cross hung a white stone image of Jesus. This vivid juxtaposition spoke eternal truth to me. We are a human race who sins. We are a people who break our Lord's heart by what we do. Yet we can be forgiven.

Thank You, God, that You so loved the world that
You gave Your one and only Son, that whoever believes in Him
shall not perish but have eternal life.
—Kim Henry

Digging Deeper: Psalm 2; Romans 4:25, 15:13

"The steadfast love of the Lord never ceases; his mercies never come to an end; they are new every morning...." —Lamentations 3:22–23 (ESV)

D ad, I'm not sure why you put on this twenty-four-hour hold," Johnny said. "I was ready to close the deal."

He had been talking with the Realtor about the house he wanted to buy. Since this was his first home purchase, I was there to coach him if needed...a "silent" observer in the room. Sensing he was about to make an offer, I blurted out, "We'll sleep on it and get back together tomorrow." So much for being silent!

As we drove back to the hotel, I explained that I found it helpful to create space to think through the options and allow new insights to come when making a major decision. My son seemed receptive to it, though his question reminded me that this was his deal, not mine.

Over dinner, we continued talking about the house, its location, and price. Everything about it seemed perfect for him. Were we missing something?

Still on my mind as I went to bed, I asked God for insight, and early the next morning I awoke with a new idea. The house was move-in ready. Why not ask the builder for a lease agreement until the closing? Johnny could eliminate a hotel stay, avoid his possessions going into storage, and the builder would get rental income. Johnny liked the idea and made his offer, and the builder agreed.

My son did not need much help in buying his first home. If he takes only one lesson away from the experience, I hope it is the difference that the twenty-four-hour hold made and the value in seeking God's guidance and then waiting for insight.

Dear Lord, thank You for taking the stuff lingering in our minds at day's end and planting within us fresh insights for the new day. Amen.
—John Dilworth

Digging Deeper: Proverbs 3:1–6; Isaiah 40:30–31

Saturday, July 28

He telleth the number of the stars; he calleth them all by their names.
—Psalm 147:4 (KJV)

Sometimes I feel like I've been forgotten. I wake up during the night and wonder, *How can I keep doing all the things I have to do? There's Zimbabwe: we take on more children every year to feed, clothe, educate. What if our resources dry up?*

And there's the community group I organize—speakers and meeting places every month. I don't want to let anyone down but...

And my family and friends who need me—I don't have enough time.

And on it goes. Finally I pull myself out of bed and walk around the house.

I'm pedaling as fast as I can, God. Will I ever get to a stretch of easygoing, where I can coast?

Still not ready for sleep, I wander out to the porch. A train passes in the distance. A slight breeze rustles the trees, and beyond their branches I see a slice of moon, a scattering of stars.

The darkness is calming. I reach past the worry and breathe deeply. In the stillness, something greater than myself and all my fears waits. I recall the times I've let go and trusted God. I remember how solutions beyond my understanding seemingly come out of nowhere.

The sky above is infinite, and if God's Word is true, He has every single one of those stars named. In ways I can't understand, He sees everything...even me, as I sit in the night. God will never forget me. My problem is this: sometimes I forget Him.

Father, save me from my worries.
I know that if You stay close, I can coast.
—Pam Kidd

Digging Deeper: Job 28:20–28

"The Lord will fight for you; you need only to be still."
—Exodus 14:14 (NIV)

My best friend came to visit me in New York. It was her first time to visit, so I wanted to pack all the sights, food, and fun I could into our four days together.

The first day we took a train into Manhattan at ten in the morning. We walked crosstown, hopped on the subway, and headed uptown to the Cloisters. It was a meditative spot to start our adventure. Then, back on the subway, we went down to the Metropolitan Museum of Art. We both love Impressionist painting, so we spent time gazing at the works of Edgar Degas and Vincent van Gogh. Next, we headed farther downtown to a favorite barbecue place. Along the way, we window-shopped and gawked at the towering buildings. Finally, we took a train home at ten thirty that night.

My friend was pooped, not used to so much walking. She suggested we stay closer to home the next day.

In the morning, she came down for breakfast with her knitting in hand. She suggested we sit on the patio and knit. I put on a pot of tea, and we spent all morning catching up and renewing our friendship.

My agenda for the visit had been to rush around and see as much as possible. I forgot that what I needed most was time with my friend.

> *Slow me down, Lord. Open in me the desire to spend time*
> *with You and my friend. Amen.*
> —Lisa Bogart

Digging Deeper: 1 Samuel 12:16; Nehemiah 8:11

Monday, July 30

And the Lord's servant must not be quarrelsome but kind to everyone....
—2 Timothy 2:24 (ESV)

After more than seven hours in the car, we see the sign welcoming us to Cape Cod. *We're here!*

The rental house won't let us in until after 2:00 p.m., so we park at the ocean. Our dog Soda tugs at his leash, which stretches near the sandy ridge. The ocean air is glorious, and I take in a big belly-breath and let it go. "Come on, boys," I say to Solomon and Henry. Henry brushes off the juice boxes and snack crumbs. He announces he managed to do the whole trip without going to the bathroom. But now he has to go!

"Ouch!" he says as his feet hit the hot parking lot pavement.

"Shoes," I say. "Henry, where are your shoes?"

"This morning when I was on the couch, you said, 'Henry, get in the car,' so I did."

"You weren't wearing shoes?"

Henry widens his eyes and shakes his head.

"Back in the car!" Tony says. "Everyone, back in the car!"

I pull Soda back, away from his new wonderland, and he scuffs backward, not wanting to leave.

"We're going home?" Henry asks.

Just down the road, we pull into a souvenir shop and pay three times more than we should for flip-flops. Henry smiles. He likes the ones his dad picked out. These are his favorite color, bright yellow.

I look in the side-view mirror and catch myself smiling. *We're here!*

Dear God, thank You for getting us to this place—right now—where we can handle a mishap without argument or blame and move ahead with grace and love.
—Sabra Ciancanelli

Digging Deeper: Proverbs 15:1; Ephesians 6:4

RELYING ON GOD'S UNFAILING LOVE
Giving Thanks...Even for Fleas

Give thanks in all circumstances; for this is the will of God in Christ Jesus for you. —1 Thessalonians 5:18 (ESV)

It was one of those grumbling days.

You know the ones. Days when a lost backpack makes you late for school drop-off. When there is nothing left in the fridge except for an old apple and an almost-empty gallon of milk. When appointments are missed, plans get canceled, important documents get lost.

I texted my husband that nothing was going right. That I was in a bad mood. And that I was tired of the frazzled, crazy, lukewarm way I was feeling.

Then I opened up Facebook.

My friend Sarah, the one battling breast cancer, the one who laughed as her husband shaved her balding head, had posted on Facebook about reading Corrie ten Boom's book *The Hiding Place*. There is a story in the book in which Corrie and her sister stand together in the middle of their desperation and thank God for the fleas in their room.

In her own post, Sarah gave thanks for her own "fleas"—for the cancer that had changed every "what should have been" in her life, that had stolen her hair, her health, her way of living. Yet she was thankful. Because God had used those "fleas" to help her to trust in Him.

So I got onto my knees and thanked God for my own fleas. For mistakes, for problems, for niggling issues that seem to overtake my days. And while my "fleas" aren't nearly as awful as those of Sarah or Corrie ten Boom, I know that God wants me to be grateful, not grumbling, no matter what circumstances come my way.

Lord, help me to be thankful even for the "fleas" in my life so that I can honor You and find hope in Your grace. Amen.
—Erin MacPherson

Digging Deeper: 1 Chronicles 16:34; Colossians 3:15

July

GOD'S UNFAILING LOVE

1 _____

2 _____

3 _____

4 _____

5 _____

6 _____

7 _____

8 _____

9 _____

10 _____

11 _____

12 _____

13 _____

14 _____

15 _____

16 _____

17 _____

18 _____

19 _____

20 _____

21 _____

22 _____

23 _____

24 _____

25 _____

26 _____

27 _____

28 _____

29 _____

30 _____

31 _____

AUGUST

Above all, keep fervent in your love for one another, because love covers a multitude of sins.

—1 Peter 4:8 (NAS)

"But seek first the kingdom of God and his righteousness, and all these things will be added to you." —Matthew 6:33 (ESV)

A storm brought us together.

Lonny and I huddled in the living room with our sons. The power was out, and the younger boys were restless. Their flashlights threw beams of light.

"Let's make shadow animals," one boy said. That lasted ten minutes.

"I know," another son said. "Let's sing 'Row, Row, Row Your Boat' in a round." He started singing, and the brothers joined in. Lonny and I came in at the end, and our choruses melded together every time.

"See," my husband whispered, "we can't stay apart. We meet even in a song."

I pressed into his arms, on our old sofa, in our home filled to the brim with boys. Just a few moments together made me understand that we'd been missing out.

It can be the same with God. I have every intention of beginning each day with Him. I have a special chair. My Bible is page-marked. But sometimes I hit the Snooze button. Or I wake and want to tackle dirty dishes from the night before.

It's when I go back that I understand how I've missed God. His Word becomes the heartbeat that draws me in, and I'm content and filled, settled and stilled. Focused time in His presence is the sustaining grace I need.

Lonny's arms stayed strong around me, and we waited out the storm. One of our sons found a favorite book and read out loud. I tried, but I couldn't follow. I was lost in thoughts of God's love.

> *Lord, may time alone with You be something*
> *I can't do without. Amen.*
> —Shawnelle Eliasen

Digging Deeper: Psalms 5:3, 119:47; Mark 1:35

Thursday, August 2

"Don't bargain with God. Be direct. Ask for what you need. This isn't a cat-and-mouse, hide-and-seek game we're in...." —Matthew 7:11 (MSG)

The phone rang early. Barely light. My new friend Eleanor was calling. She always phoned early as her days were long and hard. She rescues cats and dogs that have been abandoned or hurt, and, if they're mamas, she helps their babies. She has all of them spayed or neutered. She never stops. No project is too large for her. Money is tight. But the animals come first.

We'd bonded immediately upon a happenstance meeting. We were new but very close friends. I suspected that her call concerned an animal situation she wanted me to pray about.

"Good morning, Marion. How are you? Your kitties and dog?"

Normally Eleanor would relate a story about an animal she'd rescued, but this time she said, "Will you pray for me?"

I was stunned. She'd never requested prayer for herself.

"I have something very painful in the back of my mouth. Doctor is sure it's cancer, but he's sending me to a specialist. I'm going to ask you to pray for one minute every morning, when you first wake up. No more. Just do that. I'm in God's hands and not afraid," she stated matter-of-factly. "Just whisper my name and a prayer. Lift me to the throne room. He'll take it from there."

What she'd asked me to do surprised me—such a tiny request for such a big health issue. But, of course, I would pray for her. And, of course, God could work a miracle.

> *Father, may I have a minute of Your time?*
> *My friend Eleanor needs You.*
> —Marion Bond West

Digging Deeper: Psalm 107:28–30; Jonah 2:2–7; Matthew 7:7

"The owner's servants came to him and said, 'Sir, didn't you sow good seed in your field? Where then did the weeds come from?'"
—Matthew 13:27 (NIV)

We'd been away on vacation for several weeks, so I was anxious to see how our yard had fared in the hot Florida sun. I strolled through the yard, inspecting the shrubs and flower beds for progress or damage.

I was happy to discover that we'd had a lot of rain, so all the plants were healthy and growing. The roses were blooming, as were the vincas and hibiscus, and the Mexican petunias had grown another foot. Everything was flourishing...even the weeds.

I grabbed my gardening gloves and pruning shears and headed out to get rid of the intruders.

"Can I help?" asked Logan, my young grandson.

As we set to work attacking the weeds, I was overwhelmed by the amount. How had so many unwanted plants appeared in so short a time? Where did they come from? As I tugged and jerked to remove them, I thought about weeds in my own life that needed pulling.

For example, I'd been too critical of others lately. *Tug!* Pull that weed out of my life. I hadn't shown forgiveness to my family for little things. *Pull!* Get rid of that! I'd lost my temper with my son. *Snap!*

Once Logan and I had pulled out the weeds, I had room to plant more good plants. The same is true in my own life. Instead of bitterness, unforgivingness, and anger, I can plant mercy, kindness, and self-control.

Lord, please point out the weeds in my life and
remove them so only good will grow.
—Marilyn Turk

Digging Deeper: Matthew 13:1–8, 18–22

Saturday, August 4

A good man leaves an inheritance to his children's children....
—Proverbs 13:22 (NAS)

D addy, what time are we going to the drive-in?" It must have been the forty-seventh time Mary Katherine had asked.

I maintained what I felt was an admirable level of patience, as I answered, "Not much longer."

Balancing work, hobbies, and family was stressful, and often I found myself wondering how we could raise our children with a bent toward simple human kindness. Patience, I was thinking, was a good first step.

Soon we were on our way to the drive-in, not far from our cabin in Alabama. Tonight a G-rated movie was featured, and Mary Katherine was ecstatic.

We pulled into a great spot, next to a beat-up truck. Five raggedy chairs were lined up in the truck bed, where four kids and a man about my age sat laughing and talking. As the man joked with his kids, he looked sweaty and dirty as though he had just come in from the fields.

Mary Katherine rolled down her window and caught the eye of a boy about her age. She waved to him in that sweet way children have. He waved back.

I thought of distracting her, but it was too late. The man leaned down and retrieved a pizza box and held it up toward us. "We have plenty if y'all would like some." He had a kind glow that I had missed before.

I felt like laughing out loud as I gave the man my biggest smile and reached for a slice. Funny, how God answers prayers.

> *Father, the legacy I want to leave my children starts here,*
> *with the lesson of receiving kindness.*
> —Brock Kidd

Digging Deeper: Proverbs 22:6; Matthew 19:14, 21:16

They appointed elders for each church. With prayer and fasting, they committed these elders to the Lord, in whom they had placed their trust.
—Acts 14:23 (CEB)

W hen my tiny congregation learned we would be without a pastor for a whole year, we worked to provide worship services pleasing to God and helpful for us. Our pulpit rotation included three people with pastoral experience and two young lay speakers. I chose music and prepared bulletins; Blake and John were liturgists; others contributed children's stories and music.

The church continued giving and serving. A group of women made breakfast and supplied devotionals for the high school prayer group plus refreshments for the grade-school Joy Club. Joan coordinated bimonthly blood drives and cooked meals for donors.

Attendance improved. Spirits revived. Hearing the Word deepened our faith. We learned and sang new songs. Fanned by fervent prayers, a wisp of hope for survival became a tiny flame of assurance that we could thrive.

Perhaps we grew smug about our efforts and became set in our ways. At least, that's how the church authorities saw it. They would soon assign a pastor to our church. Furthermore, we were to share that pastor with two other congregations. We didn't like it, but change was on the way.

We're still praying for the pastor who will come. We are also praying for wisdom to work out emotionally charged logistics concerning worship times, pastoral time, and budgets. Sometimes I despair. Then I remember that this is not my church, but Christ's. He reminds me: "Don't be afraid, little flock, because your Father delights in giving you the kingdom" (Luke 12:32, CEB).

Lord, help me embrace new leadership and changes that can nourish our faith and grow our church. Amen.
—Penney Schwab

Digging Deeper: 1 Corinthians 14:26; Colossians 1:18–20;
Revelation 3:19–20

Monday, August 6

God is our refuge and strength, a very present help in trouble. Therefore we will not fear, though the earth should change, though the mountains shake in the heart of the sea. —Psalm 46:1–2 (NRSV)

It's Frances's first time at sleepaway camp. The drive is beautiful. The kids work out their nervous tension playing silly games in the back seat. Kate and I sit quietly with our mixed feelings.

Frances is nine. She has become a poised, mature, independent girl. We know she'll do fine, though we can tell she's masking her nervousness. Maybe we're more nervous, not so much that she'll get homesick or fail to make friends, but that life is changing. The past, when the kids were little and depended on us for everything, is ebbing away. Next year Benji will be seven, old enough to attend camp too.

Our lives have revolved around the kids for so long. Now we have to let them grow up, explore things on their own, encourage them to become their own independent selves.

We arrive at the camp. Frances gathers with a group of kids heading to the lake for a swim. She hugs us several times, then gamely trudges off. She turns to wave, and we can see anxiousness in her smile.

Well, at least she's not glad to see us go! She, too, understands this is a big moment, a venture into the unknown.

Then I remember what we loved about this camp when we visited. They held a prayer service for visiting families in the woodsy outdoor chapel.

We'll all be fine. God is here, holding us through every change.

> *Lord, we change, but You don't.*
> *Help me to remember that.*
> —Jim Hinch

Digging Deeper: Numbers 23:19; Malachi 3:6; Hebrews 13:8

Then the peace of God that exceeds all understanding will keep your hearts and minds safe in Christ Jesus. —Philippians 4:7 (CEB)

I t's a little hard to describe what I actually do when I pray. I note with some relief the willingness of others to reach for metaphors to convey their process. "It's like I'm letting go of all these little pieces of paper with my anxious thoughts and putting them in God's hands," someone will say. Or another person will describe it: "I try to imagine I'm floating in a warm bath and being washed by God's love." "I picture myself being held like I hold my dog when he's scared during a thunderstorm," someone else offers.

How can I explain what happens when I sit on the sofa in the morning and close my eyes and pray? One day I was on the computer, organizing some files on the screen, dragging my mouse across my desk to put documents in one file and then that file into another file, when it came to me: praying is like dragging and dropping. That was it.

In the morning I close my eyes and documents come up with different labels and varying degrees of urgency. "Get to this immediately!" "Worry about this now!" "Fret for unending hours about this remote possibility!" "Feel scared…or sad…or desperate about this news!" The process is to drag all those unnecessary mental distractions and put them into a big file that says "God to handle," where they can stay. The idea is to drag and drop and then drop for good.

Until the next morning when somehow a whole new set of urgent documents—and even some of the same ones ("Didn't I put you in the God file?")—fills my head. It's just like work. I need to drag and drop every day.

Lord, I am grateful to you for reordering the files of my mind.
—Rick Hamlin

Digging Deeper: Psalm 55:22; 1 Peter 5:7

Wednesday, August 8

"You heavens above, rain down my righteousness; let the clouds shower it down. Let the earth open wide, let salvation spring up, let righteousness flourish with it; I, the Lord, have created it."—Isaiah 45:8 (NIV)

Water droplets streaked the glass. Rain again. Our trip to a north Georgia lake was besieged by rain, so we had hoped that the fifty percent chance for precipitation on day three might come out in our favor. It was not to be. We found ourselves facing another day stuck inside the cabin. "At least it's not storming," my husband, Brian, said.

Olivia tumbled into the kitchen as only toddlers can, felling spices, rattling pots, and shining smiles all the way. "I want go in my boat," she said, referring to the bright red kayak that Poppa had tethered to his own orange canoe the last time we'd been at the lake.

"You know what?" I said. "Let's do it! We'll be wet anyway."

Grandparents, parents, uncles, aunts, and Olivia got dressed and made their way through the drizzle down to the dock, where we dragged out the paddleboards, tethered the kayaks, and took turns cannonballing into the smooth waters.

We splashed, squealed, and swam until we were exhausted. The pictures I have from that day show Olivia beaming from the back of Poppa's paddleboard, a tiny ray of light on a dreary day.

Every so often I am reminded to be grateful, to think outside of myself, and to have some perspective. What's a little rain when spending a vacation surrounded by loving family, warm and safe in our cabin? We often talk about that day and how Olivia reminded us all of what was really important.

> *Lord, without the rain and shadows, I'd never appreciate*
> *the warmth of the sun. Thank You.*
> —Ashley Kappel

Digging Deeper: Deuteronomy 11:14; Job 5:10; Jeremiah 51:16

A new heart also will I give you, and a new spirit will I put within you: and I will take away the stony heart out of your flesh, and I will give you an heart of flesh. —Ezekiel 36:26 (KJV)

I grow weary of talking about the need for racial reconciliation, but I keep writing and praying about it because our failure to love one another grieves the heart of God.

Stacey sits down at the table across from me. I see her only in the summer when I come to Bible Witness Camp in rural Illinois. Her twin daughters are campers, and Stacey shares her creativity and resources planning special moments for the girls. We smile, exchanging pleasantries and catching up. "I've been living on a cul de sac for ten years," she says to me. "When we moved in, the woman across the street wouldn't speak to us. The twins would wave, and she would turn her head or rush back into her home."

I see the pain in Stacey's eyes, pain that we hoped our children would never know. "And I knew she was a Christian. She would have yard sales to benefit her church."

Stacey and I have never talked about race. I take a deep breath. *Lord, can't one heart change?*

Stacey continues. "Recently, I was outside and my neighbor called to me. She said she needed to talk. She apologized. She said she owed my husband and me both an apology for how she had treated us. She said I had a nice family and that she was wrong for how she had behaved. My neighbor and I were standing in the middle of the street, crying. And she kept her promise. She came over and apologized to my husband too."

"How miraculous!" I say through tears. "God is amazing!" Her neighbor's apology and Stacey's willingness to tell the story warm my heart and encourage me.

> *Lord, thank You for reassurance. Help us to love.*
> *Turn our hearts of stone to hearts of flesh.*
> —Sharon Foster

Digging Deeper: Luke 10:27; Galatians 5:14, 6:9; 1 John 4:20

Friday, August 10

Let the heavens be glad, and let the earth rejoice; let the sea roar, and all that fills it; let the field exult, and everything in it. Then shall all the trees of the forest sing for joy. —Psalm 96:11–12 (NRSV)

My neighbor, Jim, sits on his porch in northern New England every summer evening at dusk, waiting for the deer to arrive. He lives on the southern edge of state forest land, and there's a small pond behind his house, surrounded by a birch grove. That's where the deer come each evening, and there on the porch sat Jim, as usual, at dusk in early August, when he began to hear a snorting sound.

Now, deer don't usually snort. One generally sees a deer long before one hears it make any sound at all. This was not, of course, a deer.

Jim's eyes popped when he looked to his left and witnessed a bull moose pulling up to the pond. In fact, he gasped. The moose looked up and saw Jim sitting there. A bull moose is worth about four or five Jims, and an aggressive one is not to be quietly "watched." That's an animal to run from! But Jim was safely on his porch, and did I mention that his porch sits about ten feet above the lawn and the pond below? It does. So, Jim had the strange experience of being a bit terrified, even as he knew that there was no real danger.

"The feeling of being in the presence of that animal was something I can't even describe," Jim told me. "Awesome: that's the only word for it."

You are awesome, God. If you didn't love me, and I didn't know it,
as I do, I might be afraid. Instead, I'm just in awe.
—Jon Sweeney

Digging Deeper: Job 12:7–10

"If you forgive people their sins, your Father in heaven will forgive your sins also." —Matthew 6:14 (NLV)

Today at the grocery store I ran into my very first boyfriend. He was doing his job when I saw him at the end of an aisle. I knew him from the back of his head all these years later. It's so strange how memory is.

Seeing him stopped time. On reflex, I backed my cart down one aisle and then around another, catching my breath and bringing me back to the days when I was a teenager and he was abusive.

I was with him for a few months before things turned bad. Once they did, I was caught in the relationship and deeply confused about love. Breaking up with him wasn't easy, but after many attempts I was finally free.

I found myself in the last aisle of the store with nothing in my cart from the moment that I recognized him. What had just happened? Had I imagined it all?

I retraced my steps cautiously. Rounding a corner, I looked at his face to make sure it was him. It was. I looked at him—really looked at him.

He didn't meet my eye, and I left before he could. *We were young,* I thought. *I don't know what happened in his life. I forgive him.* I sighed, a heavy sigh that let out something I'd been holding on to for a very long time.

> *Dear God, thank You for showing me that forgiveness heals.*
> *Even after all these years it makes a difference.*
> —Sabra Ciancanelli

Digging Deeper: Matthew 5:44; Colossians 3:13

Sunday, August 12

"Can you lead forth a constellation in its season...? Do you know the ordinances of the heavens, or fix their rule over the earth?"
—Job 38:32–33 (NAS)

The annual August Perseid meteor shower was coming to town—or *above* town—on a clear moonless night. I planned a "Perseid party" for neighbors. But amid the fun I had a hollow spot inside. My husband, Terry, was in such continuing discomfort and hampered by limited mobility from a back problem that he couldn't join us.

Prior to the party I read up on the Perseid event. Debris from Comet Swift-Tuttle hits Earth's atmosphere sixty miles up at thirty-five miles per second. Before the constellation rises too high in the sky, it's possible to see *earthgrazers*—meteors that travel in a long, low, colorful horizontal line. The extrabright meteors—or *fireballs*—weigh about as much as a walnut. Most of what zips across the sky is, amazingly, only pea-size.

Our group uttered exclamations late into the evening, awed by God's glory on display. The experience recalled words from Psalm 46:10 (NAS), "Cease striving and know that I am God....I will be exalted in the earth." And another passage in Romans 1:20 declaring God's eternal power is clearly seen through what He has created.

Taking time from the stress and difficulty of dealing with Terry's persevering daily struggle—repositioning to focus on God and look up—I saw the Lord of all Creation light up my sky. *How great You are! How You sustain us! How Your power is at work in and around us! I lift You high!*

It's that simple, isn't it, Lord?
Taking time out to look to You, my God.
—Carol Knapp

Digging Deeper: 1 Chronicles 16:10–11; Job 38; Psalm 14:2;
Hebrews 11:6

"They seized him, put the cross on him, and made him carry it behind Jesus."—Luke 23:26 (GNT)

It's hard for me to ask for help, but it's not just because I am a stubborn male. It's because I find so much pleasure in doing my own work.

So when the willow tree outside our kitchen window died, I decided to take it down myself. I have cut down trees so many times that I have a system.

I climbed the ladder and cut off the limbs with my chain saw. I was left with the trunk, about ten feet high and eighteen inches thick. So I dug around the base of the tree, exposing the roots, which I severed with an ax.

Now all I have to do is push this trunk over and I'm done. But when I shoved it, I nearly broke my wrists. I spent the rest of the day pushing and pulling on the trunk with a variety of ropes and pulleys, pry bars, sledgehammers, and a homemade battering ram. At last I slumped to the ground, exhausted, and prayed for mercy.

Then I heard a voice behind me. It was my neighbor John.

"I can pull that out for you with my four-wheel drive."

I nearly fell on my face in worship of him.

The powerful truck wheels clawed at the driveway. The rope tightened, and the tree trunk slowly ripped out of the ground.

"John," I sang out, "you are an angel from heaven! Thank you!"

He grinned proudly, as if I had done him a favor by accepting his help.

Now I can see that work is not a matter of either doing it myself or hiring someone to get it done. It's more about knowing when to ask for help.

Lord Jesus, even You needed help to carry Your Cross.
I need Your help with today's burdens.
—Daniel Schantz

Digging Deeper: Proverbs 27:1; Isaiah 11:6

Tuesday, August 14

Better is the end of a thing than its beginning....
—Ecclesiastes 7:8 (ESV)

I admit that in the grand scheme of life, the placement of a septic tank should be a minor consideration. But when I arrived at our cabin in Alabama and discovered that a new tank had been put in our front yard, I was distraught. There on the grass-covered drive that wound around the front of my "place of peace," two large, ugly green lids rose a foot aboveground.

How could my eyes ever get past such ugliness to rest on the lake beyond? Was the sacred space where my father before us had watched the sunset spoiled forever?

The more I thought about this terrible intrusion, the more agitated I became. It was an eyesore. The grassy drive was useless. I couldn't let go of my discontent.

And then one day a pile of boards appeared.

"I'm building a deck over the septic tank," David announced.

"A deck?"

Soon, he was hard at work, digging footings, measuring and sawing boards, setting posts. The structure rose up over the tank and quickly became a part of the landscape.

I bought four red lawn chairs and arranged them on the finished deck.

"This is the most perfect spot I've ever seen for viewing the sunset," a friend exclaimed as we sat watching the explosion of color dancing across the lake.

"Yes, it is," I answered, casting David a mischievous smile. "We call it our 'sunset deck.'"

> *Father, Your love never fails as You turn bad into good.*
> —Pam Kidd

Digging Deeper: John 16:20; Romans 14:19

Let the words of my mouth and the meditation of my heart be acceptable in your sight, O Lord, my rock and my redeemer. —Psalm 19:14 (ESV)

I was rushing across the lobby of my apartment building, lugging a bunch of groceries and hoping to make it into the waiting elevator when the sole occupant of said elevator allowed the door to close in my face. And out of my mouth came a word I don't like to say and won't repeat here.

Sooner or later most of us give in to the occasional swear word, even if it's under our breath. I'm never happy about it. God gave us the gift of language and we shouldn't debase it by cursing.

Experts say swearing is a part of every culture and remarkably consistent in its content. Even stroke patients who have lost the capacity for speech have been known to let fly with a volley of obscenities. My own mother—in the final stages of Alzheimer's—let loose with a few choice words I never even dreamed she knew.

Linguists speculate that this is because the area of the brain that controls swearing is different and more primitive than the part that controls normal speech. It is connected to emotions like anger and fear, a kind of verbal safety valve, supporting the theory that swearing was a way to circumvent more violent responses in early humans. Still, we hear so much of it these days that swearing has become offensively commonplace. Common curses in the eighteenth century included "Gadzooks" (for God's eyes) and "zounds" (God's wounds).

Like most bad habits I struggle to break, the only solution is to humbly ask God for help. He hears all, even the whispers of our hearts.

Father, our tongues are meant to praise You.
Please help me keep mine pure.
—Edward Grinnan

Digging Deeper: Psalm 34:12–14; Colossians 3:8–10; James 3:5–6

Thursday, August 16

"The stone the builders rejected has become the cornerstone."
—Luke 20:17 (NIV)

It may be the most famous statue in the world. It's certainly one of the hardest to see! You wait in a long line outside Accademia Gallery in Florence, Italy. Inside at last, you inch your way through the crowd toward the niche where it stands on a marble pedestal.

Even if I was here alone, I thought, the day I visited the Accademia, *would I really see it?* Its very popularity has robbed its impact. It's everywhere you look—an exact replica in front of the Palazzo Vecchio where the original stood for four hundred years; a colossal one towering from a hilltop; *David* postcards in every newsstand; miniature *David*s in every souvenir shop.

All this since a twenty-six-year-old sculptor was handed a seemingly impossible challenge: to carve a larger-than-life David from an "unusable" block of marble. The enormous piece of stone that Michelangelo was given to work with had already been hacked and carved and chipped at by two previous sculptors, each of whom had given up, stymied by the marble's unyielding imperfections. And so the huge flawed stone was abandoned. Nicknamed "the Giant," it had lain in the stonemasons' yard in pouring rain and searing heat and winter freezes for thirty-five years.

And young Michelangelo? He studied the sleeping giant until a graceful form appeared in his mind that would take advantage of the very imperfections that had to be cut away, and of the nicks and gouges left by the previous sculptors too. The form of a young man at the instant of turning, hips and shoulders twisting, a figure poised on the verge of action, as David had never been portrayed before. Flawed marble? Or the inspiration that limits themselves call forth.

Father, show me in the flawed marble of my life
the unique form that You all along have seen.
—Elizabeth Sherrill

Digging Deeper: Jeremiah 18:1–6

CONFIDENCE IN DIFFICULTY: Declare God's Glory

Sing to the Lord a new song.... —Psalm 96:1 (NIV)

We need to talk discharge," the social worker said. Maggie had been an inpatient for five weeks, three times longer than insurance normally allows. Being on the unit had triggered panic attacks, a suicide attempt, and rage. In many ways my daughter was in worse shape than when she was admitted.

We were told that Maggie couldn't return to outpatient treatment until she completed a step-down program, yet none of the programs in New York City would take her. Our choices were to send Maggie to a state facility in the Bronx, which we couldn't tour and no one would talk about, or to a twenty-eight-day private program in Connecticut that cost a staggering amount of money.

The social worker told us to apply to both places because a bed wasn't guaranteed in either. We agreed and prayed for a cloud to lead us through the desert. Days passed. "I'm trying to follow Your will, Lord," I prayed testily, "but I can't see it! Could You at least show me the way *not* to go?"

I turned to Psalm 96, one of my go-to Scriptures when I'm stuck. Sometimes the best way through a knot is to hold on to what I do know, rather than fret over what I don't. I find comfort in praising the Lord, even if I don't always understand what He wants.

The following day I spoke with a doctor who had heard about our discharge dilemma. She was quiet and then said carefully, "Well, I do know *some* kids who have come out of State okay."

I went home and, using the profits from the sale of our apartment the previous summer, wrote out a very large check for the hospital in Connecticut.

Father, I will sing Your praises even—especially—when I feel lost.
—Julia Attaway

Digging Deeper: Psalms 34:1, 62:8

Saturday, August 18

My friends scoff at me, but I pour out my tears to God, pleading that he will listen as a man would listen to his neighbor. —Job 16:20–21 (TLB)

I live in a close-knit neighborhood of six hundred homes and condos. Because we all belong to the same association that supports our clubhouse, swimming pool, pier, and tennis court, we know many of our neighbors. That's why whenever I've been in my condo alone for too many hours I'll step outside and take a walk around the block just to see another face. I always smile and greet anyone I see on the sidewalk, but usually it's just a quick "Hi" or "Nice weather, eh?" and I move on.

One day when walking alone, I wondered what Jesus said to people as He walked from town to town. I'm sure He did more than chitchat about the weather.

I decided to try something new during my walks. Whenever I met someone, I asked at least one question that would let the person know I was offering more than a quick hello. Or I asked something that would help me get to know him or her better.

"Ginny, now that you've sold your car, do you need a ride to the store or church?"

"So sorry about your wife's death, Bob. Do you need any help with meals or taking care of your yard? Remember, the neighborhood pot-luck dinner is this Friday. Hope you come."

"Lou, now that you're living alone, do me a favor and every morning raise the shade on your kitchen window so I know you're up and doing okay."

Father, remind me to step out of my own needs when I'm out walking and concentrate on the needs of my neighbors who have become my family.
—Patricia Lorenz

Digging Deeper: Romans 13:9–10; James 2:8–9

But Jesus said unto him, No man, having put his hand to the plow, and looking back, is fit for the kingdom of God. —Luke 9:62 (ASV)

I once met a talented artist from Romania. When she was young, she escaped Communist oppression and immigrated to the United States seeking freedom and education. Her first few years were difficult. I asked her how she adjusted. She replied, "At first I was miserable and lonely. Then I decided that I would never go forward as long as I looked backward."

I knew I was hearing words of deep truth. In my youth, I had a similar experience. I grew up in the Philippine Islands where my parents were missionaries and teachers at a seminary. When I was fourteen, my father died from a heart attack. We returned suddenly to the United States to settle in my mother's hometown of Fort Valley, Georgia. I felt like my world had collapsed and I would be adrift forever.

Starting high school, I yearned to return to the small and intimate school I attended in the Philippines. Finally, I accepted that this would not happen. I began to live in the present moment. I had discovered the same truth as my friend.

There are moments in life when I want to retreat to the past. But life loses inertia and vitality when I take my eyes off of the present.

> *Lord, keep me focused on the tasks for this day.*
> *Help me plow a straight furrow. Amen.*
> —Scott Walker

Digging Deeper: Genesis 19:12–16, 24–26; Philippians 3:12–14

Monday, August 20

"My harp is turned to mourning, and my flute to the voice of those who weep." —Job 30:31 (NKJV)

People in mourning sometimes turn to alcohol or vice or something else that shouldn't be turned to. I turn to Craigslist.

For the uninitiated, Craigslist is an online trading service. One category is Free Stuff, featuring my all-time favorite adjective. After my father passed, I went from fan of free stuff to virtual addict. I brought home shipping crates (to store firewood); three printers (one actually worked); and a used futon that (1) will be rebuilt as a backsplash and (2) already threatens my marriage because it currently resides on the back porch.

Why the sudden need to recycle every last discarded item? After many fevered pickup trips, it occurred to me that maybe my efforts to rescue everything were a vain attempt to resurrect what I myself cannot resurrect: my father, who was a kid from the Depression and saved and reused everything. In my grief, I did the same, an unwitting attempt to reclaim what was lost to me.

Yes, I realize that there's another Father Who saves what seems to be lost. But my dad's death may have claimed—at least for a while—a second victim: my faith. Eventually I'll recover. In the meantime, I'm waterproofing the new backsplash before I put it in. I notice it beads up with every fallen tear.

Lord, my faith isn't what it used to be.
Let me see You in what I do;
let me see You in my father's memory.
—Mark Collins

Digging Deeper: Psalm 116:1–2; Hosea 2:19–20

Surely I have calmed and quieted my soul, like a weaned child with his mother; like a weaned child is my soul within me. —Psalm 131:2 (NKJV)

Even though I've done it year after year, I can't drop off my children for their first day of school without being transported back to their first day of kindergarten. I want to stay. I want to hover. I want to be a helicopter parent.

But they won't let me. I mean my kids won't let me. They're older now. They're pros at going to school. But I'm not. I think of that future day when they will fly from the nest for good. I hold back tears.

The kids wave good-bye, turn their backs, and head into the high school. I drive away reluctantly. *It's for their good,* I'm thinking. *They need this.* But I'm not convinced. To me, they still look like babies wearing cartoon backpacks, trotting off to a land of crayons and wall art.

"Like a weaned child," I read in Psalm 131:2 (NKJV), "is my soul within me."

A weaned child—it's beautiful and tragic all at once. It isn't only this way with me and my kids, I realize. It is this way with all of life. We come into this world with nothing, and that is how we depart.

I feel that: the weaning, the separating, the letting go is an inevitable part of parenthood. I don't like it, but I need it. My kids need it. It is God's way for us in this world. A lump forms in my throat. I drive around the block to make sure they're okay...and to pray. It is, after all, the first day of school.

Lord, wean me gently of all things, that I might cling to the one thing I can never lose—my life with You, forever.
—Bill Giovannetti

Digging Deeper: Matthew 10:39

Wednesday, August 22

Therefore encourage one another and build each other up, just as in fact you are doing. —1 Thessalonians 5:11 (NIV)

A while back, I wrote a *Daily Guideposts* devotion about how I needed to be more gentle—one of the fruits of the Spirit. This came about after visiting two local congregations within the same week and listening to two sermons on Scripture about living by the Spirit (Galatians 5). I shared how growing up in New York City showed me that being tough was the survival spirit.

Soon after it was published, I received a letter from Julie, a former parishioner. "Today I read your devotion in *Daily Guideposts.* You questioned the quality of gentleness in yourself. Pablo, you certainly are gentle. I have witnessed that gentleness in you as a pastor, husband, and father." She reminded me that she and her husband grew up in New York City, and they, too, learned that having a tough manner was the way to survive.

Julie's letter touched me deeply. She took time out of her day to write and encourage me. Sometimes we forget that others are watching us as we carry out our faith, vocation, and lives.

I was being too hard on myself. Julie helped me to identify why I felt the need to have a more gentle spirit. It wasn't because my actions and personality were lacking in gentleness. It was because of where I came from and what I did to protect myself.

Lord, thank You for the people who care and encourage us and for the ways they do so in our lives.
—Pablo Diaz

Digging Deeper: Proverbs 27:17; Hebrews 3:13

THE BEAUTY OF SIMPLICITY: Truth Defeats Fear

Give thanks to the Lord, for he is good; his love endures forever.
—Psalm 107:1 (NIV)

When Thomas was born, an unexpected fear hit: I was afraid to trust God. Two years earlier, we'd lost a full-term baby boy, Robbie, who was born without a brain. The grief cut so deeply that we didn't plan to have any more children. But the following spring, we decided to try one more time.

And now, I held sweet, perfect Thomas in the delivery room. Terrified that something might happen to him, I became a helicopter mother—hovering, cautious, overprotective.

When Thomas was two months old, I noticed that his left foot curved inward and I rushed him to the pediatrician. Dr. D had taken care of Thomas's older sisters since birth. He knew we'd lost Robbie.

"Something's wrong with his feet," I said. "What if he can't walk?"

Dr. D held Thomas over the examining table, his bare legs dangling beneath his diaper. Touching my son's tiny ankles, he placed each foot in the palms of his hands.

Love is a scary thing. I'm afraid to be his mother. Could God really be good enough to give us another baby who's okay?

"Julie, there's nothing wrong with his feet. He'll be running before you know it." He handed me my baby boy. "Relax. You're a good mama. It's going to be fine this time."

His words went straight to my nervous-worried-mama heart. I knew he'd spoken the truth. Instantly my fear shifted into place, trusting in God's goodness.

P.S. Thomas turns twenty-seven this year. He runs a mile in under six minutes and wears a size eleven-and-a-half shoe.

You are good, all the time, Lord. All the time, You are good.
—Julie Garmon

Digging Deeper: Psalms 31:19, 107:1

Friday, August 24

Jesus said, "Let the little children come to me, and do not hinder them, for the kingdom of heaven belongs to such as these." —Matthew 19:14 (NIV)

I looked at the text message twice to make sure I'd read it correctly. My "shero" had just passed away. This amazing woman was a brilliant psychologist, an expert in the adoption and foster care world. I had never met Karyn personally, but her writings, conferences, and methodologies for caring for at-risk children had been invaluable in my life after having adopted two of my four children. I felt like I'd lost a mentor and friend.

Wiping my tears, I considered how I could honor her legacy. How could I continue the work she'd begun in the field of child welfare? After thinking and praying for answers, I began writing an e-mail message to the director of a local adoption agency. I offered volunteer hours, specifically for a program that serves families in crisis and has found great success in preventing children from going into the foster care system.

When I pressed Send, I could feel God's approval. I knew this would have made my mentor proud. I knew she would be overjoyed to see her protégées seeking ways to serve vulnerable children. I imagine her in heaven now, passing on the ministry baton to all of the child advocates here on earth.

I have no idea how many days I'll be given here on this side of heaven. I don't know when I'll live my last day. What I do know is this: I want to spend my days serving at-risk children in desperate need of safety, care, and love. It's the least I can do to honor this wonderful woman's work. It's the least I can do for God.

Lord, give me the desire and strength to love and serve the least of these, honoring the legacies of those who have gone before me.
—Carla Hendricks

Digging Deeper: Proverbs 19:17; Matthew 25:39–45

Let love be your guide.... —Ephesians 5:2 (CEV)

I paused in the grocery aisle to scratch the nearly four-inch-long jagged wound from the recent surgery I'd had on my broken arm. I sighed, then pushed the cart toward the meat case while my mind tumbled over the encounter I'd had with Katie at church earlier today. Katie had special needs and I'd been trying to reach out to her for weeks. Sometimes she'd joyfully give me a hug and would welcome conversations. But today, she seemed to have crawled deeply into a shell that served as a fortress to keep everyone out—even me. Her rejection hurt my feelings.

Steering the cart between a couple of people, I parked next to the meat case and reached for a package of hot dogs on the top shelf. When I did, my sleeve slipped toward my elbow, revealing the lesion, which puckered with stitches and scabs—and still had lines of blue permanent marker that the surgeon had drawn to guide his incision. The woman next to me gasped.

I put the hot dogs in my basket and chuckled to myself. *Lady, if you think that looks bad, you should have seen that scar a few weeks ago. You have no idea how far I've come.*

And that's when it hit me: in my desire to help Katie, I had forgotten how far she has come. I might not always see changes in her, but healing is happening. She hasn't given up and neither should I.

> *Lord, help me to have faith in the profound effect*
> *of Your love. Amen.*
> —Rebecca Ondov

Digging Deeper: Romans 12:10, 13:8

Sunday, August 26

Carry each other's burdens, and in this way you will fulfill the law of Christ. —Galatians 6:2 (NIV)

I should remember this!" she complains.

"I can't log into Facebook," my eighty-eight-year-old mother said. "I've tried for four hours."

"Okay, take a breath," I replied. "We're coming over for a visit tomorrow. I'll see what I can do then."

"I don't want to waste our visit fighting with the computer."

"I'm sure it won't take four hours to figure out. Don't worry." I said that with more confidence than I felt because I'm no good at teaching Mom what to do.

My son and husband and I had a lovely visit with her the following day. Dinner was delicious, and we laughed a lot. It was getting to be time to go so my husband asked, "Shall we take a quick look at your Facebook account?"

"Oh, there isn't really time now," Mom said.

"Let's take a look anyway," he coaxed.

Mom pulled out her tablet and he quizzed her a little on what she'd been doing. My twenty-something son got into the act too. With the tablet between them, they sat there working on the problem, maybe fifteen minutes, and they figured out how to get Mom into her account.

Then they went a step further. They shut it all down and watched as she opened up the application and got herself back in. Mom nearly cried and so did I. My guys helped Mom without making her feel stupid. They cared about her and wanted her to feel at home in the tech world.

Lord, let me be willing to carry any shape of burden
for another today with a gentle heart. Amen.
—Lisa Bogart

Digging Deeper: Philippians 2:3–4; 1 Timothy 5:1–3

For whosoever shall give you a cup of water to drink in my name, because ye belong to Christ, verily I say unto you, he shall not lose his reward.
—Mark 9:41 (KJV)

What started as a time-saver has become an integral part of my hospitality ministry.

At my church, I often help to prepare refreshments for funeral receptions. Our experienced team seamlessly provides food (hot and cold), beverages, and even fresh flowers for the tables. Of course, we rarely know ahead of time how many people we will serve, so we estimate to the nearest twenty-five, usually accurately.

This sultry summer afternoon, we're prepared for a funeral party of about two hundred. Two tables hold platters of veggies and dip, sandwiches, grapes, and cheese. Another table holds desserts, and yet another the coffee and tea. I set up a fifth table, just for iced lemon water, to avoid a bottleneck at the beverage service. To save time before the capacity crowd arrives, I pour the water to have a dozen filled glasses sitting on a tray, so no one has to wait.

The wife of the deceased approaches me with trembling smile and red eyes. I spontaneously hand her a glass and offer a smile and condolences. She effuses thanks. It seems so natural then to hand glasses to the next guests, too, instead of leaving them to serve themselves.

Suddenly, I understand. This is no time for brisk efficiency. Rather, this is the time for human touch and connection. On this difficult day, the buffet eases physical hunger, but compassion quenches parched souls.

Gracious Lord, may I never underestimate
the healing power of simple kindness.
—Gail Thorell Schilling

Digging Deeper: Luke 10:33; Hebrews 13:2; 1 Peter 3:8

Tuesday, August 28

Blessed are the merciful: for they shall obtain mercy. —Matthew 5:7 (KJV)

A friend of mine no longer drinks alcohol. "It's a good thing I don't drink," she says. "I drank way too much way too often." That's a polite way to say disaster and chaos and danger and smash.

"The thing is I tried to stop. Each time I started again I felt about one inch tall. But I always felt that some great gentle attentiveness was waiting for me with tenderness and patience. The only thing that drove me to stop again and again wasn't sense and reason and court and cost, but that deep feeling that some force, some coherent loving thing, was waiting for me with open arms.

"Use the word *God* if you want. I have grown very leery of words. People begin to think that words define or explain things that they can't come anywhere close to explaining or understanding. *God* is one of those words. *Love* is another. But I felt that patient relentless mercy very powerfully. I felt it waiting for me to finally stop and stay stopped.

"*Miracle* is another word we throw around, but I am a miracle. I would have gone to prison, or died, or both. I couldn't have stopped without that patient tender mercy being there. I wake up every day and talk to the mercy. I ask for help.

"Everyone wants to explain or dismiss miracles, and my attitude is why not just enjoy the fact that such things happen all day, every day, everywhere in the world? Why get fussy about the words for it? Why argue about other people's words for it?

"There was some endlessly patient unquenchable tenderness there for me. Believe me, I know what I am talking about."

> *Dear Mercy, not just her but me and we? Lend us*
> *Your mercy moment by moment so that we can learn to share it, too,*
> *profligately, unthinkingly, unstintingly.*
> —Brian Doyle

Digging Deeper: Matthew 9:13; Luke 6:36

Know this, my beloved brothers: let every person be quick to hear,
slow to speak, slow to anger; for the anger of man does not produce
the righteousness of God. —James 1:19–20 (ESV)

I had the best intentions. Really, I did.
I wanted to hold up my friend in love, to do the right thing, to
help in the right way. I wanted to support her when she needed support. To be there when she needed a friend.

But I really botched it.

While my heart had been in the right place, my actions surely weren't.
Words were said that shouldn't have been said and those words flew
into rumors, making their way through our community. Reputations
were scarred. Friendships grew awkward. And days were lost in a whir
of he-said, she-said, and I-don't-know-what-to-say.

But then she broke the ice.

"Erin, we have to repair this. Let's talk. Let's fix it."

And so we did. Over steaming cups of tea in a cluttered living room,
we shared our feelings, our thoughts, our intentions, our hopes. We
worked through. We understood. We stretched. We forgave.

God is infinitely faithful to us. He forgives when we don't deserve it.
He listens when we cry out. He lets go when we need grace.

We must do the same for our friends, for those perfectly imperfect
people whom we love, the ones who hurt us, who scar us, who do those
things that cause so much pain on days when we just need mercy.

We must love when we don't want to. And forgive without hesitation.

Father God, thank You for forgiving me when I don't deserve it and
for giving me friends who are willing to do the same. Help me
to forgive and to love like You do. Amen.
—Erin MacPherson

Digging Deeper: Ephesians 4:15–16; James 5:16

Thursday, August 30

I prayed to the Lord, and he answered me. He freed me from all my fears. —Psalm 34:4 (NLT)

I'm ready to start middle school." Micah held her new backpack filled with notebooks, binders, and a pencil bag.

But I wasn't. My mind churned with apprehension. *Could she find the right classroom when they rotated? Would she remember her locker number? Would she find kind friends? How could she manage the homework? What if she was exposed to peer pressure?*

Maybe I was overprotective and letting my own experiences color how I felt. Growing up, I was the "new kid" at school seven times before I went to college. Walking the halls of Sapulpa Junior High, I felt small and insignificant trying to find my classrooms. When I forgot my locker combination, I was too embarrassed to say anything. I lugged around a stack of books for weeks.

Luckily, Micah wasn't shy like me. She knew most of the students in her class. Still, I worried that no one would be there to help her.

The afternoon before the first day of school, another mother e-mailed me. "Meet tonight in front of the school to pray before the new year begins."

That evening, I circled up with five moms on the sidewalk in front of the middle school building. We closed our eyes. Peace replaced my anxiety as I poured out my fears to God. I wanted my child to be protected and I couldn't be there to do it. But God could. He was more capable than any of us moms.

Micah was ready to start middle school. So was I, thanks to my back-to-school group prayer reminder.

> *Lord, help me to remember that my school assignment is*
> *a mother's prayer for her child every day.*
> —Stephanie Thompson

Digging Deeper: Isaiah 41:10; Philippians 4:6–7

And whatever you do, whether in word or in deed, do it all in the name of the Lord Jesus, giving thanks to God the Father through him.
—Colossians 3:17 (NIV)

I spent the summer working in the garden center of a home improvement store, which was frustrating, considering that I had just finished my theology degree and had been accepted to law school. I wanted to do something important, consequential—not stack bags of mulch and organize plants.

"Logan, there's a woman by the patio pavers looking for you," my walkie-talkie warbled.

I headed in that direction, and a woman who came by the store regularly waved at me.

"I wondered when you would come by," I said. "I've missed you this week. Twenty of the red pavers?"

She smiled and nodded; she didn't speak much English.

"I'll grab these for you, then meet you out front like usual."

She nodded again, and I loaded a flat cart with the bricks and rolled them toward the curb.

The woman pulled up her car and popped open the trunk. I positioned the bricks so that she could easily remove them when she got home. As I slid the last one in, something tugged on the pocket of my cargo shorts. I turned around to see her withdrawing her hand.

"I ask for you because you're a gentleman," she said and got in her car and drove off.

I reached into my pocket and pulled out a tightly folded bill. As I ran my thumb over the crease, I thought of my wish to have an impact on people's lives, how unimportant I had felt my job was, and how every activity I do is an opportunity to let goodness shine through me.

> *Lord, let my actions—big and small—reflect Your love.*
> —Logan Eliasen

Digging Deeper: Matthew 5:16; 1 Corinthians 3:16

GOD'S UNFAILING LOVE

1 _____

2 _____

3 _____

4 _____

5 _____

6 _____

7 _____

8 _____

9 _____

10 _____

11 _____

12 _____

13 _____

14 _____

15 _____

16 _____

17 _____

18 _____

19 _____

20 _____

21 _____

22 _____

23 _____

24 _____

25 _____

26 _____

27 _____

28 _____

29 _____

30 _____

31 _____

SEPTEMBER

*Beloved, let us love one another, for love
is from God, and whoever loves has been
born of God and knows God.*

—1 John 4:7 (ESV)

For now we see through a glass, darkly....—1 Corinthians 13:12 (KJV)

My little nephew Stewart is so cute I can hardly stand it. Adorable as an infant, he became even cuter when he turned two and developed his unique personality. He's a natural-born comedian and keeps us all in stitches with the funny things he says, but it's when he's serious that he comes up with some of his best lines.

For my mother-in-law's birthday gift, we made a video of all the kids. At the birthday party, everyone was enjoying the show, oohing and aahing over all nine of the grandchildren as each took his or her turn offering good wishes. Stewart was in the room while the video played on the TV screen, but he was too busy playing with his little cars and trucks to be bothered with watching the show.

"Stewart," my sister-in-law said when he appeared in the video. "Look! Who's that sweet baby on the TV?"

Stewart looked at the screen for a moment, puzzled...then boldly proclaimed, "I want my face back." It wasn't a tantrum, just a simple declaration based on his perception of events.

Such toddler logic makes for an entertaining anecdote, though I couldn't help but consider the spiritual significance. Stewart was making sense of his world in the best way he knew how...just as we all do. When I think of the many things I don't understand, the many ways I misinterpret or even completely miss what God wants to show me—all the times when I've questioned Him about the negatives instead of noticing the positives, all the times He's had a much better plan than what I have in mind—I realize I'm not so different from my little nephew. Sometimes when God says to me, "Look!" all I can think about is wanting my face back.

Father, help me to remember that there is so much I still don't understand. And thank You for the often startling wisdom that comes from children.
—Ginger Rue

Digging Deeper: Proverbs 2:2–5, 3:5

Sunday, September 2

"Watch out! Be on your guard against all kinds of greed...."
—Luke 12:15 (NIV)

Afternoon sunlight seeped through stained glass, casting pastel shadows on the church walls. The ethereal soprano soared above the choir and organ with her "Gloria" during this special service of evensong. The sanctuary filled with soul-stirring music, but all I could think of were the cookies at the reception to follow.

Perhaps if I had eaten a more filling lunch, I could have staved off my hunger and more fully entered into the spirit of worship instead of thinking about lemon squares. Time and again, my mind drifted from the liturgy to treats already amassing when I had dropped off my strawberries and madeleines.

"Amen." *Over. Cookies!*

I didn't exactly elbow folks out of my way, but I moved right along to the reception. The lavish spread covered four long tables. My paper plate was small but it would do. A few cashews and a deviled egg—good protein. Perfect strawberries, grapes. Chips. Salsa. *Aha!* There are the lemon squares. My plate flexed slightly. Maybe a cup of this punch could support it.

Then I spied the shortbread dipped in chocolate. As I placed it on my teetering mound and turned for just one more, my cookies began to slide off my plate and smash at my feet. When I knelt to wipe up the mess, chips and cashews cascaded to the floor. Red-faced, I slunk off into a corner with what remained of my plate, but I had lost my appetite and slipped out of the hall without eating.

Since that embarrassing episode, I now stick with single layers of treats—and second helpings of self-discipline.

> *Father of plenty, forgive me when I take more than I need.*
> *Teach me to savor what I have.*
> —Gail Thorell Schilling

Digging Deeper: Job 23:12; Proverbs 23:20–21; Zechariah 7:4–6; Luke 12:15–21; Philippians 3:19

So we have not stopped praying for you since we first heard about you....
All the while, you will grow as you learn to know God better and better.
—Colossians 1:9–10 (NLT)

My phone rang at work the other morning. My wife, Julee. She was close to tears.

"She destroyed another pillow," Julee said. "There were feathers all over the living room. It looked like a hurricane hit a chicken coop."

I knew how she felt. Among the items Gracie, our adorable young golden retriever, has gleefully masticated are a number of TV remotes. Just that weekend I spent half of my Saturday waiting for the cable guy to show up so he could replace two more remotes that Gracie had attacked.

Gracie is as sweet and playful a dog as you will ever meet. But left to her own devices (I know, I know), Gracie will gnaw on almost anything—remotes, phone chargers, credit cards, cell phones, rugs, gloves, a shower curtain.

"When will she grow out of this?" Julee wailed before hanging up. I'd asked the Lord that same question, many times.

I got home that night and took Gracie to the park. I talk to my dogs, and I talked to her about my worries over her chewing. We found a bench and I invited her up. With a seventy-five-pound puppy sprawled across my lap, I sat there speaking and gesturing quite earnestly. Perhaps I looked crazy.

Suddenly, Gracie jumped up. I saw what she saw—one of those Styrofoam clamshell boxes that sandwiches come in. She tore off in its direction, me after her. All at once she veered away and fell upon a stick, taking it in her mouth and rolling happily on her back. A stick. This was progress! And a reminder: dogs do grow up eventually. We all do.

Father, all my life You have helped me grow up and out of temptation.
I know You will help Gracie because I know You love all Your creatures.
—Edward Grinnan

Digging Deeper: 2 Corinthians 9:6–10; 2 Peter 3:18

Tuesday, September 4

"Give us today our daily bread."—Matthew 6:11 (NIV)

I was complaining to my husband one day about the rising cost of groceries. "When I was a teenager, I worked as a checker at a grocery. A big brown paper bag full of groceries only cost around five dollars. Now when I go to the store I can barely fill one bag for under fifty dollars."

Not long after, I came across a receipt in an old photo album of my dad's. In January 1907, a man by the name of C. R. Aldrich sold his farm in Tampico, Illinois, to my grandfather, Henry Sebastian Kobbeman, for $92.50 an acre. In 1932, during the Depression, my grandfather lost the farm because corn was selling for only eight cents a bushel and he couldn't even pay the interest on the mortgage. Today that same land is worth over $14,000 an acre and few farmers can afford to buy land to grow crops.

Learning how my grandfather lost his farm and seeing how prices have changed in my lifetime helped me to understand the high cost of my groceries. I began to appreciate everyone—from the farmer to the food processor, the packager, and the people working in my local grocery.

Now, instead of complaining about the cost of groceries, I try to be more aware of how many people it actually takes to put a meal on my table. I also added a line to our daily prayer before meals: "Bless the farmers and all the workers who struggle financially to provide food for us."

Lord, keep me from becoming an old curmudgeon and
remind me daily of all the people who make
the wheels of my life turn perfectly.
—Patricia Lorenz

Digging Deeper: Psalms 145:13–16; Jude 1:16

FALLING INTO GRACE: Greater Trust in God's Plan

Rend your hearts and not your clothing. Return to the Lord your God, for he is gracious and merciful, slow to anger, and abounding in steadfast love, and relents from punishing. —Joel 2:13 (NRSV)

Everyone had advice. "Find a chiropractor. Smartest move I ever made." "Try this pain reliever. I couldn't get through a day without it." "Physical therapy is the answer." "Stretching exercises work for me."

I couldn't pretend any longer that this new pain didn't exist or that I had just stepped off a curb the wrong way. I felt it in my left side and leg. Friends said it was because I'd been off-kilter for so long after my fall that my body was misaligned, and now that I was resuming a relatively normal routine I was feeling pain associated with my body overcompensating for my injuries.

My spirits plummeted. Just when I was starting to feel good, I hit this obstacle. This was not the outcome I wanted.

But then I encountered Mother Teresa on my way down this path of self-pity and desolation. I read an article about her diary, which revealed that she had often struggled with feeling separated from God. After dedicating her whole life to doing God's work, she still felt bereft of Him. Surely that was not the outcome she wanted either, and yet it was the outcome she accepted as part of His plan for her. She didn't give up or feel resentment. She struggled on, never flagging in her commitment.

I know I'm no Mother Teresa, but it did occur to me that learning this about her at the very time I was struggling was part of the Lord's plan for me. And it helped me to step off the path of despair. I could at least wait beside the road and take comfort in knowing I was not alone.

Lord, forgive my stubbornness as You lead me to trust in You.
—Marci Alborghetti

Digging Deeper: Job 40:3–5; Ephesians 3:14–21

Thursday, September 6

*Whoever is patient has great understanding.... —*Proverbs 14:29 (NIV)

Ticktock. Putting away the dishes, I notice the sound of the cuckoo clock beside me. Another challenging morning, after the long summer vacation, proved to be an exercise in patience. Finding backpacks, packing lunch boxes, and remembering homework were all habits we'd easily cast aside, and now we found ourselves stressed, simply trying to get back into the routine.

This morning one of Henry's library books went missing, and a frantic search left the living room a mess, couch cushions misplaced, the contents from the shelf beneath the coffee table spread out on the carpet. All that chaos, and the book was exactly where it should have been—tucked safely in his backpack.

Ticktock, and the maiden on a swing goes back and forth. It was over a decade ago when I spotted the small clock in a shop window while we were on vacation in Vermont. I mentioned to my husband how I adored it, but the store was closed and we were only visiting the town for a day, so I forgot all about it until my birthday came months later. And there it was—the cuckoo clock.

Tony explained how he went back to the store later that day without my noticing. I was amazed at his patience. How had he kept this great gift a secret? So unlike me—I can't wait to share a perfect present, and here he'd managed to save it for just the right time.

Ticktock. I feel myself shift from stressed to blessed.

> *Dear Lord, when the chaos of family life overwhelms me,*
> *guide me to my blessings and help me to remember*
> *that love is patient.*
> —Sabra Ciancanelli

Digging Deeper: Romans 8:25; Galatians 6:9

"Follow me, and I will make you become fishers of men." —Mark 1:17 (ESV)

As a professor, I often say to Mercer University students, "One thing more important than an academic degree is to know an experienced mentor who encourages and teaches you to become your *best self.*" Dr. Bill Hale was such a mentor for me.

I met Bill Hale forty years ago when I graduated from seminary and became the Associate Pastor of the First Baptist Church of Athens, Georgia. The home of the University of Georgia, this vital community is filled with creative people. On our first Sunday at First Baptist Church, Bill Hale greeted Beth and me with a big smile and an enthusiastic handshake.

I didn't realize it, but on that first Sunday so long ago, Bill made a quiet commitment to be my friend and mentor. When I preached, he often invited me to coffee to discuss my sermon. Together we planned youth retreats, chaperoned mission trips, taught college student seminars, and spent hours discussing theology and life in general. Later, Bill served on my dissertation committee as I completed my doctoral studies at the University of Georgia. He challenged me to strive to be *my best self!*

Bill died recently, having remained active and "full of himself" until his mideighties. When his son, Billy, called to tell me that his father "had gone home," I wept and rejoiced at the same time. And then I blurted, "Billy, what am I going to do? Your father was my last living mentor!" Billy quickly shot back, "Well, Scott, I'll tell you what you're going to do. This means it's your turn now! It's your turn to be a mentor too! Daddy taught you how. Now go do it!"

Father, may I be a mentor to people You bring my way. Amen.
—Scott Walker

Digging Deeper: Philippians 4:9; Hebrews 13:7

Saturday, September 8

But Jesus beheld them, and said unto them, "With men this is impossible; but with God all things are possible." —Matthew 19:26 (KJV)

I was retiring from my nursing job of thirty-eight years, embarking on the "second act" of my life. At long last, I'd get to do what I enjoy on *my* terms.

The only thing I needed was a more dependable vehicle. Make that a dependable vehicle on a limited budget. "Lord, please help me find a low-mileage car in great condition for a great price," I prayed every day as my retirement approached. "Something a little old lady has just driven to the post office."

Then one Saturday morning, my sister suggested we drive to an estate sale in a town we'd never visited. The address sounded like it was way out in the country and would take forever to find. I plain didn't want to go. But armed with the GPS, we were on our way.

Word was that the woman who lived there had been diagnosed with early Alzheimer's disease and was now residing in a nursing home. The man conducting the sale said to me: "I know you're not looking for a car, Roberta, but if you were, I have an incredible deal out in the garage. And the price gets reduced a thousand dollars in ten minutes." He then added words that sent a chill up my spine. "Hard to believe, but it only has nineteen thousand miles on it. The woman just drove that baby to the post office."

Later, when I picked up the car, there was a golden placard hanging on the rearview mirror. On it were the words from Matthew 19:26: "With God, all things are possible."

Thank You, Lord, for incredible people who remember You during difficult transitions.
—Roberta Messner

Digging Deeper: Luke 1:37; Philippians 4:13

There remains, then, a Sabbath-rest for the people of God; for anyone who enters God's rest also rests from his own work, just as God did from his. —Hebrews 4:9–10 (NIV)

"Yᴏu're kidding me, right?"

The well-dressed Realtor stood at my door, shaking his head and staring at his toes. The silver SUV behind him sat running, with two passengers leafing through papers.

"No, I'm sorry," he said. "They decided not to come in. They didn't like the location."

The potential buyers were already late. Hours of staging. Another hour of waiting. Numerous prayers. And they didn't have the courtesy to even walk through our home!

The Realtor apologized again. "Your house really is incredible," he said. He turned and drove off.

Anyone with a house for sale understands the work of preparing for a showing. This work was for nothing. As I dialed my wife, I sensed a whisper from heaven. *Bill, in your relationship with Me, the work has already been done.*

I'd gotten myself into a trap. Prayer, Bible study, service, activity for Jesus, imagining I could somehow buy the blessing of a fast house sale from Him. In that disappointing moment, God reminded me that His blessings are not for sale. They are neither paychecks for service, nor rewards for good behavior. They are, rather, gifts of grace, paid in full by my precious Savior and His finished work.

Why was I laboring so anxiously to obtain a blessing that God would freely give?

We still work to stage our house for showings. But our hearts are at rest in God, knowing with Him the labor is already done.

Gracious Lord, teach me to rest my weary heart in Your never-failing love.
                        —Bill Giovannetti

Digging Deeper: Matthew 11:28–29

Monday, September 10

First of all, then, I ask that requests, prayers, petitions, and thanksgiving be made for all people. —1 Timothy 2:1 (CEB)

I'd been thinking all week about a prayer request that came to Guideposts. "Pray for everyone," it said. We did that on Monday morning when we gathered for prayer but I'd been mulling it over ever since. Pray for everyone...for what? Anything specific?

Friday at midday, I was heading out of the glass door of our offices on the ninth floor when I intercepted a delivery man. "Would you sign for this?" he asked. "Sure," I said. I scribbled my name on the dotted line and was ready to take the package back inside, when the young man paused and I paused, my foot holding the glass door open.

"Are you a Christian?" he asked.

"Yes," I said. "I try to be."

He stood silent for a long while, struggling for words. "I have faith," he said.

"I'm glad." *What did he want?* "Would you like some copies of our magazines?" I gestured to the stack by the door.

"I've taken some already." Clearly there was something else on his mind. He paused for a while longer, then asked, "Would you pray for me?"

"Sure," I said. "We gather to pray for others every Monday morning. What would you like us to pray for? A stronger faith?" Maybe that was it.

"My faith is strong," he said, choosing his words very carefully. "I would just like to have...less unbelief."

"What's your name?"

"Matthew," he said.

"I'm Rick," I said. "We'll pray for that." *Less unbelief.* What a profound thought. I couldn't think of two better words for prayer. For me, for Matthew, for everyone.

You put us together in community, Lord, to draw on each other for strength.
—Rick Hamlin

Digging Deeper: Mark 9:24; Philippians 2:3–4

"Let your light shine...."—Matthew 5:16 (NIV)

I don't see what difference it makes," our granddaughter Abby argued with her mother. "Nobody cares whether or not I eat in the school cafeteria."

The Nashville public school system had adopted a new policy. To avoid singling out the children who were on the free lunch program, lunch would, instead, be free to all students.

Keri, Abby's mother, felt strongly that this sort of equality was important. Abby should not set herself apart by bringing tasty, more attractive lunches.

"One person doesn't matter," Abby argued.

The next weekend I encouraged Abby to attend a gathering with me. Once there, I made sure she sat near a sweet soul named Claudia. As dinner was served, I said, "Claudia, would you tell Abby your lunchroom story?"

Soon, Abby was taken back to the time when Tennessee schools didn't provide food. Claudia arrived at school every morning with a packed lunch. But soon she noticed that when noon came, several of her friends had nothing to eat.

So Claudia went on strike. She refused to eat the lunches her mother provided. Day by day, her parents became more upset, but Claudia stood her ground. Finally, her father was moved to go to the local school board. Because of one little girl, a school lunch program for all the children in the county was organized.

"So what do you think about Claudia's story?" I asked.

"Oh, Mimi," she answered, "I get it. One person does matter. And not just the lunch thing.

"Standing up to bullies and being nice to kids who are shy or lonely or different. I want to matter just like Claudia."

And so do I, Abby. So do I.

> *Father, show us Your way... a way that matters.*
> —Pam Kidd

Digging Deeper: Psalm 143:10; John 13:15; Hebrews 10:24

Wednesday, September 12

"And you will know the truth, and the truth will set you free."
—John 8:32 (TLB)

"Mom," came the call from the living room, "buried treasure! In the wall!"

I've lived with pirates for years. When the boys were smaller, their bunk bed was a mighty ship. I was Mama Red, and Gabriel, after an unfortunate tumble, was Captain Ghost Tooth. Isaiah was Oceanus, named after a pilgrim-babe, not a pirate, though he didn't mind. Eventually, the ship stilled, but the pirates remained.

I found my sons fast.

"Look," ten-year-old Gabriel said. He knelt in front of the fireplace and removed a loose tile. "We can slip our money in here." Isaiah stood beside his big brother, green eyes shining with pirate pride. "What do you think?" Gabriel asked.

I nodded and decided that a life with pirates was the sweetest under the sun. But I also began to think about what we hold dear. For my pirates, it was a few dollars tucked away. For me, it was God's living Word, hidden in my heart.

As a mother, I'm still working through tough times. A son wrestles to believe God's promises, and the reality scrapes my own soul. God's been faithful to speak to me, though. When I turn to His Word, He offers hope. When I commit truth to memory and hold it to circumstance, the hope sustains me. Standing there with my sons, I was suddenly thankful that when worry comes strong, the Spirit brings Scripture to the surface. It's light that dispels darkness. It brings peace to panic and faith to fear.

Soon there were footfalls. As my boys bolted to make a map, I prayed that one day their treasure would be God's Word too.

> *Lord, help me to hold Your Word in mind and heart. Amen.*
> —Shawnelle Eliasen

Digging Deeper: Psalm 1:2–3; Matthew 4:4; John 17:17

He forgives all my sins and heals all my diseases. —Psalm 103:3 (GNT)

I have healed beautifully from a six-hour surgery to remove a benign lump from my left jaw. There is not the slightest scar.

Watching my face heal reminded me of other illnesses I have survived, starting in childhood: mumps and measles, chicken pox and whooping cough, strep and flu, and a rare blood disease that almost took my life in the first grade.

I look at my arms and hands. From a lifetime of working on cars and pruning trees, my arms have been bruised, burned, lacerated, punctured, crushed, sprained, and sliced to the bone many times over. Yet my arms look about as smooth and clean as they did fifty years ago.

How clever of God to give us smart bodies with a self-healing app installed at birth!

The wounds that bother me most, however, are the invisible wounds of the heart. Times when I was crushed by harsh criticism from bullies at school. Even worse is the shame I feel over my own careless words that hurt the people I love the most.

"That's where God's grace comes in," my daughter Natalie reminds me.

"I know, and I'm grateful, but I would rather I had never said those things."

"Don't we all," she says laughing. "But you learned something from your mistakes, and that's important."

I look again at my arms. They are still strong and useful, after all the insults they have endured; and if my heart looks as good as they do, it's only because of God's healing grace.

I thank You, Father, for healing me within and without so that
I might continue to be strong and useful to those who depend on me.
—Daniel Schantz

Digging Deeper: Psalm 131; 2 Corinthians 12:8–9

Friday, September 14

The Lord said to him, "Who gave human beings their mouths? Who makes them deaf or mute? Who gives them sight or makes them blind? Is it not I, the Lord? Now go; I will help you speak and will teach you what to say." —Exodus 4:11–12 (NIV)

It's my first semester of law school. The lecture hall is stifling because of the seventy students crammed into it. I lean over my casebook, highlighter cap between my teeth, and I strike the text with neon blue.

"Let's take a look at the dissent," the professor says. "Why don't you walk us through the argument, Mr. Eliasen?"

The cap falls from my mouth. My face burns. It's not that I'm unprepared. I read the case three times last night. But I'm a quiet person, and seventy sets of eyes are on me now.

I'm humble; it's one of my better qualities. But sometimes our greatest strengths don't dwell far from our deepest weaknesses. My humility borders a place where feelings of inadequacy lurk and I can sense those thoughts in the back of my mind: *You're too quiet. You don't have anything worth saying. You're not a speaker.*

Then I think of Moses. The man who stood before the fiery presence of God and explained that he was too terrified to speak to a human king.

"I will teach you what to say," promised God.

I flip the pages of my casebook and then clear my throat. I'm ready to reject my fear of inadequacy. I'm ready to claim God's promise.

> *Father, I'm so grateful that I can trust You*
> *to fill my mouth with words.*
> —Logan Eliasen

Digging Deeper: Jeremiah 1:6–8; Luke 12:11–12

Therefore if anyone is in Christ, the new creation has come. The old has gone, the new is here! —2 Corinthians 5:17 (NIV)

It was a hectic Saturday at the events center. I'd stopped by to drop off a deposit to reserve one of the reception rooms. There was a line of people waiting to speak with the receptionist when I arrived. A florist wheeled in a cart filled with flower arrangements and asked where to leave them for the wedding scheduled in a few hours. The young girl at the reception desk looked harried. She was on the phone with what was probably a difficult customer.

She looked up and abruptly snapped at the florist. "Look," she said, "I don't have time to get with you right now. The owner is on her way. You'll have to wait." She turned her back to finish her phone conversation.

Those of us in line looked at one another in disbelief at the curtness of the receptionist. The florist replied with an understanding smile, "No problem. I can wait."

The receptionist finished her call. The florist asked her, "Would it be okay to place the flowers over here in the meantime?"

"I suppose so," she replied curtly. The florist rolled her cart over to a spot out of the way and busied herself with a few last-minute tweaks to her arrangements.

At church the next day, my pastor spoke of the empowering love of Jesus that allows us to live as Christ did and to embrace those less perfect with compassion and understanding. *That's a tall order,* I thought. But then I recalled the kindness and compassion of the florist. She had been a role model for Jesus, showing only love and compassion.

> *Dear Jesus, I want to know You so completely that*
> *when people see me, they see You in me.*
> —Melody Bonnette Swang

Digging Deeper: John 13:34–35; 1 John 2:9–10

Sunday, September 16

But you, O Lord, are a God merciful and gracious, slow to anger and abounding in steadfast love and faithfulness. —Psalm 86:15 (ESV)

Yes, the Lord is slow to anger and abounding in steadfast love and faithfulness, but I am not.

Why? you might ask.

Well, because there is a slab of kitchen countertop in my living room.

It's been there for nine months, twenty-four days, and seven hours to be exact. Not that I'm counting. But that's how long it has been since we began the home-improvement project to renovate our attic into a home office. That's how long I've been working out of my bedroom. That's how long all of the boxes and bookshelves and tidbits from the attic have been sitting in the hallway.

It all started when the contractor's bid for the project came back at twelve thousand dollars and, in a moment of panic, my husband said the nine most terrifying words a woman can hear: "I think I can do it myself for less."

I should have said no. I should have started saving up that twelve thousand dollars. I should have reminded him that my steadfast love and faithfulness has a breaking point, and that point likely coincides with the 322nd time I stub my toe.

But I didn't. I said, "Give it a try." And the next day I found myself living in a construction zone.

Needless to say, I've been a tiny bit impatient about this whole thing. And last night I lost it. I screamed, "If I have to see that countertop just one more moment, I am going to lose my marbles!"

Cameron looked at me calmly and said, "Oh, why didn't you tell me it was bothering you? I'll move it into the garage."

And he did.

Lord, help me to be more Christlike in everything I do, even when things
don't happen the way I expect them to. Amen.
—Erin MacPherson

Digging Deeper: Colossians 1:11–12; 2 Peter 3:9

CONFIDENCE IN DIFFICULTY: Led by a Sovereign Teacher

"But the Advocate, the Holy Spirit, whom the Father will send in my name, will teach you all things...."—John 14:26 (NIV)

My son John came in from walking the dog. "We have an audience in the hallway," he said drily. That wasn't surprising: his sister Maggie was blisteringly angry, bellowing threats. The doctor in Connecticut had sent her home after two days, suggesting she attend a therapeutic wilderness program instead. "She's had a traumatic hospital experience and will do better in a different kind of setting. It will only take a couple of days to get in," he advised, "and she's psychiatrically stable."

Except she was not stable, as we—and now our neighbors—knew. I was applying four self-reminders I'd learned in twelve years of managing John's mood swings and anxiety to keep from having to call 911.

1. Nothing good comes from getting stressed.
2. Respond to Maggie's feelings instead of reacting to her tone and behavior.
3. Pray before speaking: "Holy Spirit, guide my words."
4. Stay focused. Ignore the gawkers, embarrassment, and fear.

I did all this, yet things were getting scary. "Holy Spirit, show me how," I pleaded in a split second between eruptions. On cue, I remembered I was hearing the illness talking, not my daughter.

Almost imperceptibly, the tide began to turn. I listened better, responded better, focused better. After more than an hour of intense effort, Maggie's rage tapered off.

I breathed out a silent thank-you and thought back to the years when John's mood swings and anxiety had caused our family so much distress. I could see now that something else had happened during that time: I'd been prepared for surviving today.

Thank You, Lord, for every hard lesson I never wanted to learn.
—Julia Attaway

Digging Deeper: Psalm 119:77; 2 Corinthians 12:10

Tuesday, September 18

"Do not fear them, for it is the Lord your God who will battle for you."
—Deuteronomy 3:22 (JPS)

I am uneasy about things with more than four legs, so I have always run away when confronted by spiders. I know they serve a purpose in the great scheme of things, but I'm much more comfortable when they're serving that purpose someplace I'm not. My husband, Keith, understood. All I had to do was yell, "Spider!" and he would come to my rescue.

After Keith died, I learned to do a lot of things that he used to take care of: trim the blackberry bushes, change lightbulbs in the cathedral ceiling, clean snow off the satellite dish, trap mice. These tasks were easy compared to the first time a spider challenged me. (Throwing things at spiders is not very effective.)

If I could not conquer my fear of spiders, I knew I would always be afraid they would crawl over me at night. And some of our spiders were big enough that even the cat didn't want to have anything to do with them.

I had to make myself get close enough to them to squash them. I still yelled, "Spider!" but now it was a prayer, not a condemnation. I was learning that the only way to conquer the fear was to understand I still had support when I was scared, even if it was invisible, and even if I had to do the active rescuing myself.

Lord, thank You for being there when I face my fears, because
I never have been able to do that without Your encouragement.
—Rhoda Blecker

Digging Deeper: 2 Kings 6:16

Don't jump to conclusions.... —Proverbs 25:8 (MSG)

I glanced at the e-mail announcing a meeting Darcy had put together for a group of us. Once again she'd scheduled it for 3:00 p.m. on Wednesday. I groaned. *She does this every time! She knows I can't come until 3:30.* My mind turned sour. *Could she be doing this on purpose because she doesn't want me there?* My thoughts drifted out the window where the horses stood begging for their morning feeding.

After I tossed flakes of hay in the feeder, Sunrise, my golden retriever, traipsed alongside me as I dragged the hose around the corner of the house to water the garden. My heart sank when I saw a few of the sugar snap pea stems chewed in two, and over the next few days more pea vines disappeared; rodents called voles like my sugar snap peas as much as I do!

Wednesday morning I sat at my computer, wondering if there was a way to get out of the meeting. I peeked out the window and witnessed Sunrise trotting toward the garden. She glanced over her shoulder as if she was looking for me, then slunk in among the peas and chowed down. My jaw dropped. After scolding Sunrise, I shook my head. *Boy, I jumped to conclusions on that one! I never suspected her.*

But that wasn't the only thing I'd jumped to conclusions about. When I walked into the meeting, Darcy looked up and greeted me: "I know that this isn't a good time for you, but I'm glad that you could come. You're one of my favorite people."

> *Lord, please continue to show me when*
> *I jump to wrong conclusions. Amen.*
> —Rebecca Ondov

Digging Deeper: Proverbs 3:7; 1 Corinthians 4:5

Thursday, September 20

"He heaps up riches. . . ." —Psalm 39:6 (NKJV)

"Never let the things you want make you forget the things you have." It was a telltale sign, for sure, posted at a gas station where we stopped for fuel.

My husband and I had been invited by our friend Mike for a tour of the multimillion-dollar megaranch where he worked. We drove through sweeping green fields rimmed with forests. The ranch had a fancy house and a shop that would make a mechanic faint from pure happiness.

"What a beautiful ranch," Randy remarked. "Mike's lucky to work here." The guest cabins and the cow barn, with its dining hall, entertainment room, sale ring, and full kitchen catered to cattle ranchers who came to buy breeding stock. I stared dreamily at the efficient layout of the corrals. We both loved the secluded meadows and lakes. It was enough to dull the sheen off of our own modest ranch.

We drove past a fleet of new tractors that dwarfed our pickup. Randy and I didn't have a fleet. Recently we'd scraped together enough for a used backhoe that we'd needed for years.

"Wouldn't you like to own this place?" we said to each other as we left. But as we nosed the pickup toward home, Randy held my hand. I thought about what Mike had said about the owner: he was divorcing for the fourth time, his kids were suing him, and he didn't have time to come to his own ranch. As if reading my thoughts, Randy said: "We're the lucky ones."

"Yeah," I agreed, "we truly are blessed."

> *Lord, keep reminding me of all the blessings in my own life,*
> *especially when I'm tempted to discount them.*
> —Erika Bentsen

Digging Deeper: Matthew 13:22–23; Luke 12:13–21;
John 6:27; Galatians 5:13; Philippians 3:19

How many are your works, O Lord! In wisdom you made them all; the earth is full of your creatures. —Psalm 104:24 (NIV)

My dogs, Sage and Montana, smile when I scratch their tummies. Their look of bewilderment is clear when I give one a treat before the other. Their delight when we embark on a walk is expressed in barks and gleeful leaps. And their downcast eyes when I leave them behind inflict a twinge of guilt. But their God-planted sensitivities go even further.

Each morning I arise before dawn and let Sage and Montana outside. They bolt into the fields surrounding our home while I head to the coffeemaker. I look through a window as they cavort in the murky light. I chuckle at their antics. But what I enjoy most is their ritual of plopping down on a small hill near our driveway and watching the sunrise together. Most days, just as that golden ball is about to edge up over the horizon, Sage and Montana sit facing east and gaze at the sky just as the sun appears.

The other day I looked at their elevated spot, and it was empty. My eyes searched the fields. Sure enough, there were Sage and Montana, below and to the right of the hillside. They were on their stomachs, paws outstretched, heads alert, eyes on the horizon. From this position, they were better angled to watch the sun's ascension. As the seasons change, the sun's rise gradually shifts from northeast to southeast. Sage and Montana were rotating their front-row seat accordingly.

> *God, it's clear our dogs feel emotion. But to think that
> You instilled in their hearts awe at a sunrise, to realize
> they enjoy its wonder, is pretty amazing.*
> —Kim Henry

Digging Deeper: Genesis 9:16; Psalms 40:5, 145:21

Saturday, September 22

THE BEAUTY OF SIMPLICITY
Taking a Break from Social Media
"You shall have no other gods before me." —Exodus 20:3 (NIV)

I didn't want to admit it, but my cell phone had gotten way too important to me.

As soon as my husband, Rick, and I went to run errands, I whipped out my phone. Sure, I liked keeping up with Facebook, Twitter, and Instagram, but I wasn't addicted to them, or even obsessed with them.

Inside the restaurant, there was a TV in every corner, which meant Rick would have something to do. After we were seated, he glanced at the football game behind my head. The familiar urge came over me. I slipped my phone from my purse.

"Do you realize how much time you spend on your phone?" Rick commented.

"What difference does it make? You're watching the game."

"I checked the score."

Irritated, I put down my phone.

The next morning at church our pastor mentioned that his smartphone had become a huge time drain. He said he was guilty of obsessing over how many "likes" he'd received on a recent status update. I fidgeted in my seat and didn't dare look at my husband.

On the way home, I left my phone in my purse, but it was like having a terrible itch and not scratching. I didn't know what to do with myself.

Two days later a friend called. "Julie, I have a confession to make. I've been spending time on social media rather than living real life."

The truth pricked my heart. "Me too."

"I've decided I've had enough. Now I only check social media twice a day. It feels wonderful. I'm free!"

> *Lord, anything and everything can take Your place,*
> *even social media. I'm sorry. You alone are God.*
> —Julie Garmon

Digging Deeper: Isaiah 26:3; John 8:36; Romans 12:1–2

Let the trees of the forest sing for joy before the Lord.
—1 Chronicles 16:33 (NLT)

There are two sets of trees, one pointing up and the other down. The only imperfection in the forest's mirror image along the shoreline of the St. Lawrence River comes from the ripples that spread when a cormorant lights on the water's surface. The lunch bell is ringing on the small passenger ship I'm sailing on, but I forgo lunch. I can always eat. But I have no idea how long this wing of the Almighty's art gallery will remain open.

The fall foliage paints the river with strokes of copper, canary, russet, and a regal shade of purple I've never seen before on a palette of autumn leaves. With everyone else downstairs in the dining room, the only sound on deck is the click of my camera's shutter.

As pure and sacred as singing "Amazing Grace" or praising God for all of the little ways He lets me know He's near, photography is one of the pursuits I've found where I can worship with childlike abandon. As I play with light and shadow, pattern and perspective, color and contrast, I've developed a habit of whispering a word of thanks, praising God for His handiwork right along with every photo I take.

Whether I'm focused on the changing seasons in Canada, an Arizona sunset viewed from my front porch, or the light in the eyes of someone I love, I can worship God through my lens as well as I can on my knees.

Lord, everywhere I turn, the intricacy, diversity, and creativity
You've woven into this world point toward You, the Almighty Artist
and Creator. Thank You for delighting my heart with
a fresh dose of beauty each and every day.
—Vicki Kuyper

Digging Deeper: Psalm 86:9–10

Monday, September 24

As we have opportunity, let us do good to all people, especially to those who belong to the family of believers. —Galatians 6:10 (NIV)

What just happened? Working on my computer, I simultaneously hit three keys that together provided a shortcut for a long dash. My fingers had made this maneuver a dozen times a day, for years. But this once, my right hand slipped and fell short of its mark. I hit a wrong key and, in a blink, my entire computer screen turned ninety degrees clockwise.

I gasped. I gulped. I stared. But in that moment, when my world turned upside down, I didn't panic. Several age-old coping mechanisms kicked in.

I prayed for guidance. "God, what do I do now?"

Then I posed and answered a question that lingered from my childhood: if my dad were here, what would he do? If he knew a problem's solution was beyond his ken, he'd reach outside of his four walls to a wider network: his church friends, professional colleagues, fix-it neighbors, or local business owners. The community, working together, would usually find answers.

Those were simpler days, some will say. And they're right. Friends are preoccupied and expect us to Google our own questions. We may not feel connected with fellow parishioners or neighbors. We frequent fewer small, friendly mom-and-pop hardware stores or repair shops.

But I went ahead and gave it a try, relying on my personal network. The first friend I called provided a quick fix, giving me three key strokes that set my screen aright. "Oh, Dan, thank you!" I exuded. "If I can ever be of help, let me know. One good turn deserves another."

God, remind us to appreciate and value the networks
that help stabilize our daily lives.
—Evelyn Bence

Digging Deeper: Romans 15:1–7

*"But I have called you friends, for all things that I heard from
My Father I have made known to you."* —John 15:15 (NAS)

I sat on the playground with my granddaughter Grace—her invited
guest at an autumn class picnic. "How are you liking your new
school?" I asked.

It's not the easiest thing to move to a new locale when you're going
into first grade. When you've lived in small-town Alaska and gone to
preschool and kindergarten at the same rural site.

You land in the "big city" and, come September, must walk into a
building populated many times over from what you've known.

"Well," Grace said with a faraway look, "at first when I played outside on the swing I wished I could fly high up into the sky and get on
an airplane and go back to Alaska. But now I don't want to go back—
because I have friends."

Friends are so important that Jesus surrounded Himself with them in
His three-year public ministry. He dined in homes, attended weddings,
had traveling companions, held children, spent hours in conversation
with others. He immersed Himself in the lives of people and welcomed
many of them into His life.

In fact, He felt so strongly about no one being alone that He taught,
"I was a stranger and you invited Me in" (Matthew 25:35). He said that
to whomever we extend friendship, it is as though we have befriended
Him.

Offering friendship—particularly for someone who might otherwise
be alone—is nothing short of royal service for the King!

*Thanks, Lord, for looking out for a little girl who needed a friend.
Keep me on the lookout for someone I can "invite in"
through the welcoming act of friendship.*
—Carol Knapp

Digging Deeper: Proverbs 27:10; Ecclesiastes 4:9–12;
Matthew 25:34–40

Wednesday, September 26

"Blessed are the pure in heart, for they will see God." —Matthew 5:8 (NIV)

I could've done that," I said to my friend as I stared at a half-massaged lump of clay in the Guggenheim Museum.

"Yeah, but you didn't," she replied, and we chuckled.

The whole art exhibit up to that point had felt like a clever trick by the artist: get a bunch of people to pay to look at pieces of "art" that essentially amount to a large gray cylinder, or something that looks like a giant gray macaroni noodle, or a photo of cut-up hot dogs and household items stacked on top of each other.

But as we continued around the museum, we found pieces with which we really connected.

At the very top floor was the last display in the show. The room was dark and at the top of one wall was a row of projectors. The projectors cast questions in different directions and different languages on the other three walls and the ceiling. Just as winding as the writing were the questions. They ran the gamut—love, life, self-awareness, the universe. Some were silly while others hit so close to home that they were gut wrenching. It was the single most authentic creation of human experience that I had ever witnessed with any art form.

Michelle and I—in awe of this brave, honest display of vulnerability— sat on a bench in the back of the room under the projectors and read each and every question.

God, thank You for showing me examples of people who are willing
to be bravely vulnerable and who reveal their hearts.
May we all receive each other and our vulnerabilities
with awe, compassion, and love.
—Natalie Perkins

Digging Deeper: 1 Samuel 16:7; Psalm 139:14–16; Romans 12:1–5

Bear with each other and forgive one another if any of you has a grievance against someone. Forgive as the Lord forgave you. —Colossians 3:13 (NIV)

My ex-husband and I stood over our boys with smiles for the birthday picture. Brandon was fixated on his cake, while my little one turned around and excitedly exclaimed, "The whole family!"

This was our first family picture in five years. For all that time, we had not occupied the same space for more than a few seconds and we barely spoke. Now we were celebrating our son's birthday for the entire weekend in a rented vacation house with my ex's family.

That night, I kept looking at the picture with tears in my eyes. "Thank You, Jesus," I prayed. "Thank You for getting us through all the pain and bringing us here."

I thought about this restoration of friendship with my ex-husband, I thought about the memoir I wrote of my journey to single motherhood, which would soon be published. The sweetness of those recent moments all came from pain and the act of facing it, wrestling with it, letting it go, and moving on from it.

It's easy to snuggle up with hurt and anger and defend it as a right. It feels good. But as the four of us sang "Happy Birthday" to our little boy, surrounded by family, I knew that this place of forgiveness was so much better.

Lord, thank You for the power of forgiveness.
—Karen Valentin

Digging Deeper: Ephesians 4:31–32

Friday, September 28

"For in the resurrection they neither marry nor are given in marriage, but are like angels in heaven." —Matthew 22:30 (RSV)

I was asked to teach a premarital class at my church for a group of newly engaged-to-be-married members. I froze before answering. I suspect that most couples view these types of classes as an obligation. But when done well, premarital classes can be an eye-opening introduction to the challenges of married life, especially for people of faith.

I froze because, after thirty plus years of marriage, I didn't know what to say. I could give scads of advice, mostly beginning with the words *I used to think...* but what advice could I give now?

After weeks of flailing, here was my gift to sixteen couples prepping for a lifelong sacrament—a travelogue:

"Ladies and gentlemen, here are photos of my trip to China. Here's Beijing—or one small part of Beijing, which is one small part of the colossus known as China. Here we are at the Great Wall—well, one small part of thousands of miles that was built over centuries. Here's our group in Inner Mongolia, which was as different as another planet.

"After visiting China, I know less than when I started, because I now realize all I didn't know. To know something well, you have to live with it, learn the language and traditions and history.

"Marriage is a foreign country. You have to learn how to adapt, to communicate. You have to know why the walls were built and where the gaps are. Most important, you cannot do it alone. If you, as a couple, think you can have a marriage without good fortune and help from above—well, I wish you the best. You'll need it."

*Lord, watch over these sixteen couples and
the holy and foreign country they now enter.*
—Mark Collins

Digging Deeper: Psalm 63:7–8; Matthew 19:4–6

So do not fear, for I am with you; do not be dismayed, for I am your God. I will strengthen you and help you; I will uphold you with my righteous right hand. —Isaiah 41:10 (NIV)

My daughters, Jennifer and Julie, and I were driving to a nearby big city to try to meet up with my son Jon. We remembered happier times when he was stalwart, funny—with a bizarre sense of humor. We remembered him scoring touchdowns and basketball goals and homeruns. The girls could even remember my bringing him and his twin brother, Jeremy, home from the hospital and placing a baby in each of their outstretched arms. Jon was now homeless.

Jennifer, who was driving, screamed, "There he is!"

I put my hand on the handle of the car door. "Don't you dare get out until I stop," she ordered.

It was Jon's birthday. Parking by a blue Dumpster, we climbed out of the car. He sat on the sidewalk, leaning against the brick homeless shelter in the warm sunshine, eyes closed. We plopped down with him. He opened his eyes. "Well, happy birthday," he said softly, smiling.

"To you!" we answered. At six feet two inches, his frame was thinner than the last time we'd seen him.

"I'm fine," he offered. His eyes crinkled with momentary joy, like the old Jon. He'd never complained about anything growing up. He was wondrously kind and loved Jesus.

We knew he'd end the visit soon. He never wanted us to stay longer than several moments—or even not come at all.

Someone said something funny, and the four of us laughed like old times. Belly laughs. Then he gently dismissed us.

The only way I can walk away, Father, is to know that You don't.
—Marion Bond West

Digging Deeper: Isaiah 26:3; John 14:27; Romans 8:37–39

Sunday, September 30

Rejoicing in hope; patient in tribulation; continuing instant in prayer.
—Romans 12:12 (KJV)

I found the perfect anniversary card for you and Dad," our daughter Rebecca said. The front featured a man driving, his wife in the passenger seat. She thinks they are lost. He says they are not. She wants to ask for directions. He refuses. She prays silently for strength while he prays silently for patience. Inside are the words "The couple who prays together stays together."

My husband, Don, and I have been lost in Baltimore, Dallas, and other cities too numerous to list. We both have squeaky-clean driving records but don't trust each other's driving. I think Don drives too fast. He thinks I drive too slow. He gets irritated when I nag because he's speeding or changing lanes abruptly. I get irritated when he says I'm impeding traffic and better speed up. But since we like to visit family and friends, we are stuck with each other. I won't drive in heavy city traffic, and Don gets sleepy on long stretches of interstate.

We'd argued during a recent trip to Colorado, then spent an hour hunting for our hotel. We arrived tense and upset, and it was obvious that traveling together meant making changes. The next day we bought a navigation system with maps and clear verbal instructions, best route, and construction information. Don has slowed down (most of the time), and I'm trying to remain calm and silent. I'm keeping pace with traffic (most of the time), and Don isn't urging me to speed up. We're traveling…and praying… with more trust and peace.

Dear Lord, thank You for a husband who prays with me and for me,
even when he prays for patience while I'm praying for strength.
—Penney Schwab

Digging Deeper: Psalm 19:14; Matthew 18:20; Ephesians 5:31–33

GOD'S UNFAILING LOVE

1 _____

2 _____

3 _____

4 _____

5 _____

6 _____

7 _____

8 _____

9 _____

10 _____

11 _____

12 _____

13 _____

14 _____

15 _____

September

16 _____

17 _____

18 _____

19 _____

20 _____

21 _____

22 _____

23 _____

24 _____

25 _____

26 _____

27 _____

28 _____

29 _____

30 _____

OCTOBER

The Lord hath appeared of old unto me, saying,
Yea, I have loved thee with an everlasting love:
therefore with lovingkindness have I drawn thee.

—Jeremiah 31:3 (KJV)

Monday, October 1

Then as a widow to the age of eighty-four, she never left the temple but worshiped there with fasting and prayer night and day.
—Luke 2:37 (NRSV)

Every three months, my family made the two-and-a-half-hour trek to visit my husband's grandparents in Marietta, Oklahoma. Nana was in the early stages of dementia, and Grandpa, a navy veteran of two wars, was a two-time cancer survivor who was only able to breathe with the help of an oxygen tank.

Rocking in his recliner, Grandpa lamented their condition. "We're in overtime," he admitted. Nana nodded.

Then Grandpa died. Nana couldn't stay alone; she moved to an assisted-living center in our town.

I monologued to her about the positives: now we could visit weekly instead of every three months. She'd also get to know our daughter, Micah, her only great-granddaughter, more intimately. Every Sunday my in-laws could take her to church and dinner. Still I worried: How did she feel now that her body and mind were betraying her?

Gently, I tried to persuade her to talk about her circumstances. Nana shook her head. "I'm in overtime" was all she said, as if to indicate she had nothing left to live for.

One Saturday, Nana came over to watch her beloved University of Oklahoma Sooners play football. At the end of the fourth quarter, the score was tied. We cheered as the Sooners prevailed and won in overtime.

"You know," said Nana with a gleam in her eye, "the best games always go into overtime."

I nodded and smiled. Nana was still in the game.

Lord, thank You for Nana's wisdom. Help me remember that we all can serve You until our final minute.
—Stephanie Thompson

Digging Deeper: Deuteronomy 33:25; Psalms 71:18, 92:14

Love each other. —John 15:17 (NIV)

I knew my father-in-law only after he lost his sight. So I had to imagine what it was like for this respected professor of theology to be told at age forty-nine that he would be blind in a matter of weeks.

It was 1942, wartime. His son John (my husband-to-be) was completing basic training in Camp Wolters, Texas. The Red Cross obtained four days "compassionate leave" for John to return to Louisville, Kentucky, so that his father could see him for the last time. "I expected to find Dad grieving over the end of his career," John remembers.

Instead, he found his father preparing to carry on exactly as before. Already, he was learning Braille, training his fingers to take on the hours of reading his courses required each day. "What seemed to worry him," John told me, "wasn't his own loss but that his blindness might be a barrier for his students." With John's mother, he was practicing locating a speaker's eyes from the direction of his or her voice. He was walking with his wife around the seminary with his eyes closed, so he wouldn't need a cane.

John was fighting in Italy when his father wrote that he'd discovered a wonderful new resource: "Talking Books." With these, his Braille books, and his extraordinary memory, he was able to retain entire texts, so that in front of a class he would appear to be reading. Years later, when I wrote a story about him, I got a furious letter from a man who studied under him in 1951. "How can you write such lies! Dr. Sherrill could see as well as I can!"

Certainly he *seemed* to see. "How lovely you're looking today!" he'd say to me. And though I knew it was not my appearance but his own loving spirit speaking, I would *feel* lovely.

Dad Sherrill taught more students and wrote more books without his eyes than with them. "There are many ways to see," he told me once. "The important thing is to look with love."

Father, teach me to see.
—Elizabeth Sherrill

Digging Deeper: Colossians 3:14; 1 John 4:7

Wednesday, October 3

Let not mercy and truth forsake thee... write them upon the table of thine heart. —Proverbs 3:3 (KJV)

"O h no," I groaned one morning as I negotiated the traffic on my way to work. On the radio, the newscaster was reporting on an effort to "rid the streets of those homeless 'paper-people.'" He reported on a local newspaper called *The Contributor*. Like other papers, it covers a range of subjects from lifestyle articles to important issues facing our city. But one thing makes this paper different: it is written, illustrated, and marketed by Nashville's homeless community.

In so many ways, I'm proud of Nashville. It's been nationally ranked as one of the "It Cities," with a strong economy and rich diversity. Many move here for Nashville's friendly lifestyle and varied career opportunities. But there is another side to our city. People have been left behind, marginalized by our fast-paced growth. *The Contributor* is one way that those who are down on their luck can lift themselves up.

Driving through Nashville, you'll see *Contributor* salespeople on many street corners. In freezing cold rain and in the sweltering heat of summer, they are there. Offering their papers to passing motorists, they smile, dispensing friendly words and frequent "God bless you's."

It made me sad that a few unhappy folks wanted to make their streetside selling unlawful.

All of us Nashvillians did what we could: made donations to support the paper, and let our friends and family know to do the same. In the end, the "It" city responded with a resounding, "Yes! Our *Contributor* vendors are important. We want them to stay."

I'm proud to say that mercy and truth trumped cold hearts and our *Contributor* salespeople still grace Nashville's streets with hope.

> *Father, empower us to create a city and a world*
> *where all are allowed the mercy of Your love.*
> —Brock Kidd

Digging Deeper: Psalm 85:10; Hosea 12:6; Matthew 5:7

Strength and honour are her clothing; and she shall rejoice in time to come. She openeth her mouth with wisdom; and in her tongue is the law of kindness. She looketh well to the ways of her household, and eateth not the bread of idleness. Her children arise up, and call her blessed; her husband also, and he praiseth her. —Proverbs 31:25–28 (KJV)

Two days and one night a week, my wife goes up the tallest hill in our city to the hospital there and spends hours with kids who are being hammered by cancer. The ward is called Ten South, and people speak those two words in hushed, frightened tones.

"The mothers are there all the time," says my wife. "They used to sleep on the floor next to their kids, but finally we have cots for them. The mothers never give up, never quit. They go to weep in the chapel or the bathroom or the stairwell. When they say they are going out for a walk that means they are going out to cry.

"The fathers and brothers and sisters and cousins and aunts and uncles and grandparents come in waves, sometimes a dozen at a time, but the mothers are always there. I don't know how they do it. Most of them have jobs. But when your kid is on Ten South, you are too.

"The mothers are so tough and brave and relentless and attentive and tireless. They are love, you know what I mean? We say 'mother-love,' but that's an awfully weak phrase for something so strong and roaring and unquenchable and holy.

"Sometimes they break down in the elevator, and I just hold them while they cry.

"You are in the word business," my wife says to me. "Find me a word for how brave and haunted and fierce those mothers are. Find me a good word for that."

> *Dear Source from Which All Love Floweth Like Water, the only word I can find that has any weight at all for them is divine.*
> —Brian Doyle

Digging Deeper: Isaiah 66:13; 1 Corinthians 13:13

Friday, October 5

FALLING INTO GRACE: Seeds of Compassion

"But I say to you, Love your enemies and pray for those who persecute you, so that you may be children of your Father in heaven...."
—Matthew 5:44–45 (NRSV)

He looked so ill I almost didn't recognize him. The old man shuffling down the aisle at church was a former city official who'd opposed our city's homeless shelter at every turn. I'm not proud to admit that I'd despised him for this and spoken disparagingly of him on many occasions.

Seeing him haggard, thin, and pale sent a different kind of pain through me, almost as sharp as those I'd been having since my fall. It was more than guilt at past harsh thoughts and words, though remorse was part of it. There was something else—a sense of empathy for someone I once thought it impossible to feel anything for but dislike.

I whispered to my husband how ill the man looked. Surprised, Charlie said softly, "I told you last year that he was sick."

I had some vague memory of this but had dismissed it because I just hadn't cared that much. Now silent in church, I began to think about God's timing. If I'd seen this man before my accident would I have experienced this compassion? I had to admit the answer was no, which left me with conflicting emotions as I faced the fact that God was shaping something good in me out of my pain.

I have been praying for this man ever since, and once I even surprised him by saying hello. At first, he looked ready to rebuff me, but then I saw a spark of recognition in his eyes. I imagine it wasn't much different from what he saw in mine.

Lord, plant seeds of empathy and compassion in me
and help me to harvest love.
—Marci Alborghetti

Digging Deeper: Isaiah 32:16–18; 2 Corinthians 6:1–2

You forgot the God who gave you birth. —Deuteronomy 32:18 (NIV)

While shopping recently in the hot, dark basement of an old white frame house, I spotted the most charming porcelain kitchen table. Though it was laden with dog-eared cookbooks and chipped bowls, I knew the table's art deco design was an estate sale treasure. What I especially admired were the extendable leaves with lovely pots of red flowers stenciled in each corner. They would make perfect shelves for my log cabin kitchen.

The price scribbled on a scrap of masking tape was even better. Ten dollars! Everyone had passed on the table because its chrome legs were pitted. But those leaves were pristine. If only I had a screwdriver. That's when a middle-aged man named John entered the scene wearing a canvas tool belt. "For times like these," he said with a laugh.

For forty long minutes, John and his wife, Donna, labored over my find. Time they could have spent heading to the next estate sale. Donna held everything in place while John operated his ragtag assortment of tools.

When the leaves were finally separated from the table, I tried my best to compensate the couple for their efforts. Yet when I offered them enough money for lunch, they insisted that I enjoy lunch at my favorite restaurant instead. That's when I remembered a box of beautifully illustrated books on prayer in the trunk of my car. But my quiet offer garnered a vehement "No! We don't get into that God stuff," Donna said, shaking her head. John climbed into the cab of his rusty truck without even saying good-bye.

I was so sorry I had offended them and even sorrier that such good-hearted folks didn't recognize the Source of the love they so generously offered to others. Ever since, I've prayed for John and Donna and others like them in my world:

Please nudge resistant hearts to welcome You, Lord.
—Roberta Messner

Digging Deeper: Jeremiah 3:19; Luke 12:9

Sunday, October 7

"When you walk through fire, you will not be scorched, nor will the flame burn you." —Isaiah 43:2 (AMP)

The phone rang near midnight. A deacon from the church I am temporarily pastoring told me that the home of church members Bob and Diane was on fire. An old, historic wooden dwelling, it is a beautiful farmhouse perched on a hill. Generations of the same family have called this place home.

Jumping into my car, I drove into the heart of middle Georgia. I could see a glow in the sky before I arrived. Fire trucks and volunteer firefighters surrounded the house. In the countryside, there are no fire hydrants, and tanker trucks had trouble supplying water. Now, however, the fire had finally been subdued and the damage contained.

Walking inside the scorched kitchen, I saw Bob in the smoky darkness and realized there were no words to say. All that felt right was a heartfelt hug and a gaze between two men who have both known tragedy. Then we lost ourselves in frantic action. Though ceilings were collapsing from the weight of water, there was still time to drag antique furniture into the yard. As we moved through the dining room, we walked on shards of broken heirloom china. Paintings could still be taken from walls and personal possessions thrown into bags to be sorted later. As dawn broke, the fire trucks left, a guard was set, and most of us drove away in stunned stupor to get some sleep.

Driving home, I knew that Bob, Diane, and I would always be friends. There is nothing more bonding than being with one another in times of tragedy, joy, birth, and death. We often cannot prevent adversity, but we can walk through it together.

> *Father, may I be present amid the needs of others today. Amen.*
> —Scott Walker

Digging Deeper: Psalm 23; Proverbs 17:17

Every good and perfect gift is from above, coming down from the
Father of the heavenly lights, who does not change like shifting shadows.
—James 1:17 (NIV)

I had worked with the same staff for many years; they had become my family. Then, out of the blue, a series of resignations began taking place. Most were responding to a new call in their life; some left for better opportunities or retirement. When I thought the leave-taking finally had ceased, I was surprised by one more. This individual had been with Guideposts for eighteen years and then decided to switch fields. All of these changes occurred within eighteen months.

I developed wonderful relationships with each and every one of these people. They not only became my friends, but they also helped me to become a better leader, manager, and person. They were a gift to our ministry and proved that a mission is accomplished through the efforts of a team.

I know that God ordains each of our steps, but seeing colleagues leave is never easy. As each person moved on, I prayed for God to bless them. This was a season of change.

From where I stand now, I can look back and see that God had everything under control. Today's ministry is stronger than ever with new and old staff members working together. My hopes are high because God will guide us.

Thank You, Lord, for watching over my colleagues, old and new.
May our work always be for You.
—Pablo Diaz

Digging Deeper: 1 Corinthians 3:9; 2 Corinthians 6:1

Tuesday, October 9

Remember the wonders he has done, his miracles, and the judgments he has pronounced. —Psalm 105:5 (NIV)

My faith was small the day my son Jeremy had to appear in court. Because of the exemplary manner in which he'd performed the tasks assigned to him, his pro bono lawyer requested that the ankle monitor come off two weeks early. That very day. He'd worn it for almost six months and was under house arrest. His attorney requested that family and friends come to support him: my husband, Gene; Jeremy's sister Julie; Pastor Tom; his Sunday school teacher and wife; and one of his lawn care customers. Even his state counselors showed up.

The prosecutor presented an excellent case for why Jeremy shouldn't have the monitor removed. When he was off his bipolar medications, he'd had a car wreck and received a charge for driving under the influence. My hopes sank even lower. Standing behind Jeremy in court, I saw his shoulders tremble slightly and his head drop a bit. Then his lawyer presented the defense. The judge acknowledged us, his support group. We stood erect like soldiers behind Jeremy. She repeated Jeremy's offense, looking directly at him, and added, "I'm going out on a limb, Jeremy, to rule in your favor."

His shoulders squared and his response was quick—emotional: "I won't let you down, Your Honor."

We all contained ourselves properly in the courtroom, but once out-side we hugged each other fiercely. Then Pastor Tom gathered us in a circle to praise and thank God. Afterward Jeremy wiped his eyes quickly. I did too.

Oh, Father, You show up anywhere—courtrooms, jails, hospitals. Thank You for not limiting Yourself to houses of worship.
—Marion Bond West

Digging Deeper: Deuteronomy 6:12; Psalm 103:2

With the measure you use, it will be measured to you.
—Matthew 7:2 (NIV)

A retired relative of mine was widowed some years ago. When we talk on the phone, we always discuss her "purpose in life." Before her husband died she never really thought about her purpose, she says. Now she realizes her purpose was being with him: going on trips, sharing meals, talking, collaborating on the Sunday crossword puzzle.

We discuss other purposes that she might consider: friends, volunteer work, church, getting a job. None of these is an adequate substitute for what she's lost, she says. Sometimes she cries. I never know what to say, how to comfort her, except to listen.

And beneath the listening, I'm worrying. Is this me? Is my husband effectively my purpose in life too? How would I spend my days if Kris died? Who would I talk to when I got home from work? Sure, I have friends and relatives, but they'd have their own families to occupy them. Would I be okay on my own, with nobody to eat dinner or play a game with before bedtime, nobody who even knew my schedule?

When I got off the phone with my relative, I kept pondering this idea of my husband as my "purpose in life." Initially, it made me uncomfortable, but the more I thought about it, the more the thought of losing him made me nervous. And I realized why: after creating the world, the only part God called "not good" was for Adam to be alone. If it wasn't good for Adam, it's probably not good for anyone.

Our assigned purpose in life, I concluded, is to counteract others' aloneness—by eating together, talking on the phone, sharing our days.

Father, help me to remember others in their aloneness and
let me be remembered in mine.
—Patty Kirk

Digging Deeper: Genesis 2; Psalm 68

Thursday, October 11

I can never be lost to your Spirit! I can never get away from my God!
—Psalm 139:7 (TLB)

Our three youngest sons had never seen the ocean. So when I was invited to a writers workshop in Florida, Lonny and I took them along. We piled into the van and drove south for days. When deciduous trees turned to palms, the boys cheered. We stopped, and they ran their hands over the trunks.

"Will the ocean taste salty?" a boy asked.

"Will it be cold like the lake?" asked another.

Mile after mile, we anticipated the ocean. I couldn't wait to see my sons witness the end-of-day glory—sun slipping into water from a pink-orange sky. But as we neared our beachfront hotel, raindrops splattered the windshield. The sky went broody and bruised.

"I'm sorry, guys," I said. "We'll watch the sunrise in the morning."

We checked into our hotel and took the elevator to a high floor. The boys bolted inside the room, opened the sliding glass door, and stood on the balcony.

"Mama," seven-year-old Isaiah called, "quick! Come see!" The ocean stretched wide, and a rainbow curved across the sky.

I'll never forget the faces of three boys as they stood under the great drape of God's glory. I'll also never forget how that image spoke to my soul. I often grow weary from an ongoing family struggle. I see darkness; it's as threatening as an ominous sky. But the Lord is faithful and gracious to remind me He is there—a promise from His Word; encouragement from a friend; an unexpected, hope-birthing smile from my struggling son. God's love is light that pierces panic.

"It's the prettiest thing I've ever seen," Isaiah said that night. Glory over darkness. I'd have to agree.

Thank You, God, for reminding me that You are here—always. Amen.
—Shawnelle Eliasen

Digging Deeper: Exodus 33:14; Matthew 28:20

Be still, and know that I am God.... —Psalm 46:10 (KJV)

I slid into the driver's seat and checked the clock—five minutes behind schedule. I might still make it to class on time if I didn't hit any red lights. I pulled out on to the road; it was packed solid.

As I joined the ranks of unmoving vehicles, I could feel my heart thumping. I glanced at my mirror, and my reflection stared back with shadowed eyes. I looked like I hadn't slept in days, which was accurate.

Law school was difficult. My days were crammed with intricate assignments and dense casebooks. At night, I couldn't shut off my mind. My brain kept trying to connect statutes and cases while I tossed back and forth.

I looked out at the line of brake lights and drummed my fingers on the steering wheel. What a waste of time! I could be skimming my notes or working on tomorrow's readings. Instead, I was forced to sit here, forced to be still.

I ran a thumb over my stubbly cheek. When had I last taken the time to be still? When had I last rested in God's strength?

I steadied my breathing and cleared my mind of all the work I had to do. It could wait. In the busyness, I had forgotten that though I am just Logan, God is God. These burdens were too heavy for me, but not for Him. Remembering that lifted some of the pressure off my chest.

The van in front of me began to move forward, and I eased off the brake. I knew I was driving toward a full day, but that moment of stillness anchored me in the One Who would get me through it.

Lord, show me Your peace when I am restless.
—Logan Eliasen

Digging Deeper: Psalm 29:11; Matthew 11:28–30

Saturday, October 13

When my heart is overwhelmed: lead me to the rock that is higher than I. —Psalm 61:2 (KJV)

When I need to clear my mind, find perspective, or just escape wearying routine, I head for the hills. Luckily, I live about an hour from White Mountain National Forest just north of my home. From several overlooks, I ponder the reassuring bulk of Cannon Mountain, a granite dome 4,080 feet high. Even from a distance, the mountain helps me to feel secure and calm.

If I visit midweek, tourists are fewer and my expedition feels more spiritual than recreational. A fifteen-minute ride on the aerial tramway to the summit exposes me to a panoramic vista of three states and Quebec, and weather drastically different from the base. On a mild autumn day, for example, a snow squall may blast me on the observation deck. Even on a pretty June afternoon, the temperature can drop twenty degrees at the summit.

Yet here, so high up the mountain that cars in the parking lot below look like specks, peace returns, even as manic wind tears at my clothes and lashes out at my hair. Perhaps it's just the altitude or escaping distractions that I find so soothing. After all, even Jesus needed time apart.

I learned the security of high ground from hiking with pack goats in the Rocky Mountains. These obliging, social creatures followed us, carrying our gear in minipanniers. When we camped at night, however, the goats instinctively sought the highest ground for protection against predators.

Like the goats, I eventually need to descend the mountain and return to daily life and all its niggling anxieties and obligations. Mountaintop getaways keep me grounded.

Lord, thank You for the ways Your creation refreshes our souls.
—Gail Thorell Schilling

Digging Deeper: Mark 6:31; Luke 6:12–13

Remember this, my dear brothers and sisters: Everyone should be quick to listen, slow to speak, and should not get angry easily. —James 1:19 (GW)

"Hi, Mom. It's me." It's a Sunday night, and I call Mom. I always call Mom on Sunday nights. Eight o'clock, my watch says. That would be five o'clock for Mom out in California.

"Oh, it's you," she says, sounding pleasantly surprised, as though she didn't expect me. "I don't know if you tried earlier. I was out in the garden. I wanted to clip some roses."

"How are the roses?"

"They look good this year, although it's been a hot October. I even had to turn on the air-conditioning." The weather, we always spend a few minutes on the weather. "Is it getting cold back there in the East?"

"It dropped down to the fifties."

"That sounds cold to me." Mom, the eternal Californian. We go from the weather to bridge and how she and her partner played at the bridge center. "I thought we weren't doing very well at all, but we got on the board. You never know. We must have played our hands well."

We enter into the minutiae of her life, what her friend brought her from the market, the book she's reading, what the physical therapist said about her leg, what happened at church that morning. At once I had the memory of calling her when our boys were little. Then I was the one rattling off details about her grandsons, the minutiae of *their* lives, to her delight. How glad I was to be the one listening now. This is what we do for those we love. We share in their joys by listening. A well-played hand at bridge is something to be happy about.

"Love you, Mom," I say, signing off.

"Love you," she says before hanging up.

Let me practice Your presence, Lord, by listening to those we both love.
—Rick Hamlin

Digging Deeper: Exodus 20:12; Psalm 16:11

Monday, October 15

The path of the just...shineth.... —Proverbs 4:18 (KJV)

I want you to take these to your teacher tomorrow," my mother was saying as she wrapped my beloved alligator shoes in tissue and put them in a bag.

"They're like new because you only wore them on Sundays," she continued.

"*Noooo*, not my alligator shoes! I love those shoes! I want to keep them forever!" I wail.

"They are beginning to hurt your feet," my mother explained, "and your teacher said there's a girl in your class who needs nice shoes for your Christmas program."

It was true: the shoes were too tight for my fourth-grade feet. But my alligator shoes—nobody I knew had shoes as beautiful as these.

"We'll get you new Sunday shoes. But right now you need to remember that there are girls in your class who aren't so lucky." My mother's look erased my pout.

"Pamela, it's what we do in this family. We care about others. When the world's not fair, we try to help."

The next morning I dutifully delivered the package to my teacher. And on the night of the program, I spotted my alligator shoes dancing across the stage. I didn't say a word, but I felt like my entire being was one giant smile.

In this life I will never again have anything as grand as those alligator shoes. Because, you see, they are always out there in front of me, buckled on the feet of a dancing girl, leading the way down the shining path my mother set for me.

Father, keep me on the path. Let me be a bringer of justice
to those who need what I can give.
—Pam Kidd

Digging Deeper: Psalm 82:3; Proverbs 21:3; Philippians 4:8

"Arise, shine, for your light has come, and the glory of the Lord rises upon you."—Isaiah 60:1 (NIV)

I love social media. You can share that gorgeous cake you decorated, snap a shot of your just-planted garden, or even send a quick video of your latest fun dinner out. But social media has also changed how we spend our downtime. Instead of grabbing a magazine or book, or lingering over the sunset, we tend to reach for our phones and try to capture each moment or scroll it away as we idly browse updates.

While that can be harmless, it can also be disheartening. Social media is a highlight reel, one that slants toward winning moments.

This year, I decided to be more authentic. I shared the photos that showed my kitchen in a less-than-perfect state, talked about my miscarriages, and opened up to display my wonderfully, painfully imperfect life. In return, I received a wash of renewed, deepened connection. While we think we want to see perfection, we in fact strive to know the real us.

Our online life is an ever-present ministry, one that is worth being authentic in daily.

> *Heavenly Father, thank You for loving me in my shining moments*
> *and in my dark nights. Life is beautiful and*
> *hard and oh so worth it!*
> —Ashley Kappel

Digging Deeper: Matthew 5:13–16; John 8:12; 2 Corinthians 4:3–6

Wednesday, October 17

CONFIDENCE IN DIFFICULTY: My Hope Is in the Lord

Be strong and take heart, all you who hope in the Lord. —Psalm 31:24 (NIV)

"Get me out of here!" Maggie demanded. My daughter was back in the Connecticut hospital after her meltdown, awaiting word from the wilderness program. The readmission set off new waves of trauma, with flashbacks from the awful hospitalization in New York.

A week's worth of hospital bills later, the wilderness program said they didn't think they could meet Maggie's needs. "Now what?" I wailed to the doctors and God. A mad scramble ensued. The hospital finally found us a spot in a day program in New Jersey. It meant a two-hour bus commute each way, five days a week, but we took it.

Maggie came home Friday, and we went to the intake interview on Monday. My daughter's needs were too complex; the program said they couldn't take her.

I immediately called Connecticut for help in formulating another plan. They didn't call back for two days. When they did, it was only to say a bed wouldn't open up there for almost two weeks.

Other problems surfaced: my daughter Elizabeth moved back to the Midwest and was struggling; my son John became depressed and dropped out of college; my daughter Mary's foot became infected; my son Stephen was wildly anxious; my husband, Andrew, withdrew emotionally.

"Pray for us," I e-mailed my friends. They did—and also sent meals. I was positive God could untangle my family's knots, yet that didn't seem to be part of His plan. What was I supposed to do if God wasn't going to fix this nightmare? Framed that way, the answer was clear: I had to figure out how I would go about loving God, serving Him, and trusting Him in the midst of it.

Father, I put my hope in You rather than in what You can do for me.
—Julia Attaway

Digging Deeper: Psalms 118, 136

When I was a child, I talked like a child, I thought like a child, I reasoned like a child. When I became a man, I put the ways of childhood behind me. —1 Corinthians 13:11 (NIV)

My youngest son lost his first tooth, and he flashed the biggest smile to show off the empty space. His excitement collided with my heartbreak. The disappearance of his sweet baby smile hit me harder than I expected. This was my last child. His small, straight, perfect teeth would soon be replaced by clumsy, giant ones—too big for his little face. They'd probably grow in crooked like mine did—grown-up teeth and their grown-up teeth problems.

The infant who used to curl into a ball on my chest was growing up. Soon he'd be a teenager, then a man. His life so far has been as perfect as his little boy smile. He is loved, protected, clothed, sheltered, and nurtured. He's never lost a loved one in death, never known tragedy or violence. But now the open space in his mouth represented the open space of the unknown. What would the next chapters of his life look like? As much as I want to protect him, my job is also to prepare him for the harsh realities of life. I don't want him to experience heartache and pain, but I know trials grow us into the people we're meant to be.

"Oh, my baby," I sigh. But he's not a baby anymore. The proof is under his pillow. A tiny, perfect tooth, now just a souvenir of his childhood.

Life can be difficult, Lord. I want to protect the ones I love, but help me to let them go as You mold them into the ones You've called them to be.
—Karen Valentin

Digging Deeper: Isaiah 40:11

Friday, October 19

... The little foxes, that spoil the vines.... —Song of Solomon 2:15 (KJV)

One of my vehicles suddenly developed a rattle under the dashboard that sounded like a half-dozen marbles in a wooden box. "Just ignore it," my wife said, ever helpful.

And I tried, but the noise seemed to get louder each day, until it felt like the marbles were actually in my head. But my wife assured me that I had lost all my marbles years ago.

From long experience with cars, I knew that the source of the rattle was likely to be something simple but that finding it could be wicked hard.

While Sharon drove the car over bumpy roads, I probed under the dash with a stethoscope and a variety of lights and mirrors, but found nothing. At one point I actually "laid hands" on the hood and prayed: "Lord, help me find this rattle before I have to be led away to rehab."

In the end, I gave up. I just turn up the radio on bumpy roads.

Car noises are one thing, but a squeak or a rattle in a relationship is more serious. I once had a student who was the sweetest, most cooperative student ever. Then, abruptly, she began to complain about everything I did and said. Not until the end of the semester, when I got my student evaluations, did I find out the problem. I had said something in class that hurt her feelings. So I went to her and apologized, and she forgave me with a hug and tears.

It's not easy, finding the "little foxes" that are spoiling the vines, but it's worth the trouble, I think.

Lord, help me to not ignore the noises in my friendships.
Give me the courage to find out what's wrong and to fix it.
—Daniel Schantz

Digging Deeper: Proverbs 17:14; Romans 12:18

*For we are His workmanship, created in Christ Jesus for good works,
which God prepared beforehand so that we would walk in them.*
—Ephesians 2:10 (NAS)

Eight-year-old Benjamin and his family are temporarily living with
my husband and me. The morning after a gigantic windstorm
blew through, I walked with Benjamin and his older brother Simon
down the mountain road to the bus stop. Pine branches and big sticks
littered the ground.

Picking up a supple branch with a cluster of needles at the top, I held
it high and asked, "Who am I?" Simon called out, "Statue of Liberty!"
A good guess since his family has lived in New York City.

Ben jumped into the game. Back and forth went our charade parade.
A bent stick became a big fish on the line. Another branch turned into
a hose dousing a fire. More strands of needles swayed like a hula skirt.
Ben was Gandalf from *Lord of the Rings*, leaning on his staff. I was an
Olympic javelin thrower.

The wooded bus stop transformed into an earthen stage where we
imagined ourselves characters—even heroes—in far-flung places. We
were so involved we might have waited for the bus all day had someone
not driven by and told us there was no school because of the storm!

This little drama brought me such joy. I felt I had fulfilled my purpose on that day—like when the Apostle Paul wrote Archippus, "Take
heed to the ministry which you have received in the Lord, that you may
fulfill it" (Colossians 4:17, NAS). I'd made memorable a moment that
might have been easily overlooked and encouraged a sense of discovery
and imagination in two young boys. One's purpose can be found in the
simplest of acts.

Lord, make known to me even the smallest service I can carry out for You.
—Carol Knapp

Digging Deeper: Zechariah 4:10; Mark 4:30–32; John 6:8–9

Sunday, October 21

"So do not be afraid; you are of more value than many sparrows."
—Matthew 10:31 (NRSV)

When my kids were teenagers, they were incredibly self-conscious. Their hair, their skin, their voices, their feet—every aspect of them seemed to suffer in light of their own narrow view of what was "good." *Everything* was embarrassing.

"Dad, that is so embarrassing!" was their constant refrain.

This all began to change for my son one day in Boston. I took him to the somewhat rough neighborhood where I had worked twenty-five years earlier. As we were walking past a graffiti-riddled brick wall, we almost stumbled upon a man who was out cold in the gutter.

We looked at him for a minute. My boy had never seen this sort of thing. He had never witnessed this kind of real embarrassment.

"Grab him under one arm," I said.

"What?"

"We're going to help him up," I said. "Grab him under the arm." And then I bent over to do the same on the other side. Within a few seconds we had him up, and after a brief conversation the man had a cup of coffee and a doughnut from the place on the corner and was sitting on a bench. "Go along. Go away. Thanks," he told us, and that was fine. I hope he had a better day than his night had been. I was grateful for the lesson he provided my son. I don't think my son ever worried about his self-image in the same way again.

In fact, "Let's find someone else to help up!" he said, as we rounded the next street corner.

Remind me today, Lord, who I am in Your eyes.
—Jon Sweeney

Digging Deeper: Psalm 139:13–14

THE BEAUTY OF SIMPLICITY: God Knows Everything

We never really know enough until we recognize that God alone knows it all. —1 Corinthians 8:3 (MSG)

We live way out in the country and often have no phone or Internet service. To complicate matters, our long gravel driveway gets muddy when it rains. I work from home, and to communicate by cell phone I have to walk to a certain spot in the driveway and hold my head at just the right angle.

After several days of this nonsense, I became unglued. I'd been waiting for an important e-mail regarding a project I'd completed. Had my colleague tried to reach me but couldn't?

Our home phone service had been out multiple times. Now the cable that was buried under our driveway had broken because the cable repair workers had plowed a ditch through the middle of the driveway.

I decided that my car wouldn't make it through the deep grooves and mudslide, so I crawled into my son's pickup to weave my way through the machinery and workmen toward civilization and Wi-Fi. But there were no keys in his truck, and he wasn't home. I slammed his door and marched through the chaos, swatting flies and mosquitoes, hoping I could find one spot where we had service. Walking toward our mailbox, I clicked the e-mail icon on my cell phone. Hallelujah! I was connected. But there was no response on my project.

I typed out a long-winded e-mail to my colleague and explained the dire situation. Seconds later, I received a calm, gracious reply: "Julie, sorry you're having a disconnected and discombobulating day. I should have an answer for you in the next week or so. Hope your day improves."

Lord, You had it under control the whole time. You always do.
—Julie Garmon

Digging Deeper: Psalms 23:1–3, 139:5–6

Tuesday, October 23

"This is My commandment, that you love one another as I have loved you." —John 15:12 (NKJV)

It was a stormy night, and most people had already filtered out of Bible study to head home. As the pastor, I'd spoken with a man who was at our church for the first time and welcomed him. I'd been teaching about grace and how weirdly resistant we can become to God's good news.

We had a nice conversation and then he left. But he returned a few moments later; his car battery was dead and he asked if anyone had jumper cables. I always keep some, so I volunteered.

I followed him out to the car. Rain splatted against us as I handed him the cables and went to open my hood. He hooked them up to his battery and handed me rain-slicked cables to hook up to mine. I double-checked first: "Red to positive, right?"

"Right," he said. "Red to positive."

The instant I touched the clamp to my battery, sizzling sparks and a loud pop told me something was wrong. We both jumped back. I took a deep breath and checked under his hood; he had put red to negative. *Doesn't he know that reversed polarities can make a battery explode?* I was mad but held in my anger.

We righted the cable connections, got his car started, and off he went. As I drove home, God's Spirit gently nudged me and made me think. *Can my heart have reversed polarities too? Can I be weirdly resistant to grace? Am I shooting off my own sparks by getting angry?*

I reconnected my heart to God's grace: receiver to Giver, child to Father, forgiven one to Savior. By the time I got home, the storm was over.

> *Loving One, shelter me within Your grace and teach me*
> *to show others the same grace You've shown me.*
> —Bill Giovannetti

Digging Deeper: Colossians 4:6

"I was a stranger and you did not take Me in...."
—Matthew 25:43 (NKJV)

Like many universities, "Pitt," where I teach, is blessed with faculty from around the globe. Dr. Li is from China, and during our initial meeting I peppered her with questions about her homeland. Her answers were patient and thoughtful. Finally she said, "You realize I don't speak for all of China."

Right. Of course. So we ventured into other topics. Turns out we are both fans of *Star Trek: The Next Generation*, especially the collective enemy known as the Borg, whose goal is to stamp out individualism and assimilate every species. Man, I miss that show!

Then Dr. Li began asking me why American men are the way they are. Finally I said, "I don't speak for all men, but let me apologize for my entire gender."

We laughed, but the message was clear: we are not the Borg. What we think we know about each other is often based on collective misunderstandings, yet we are at heart just one person on the planet talking to another person, trying to connect. Our understanding reaches for the closest stereotype, but sometimes that's also the one thing that's least able to reflect back what God sees in each of us.

"Resistance is futile," says the Borg, but they're wrong. Hope always wins. There will always be the human desire for simple conversation, faults and all. It's an ancient, familiar, often-forgotten message: love your neighbor, alien or otherwise.

> *Lord, let me see the hope that is in all of us.*
> —Mark Collins

Digging Deeper: Jeremiah 7:5–7; Ezekiel 22:29

Thursday, October 25

Behold, God is my helper; the Lord is the upholder of my life.
—Psalm 54:4 (ESV)

Outside, the trees were just turning crimson. The air had a chill. I raked leaves that had fallen and tried to convince myself that everything was okay despite having just learned that an opportunity I'd hoped would come my way had gone somewhere else.

I took in a deep breath and came up with reasons the opportunity wasn't right for me—that most likely it would be a failure anyway. When the sour grapes approach didn't work I tried to put the disappointment out of my mind altogether.

My pile of leaves got bigger, but I was still feeling bad. I took another deep breath and prayed, "I trust Your plan, Lord. Your will, not mine."

Looking at my watch, I realized that Henry would be coming home from school any minute, so I sat on the front porch. The big yellow bus roared down the road, and I smiled at seeing my son's face in the window.

He bopped off the bus steps. "We're roller-skating in gym!" he said.

"Is it fun?" I asked.

"I don't know yet," he said. "We spent the whole day learning how to fall down."

"That's a useful skill," I said, opening the door. I smiled, thinking of a gym filled with kids purposely throwing themselves on to the floor. "I'm still learning how to fall, Henry," I said.

All at once, the weight of my disappointment seemed to disappear.

Dear Lord, thank You for helping me through life's disappointments,
for picking me up when I fall.
—Sabra Ciancanelli

Digging Deeper: Psalm 42:11; Luke 22:42

I therefore, the prisoner of the Lord, beseech you that ye walk worthy of the vocation wherewith ye are called.... For the perfecting of the saints, for the work of the ministry, for the edifying of the body of Christ.
—Ephesians 4:1, 12 (KJV)

I got a message on Facebook from Diane Wilson Onwuchekwa. "Are you the author? If so, I met you years ago with my friend Tish." Of course I remembered Diane and Tish. Their book club had invited me to a meeting to discuss my first book, *Passing by Samaria.*

Diane explained that she had written a book and wanted my help editing. Would I be interested? I hesitated. The gifts I've been given are to serve God's people through the stories I tell and through helping others tell their stories, but I must be a good steward of the gifts: the stories should help others. I wasn't sure if Diane's story would meet the criteria.

"I was in a terrible car accident, Sharon. I was clinically decapitated and more than seventy-eight bones were broken in my body. They told me I wouldn't walk again."

I was speechless. I remembered Diane as being such a vibrant woman. She had spent months in the hospital and then more months in a rehab center. "My church prayed for me. And my tight-knit group of friends, my prayer team, was always there, even when I felt hopeless."

Over the course of a few months, which included interviews, research, and a lovely retreat, Diane and I worked on her book, *Teachable Moments: Spirituality and Medicine.* I lent my skill as a writer, Diane brought her story of courage in the face of incredible odds, and we shared faith in God's miracles.

When things seem impossible, I remember God specializes in the impossible.

Lord, thank You for Your miraculous gifts and healing. I pray for all those who are sick, who are discouraged, and for those who have lost hope.
—Sharon Foster

Digging Deeper: Jeremiah 17:14; Matthew 14:14; Romans 8:28

Saturday, October 27

If it is possible, as far as it depends on you, live at peace with everyone.
—Romans 12:18 (NIV)

I grew up in a politically aware family. Political arguments were a part of life in our household, especially between my liberal mom and my conservative dad. We debated everything and were never afraid to say what we believed, loudly and proudly. We subscribed to three daily newspapers and two news weeklies. My parents never went to bed until after the 11:00 p.m. local newscast.

Lately, though, our national discourse has grown increasingly rancorous, even toxic. People aren't just wrong or misguided—they're evil and nefarious. We vote our fears rather than our convictions.

How did we come to this? It's not altogether new. Jesus joined the human race at one of its great boiling points. Jerusalem was a hotbed of political strife. Imperial Rome was an oppressive occupier of Jewish lands and ruled from afar with a merciless hand. Herod and his family were ruthless and corrupt. Revolution was in the air and violence was never far. Nazareth was poor and overpopulated and crime-ridden. The Zealots were already plotting insurrection.

It was into this roiling political cauldron that Jesus deliberately came, had planned to come at this exact moment since the very beginning of time. His message of peace for all humankind was a rank political contradiction. His command to love one another was an historical absurdity.

Yet it was the message that endured through the ages, the gospel of love and not hate, of peace and not strife. The word of Jesus still prevails, then as now. I have to listen closely to hear the eternal message of a peace that surpasses all understanding.

> *God, Your peace is beyond human comprehension.*
> *Teach us not to hate, but to disagree*
> *as brothers and sisters, not enemies.*
> —Edward Grinnan

Digging Deeper: Isaiah 9:6; Philippians 4:6–7; 1 Peter 3:8–9

Satisfy us in the morning with your unfailing love, that we may sing for joy and be glad all our days. —Psalm 90:14 (NIV)

I slap the alarm button before the noise awakens my husband. Forcing myself out of bed, I stumble through the house, following the cat whose meow demands food, silencing him before he wakes my grandson.

Going through the motions of my routine, I'm like a toy robot whose batteries are running down. I stare through the kitchen window as the coffee brews to wake me up.

I am definitely not a morning person. But I made a commitment years ago to spend time with God before my day got started. The only way to find the time was to get up earlier, before anyone else did. As a result, my life became more peaceful.

It still wasn't easy, and often I battled with my self-will to maintain the routine.

Clutching a cup of coffee, I sit at the table, then open my devotional book and journal. The house is quiet, and the solitude alarms me. "Lord, are You awake yet? Did You remember our appointment?"

I feel someone looking at me and glance toward the hallway to see if my grandson has sneaked up on me. But no one's there. Then I look toward our sliding glass door to the backyard, and I see him: Mr. Squirrel. He (or maybe she) is a squirrel we've been feeding for several years. He's become so familiar with us that he will take a peanut out of our hands.

I smile because he knew I would be there, and he was waiting patiently for me to give him my attention.

Lord, thank You for the smile You gave me this early morning
and for always waiting patiently for my attention.
—Marilyn Turk

Digging Deeper: Psalms 5:3, 65:8, 143:8

Monday, October 29

May the God of peace be with you all.... —Romans 15:33 (ESV)

My grocery store has been giving out stickers that customers can paste into a folder, one sticker for every ten dollars spent. Collected over several months, they can be redeemed for kitchen utensils. "What a great marketing idea!" I enthused to my friend Michelle.

She wasn't convinced. "What a gimmick, so people will buy more." Her comment tamped my enthusiasm but not by much. I eagerly played the game, calculating a trip's purchases so they would bump up to the next ten dollars.

At the checkout, I awaited my reward. When I didn't receive it, I responded like a kindergartner: "Ma'am, where's my sticker?"

Hearing that I'd miscalculated, I grimaced. "Can I go find something else and come back?" The cashier said yes.

That's when I noticed the next customer in line. Her presence brought me to my senses. "Oh, never mind. Forget it." I pushed my cart to the car, thinking: *This is ridiculous. So childish. Grow up!*

"Oh, there you are. I found you," the woman who'd stood behind me at the register said cheerfully. "Here. Take my sticker. I'm not participating."

Momentarily I felt ashamed and said, "It's so easy to get caught up in a game...." But as she handed me the stamp, I sensed only kindness and was calmed by this stranger, sent by the Spirit of peace.

Lord, in all aspects of life, help me to maintain a level of participation that promotes peace in my spirit and in my neighborhood.
—Evelyn Bence

Digging Deeper: 1 Thessalonians 5:23; Hebrews 13:20–21

If I take the wings of the dawn, if I dwell in the remotest part of the sea, even there Your hand will lead me, and Your right hand will lay hold of me. —Psalm 139:9–10 (NAS)

I'm grateful for the name my parents chose for me. Deborah was a wise woman of the Bible who led men into battle. She was a leader, a woman of deep faith. Deborah means bee, chatty, vibrant, busy. Yup, that's me all right. Then I had foot surgery and was forced into a long period of nonactivity.

I came through the surgery without a problem, but then the lengthy healing process started: six weeks in a wheelchair followed by six to eight weeks in a walking cast. When the doctor mentioned the prolonged recuperation time, it hadn't sounded so bad. Because I usually travel so much, I was actually looking forward to an extended time at home. And for the first week or two it wasn't bad. The wheelchair was a hassle, but I managed.

Soon, however, I was bored, miserable, and feeling sorry for myself. I've heard through the years that I needed to slow down and smell the roses. There were roses? I didn't see any roses.

I don't know that I could have gotten through this time if not for God. Despite the physical limitations, these were rich spiritual weeks. I read my Bible, studied His Word, and felt His presence in a profound way while my heart and mind quieted. While I felt hidden from the world, buried in the deepest part of the sea, God was there. His hand was upon me. He held me close to His heart, comforted me, saw me through those dark days. It didn't take long for me to smell the roses, the sweet scent of God's love and care for me.

Lord, You needed to slow me down, take me away unto myself so that You could get my attention. Only You could take my physical limitations and use them as a time of spiritual renewal.
—Debbie Macomber

Digging Deeper: Mark 1:35; Hebrews 4:15–16

Wednesday, October 31

"Blessed are you who weep now, for you will laugh." —Luke 6:21 (NIV)

My friend Carol was invited to her dear friend's birthday party. Since the party was so close to Halloween, the women talked about coming in costume. Carol borrowed one from a friend, a big vinyl blow-up version of a very fat cartoon character wearing a bikini and a shirt that said *Workout Trainer* across the front. Carol said she looked more like an overstuffed version of the Pillsbury Doughboy.

When she arrived at the restaurant, she pulled the costume up to her neck, pushed the blow-up button, inflated herself into blimp size, and waddled past all the dressed-up customers in the upscale restaurant. When she finally reached the back room where the party was, she opened the door and was mortified to discover that she was the only one wearing a costume. Carol was so upset and embarrassed that she had to take a deep breath and think about what her response would be. She could get angry and blame the others for the situation she was in or she could play nutty to the hilt, join in on the laughter, and make light of her ridiculous look. That's exactly what she did.

Not long after Carol told me that story, I was upset with my neighbor for removing my clothes from our community dryer two minutes before I arrived to do the job myself. I thought about Carol's reaction and decided to play it cool. I never mentioned it to my neighbor and gave her a big smile and an extrafriendly hello the next time I saw her.

Lord, thank You for the ability to think twice before I react to anything. Keep my funny bone at the forefront, so I can laugh my way through anger or embarrassment.
—Patricia Lorenz

Digging Deeper: Psalm 126:1–3; Proverbs 1:22–23

GOD'S UNFAILING LOVE

1 _____

2 _____

3 _____

4 _____

5 _____

6 _____

7 _____

8 _____

9 _____

10 _____

11 _____

12 _____

13 _____

14 _____

15 _____

October

16 _____

17 _____

18 _____

19 _____

20 _____

21 _____

22 _____

23 _____

24 _____

25 _____

26 _____

27 _____

28 _____

29 _____

30 _____

31 _____

NOVEMBER

For you, O Lord, are good and forgiving,
abounding in steadfast love to all who call upon you.

—Psalm 86:5 (ESV)

Thursday, November 1

He that loveth not knoweth not God; for God is love. —1 John 4:8 (KJV)

My brother Kevin died just before the sun went down. I understand the theory that he is gone and what is left of his earthly vessel is in a stone box under an oak tree in Illinois, but it seems inarguable to me that his love for me, and mine for him, persists, even though I do not have the same long, tall, grinning target for my love like I used to. Yet his memory is something that is with me all the time.

I saw a heron the other day, and it was Kevin. I saw a big guy lumbering diligently on a basketball court, and he was Kevin. We are so sure we know what is possible and impossible, and we are pretty much wrong about that. I think love wanders among generations and probably galaxies. I think love is the greatest thing ever invented, with all due respect to water and butter and my wife. I think if you love and were loved, then you lived the best life ever. I weep for people who were never loved and never got the chance to love other people. So very many people who never bathed in love and never cast their love into the hearts and souls of others.

Love is so much bigger than romance. Love is reverence and responsibility and respect and tenderness and patience and attentiveness. "There is compassion and then there is everything else," said a brilliant man to me once, and he was talking about big love, the ocean of love, about which my brother taught me so much.

Dear Lord, as You know, I used to curl up against my vast brother when I was little, and he taught me basketball and chess, and he was my hero, and we were blessed to grow to be dear friends as men, and now he is with You, and that's good. But thanks so much for letting the memory of him stay with me. I can't explain how much that means.
—Brian Doyle

Digging Deeper: 1 John 4:7–11, 16

"For my thoughts are not your thoughts, neither are your ways my ways,"
declares the Lord. —Isaiah 55:8 (NIV)

My wife, Elba, and I were enjoying a TV program when the phone rang. It was our daughter, Christine. I tried to keep my focus on the show, but I heard Elba crying. "What happened?" I asked.

She turned to me and said, "Christine and Taun got engaged!" I was delighted to hear the news.

Two months earlier, Taun had come to our home without Christine to tell us he would be proposing to her. We embraced him with open arms and gave him our blessings. He asked that we keep this to ourselves because he wanted to surprise our daughter. We didn't have any idea when he would propose, but nonetheless we were excited for them.

Since our children were young, Elba and I have prayed for their education, spiritual life, college choice, dates, and their marriage partner. Many years ago, before Taun and Christine met, my mother-in-law said to Christine, "Your true love is coming from afar." To this day, we all joke about this because Taun moved to New York from South Dakota.

As one of my colleagues says, "God has better plans for our children than we could ever plan." Indeed.

Lord, help us to trust Your ways.
—Pablo Diaz

Digging Deeper: Deuteronomy 7:9; Psalm 100:5

Saturday, November 3

There is a time for everything, and a season for every activity under the heavens. —Ecclesiastes 3:1 (NIV)

The knock at my door was soft but lasted much longer than the average knock. It was a little-boy knock. I opened the door to find my six-year-old brother on the other side. My family was taking me out for dinner to break up an exhausting weekend of studying for college finals, and Isaiah must have run ahead.

"Well, hello," I said.

Instead of his usual hug, Isaiah opened his mouth wide and pointed at two gaps in his smile. "These teeth will never grow back."

I stifled a laugh and wrapped my arms around him. "Who told you that?"

"I just know."

I pulled back and saw the concern twisted into his face. "Have you ever lost baby teeth before?"

"No," he answered.

"Well, I have—a whole bunch. And I can tell you that new ones will come in."

Isaiah nodded but pulled his lips tight over his gapped set of teeth.

"God didn't make those little teeth to last you forever," I told him. "They have to fall out so that there will be room for your grown-up ones."

Two more brothers made it to the door, and the moment was over. But Isaiah looked relieved. I was sure he couldn't wait for his smile to fill in, but now he knew that it would happen.

I felt reassured as well. Confident that, despite the overwhelming stress of finals, this, too, would pass. God had appointed a time for gappy smiles and for finals, and in His goodness, new teeth would show and exams would disappear.

Lord, thank You that Your timing is perfect.
—Logan Eliasen

Digging Deeper: Psalm 31:15; Acts 1:7

As iron sharpens iron, so one person sharpens another.
—Proverbs 27:17 (NIV)

On our way to church, my husband, Chuck, asked, "What's your class studying?" I lead a women's group, and Chuck leads another study.

"Women in the Bible who followed Jesus. Today, we're talking about Mary Magdalene. I love learning about people in the Bible."

"I do too," Chuck said. "There's always some new fact to discover or concept I hadn't considered before."

Suddenly, my enthusiasm dimmed.

"I hope Alice doesn't come to our class this morning," I said. "She's always so negative and contentious. I think she asks questions just to argue. Maybe she'll go to your class instead."

Guilt pinched my heart as I spoke, as I realized how inhospitable I sounded. *Shouldn't I welcome everyone to class? Why am I so afraid of her questions?*

Although Chuck seldom has anything negative to say about anyone, he, too, had experienced Alice's hostile presence. She frequently dropped in on different classes, voicing her opinions that usually ran counter to the lesson being taught and sometimes offending others.

So when Alice walked into my class that day, I was filled with dread. True to form, she interjected her critical views about the study. When she challenged me on a point in the lesson, I silently became defensive and prayed for the right words to say.

The next time I planned my lesson, I did extra research so I'd be ready to answer questions that Alice, or anyone else, might ask. And then I realized why she was there. Her questions made me spend more time preparing for the class, thus making me a better teacher.

Thank You, Lord, for sending Alice, whose presence prepares my heart and mind to teach Your Word and love all Your children.
—Marilyn Turk

Digging Deeper: 2 Timothy 2:15; 1 Peter 3:15

Monday, November 5

When he is dealing with the arrogant, he is stern, but to the humble he shows kindness. —Proverbs 3:34 (NAB)

"We're reassigning you and putting you on probation," my supervisor was saying. My heart went cold. My vision went fuzzy around the edges. I heard her words as if they were wrapped in cotton. "If your attitude and performance don't improve in a month's time, you will be fired."

Even in the midst of that hot, shame-filled moment, paths opened before me. I could tell my supervisor how she was wrong, how this was unfair, and how I was misunderstood and maligned. But God graced me in that moment with humility. I had taken this job because it didn't challenge me and it was easy money. I admitted to myself that I had put little thought or prayer into how I wanted to apply my skills and passions.

Humbled, I bought Richard Bolles's *What Color Is Your Parachute?* I followed every instruction in that book and researched jobs that sounded like they'd be fun and challenging. I was especially drawn to the job of radio commentator, and a year and a half later I was working at a public radio station, my first full-time position in what turned into a rewarding twenty-five-year career.

I was stunned by the stern discipline I had received that day in my supervisor's office. But my punishment was fair. I had harmed my employers with my arrogance and defiance. Acknowledging that behavior provided God with the opening He needed to shower me with kindness and wisdom.

God, help me to learn humility from my humiliations.
—Amy Eddings

Digging Deeper: Psalm 51:17; Ephesians 4:2; Philippians 2:8–9

Jesus said to her, "I am the resurrection and the life. Whoever believes in me, though he die, yet shall he live." —John 11:25 (ESV)

Watching all the media buzz surrounding the last national election, I felt a sadness mounting inside. I was missing my dad, who had passed away. My dad had been a political enthusiast, having run for city council and mayor of Baltimore, Maryland, my birthplace.

Growing up in a politically savvy family made election season fun. I remember countless times when my dad, mom, two older sisters, and I circled around the dinner table, discussing politics with the fervor of a congressional hearing. We would debate issues as passionately as the candidates.

This election season marked the first without my father. I missed hearing his daily commentary on the candidates' campaign antics and verbal attacks on their opponents. I missed hearing his views on each candidate's qualifications or lack thereof. I missed chuckling as he ranted about his least favorite candidate. I missed *him*.

On the day of Maryland's state election, my sister Sherri called to discuss the recent election footage we'd been following. We discussed the front-runners, and she had lots of opinions on each of them. Her endorsement for her favored candidate was so compelling, I laughed, thinking her candidate would do well to add Sherri to the payroll.

Then it hit me. My father was no longer here, but a part of him lived on in each of his daughters. He left me a compassionate and sensitive heart. My sister Lori embodies his protectiveness and care. He passed along his love for politics and public service to Sherri.

Now I don't feel the sadness as I did before. My father's spirit lives on, and for that I am grateful.

> *Lord, thank You for blessing us with loved ones who*
> *continue to be with us long after they've passed.*
> —Carla Hendricks

Digging Deeper: John 1:4, 3:16–17

Wednesday, November 7

FALLING INTO GRACE: Giving Thanks
He [Jesus] said to them, "Why are you afraid? Have you still no faith?"
—Mark 4:40 (NRSV)

I kept my eyes closed for a moment after waking. I wanted to savor the feeling of thankfulness. God had been healing me, and I had been learning to live with the changes and continuing pain from my fall. The journey since my broken collarbone and cracked rib led my husband, Charlie, and me to put our condominium on the market. We were better at trusting God and had accepted an offer for the purchase price, a blessing in our recession-struck city. Today, I felt a moment of bliss.

Then Charlie walked into our room. "The buyer pulled out."

"No!" I closed my eyes and howled in sadness and frustration. I could see the future we thought God had provided us collapsing into one big mess. Another fall. Another mistake. Another accident. The doubts and depressing thoughts overwhelmed me. I was tired of trying to think positive. What did God want from me? What was I supposed to learn from this?

I opened my eyes and saw Charlie seated on the edge of the bed, head in hands, his back to me.

Abruptly, the packed boxes, the vision of Christmas in the gleaming new apartment, my self-pity were all swept away. This man, who had done so much for me, loved me through everything, was hurting as much as—maybe even more than—I was. He counted on my faith to strengthen his.

I wrapped my arms around Charlie. "It's Thanksgiving time. We're together. And I can hug you with both arms. Who knows what God has planned for us next?"

Lord, when it rains, it pours. Please remind me that this is part of Your plan.
                                        —Marci Alborghetti

Digging Deeper: Psalm 71:1–6; Proverbs 2:1–11

But You, O Lord, are a shield for me, my glory and the One who lifts up my head. —Psalm 3:3 (NKJV)

Jogging this morning, I found a pretty feather—buff-and-brown-striped, probably from a hawk. The first feather I'd found in a long time.

I became interested in birds after finding a dead roadrunner on the roadside over a decade ago. I took some of its long, slender, white-tipped tail feathers, and my teenage daughters, who are part Cherokee, made them into dream catchers and hung them in our kitchen window.

I have glass vases full of fancy feathers I've collected since then: red cardinal and tanager feathers, blue bunting and jay feathers, striped and speckled feathers from woodpeckers, ducks, doves. I've used some in crafts, but mostly I forget them until some visitor comments.

That's why it seemed odd not to have found one in so long. Years, probably.

What changed? I pondered as I jogged, scanning the trees for warblers. *Are fewer birds dying? Are buzzards snatching them up before I find them? And if so, why?*

Finally I figured it out. Back when I first started running, I ran, my athletic daughter Charlotte pointed out, "wrong": my shoulders hunched, my head down.

"Running that way's bad for you! Throw back your shoulders! Lift your head!" she counseled. I found following Charlotte's advice nearly impossible. It seemed to take all my effort just to keep moving forward.

Now, though, those creatures that God made to "fly above the earth in the open firmament of heaven" (Genesis 1:20, KJV) keep me peering up into the tree canopy and out over the fields. Without meaning to, I run "right" these days. Getting exercise has morphed from a chore to a delight. My whole outlook has changed: I no longer notice dead birds, only live ones.

Thank You for lifting my head, Father. It seems a much better way to proceed.
—Patty Kirk

Digging Deeper: Ephesians 6:10–18

Friday, November 9

"Prepare yourself and be ready...." —Ezekiel 38:7 (NKJV)

I glanced at the fuel gauge: three-quarters full. We lived thirty-five mountainous miles from town, but there was plenty to make it home and back before the pickup needed refueling. I was tempted just to go home.

With a foot of snow on the ground, shopping in town had taken forever. My husband always kept the tank topped off, especially in winter; he's more of a stickler about that than I am. But I was using his pickup, so I needed to do it. I pulled into the gas station. "Lord, please give me patience when I have to do the right thing." It was more of a grumble than a prayer.

It sounded to me like my faith tank needed to be topped off, too, so when I got home, I pored over Scriptures about patience.

The next day, Randy and I were nursing our predawn coffees next to the woodstove, when the phone rang.

"Sorry to call so early," a friend said, "but I was driving in the woods and there was a creek flooding the road under the snow. My rig is buried. Could you come pull me out?"

I glanced at the thermometer: minus twelve degrees. There wasn't a moment to spare. He was more than seventy miles away, in the opposite direction from town. I filled the thermos and helped Randy load the chains and gear for rigging out our friend's truck.

"Thank You, thank You," I repeatedly prayed, grateful that I'd taken the extra few minutes to fuel up in town. Being stuck far from civilization can be a death sentence during our brutal winters.

Our friend was glad to see us. It took us over an hour, but we finally winched him out to higher ground.

Thank You, Lord, for reminding me to keep my faith primed and my tank full. You alone know the future. Help me to be prepared for the jags in the road I cannot see.
—Erika Bentsen

Digging Deeper: 2 Corinthians 9:5; 2 Timothy 4:2; 1 Peter 3:15

For I desired mercy, and not sacrifice; and the knowledge of God more than burnt offerings. —Hosea 6:6 (KJV)

I was sitting with my sister in Michigan Stadium—known as the Big House to those of us who bleed maize and blue—when the opposing team failed to make a desperately needed first down and had to turn the ball over to the Wolverines. "I'm beginning to feel sorry for them," Mary Lou said.

"Never, Mary Lou," I said. "Never feel sorry for the other team. They don't feel sorry for you when things are reversed."

"But Michigan is killing them," she said.

"That's the object of the exercise," I said. "You don't let up until the final whistle. There is no room for mercy."

Michigan was playing a team that had suffered a terrible scandal a few years before, one of the worst scandals in the history of collegiate sports. The university's football program, once one of the greatest in the nation, nearly collapsed. There was even talk of discontinuing it. It was still very difficult to recruit good athletes out of high school to come play for the university. So it was no wonder that Michigan was trouncing them.

I looked over at my sister, who has such a good heart, a heart that is soft and kind and merciful. *Had I really used that phrase "no room for mercy"? Really?* Faith teaches me that mercy is one of the great qualities of God the Father, and that He expects us to practice it.

Even for a football program that had fallen on hard times through no fault of the current staff and players.

As I was pondering all this, my Wolverines scored again and the crowd exploded. I put my arm around Mary Lou and said, "Want to go? I'm beginning to feel sorry for these guys."

Father, You are infinitely merciful in order to teach us to be merciful to others. We live in such a cutthroat, competitive world. Never let me forget that the quality of mercy is divine.
—Edward Grinnan

Digging Deeper: Psalm 103:8; Micah 6:8; 2 Corinthians 1:3–4

Sunday, November 11

Greater love has no one than this: to lay down one's life for one's friends.
—John 15:13 (NIV)

Pat and I were heading home from visiting our son in Hawaii. As we were waiting for the plane to leave Honolulu, the pilot told us, "You are all part of a very special flight tonight—an *honor flight* bringing home the remains of two missing airmen from World War II." Our pilot went on to explain that a B-24 bomber with twelve crew members was shot down in 1944 over New Guinea. The airmen had survived the crash but died in captivity.

During the trip, I kept thinking about these men, about their families, and about the unimaginable pain and turmoil they had all suffered. I wondered whether there were any living family members. Would someone be there to receive the remains?

As we arrived in Atlanta, a flight attendant asked us all to stay seated until those accompanying the airmen's remains disembarked. No one moved. Even after the military escorts, crisp in dress uniforms, deplaned, everyone kept silent. Slowly, people began leaving.

Inside the airport, a crowd gathered around the large terminal windows to watch a deeply moving tribute planeside. Everyone there had come together in gratitude to honor the airmen's sacrifice and to welcome home two American heroes after more than seventy years. Strangers became a family of the heart.

*Dear God, as we observe Veterans Day, let us always be ready to pause
and honor sacrifices made by men and women who pledge
their lives to defend the freedoms we enjoy! Amen.*
—John Dilworth

Digging Deeper: Mark 9:12, 10:45; Romans 5:7; Ephesians 5:2

Say to your brothers, "You are my people," and to your sisters, "You have received mercy." —Hosea 2:1 (ESV)

W here are you?" a young visitor asked, pointing to a picture posted on my refrigerator, then another, of me surrounded by my siblings. "Who are they?"

"Oh, they're my dear ones," I said. The phrase surprised me and prompted a twinge of nostalgia. You see, every Sunday afternoon for fifty years, my mother hoisted a Royal typewriter onto the dining room table. She inserted carbon sheets between six or more pages of bond paper and rolled them all into place. Then, modeling a hunt-and-peck method, she typed her predictable salutation: "Dear Ones."

In subsequent paragraphs she relayed highlights of the previous week's activities followed by a preview of the coming week's plans. Her letters—mailed to her parents, siblings, in-laws, and eventually to us adult children scattered across the country—represented her family ties. We knew we were her people, blessed by her lifelong commitment.

My parents passed away some years ago. I don't see my siblings often, but I talk to one, if not several, weekly. And one brother, bless him, sends out a Sunday group e-mail, summarizing his week. His closing phrase, "God is good," settles my spirit. It's the familial encouragement I see in Hosea's message: Tell your brothers and sisters that they're God's dear and beloved ones. I hear and accept the challenge. I'm reaching for the phone.

Father, thank You for Your love and mercy. It's a privilege
to share that good news with my family.
—Evelyn Bence

Digging Deeper: Philippians 4:1; 2 Timothy 1:1–10

Tuesday, November 13

As each has received a gift, use it to serve one another, as good stewards of God's varied grace. —1 Peter 4:10 (ESV)

Tonight was my hometown's local talent show. I've lived in Tivoli, New York, for most of my life, and over the years very little has changed. It's still a no-traffic-light, four-corner-center village of about a thousand people.

The slogan for our town has always been "Tivoli: 'I LOV IT' Backward." Growing up, I always felt safe and lucky, as if we lived in a secret utopia. I still feel that way.

A small crowd of us gathered on the second story of a grand brick church. Packed on folding chairs, standing room only, we faced the stage. Rays of the setting sun streamed through the stained glass.

One after another, young and old came onstage, playing instruments, dancing and singing, doing gymnastics and even puppetry. A young boy played "Old MacDonald Had a Farm" on his violin. A teenager danced and lip-synched to his favorite rock song. A woman sang tenderly to the beat of a single drum, stirring something deep in my heart.

My family scooted together in the audience. Henry—feeling a bit too old but wanting to see—sat on my lap to get a better view, and my mom, my oldest, Solomon, and my husband, Tony, clapped loudly. I found myself tearing up more than once at the generosity of the people I live among, the willingness of so many to put themselves onstage and give a gift only they could give, and the reciprocity of how that gift was appreciated, the cheers and applause that echoed off the vaulted ceiling again and again, reassuring each and every one of us: you belong; you are loved.

> *Heavenly Father, thank You for the variety of blessings You bestow*
> *upon us and the magic that happens when we share, honor,*
> *and celebrate our gifts.*
> —Sabra Ciancanelli

Digging Deeper: Matthew 6:21; Romans 12:6; 1 Corinthians 16:14

For there is hope of a tree, if it be cut down, that it will sprout again....
—Job 14:7 (KJV)

The three-alarm fire started just before midnight and blazed for over an hour. By then, the 150-year-old Grace Episcopal Church in the Bronx was a skeleton of charred wood, melted stained glass, and the ashes of its century-old organ.

Church members were not the only ones grieving as they stood before the smoking ruin that Tuesday morning in November 1993. Grace Church had been an oasis of hope in a decaying neighborhood, operating a food pantry and an after-school tutoring program for kids.

On the Sunday after the fire, the congregation gathered in front of the ruined building in the chilly air. They sat on folding chairs, sharing the few sooty and sodden hymnals salvaged from the wreckage. Father Miles, in a borrowed robe, stood behind an improvised altar and read the passage from Job about a tree that had been chopped down but was growing again.

Grace Church did grow again. The congregation moved into temporary housing for worship and outreach. The Episcopal Diocese of New York, of which my own church was a part, started a rebuilding fund. Today, where the old church stood is now a stunning glass-and-stone sanctuary.

For me, the experience was a working out before my eyes of an oft-heard truth. I remember arriving at their interim location. "Everyone's so cheerful!" I said to Father Miles. "You'd never think you'd just lost your beautiful church."

"Oh, we didn't lose the church," Father Miles said. "That was just a building." He gestured at the group. "*This* is the church! People who love Jesus and love one another. No fire on earth can destroy that."

Father, help me always to see reality beneath outward appearance.
—Elizabeth Sherrill

Digging Deeper: Acts 2:44–47

Thursday, November 15

Thanks be unto God for his unspeakable gift.
—2 Corinthians 9:15 (KJV)

A couple of years ago, I bought my teenage great-nephew some special attire to wear for hunting. I'd seen a couple of pictures of him trekking through the woods in the camouflage gear. But as time passed, I'd forgotten all about my gift to him.

Then this fall at a family get-together, Trenton gathered me in a hug. "Thanks again for the hunting clothes, Aunt Roberta," he said.

Hunting clothes? I wondered. That was at least two years ago. How would a fifteen-year-old who is consumed with school and soccer remember something so distant? Especially something that probably no longer fit.

I was still thinking about Trenton's thankfulness as I drove to work and passed a church sign. "Thanksgiving is coming," it said. "But don't just thank God one day a year."

I decided to accept the challenge and emulate Trenton. I searched my own mind for two-year-old blessings I'd all but forgotten. The freezing January night my neighbor helped me with a flat tire. The afternoon an unexpected check arrived in the same batch of mail as a second notice for a medical procedure. The resale shop that had an embroidered shawl I'd been admiring in an upscale boutique window.

Come to think of it, I'd been forgetting about the Real Source of a lot of things.

> *At Thanksgiving and always, Lord,*
> *thank You for a lifetime of blessings.*
> —Roberta Messner

Digging Deeper: Psalms 28:7, 69:30

The Lord shall give thee rest from… thy fear.… —Isaiah 14:3 (KJV)

I awoke with a jolt. I was terrified. Once again I felt like I was being smothered. I couldn't catch my breath until I got up and walked around the house. Back in bed, apprehension consumed my thoughts.

It was a relatively simple problem. For some reason, my inner nose had collapsed, making it difficult to breathe properly. A couple of times, while climbing the steep steps of a tower or dashing up a long mountain in Zimbabwe, I had actually panicked, not realizing that my erratic breathing had caused my heart to beat in double time. After extensive tests, my doctor concluded that my nose was my only problem.

All I had to do was have surgery. But that's when the real fear found root. And it was made worse by comments from friends.

It's a terrible surgery. You will think you are being smothered for days. To be honest, you'll have the sensation of drowning for an entire week.

The nasal problem was getting worse, and I wasn't helping it by ramping up my anxiety level. So I called on God and centered myself there: in His presence, one moment at a time.

I was ready.

The surgery went without a hitch. Some hours later, as I began to wake up, one thing was perfectly clear. I could breathe through my nose! My doctor had cleverly inserted tubes that allowed me this forgotten pleasure. No smothering or drowning sensations. Already I could see that my problem had been solved.

How many years did I waste? How many nights' sleep did I lose? How many hours of manufactured panic did I spend separated from the one truth that waits for us all: God is with us. What shall we fear?

Father, with every breath, I breathe Your presence. I am not afraid.
—Pam Kidd

Digging Deeper: Exodus 14:13; Matthew 6:34

Saturday, November 17

Stand this day, all of you, before the Lord your God....
—Deuteronomy 29:9 (JPS)

The phone call came in the middle of the morning. A man whom none of us knew had died at the hospital yesterday and had asked for a Jewish funeral. The rabbi was trying to put together a *minyan* (a group of Jews required for the recitation of a number of prayers, one of which is the Mourner's kaddish) in order to fulfill the man's final request.

Even though it was cold, windy, and rainy, and I had no idea who this person had been, I agreed to participate. The rabbi asked me to be at the cemetery at two o'clock that afternoon.

It was windier and colder by then, so those of us who walked to the open grave were bundled up and hunched over to try to keep warm. There were exactly ten of us, along with two Christian men the deceased had known through work, and the cemetery groundsmen.

The rabbi said that everything he knew about the man was what his two colleagues had told him, and it was all work-related. We knew nothing about his family, his history, his likes, his dislikes. Still, we wished him well on his way and prayed that he had found whatever he desired, because he was part of our community, even though he had separated himself from it until the moment when he knew he had to choose how to greet eternity. He then wanted to be a part of us, and we would not let him go any other way.

> *We are Your people, God of Life. Help us to honor You*
> *by standing together so that we don't fall apart.*
> —Rhoda Blecker

Digging Deeper: Judges 5:9

CONFIDENCE IN DIFFICULTY: Treasure God's Light

The light shines in the darkness, and the darkness has not overcome it.
—John 1:5 (NIV)

Maggie was finally back in Connecticut for a third time, though the twenty-eight-day program was a bust. We had what appeared to be a viable plan for moving forward: she was going to a different therapeutic wilderness program, in Georgia. But she flat-out refused to go.

We were advised to hire a professional to transport her. Joe was our man. When he and his partner arrived at the hospital to pick up Maggie, she bellowed, howled, threatened, and ran around in a frenzy. After half an hour the nurse said, "We'll have to sedate her."

Joe frowned and shook his head. He believed his job consisted of more than just getting Maggie from point A to point B; he wanted to make her journey a positive one, a smooth transition. Force didn't fit into that.

"No," he said, "she can make the decision to come on her own." He asked the staff to back off and give her space. Then he turned to my daughter. "Take your time, Maggie. I believe you can do this. I can wait."

She stared, wild-eyed and trembling. Deep inside her terrified heart, she heard he'd stood up for her, trusted her.

A few moments passed. My fourteen-year-old finally took a deep breath and looked Joe in the eyes. Then she said, "I can do this. Let's go." And they did.

> *Father, You shine rays of light into even the deepest darkness.*
> *Help me recognize that light, treasure it, and be thankful for it.*
> —Julia Attaway

Digging Deeper: Ephesians 4:29; Philippians 4:5

Monday, November 19

Be still before the Lord and wait patiently for him. —Psalm 37:7 (NIV)

"Mother," my daughter said gently. "Do you know that when you ask questions, you don't give anyone a chance to answer?"

"Yeah," my not-so-tactful son chimed in. "You talk a lot."

Nursing my bruised feelings, I stopped by the Athens Area Humane Society, where I'd just signed up to be a volunteer. "Welcome!" The gal in charge smiled. "We'll assign you to Precious. She's been here two-and-a-half years. Was mistreated as a kitten and now doesn't like people or other cats. Been returned by two families."

Precious had her own little room with a baby gate, which encouraged her to stay inside.

Still feeling glum, I was left to befriend Precious. I climbed over the baby gate and sat down in the middle of the tile floor, cross-legged. Precious perched atop a purple shelf and turned her head to the wall.

So I sat. Quietly. *My children should see me now.* I left Precious after about thirty minutes. A failure—but for some unknown reason, I continued to visit her.

Ours was a strange, soundless relationship. A few months later, as I sat there on the floor, she offered a distinct *"Meow."*

I caught my breath, surprised and delighted. *"Meow,"* I told her softly. Lo and behold, the huge black-and-white, long-haired beauty sashayed over to me. She stepped daintily into my lap and got situated comfortably.

She purred.

I smiled.

A short while later Precious was adopted by a family who totally understood her. I was given a picture of my feline friend standing on her hind legs, leaning against a human.

Jesus, You have the most unique methods of teaching a chatterbox like me.
—Marion Bond West

Digging Deeper: Psalm 141:3; Proverbs 17:28; Ecclesiastes 3:7–8, 9:17

Do not hastily bring into court, for what will you do in the end, when your neighbor puts you to shame? —Proverbs 25:8 (ESV)

My dog was gone.

We had searched everywhere—driving up and down neighborhood streets late into the night, scouring the neighbors' yards, trekking into the woods to see if he had wandered too far and gotten lost. But my precious, thirteen-year-old golden retriever, Jack, was gone.

I was devastated. I called every animal shelter in town asking about him, praying that somehow, somewhere, someone had found him.

Then a glimmer of hope: A woman posted on the neighborhood boards that she had a sweet elderly dog in her possession. My Jack had been found!

And then the bad news came: The woman, seeing that my old, beloved dog was scraggly and thin and that he had trouble walking, turned him over to the city animal authorities, filing a report of animal abuse against us.

Talk about a flood of emotions! Relief mixed with frustration. Anger mixed with hope. Tears followed by more tears.

We did get Jack back. Our wonderful vet came back early from a family vacation to make a full report, sending all of his previous veterinary records to the city, showing the officials that Jack was, in fact, well cared for, albeit old and partially lame. Charges were dropped. Fines were excused. Jack came home to a jubilant welcome as three kids surrounded him with hugs and beef strips.

And my neighbor? Well, I've forgiven her. It took a while. I went from frustrated to angry to finally recognizing that her reaction was a well-intentioned attempt to protect a precious animal. I now know that she meant well. And that's all we can ask of our neighbors.

Lord, give me the ability to assume the best in people.
—Erin MacPherson

Digging Deeper: 1 Corinthians 13:7

Therefore as you have received Christ Jesus the Lord, walk in [union with] Him... having been deeply rooted [in Him] and now being continually built up in Him and... established in your faith, just as you were taught, and overflowing in it with gratitude. —Colossians 2:6–7 (AMP)

I recently read a story about the first settlers who came to New England and the great hardships they suffered those first few winters. During one of their public assemblies, a member of their group proposed that they proclaim a fast and remind God of their many needs. Another man stood and declared that, instead of bombarding heaven with what they lacked, they celebrate all that they had for which to be thankful. Rather than fasting, the man suggested, they should hold a day of thanksgiving. It could be from this very meeting that we now have come to observe the tradition of Thanksgiving. I'd like to think so.

Having an attitude of gratitude is something I learned from reading Norman Vincent Peale's books. I found his words compelling enough to start my own gratitude journal. Every morning I list five things for which I am most grateful. My list isn't anything profound. This morning I noted the music of the songbird outside my window and the excitement I feel for a knitting project I'm about to begin.

I discovered that counting my blessings starts my off day on a positive note. Instead of worrying about my to-do list, I take a short pause to thank God for this day and all that it will hold. It helps me to remember how very blessed I am.

All the paper produced in the world could not contain the blessings
You have poured upon me, Lord. May I always have
an attitude of gratitude.
—Debbie Macomber

Digging Deeper: 1 Chronicles 16:34; 1 Thessalonians 5:16–18

The Lord is close to the brokenhearted.... —Psalm 34:18 (NIV)

Evie wasn't friendly or accommodating like the other servers at the Waffle House. The day before Thanksgiving, when she charged me $1.70 for an ounce of milk for my coffee, I slapped a couple of choice labels on her too. "Grumpy" was my favorite.

"You sure aren't in much of a Thanksgiving frame of mind," my sister said. "Where's all that kindness and gratitude?"

So I decided to change my tack. "You like magazines?" I asked Evie. I'd brought along a couple of home decor glossies.

"Don't have time for picture books like some," Evie grumbled.

Then she paused and took in the cover. Featured was a mouthwatering pie.

A slow smile crept across Evie's face. "Well, I'll be," she said. "A *pee-can pie.* Gimme that thing. I'm going to make my man a *peecan pie* for Turkey Day."

Another server stole a glance at the photo of the pie and at Evie. "Don't be thinking that magazine's yours," Evie said, jabbing the server's elbow. "My friend at table five just gave it to me. I'm making my Sammy one of those pies. It's his favorite, you know."

Later, when Evie brought my order of scrambled eggs and bacon, she related the story of "her man." They'd been together for thirty-five years. She'd baked him a pecan pie when they were newlyweds, and he'd raved about it ever since. But now he had end-stage lung cancer. Doctors predicted this would be his last Thanksgiving.

I'd been all wrong to judge Evie without knowing what made her the way she was. I'd thank God for her and ask Him to give her a double helping of blessings too.

Evie wasn't mean-spirited at all, Lord. She simply had a broken heart.
She can be my Thanksgiving teacher if I only let her.
—Roberta Messner

Digging Deeper: Psalm 147:3; John 14:27; 1 Peter 5:7

Friday, November 23

Then Hezekiah took the letter from the hand of the messengers and read it.... —2 Kings 19:14 (NAS)

Shortly after I sold my mom's place, the new owner called, saying, "There's a disintegrating trunk in the corner of the shed. It has some letters in it."

The trunk turned out to be filled with my grandmother's last possessions. Priceless for me were those letters—written from my mother to her mother when I was just a one-year-old.

I kept them to read on the first anniversary of Mom's death. Hearing how she felt as a young wife and mother more than sixty years earlier gave me back my mom that day. I savored each word, sorry to come to the last one.

In two of her letters, Mom revealed my toddler personality. One said I'd been sick and was feeling better—"Carol is back to her usual cheery self." I sucked in a surprised breath. Mom and I had talked often about my being her "song of joy"—the meaning of my name.

Another stated, "Carol sure does jabber a lot. I think she'll talk before she walks." How I laughed. I am a talker—much more than my mother, who was always an excellent listener. It comforted me to know that verbal expressiveness was in my makeup from the beginning—something to monitor but important to who I am.

I thought I'd known most things about Mom. But the unexpected gift of the letters in the trunk revealed more. They spoke to me of the strong tie between us that would always be there. On what might have been a despondent day, they helped me find my "usual cheery self."

Jesus, Lord of deep bonds, I offer gladness for my bond with Mom and our bond with You—an unbreakable union among us.
—Carol Knapp

Digging Deeper: Jeremiah 31:25; John 14:16-21; 1 Corinthians 13:11

THE BEAUTY OF SIMPLICITY
Never Stop Praying for Each Other

Pray without ceasing. —1 Thessalonians 5:17 (KJV)

Every morning my husband, Rick, and I pray for each other. He prays for me to be bold and courageous; I pray for him to be tenderhearted and patient.

Last week, he encouraged me to attend an out-of-state conference. I'm a homebody, an introvert. He stayed behind and took care of Clyde, our one-hundred-pound Labrador, and Ellie, our ten-pound Morkie.

Before Ellie came to live with us, we'd always had big dogs, dogs that "served a purpose," Rick said. Then our son-in-law trained a police dog who didn't like Ellie. My husband rescued her, and they've been BFFs ever since.

After the conference, I came home exhausted but filled with fresh creativity. I found Rick sitting in his recliner, holding Ellie.

"Guess who went to work with me while you were gone?" he said.

"No way."

"She looked sad when I tried to leave her."

I smiled and touched the back of his neck. "Nice haircut."

"She went with me to get my hair cut too."

Imagining the scene, I fell in love all over again. "You showed up at the salon carrying a froufrou dog?"

"Not exactly. After work, I stopped by to make an appointment. The woman offered to cut it then, but Ellie was in the car with the AC running. She said to bring her inside."

"Did she behave?"

"Of course. She sat on the sofa and watched me. Isn't that right, girl?"

My heart melted. Only a tenderhearted man would do that.

Lord, we haven't stopped praying, and You haven't stopped working.
You're tenderizing my husband and making me brave. Thank You.
—Julie Garmon

Digging Deeper: Ephesians 6:18; James 5:16

Sunday, November 25

You, therefore, have no excuse, you who pass judgment on someone else, for at whatever point you judge another, you are condemning yourself, because you who pass judgment do the same things. —Romans 2:1 (NIV)

How's my driving, Mom?"

"Pretty good."

"Yeah, but I'm too slow when I get on the freeway."

"You'll get better."

"I jumped out in front of another car in an intersection."

"True, but you are learning."

"You keep giving me the benefit of the doubt, 'cause you love me."

"So?"

"So…maybe the other drivers on the road could use a little love too."

Ouch. My son, Zach, who had recently gotten his driver's license, was right; I am not a perfect driver. I make mistakes all the time. And my biggest mistake, the one I keep making? I'm too quick to judge.

I follow traffic rules, or at least I try to. I want others to, as well. It makes life easier and safer when we do. And I like to think I am a courteous driver. Yet I don't use my turn signals every time. I don't always make a complete stop at a stop sign. Some days I have a running commentary in my car, talking to other drivers. I point out their mistakes or, at the very least, roll my eyes. *It's not your turn. Read the signs. Turn off your phone!*

Why do I become self-righteous when I am behind the wheel of my car? Maybe because I feel anonymous. I am able to judge without consequence. No one knows what I am saying or feeling about their "terrible" driving.

My son got his license, but I got the lesson. A little love and grace go a long way in keeping the roads safe. They also go a long way toward keeping my head free of ugly thoughts.

Reduce the speed of my harsh words, Lord. Pull me over and let me be compassionate behind the wheel of my vehicle today. Amen.
—Lisa Bogart

Digging Deeper: Nehemiah 9:33; Proverbs 15:3, 17:15; John 7:24

Open my eyes, that I may see wondrous things from Your law.
—Psalm 119:18 (NKJV)

Want to see something weird?"

The bus driver stopped. We were at an airport, being transported from the parking lot to the terminals. She invited us to look out the front window at a sight that made us gasp.

"It's been like that all morning." There was a skunk, wandering the parking lot, its head stuck inside a yogurt cup. It ambled in circles, bumping into parked cars and heading off in random directions, its tail standing tall at the ready.

A Good Samaritan stood by, trying to figure out what to do. My kids offered to run out and yank the cup off the skunk's head, but my wife and I persuaded them to let the gentleman have a try first.

I watched the poor little creature and commented, "I feel like that sometimes." I can't see where I'm going. I don't know what's ahead. I'm not sure of my direction. At times, I'm not even sure about God. "I get you, little one," I said. My family smiled.

Finally, the Good Samaritan made his move. He made sure the skunk's business end was pointing away from him. Then he reached out his hand, grabbed the yogurt cup, yanked it off while jumping as far away as he could, and ran.

So did the skunk...in the opposite direction, as if to say, "Thank you, sir, for rescuing me." It was a bona fide feel-good moment.

We sat down, the bus resumed its route, and I thought of how privileged I am whenever I see the blessings that God has prepared for me.

Gracious Father, please yank away the blinders that keep me from
seeing Your everyday, everywhere gifts of grace. Amen.
—Bill Giovannetti

Digging Deeper: Ephesians 1:17–18

Tuesday, November 27

Be clothed with humility.... —1 Peter 5:5 (KJV)

A new grandbaby! When Tom and Canay shared the news, I swung into turbo-grandma mode, buying baby clothes and enthusing over knitting projects with my sister-in-love, Dana. Of course, I'm not much of a knitter, but my enthusiasm outraced my ability.

First, we ordered fine merino yarn from Peru. Dana, a knitter with some experience, would craft a sweater and booties from variegated blue and green fibers. The parents-to-be wanted "something different," so I would knit a fine-gauge stroller blanket in sunset colors: indigo, coral, and violet. After all, the pattern was just an enlarged dishcloth, all knit stitches and one yarn over. How hard could it be?

Once I had knit the first six inches, I knew my piece would have many "spontaneous design elements," as the knitting circle women generously called them. To me, they looked like holes, lumps, and repair jobs. I suppose I could have started over, but I stubbornly plowed on.

By the time I finished the blanket, Baby's arrival was still five months away. I certainly could have redone my project perfectly with time to spare, especially now that I had seen the layette whipped up by Baby's other grandma, a knitting whiz. Should I scuttle my embarrassing blanket, thirty hours, and nearly as many dollars?

No.

At the baby shower, I shall offer my lumpy, love-filled artwork as a metaphor for parenting. The card will read: *"This blanket is not perfect, yet I give it to you as a reminder that parenting isn't about perfection. Baby won't care about your flaws and inconsistencies when he's wrapped in your warmth and love."*

Heavenly Father, thank You for loving us, flaws and all.
—Gail Thorell Schilling

Digging Deeper: Proverbs 10:12; Matthew 18:4; 1 John 4:17

And Jesus said, "Come." Then Peter got out of the boat and was walking on the water toward Jesus. —Matthew 14:29 (CEB)

They're my favorite socks: blue, gray, and black, with a little bit of writing on the bottom. They're warm, wooly, and I always search for them on each first cold day of the year. You can't really see the most significant thing about them unless I take off my shoes and show you the bottoms of my feet. But there, on each sock, is a bluish puddle labeled the Sea of Galilee. My friend Edward bought them for me on a trip to Israel, a fine souvenir.

"You gave them to me because I can walk on water?" I suggested.

"Because I thought you'd like them," he said.

I don't walk on water. Don't even come close. If Jesus asked me, as He asked Peter, to step out of the boat and walk with Him on the Sea of Galilee, I would surely sink at the first step, faltering in my faith, not even hearing Him call out, "Be encouraged! It's me" (Matthew 14:27, CEB). And yet I love having something on my feet to remind me, ever so subtly, to walk in Jesus's footsteps.

That cashier who was so rude to me, couldn't I have been a little nicer to her? That guy who cut me off as I tried to move into the right lane on the highway, did I really need to shout at him from behind the wheel of my car? That sympathy note I've been meaning to write, the check for the worthy cause, the get-well card: it's time to get to them tonight.

Most important, the fears that prevent me from trusting, why not give them up?

"I'm wearing my favorite socks today," I tell Edward at the office.

"Glad you like them," he says. "Nice to feel like a disciple, with the Sea of Galilee at your feet."

"Come," You said, and I come, knowing that as long as I keep Your gaze, I can walk where I never expected to go.
                    —Rick Hamlin

Digging Deeper: Luke 5:11; Romans 15:5

Thursday, November 29

The Lord will settle international disputes; all the nations will convert their weapons of war into implements of peace. . . . —Isaiah 2:4 (TLB)

Sometimes it's hard for me to love my neighbor. Especially the cranky lady downstairs who won't speak to any of us and who continually fires off nasty letters to the management. But when I see her out back, trimming the bushes, pulling weeds, and trying to make our backyard beautiful, I am reminded that I must love her in spite of her crankiness.

Loving my neighbor brings to mind one of my favorite pieces of art. It sits at the United Nations Building in New York City: a colorful mosaic, nine feet by ten feet and weighing twelve hundred pounds. It was created by Norman Rockwell and is titled *The Golden Rule.* Across the front are these words carved in gold: "Do unto others as you would have them do unto you."

The mosaic shows the faces of twenty-eight people who represent all the different people we must love: black, white, Asian, Muslim, Jewish, Christian, atheist, racist, addicted, imprisoned, gay, homeless, young, old, sick . . . the list goes on.

When I saw Rockwell's mosaic for the first time, I was stunned by its intricate beauty and even more so by the variety of people depicted in the work. The piece has since been restored and will remind visitors for generations to come that we must love, accept, and respect our neighbors—all of them.

This year, for Christmas, I'm giving my cranky neighbor a gift of one of my small paintings. It isn't much, but she is, after all, part of the mosaic of our community.

Lord, help me to love, accept, and respect my neighbor, and thank You for the variety of people You have put in my life.
—Patricia Lorenz

Digging Deeper: Hebrews 13:1–3; 1 Peter 3:8–12; 1 John 3:11–24

Happy is the man that findeth wisdom.... —Proverbs 3:13 (KJV)

My career in wealth management, my community activities, and my family involvement have opened many windows into the world as it unfolds around me. I see people who seem to have everything and others whose possessions are meager. Some almost drip with awards and accolades, while the goodness of others is never publicly recognized. I see people who shine with happiness and others who spread misery. People who are generous beyond measure and a few who cling to the first dollar they ever made.

In all of this, sizing up a successful life is more than a little elusive, and when I reflect on how I want to live my life, my thoughts fly to my father.

My dad served as a minister at the same church in Nashville, Tennessee, for thirty-eight years. Even though he was offered positions at bigger, more prestigious churches from all over the country, he felt called to remain where he was.

I can't count the number of people who consider my father "the smartest man I've ever known." In addition to his unparalleled intelligence, he forgives without hesitation and radiates a kindness that draws people to him.

I guess he's a bit like King Solomon who, when given a choice, looked beyond wealth, power, and prominence. My dad's choices, like the great biblical king's, radiate wisdom. If a contented life is a measure of success, Dad rises to the top.

So as I gaze at the panorama of life that my particular windows offer, I try to look first for the people who wisely chose happiness, generosity, and fulfillment, no matter what their position in the world happened to be. Like my father, they are God's people, and I want to be counted in their number.

Father, my earthly father reflects Your wisdom. Let me be like him.
—Brock Kidd

Digging Deeper: Proverbs 16:16, 18:19; Ecclesiastes 8:5

GOD'S UNFAILING LOVE

1 _____

2 _____

3 _____

4 _____

5 _____

6 _____

7 _____

8 _____

9 _____

10 _____

11 _____

12 _____

13 _____

14 _____

15 _____

16 _____

17 _____

18 _____

19 _____

20 _____

21 _____

22 _____

23 _____

24 _____

25 _____

26 _____

27 _____

28 _____

29 _____

30 _____

DECEMBER

"The Lord your God in your midst, the Mighty One, will save; He will rejoice over you with gladness, He will quiet you with His love, He will rejoice over you with singing."

—Zephaniah 3:17 (NKJV)

And she gave birth to her firstborn son; and she wrapped Him in cloths, and laid Him in a manger, because there was no room for them in the inn. —Luke 2:7 (NAS)

Christmas has always been my favorite time of year. Our home is decorated with five Christmas trees, one for each family. It takes an entire week to get everything set up and ready. In addition to the trees, I have collected well over fifty Nativity sets. There are mangers in every room of the house. I like to say you can't even use the guest bathroom without the Baby Jesus watching every move you make. These Nativity sets are important because I don't want anyone who visits to think I've forgotten the reason for the season.

However, it was from a sermon that I only recently learned something about the birthplace of Christ that I never knew before. Scripture tells us that Jesus was placed in a manger. What came as a surprise was to realize this wasn't just any ordinary stable or barn. This was a special one, reserved for the lambs that were to be sacrificed in the temple.

I let that sink in: Christ, the Lamb of God, chose to be born in a stable only for sacrificial lambs, foreshadowing His death upon the Cross for my sins, for yours.

Now, when I look at the Nativity sets around my house, I'm reminded even more of the reason that Baby Jesus came—to grow into the Lamb of God, Who takes away the sins of the world.

Father God, You gave us Your Son, sending Him into the world to be
an atonement for sins, Your mission statement to the world.
May my mission statement be to live for You.
—Debbie Macomber

Digging Deeper: Isaiah 53:7; John 1:29

First Sunday in Advent, December 2

LIGHT IN OUR DARKNESS: Be Still

"Be still, and know that I am God!..." —Psalm 46:10 (NRSV)

I am in a doctor's office, waiting...again.

This has become my life. What started as an injury to my left hip has escalated into injuries all over my body.

Some of it is my fault. I keep trying to return to exercise too soon. But I was also originally misdiagnosed, and the first physical therapist prescribed exactly the wrong course of treatment. Now I live every day in pain and weakness.

Just months ago, I was strong, vigorous, running and swimming each day and playing outside with my kids. I feel diminished, half a person.

I spend a lot of time waiting—to see doctors; for signs of healing; for the day to end, so I can go to bed and pretend that none of this is happening as I lie and wait for sleep.

I abhor waiting. I especially dislike being sick and unable to use my body as I want to. I keep reminding myself that God has His own timing, that He works all things for good for those who love Him. So far there is little good for me to meditate on as I sit in the office.

Then I remember a prayer recommended to me by a friend. "At night when you can't sleep or whenever you find yourself with quiet time, say: 'Be still and know that I am God.'"

I begin saying the words over and over. They don't crowd out all of my anxious thoughts or make me better instantly, but their deep truth sinks in.

When I am in pain or distress, God, I will remember that
You are God no matter what and You are with me.
—Jim Hinch

Digging Deeper: Romans 8:24–30; 2 Thessalonians 1:4–5

"For he took notice of his lowly servant girl....He has scattered the proud and haughty ones. He has brought down princes from their thrones and exalted the humble." —Luke 1:48, 51–52 (NLT)

I pulled a glossy catalog from my mailbox. Flipping through it, I saw lofty Christmas trees awash in luxurious ornaments. For a moment, I wondered whether I should replace my motley assortment of ornaments amassed over the years.

My collection includes a Popsicle-stick, pipe-cleaner, and felt skier; a white paper-plate, glitter-encrusted angel with a loose head; a yellow and black clay creation resembling a cross between a blowfish and a finger-imprinted whale; and a red construction paper heart emblazoned with "Mery Chirstmas" in blue crayon. Yes, many of my ornaments were made by our children when they were young. Some we purchased to commemorate a special trip, event, or memory. Others are from friends and remind me of fun times together.

All in all it's quite a hodgepodge. And you know what? I'll continue to choose them over the gleaming uniformity and polished precision of the ornaments in the catalog. My ornaments aren't perfect in the world's eyes, but in mine they are.

As I threw away the catalog, it dawned on me—that's how it is with God, Who chooses the lowly and humble over the proud and haughty. And He's got quite an assortment of us humans! We aren't perfect, but in God's view we are.

Thank You, Lord, for choosing me with all of my flaws and
failings and for loving me despite—
maybe even because of—them.
—Kim Henry

Digging Deeper: Psalm 149:4; 1 Corinthians 1:26–29;
2 Corinthians 5:21; James 2:5, 4:6

Tuesday, December 4

We don't know what we should pray, but the Spirit himself pleads our case with unexpressed groans. —Romans 8:26 (CEB)

I pray a lot," my friend Sharon said after we'd shared concerns about our grandsons. Kale, her youngest, was playing basketball that night even though he had a broken foot. My David, a marine, was training to swim a mile in the ocean off Pensacola, Florida, wearing a sixty-pound pack.

Praying for Kale and David was simple. Intercessory prayers for family and friends came easily because I knew their needs and pictured their faces while I prayed. Intercession for governing authorities and leaders was more difficult, but I usually had some specific information to guide my prayers. Every day brought reports of disasters—eight dead in floods; forty thousand displaced by civil war; over two hundred dead following an earthquake—and I struggled for a meaningful way to pray for victims and survivors.

Then I watched a news clip featuring a woman who fled for her life when terrorists attacked her remote village and slaughtered men, women, and children alike. She was able to save only one of her children. "We just ran," she told the interviewer. "We didn't even have time to cry."

Now, when intercessory prayer is my only gift to those who have experienced tragedy and loss, I picture that grieving woman. For me, her face symbolizes all who suffer. I rest in knowing that my prayers join thousands of others, that the Holy Spirit supplies the words, and that our compassionate God is present even in tragic situations.

> *Lord, help me to faithfully pray for all the people*
> *who don't even have time to cry. Amen.*
> —Penney Schwab

Digging Deeper: Nehemiah 1:1–11; 1 Timothy 2:1

Glory to God in the highest, and on earth peace, good will toward men.
—Luke 2:14 (KJV)

Last week I attended a class that included an interesting aspect of Eastern church icons. The leader explained how a physical act can take on spiritual meaning. "The icon artist layers paints—first a base tone, then increasingly ornate and golden—to represent a progression from the earth below to the heavens above."

When I got back home, I wearily assessed the burdensome progress of a craft project, instigated by a young neighbor. She'd begged me to make a piñata for her upcoming birthday. "It's easy. Please?" she'd implored. She named a few basic supplies: a balloon, flour for homemade glue, newspapers, and decorative tissue paper. She'd cut a bagful of strips even before I'd bought a balloon. Her enthusiasm was hard to resist.

"We can try," I finally said.

Well, what a gooey mess! By the time we'd finished plastering layer one of bits of paper to the round rubbery frame, our forearms were flecked. Two days later, we added layer two. That's what I saw drying on my splattered dining room table when I came home from the class. But now I recognized something new in the encrusted ball.

Later in the week, as we stirred up more glue and laid down more pasty strips, I envisioned that our hands were building a well-rounded life—maybe mine, maybe my young friend's, maybe a blend of both—with layers of goodwill and peace. A final fringe—bright red, yellow, orange—set my spirit soaring beyond the earthy mess, singing an ancient song about the heavens above: "Glory to God in the highest."

> *Lord, may the work of our hands and the meditations of*
> *our hearts lift us and others to new heights.*
> —Evelyn Bence

Digging Deeper: Matthew 6:9–13

Thursday, December 6

Therefore, as God's chosen people, holy and dearly loved, clothe yourselves with compassion, kindness, humility, gentleness and patience.
—Colossians 3:12 (NIV)

As our fourth wedding anniversary got closer, I began to wonder if I was taking Jack for granted. The fact that we live in two separate condos—fifty-seven steps apart—means I spend much of my time alone in my condo doing my own thing while he enjoys his own activities in his. We sleep at his condo and most of my clothes are there, but after breakfast I walk to my place where all my things are and where I am free to work, paint, pay bills, visit with friends, nap, cook, work on my hobbies, watch TV.

Then something happened when I visited my dad and his wife, Bev, in Illinois. Every evening around ten o'clock, my dad would push his walker to the kitchen, set three paper napkins on the seat of his recliner and then place two prunes, one date, and five large seedless grapes on each. Then he'd wheel our late-night healthy snack right to the sofa to serve Bev and me.

It reminded me of Jesus washing the feet of His disciples. Pure kindness and humility. It made me think about what I could do to make life a little nicer for Jack.

Back home I started asking if I could get him a fresh glass of iced tea. Or I'd lug the laundry down the steps without asking for his help. Or I'd offer to pay the bill when we went out to eat. I learned from my dad that you're never too old to learn new ways of kindness toward the ones you love.

> *Father, You have blessed me with the most amazing dad.*
> *Thank You for giving my hero such a long, happy life and for*
> *the inspiration he provides to make me a kinder person.*
> —Patricia Lorenz

Digging Deeper: Nehemiah 9:16–18; 2 Corinthians 6:3–13

He maketh the storm a calm.... —Psalm 107:29 (KJV)

It came in my Christmas stocking a few years ago, a white coffee mug with five words in red: KEEP CALM and CARRY ON.

Soon I was seeing this phrase everywhere—on T-shirts and key rings and office walls. There were variations too. Keep Calm and Live Your Dreams. Keep Calm Tomorrow Is Friday. Keep Calm and Play Soccer. *A pleasant fad*, I thought. I certainly reached often for my mug!

Then I learned the story of the original motto.

It was a slogan printed on thousands of posters to bolster British morale during the dark days of World War II. They were to be displayed on trains, buses, street corners, store windows, schools, theaters. But the British people never saw the posters. The Information Office was saving them for a "crisis." They were held for posting when German troops landed on English soil.

Since the expected invasion never came, the posters were never used, and they were disposed of after the war. It wasn't till sixty years later that a bookseller found one of them in a carton of dusty volumes. He displayed it in his shop window, passersby were intrigued, and the motto caught on everywhere.

But I kept thinking of what the British regarded as a "crisis." Not, apparently, when their country stood alone against all of Nazi-controlled Europe. Not with tens of thousands of civilians dying in nightly bombing raids. Not when submarines sank the ships bringing desperately needed food to a hungry population.

And I thought about how glibly I use the word *crisis*. What if I, too, reserved it for some supremely awful event? What if, like the invasion of England, it never happened?

> *Whenever I hear the word* crisis, *Father, help me to listen*
> *for the Voice that says, "Keep calm."*
> —Elizabeth Sherrill

Digging Deeper: Isaiah 43:2; 2 Timothy 1:7

Saturday, December 8

The sacrifices of God are a broken spirit; a broken and contrite heart, O God, You will not despise. —Psalm 51:17 (NAS)

I'd come up with *Ever True to God* for Mom's grave marker. The phrase really fit her life. Much later—discussing these words among a gathering of women—I found that no one thought their life was "worthy" of such a statement. I disagreed.

Tucked away in 1 Kings 15:5 (NAS) is the word *except*. The passage tells of King David who "did what was right in the sight of the Lord...*except* in the case of Uriah the Hittite." David had desired Uriah's wife and saw to it that Uriah was placed on the front line—and killed—in battle, clearing the way for her to become his own wife.

Another passage, 1 Samuel 13:14 (NAS), says of David the young shepherd boy, "The Lord has sought out for Himself a man after His own heart." Surely God knew the snare that lay ahead for David, the king: the slipped loyalty, the *except*. Yet He especially chose David as being someone near to His heart.

David's redeeming factor is he sought God when he was in the wrong. Psalm 51 is his anguished cry regarding Uriah. He pleads, "Create in me a clean heart, O God, and renew a steadfast spirit within me" (verse 10, NAS). I, too, have uttered this plea, more than once.

Ever true to God doesn't mean I never have any *excepts*. It means having a change of heart when I do—asking God's forgiveness—and renewing my commitment to Him.

> *Lord, I have these "excepts" in my life—*
> *yet You know my heart longs after You.*
> *Restore me to "the joy of Your salvation" (Psalm 51:12, NAS).*
> —Carol Knapp

Digging Deeper: 1 Kings 11:4; Psalm 51; Hebrews 12:1–3

LIGHT IN OUR DARKNESS: A Perfect Gift from God

Every generous act of giving, with every perfect gift, is from above,
coming down from the Father of lights, with whom there is no variation
or shadow due to change. —James 1:17 (NRSV)

Words—reading them and writing them—are my livelihood and my life.

Or at least they are half of my life. The other half is my body, which, until this year, was a source of joy for me. Now, after months of worsening pain and weakness from what seems like an endless series of injuries, I feel like I am losing my body.

But words remain. Or so I try to tell myself. To be honest, I often find it hard to read and write anymore, to derive joy from them, because I am depressed about my body. I am waiting for joy to return.

Sometimes the wait unexpectedly ends, at least for a moment. I was lying on my bed, trying to read, trying not to dwell on pain. Suddenly, my son Benji jumped onto the bed with me, holding a book we'd recently picked out at the library.

I have been reading to my son for years, ever since he was born. It's one of my joys. But this time Benji opened his book and began reading on his own. He'd learned to read about a year earlier and now could read short chapter books by himself.

I marveled at how God had led Benji to this. For a while my worrying over pain abated. I lay there reading with my son, reveling in the joy of it.

> *Lord, help me to remember that Your gifts are worth the wait,*
> *even when the wait seems long.*
> —Jim Hinch

Digging Deeper: Ephesians 2:8; 1 John 5:15

Monday, December 10

Let us consider how to provoke one another to love and good deeds, not neglecting to meet together, as is the habit of some, but encouraging one another, and all the more as you see the Day approaching.
—Hebrews 10:24–25 (NRSV)

My friend Peter is the oldest of eleven. He has two sisters and eight brothers. There aren't many families like theirs anymore.

Most amazing to me, Peter and his siblings are close to one another in every possible way. They were born on average about eighteen months apart; they all still live within a two-hundred-mile radius of each other; they spend Christmases and Fourth of Julys together in their living rooms and on their back decks, which are the envy of the rest of us— we who wish that we had friends and families so devoted.

I grew up in a small family. One brother, two parents. My brother and I jumped into careers and moved for jobs, and now he and I and my parents live in a triangle, and each side of that triangle is about a thousand miles long. We rarely see each other. We don't know each other in the way that more traditional families, I suppose, do. That is why I envy Peter.

But some of us find our "family" in other places. We make friends who become family. We live in others' homes and in each other's lives like Peter and his siblings do. Today, I'm grateful for Judith, for Michael, for Nancy, and for Debra Ann. They are my brothers and sisters, my neighbors, my family.

Lead me today, Lord, to those whom I am to love like family.
—Jon Sweeney

Digging Deeper: Ecclesiastes 4:9–10

I pray that He may grant you, according to the riches of His glory,
to be strengthened with power in the inner man through His Spirit.
—Ephesians 3:16 (HCS)

Seven Ways Alcohol May Be Good for You! That was the subject line of an e-mail from a medical Web site that popped up on my screen today. I guess they don't know E. Grinnan quite as well as they think.

There isn't a single way alcohol is good for me. The first time I held a bottle of Old Grand-Dad bourbon up to the light of a full moon and tipped it back to my doomed thirteen-year-old lips, I was an alcoholic. I was probably an alcoholic before I took that first kiss of whiskey. I had all the attitudes in place—fear, arrogance, pride, shaky self-esteem, and a screaming genetic predisposition. The booze was just the icing on the cake. The bourbon burned all the way down, like an electrical current, but when its effects hit my brain a few seconds later a light went on: *I want to feel this way all the time.*

And, oh, how I tried relentlessly through the next several decades of my life until the choice finally became a binary one: drinking or dying. I'd lost everything else...relationships, jobs, friends, homes, self-respect, and faith. I only had faith in the bottle.

When all else had been stripped from my life and I was naked before God, it was His hand that reached out to mine, the only force in the universe more powerful than my addiction. I liked the way God's love made me feel. I wanted to feel that way all the time, a day at a time.

After I got sober I was humbled to learn how many people had me in their prayers, people I scarcely knew. In the many years since, I have never doubted that those unknown prayers helped get and keep me sober.

Today and every day, Lord, let me not forget the addicted.
Let me pray for all the suffering addicts,
those I know and those I don't.
—Edward Grinnan

Digging Deeper: Exodus 20:1–3; Jeremiah 31:3

Wednesday, December 12

He has made everything beautiful in its time.... —Ecclesiastes 3:11 (ESV)

I placed the wooden dog on wheels under the Christmas tree. Even though Micah was now a preteen, I still used her cherished gift from my grandmother as a decoration.

Shopping was Grandma Caryle's passion. She traveled the world and gathered souvenirs to give as gifts. She had a knack for choosing just the right presents for the people she loved.

The year after I graduated, there was a gift under the tree for "Stephanie's baby." But I didn't have children. I wasn't pregnant or even married. For years, my nonexistent child received presents from my eccentric grandmother.

By the time I finally married and had a child, Grandma didn't know it. Alzheimer's had stolen her memories. Right before Christmas, I took one-year-old Micah with me to visit.

"Merry Christmas!" I called, kissing her cheek.

"Is it Christmas?" she asked. "Have I shopped? I need to get the baby something."

I changed the subject. Some days Grandma didn't know who I was. I doubted she understood that this was her great-granddaughter, the child she'd so desperately wanted for me.

That afternoon, I dug around the closet for extra wrapping paper while Micah napped. Buried deep on the bottom shelf, I came across a dust-covered box. Slowly, I lifted back the worn flaps. Could it be?

I gently lifted out a wooden dog on wheels from Denmark—the first gift to "Stephanie's baby" nearly twenty years earlier! It was perfect for thirteen-month-old Micah.

Once again Grandma was right on target with the perfect gift.

> *Lord, thank You for my dear grandma who loved*
> *giving gifts, and for Your perfect timing.*
> —Stephanie Thompson

Digging Deeper: Habakkuk 2:3; Galatians 4:4

Lay not up for yourselves treasures upon earth, where moth and rust doth corrupt.... —Matthew 6:19 (KJV)

In 2001, I jammed all of my belongings into a storage unit in Wyoming, then raced to New Hampshire, where both of my parents had landed in the hospital. Dad died within a year, but my resilient mother lived another fourteen. I stayed close to my family, cobbling a home from mismatched silverware, freebie furniture, and yard-sale dishes while my own earthly possessions languished in storage.

Now, years later, I begin the dreaded task of clearing out my dusty unit. Over seven days, I open every box and evaluate the contents. Decisions! Household items are easy; donate to the college apartments. Some books are easy too; donate to the new kindergarten teacher. But some items, like the jelly-bean holder Tom created from a cement block, tug at my heart. Yes, he has just graduated with his PhD, but... I photograph the relic and let it go.

By the time I finish, I have salvaged mementos like baby books and baby shoes for my children. Most of my treasures, aside from a few cherished photographs, books, letters, and kid art, I relegate to the landfill. *Why had I felt compelled to save so many reminders of happy times anyway? Didn't I trust the future?*

My children assure me they enjoyed happy childhoods and stay in close touch with me and with each other and friends in Wyoming. Now I no longer need to trap memories in a storage locker. My children and their families continuously generate more.

> *Lord, how few possessions I need when I feel loved.*
> —Gail Thorell Schilling

Digging Deeper: Matthew 6:21; Luke 2:51

Friday, December 14

But I say unto you, Love your enemies... and pray for them which despitefully use you.... —Matthew 5:44 (KJV)

A friend called with shocking news. "I ran into Mark at the doctor's today, Roberta. He was bent over double with nausea and pain. Said it was either his liver or his pancreas."

"Mark" could only be one person: my ex-husband. We had divorced nearly two decades ago after twenty-five years together. My friend didn't utter the C word, but the nurse in me fast-forwarded to a diagnosis of either liver or pancreatic cancer. In my mind's eye, I saw Mark living out his last days in excruciating pain, jaundiced, and with a distended abdomen.

"Wait a minute," I said. "I ran into Mark's girlfriend the other day. She didn't say he had been feeling bad or anything."

"Not *that* Mark," my friend corrected. Then she provided the last name of a mutual friend.

All afternoon I replayed our conversation and the specifics of my troubled marriage. I'd had to start over at midlife because of Mark's shenanigans. Relinquish a beloved home. Face a painful, catastrophic illness alone.

I thought I despised Mark for all of those wrongs and more. How was it that I still cared about what happened to him?

There was only one explanation: God. The Author of Love was moving me toward love for someone who had hurt me. It would never be the romantic love of my youth, but it could definitely be caring for another human being. A child of God every bit as cherished as I am.

Thank You, Lord, for stretching my heart in unexpected ways.
—Roberta Messner

Digging Deeper: Luke 6:27; Ephesians 4:32

Though I speak with the tongues of men and of angels, but have not love, I have become sounding brass or a clanging cymbal.
—1 Corinthians 13:1 (NKJV)

I like to test each bell," the woman said. "Some sound better than others."

It was the first time our family was staffing a Salvation Army kettle; we were eager to do a good job. The staff person who signed us up was giving us our official bell.

She took a handful of them from her little bin and started ringing. I was impatient. It was the holiday season, and I had a whole lot to get done. "I'm sure any bell will be fine," I said.

"Well, they really are quite different," she replied. She rang the first one. It sounded tinny. "Oh no," she said, "I don't like that one." My kids agreed.

"I just figured a bell was a bell," I said. "They all look the same. I never imagined there would be much difference." I felt some of my impatience melt away.

"You'd be surprised how important it is," the woman said. She jingled a second bell. It sounded dull. "Nope."

The third one offered a bright tinkling sound. It immediately made me think of the classic Salvation Army bell of days gone by. "I like that one," my daughter said.

"Me too," the woman offered. "It's all yours. And thank you for your help."

We walked out with the perfect bell, and I left smiling. I couldn't help but wonder if the sound ringing out from my life that hectic season was more like a bright clear bell or a clanging cymbal.

Gracious Lord, may my words, thoughts, and actions always sound forth the beautiful love of Christ, even when life feels too busy.
—Bill Giovannetti

Digging Deeper: Colossians 1:3–4

LIGHT IN OUR DARKNESS: A Patient, Quiet Mind
Rejoice in hope, be patient in suffering, persevere in prayer.
—Romans 12:12 (NRSV)

I've gotten several MRIs this year as doctors attempt to diagnose my hip and shoulder pain and accompanying weakness. Today it's a brain MRI. I'm inside the machine, staring up at a plastic dome, trying to pray amid the din of magnetic bangs, wails, and barks. I feel like I'm in a science-fiction movie.

I dislike all of this. I hardly ever visited doctors. I was healthy—a runner, a swimmer, strong, active. Now my life is consumed by medical procedures. This MRI is to determine whether I have some sort of neuromuscular condition, like multiple sclerosis. *Oh, Lord, don't let it be that!*

I have to lie still, especially my head. *Is this what it feels like in the last moments of life, as the body fades and the soul becomes all we are aware of?*

Then I pay attention to the machine's noises. They have fallen into a strange rhythm, almost like a piece of contemporary classical music. The sound is haunting, bordering on beautiful. There is much about this whole experience that has its own kind of beauty.

The nurses and attendants have been unfailingly kind. For years as a busy working parent, I yearned for periods of reflective inactivity. Well, here I am. And I am praying so hard. In my previous life I prayed sporadically. Not anymore.

God is at work in my life even during this time that feels so awful. I must learn to be patient, to quiet my mind, and to listen for the music in the din.

Lord, today I pray for a heart ready to accept Your will.
—Jim Hinch

Digging Deeper: Proverbs 3:5–6; Hebrews 10:36

If I have a faith that can move mountains, but do not have love,
I am nothing. —1 Corinthians 13:2 (NIV)

My colleague's sabbatical is coming up. During our weekly prayer time, Jonathan worried out loud that, instead of working on the academic writing he'd planned, he should spend his semester off on a time-intensive training program for his nine-year-old son, who has autism.

Somehow, Jonathan's quandary brought to mind a Gospel story I'd read that morning. In it, Jesus asks two blind men who've come after Him if they really believe He can heal their blindness. When they say yes, He says, "According to your faith, let it be done to you," and they can see.

I read the story out loud to the group. Evidently, I concluded, our faith shapes God's answers to our prayers. Everyone but Jonathan nodded. He understood me to be criticizing his faith, compounding his conviction that he was the source of his son's problems, and he became even more distraught.

Later, I remembered feeling exactly the same way about others' well-meant parenting advice. Indeed, though my daughters have no disabilities, I've worried Jonathan's worry throughout their development: that if I could just be the perfect parent, my girls would have no problems.

"God picked you as your girls' mom," a friend said. "He had exactly you in mind."

That's the most comforting but hardest-to-believe lesson of parenting—and of life in general—I've ever learned. God chose us for the jobs He's given us.

"God chose you as Logan's dad," I e-mailed Jonathan later. "Whatever you do in love is the right thing."

> *Father, banish my worries about doing the right thing*
> *and replace them with pure love.*
> —Patty Kirk

Digging Deeper: Luke 15:11–32

Tuesday, December 18

"Ask, and it will be given you; search, and you will find; knock, and the door will be opened for you." —Matthew 7:7 (NRSV)

It seemed so unfair to be in the midst of heartache from a recent breakup while everyone else was *fa-la-la*-ing all around me. Quite frankly, I wasn't in the mood. I wanted to stay in New York City, in my pj's and in my feelings, watching TV and crying. But my trip to Indianapolis had been booked for months. So though my heart felt empty, I put on the bravest face and brightest smile I could muster and went home for the holidays.

By the end of the trip I felt exhausted, sad, and depleted. The night before I flew back to the city, I finally confided in my brother. "I really needed someone to be there for *me* this time," I told him. I had been waiting for someone to care for me. Why hadn't anyone done that? I felt like I was always the one present for others while no one could be bothered to be present for me.

My brother asked, "Why didn't you tell me what you needed? I've got many talents but mind reading is not one of them." I chuckled and considered what he had said. Though I had told him and a few others about the breakup, I didn't ask for what I wanted or needed. But once I was clear, he was there. He then listened and let me cry. And it was just what I needed.

God, thank You for the reminders that I don't have to wait for what I want or need, but can simply ask. Thank You for those who practice Your presence and patience with me.
—Natalie Perkins

Digging Deeper: Matthew 7:7–11

"Truly I tell you, whatever you did for one of the least of these brothers and sisters of mine, you did for me." —Matthew 25:40 (NIV)

When I saw her, I knew something wasn't right. She was wearing a school-uniform shirt at least two sizes too small. She had to keep pulling down her shirt, which kept riding up above her waistline. And every time she tugged at her shirt, it tugged at my heart.

I got busy, though, directing my staff as we taped the girl's classroom for a story we were producing for the TV station where I worked. I thought about her again over the next week but would quickly dismiss it. It was nearing Christmas, and there was lots to do. But then I began hearing about helpers.

First, my daughter Misty shared how she was leading a project at church to collect donated Christmas gifts so that single parents who needed help could shop for their children at no cost.

And there's my colleague Inkie, who reaches out to a local school to find a student in need whom she can help. Sometimes the request is for a bike. Once it was to buy letter jackets for two student athletes who'd earned them but couldn't afford them.

I knew what I needed to do. I e-mailed the principal and offered to purchase the child I'd seen some new school uniforms. I asked her to find out what else I could do to help. The principal responded quickly. "Thank you! Her mother will be so grateful for your help."

I smiled, recalling a quote from Mr. Rogers, a favorite TV personality, who'd said, "Look for the helpers. You will always find people who are helping."

Thank You for giving me an opportunity to be a helper, Lord.
—Melody Bonnette Swang

Digging Deeper: Galatians 6:2; Philippians 2:3–4

Thursday, December 20

THE BEAUTY OF SIMPLICITY: Nothing More Important
It's a good thing to quietly hope.... —Lamentations 3:26 (MSG)

Something strange happens when a boy gets older. He pulls away from his mama. At least my son did. Everybody says this is normal, but sometimes I miss the relationship Thomas and I had.

Spending time with him is different from being with his older sisters. My daughters and I chat nonstop. Although Thomas feels deeply, he only talks when he has something to say. When we're together, I ask too many questions. I should be calmer. Quieter. Wait for him to take the lead.

Newly engaged, he bought his first house and accepted a position with a telecommunications company. He works outdoors, something he'd always wanted to do. He drives a company truck and climbs poles. I had so many questions. Still do. "Do you wear a uniform? What happens on rainy days? Do you have friends? Do you bring your lunch to work?"

He answered but finally said, "Enough, Mom. No more questions."

Last week he texted pictures of his house. Thomas's dad was content with that, but I wanted to see it in person. However, I decided to wait for an invitation.

On my birthday, Thomas called. "Want to see my house?"

"Sure!" I answered with such joy. "Want me to drive over?"

"I'll pick you up," he said. When I crawled into his truck, I kept quiet. Soon, we passed his middle school. "My house is on this road."

"Near the school?"

He nodded. "Sixth one on the right."

"Remember when I drove you to school?" I said softly. "I prayed for you every morning."

My son looked at me and smiled. "I remember, Mom. Thanks."

For a split second, we connected. It was all I needed.

Jesus, You're teaching me how to relate to my grown-up son. Thank You.
—Julie Garmon

Digging Deeper: 1 Corinthians 13:11–13; Hebrews 11:1

See what kind of love the Father has given to us, that we should be called children of God; and so we are. —1 John 3:1 (ESV)

So what would you like for Christmas?" my father-in-law asked my seven-year-old son, Isaiah. "Come tell me."

My little boy stood beside his grandfather's chair. He smiled at Grandpa and then glanced at his own daddy and me. "Well, I want a runner sled," he said. "More than anything. But I'm not sure it's okay."

He looked down and scuffed his wool-clad toes over the carpet. We'd been to the hardware store the day before, and Isaiah had fallen for an old-fashioned wooden sled with metal runners. His daddy said it was an accident waiting to happen. But Grandpa's grin stretched wide. He leaned close to my son. "I knew a little boy who used to have one," he whispered. "In fact, that little boy's sled is still in the garage."

Isaiah's green eyes went round. His daddy, across the room, smiled in surprise.

"If it's okay, we'll go get it," Grandpa said.

My husband, Lonny, nodded. Grandpa started to push up from the chair. But Isaiah stood still. "Grandpa, you've kept that sled a long time," he said. "Are you sure you want to give it to me?"

My father-in-law reached out and pulled Isaiah to his lap. His arms wrapped around my son. "Well, you're my grandson," he said. "Aren't ya?"

Isaiah, his brothers, Lonny, and I have spent many sunlit winter afternoons sledding at the park near our home. But even more than flying down that snow-covered hill, cheeks stained red and smiles shining from the soul, Isaiah loves to tell the story of the day the sled became his.

"And then Grandpa sat me on his lap," he says. "And he said, 'You belong to me.'"

Lord, You created us to belong. Thank You that I am Yours. Amen.
—Shawnelle Eliasen

Digging Deeper: Psalm 100:3; Isaiah 43:1; Romans 14:8

Saturday, December 22

Your unfailing love is better than life itself.... —Psalm 63:3 (NLT)

Hundreds of people jammed into the auditorium. The private school was hosting its annual fund-raiser auction. It seemed like everyone was excited except me. I'd had one of those days when everything went wrong. I was emotionally exhausted and felt broken.

I politely nodded to the people who came over to the table I staffed, which contained items up for silent auction. Most of them were gently used and donated by families in the community. Of course, volunteers were encouraged to place bids on items as well. To pass the time, I scanned the trinkets on the nearby tables.

Suddenly, my eyes rested on a treasure. A heart-shaped mirror framed with rows of real seashells, blue, pink, and white. Without hesitating, I scribbled down a bid and imagined how beautiful the mirror would look in my home.

At the close of the evening, when the emcee announced that there were ten minutes left to place a silent bid, I made sure that I was the winning bidder on the mirror. But then my jaw dropped. Some of the edges of the blue seashells were broken and others missing.

My heart sank. The mirror wasn't quite so beautiful after all.

Suddenly, I heard a still, small voice in my spirit that said, *You feel imperfect and broken, yet I think you're beautiful.* Tears welled in my eyes.

That imperfect, broken, beautiful mirror now hangs in my home, reminding me daily of God's unfailing love.

Lord, help me to look at myself through Your loving eyes. Amen.
—Rebecca Ondov

Digging Deeper: Exodus 19:5; Deuteronomy 7:6

LIGHT IN OUR DARKNESS: Welcoming God's Son

The angel said to her, "The Holy Spirit will come upon you, and the power of the Most High will overshadow you; therefore the child to be born will be holy: he will be called Son of God." —Luke 1:35 (NRSV)

It was the church's first Christmas pageant in years. Previously, they'd put on a talent show, with the kids' and the grown-ups' choirs singing and anyone else coming onstage to do something fun. My wife, Kate, had arrived as a leader in the church a little over a year ago and she said, "Let's do a proper pageant."

There was grumbling, premonitions about a boring, same old pageant like every other church's.

Our kids, Frances and Benji, were playing parts—angel and donkey—but I wasn't worried about them. They'd do fine. But what about the church? What about Kate? What if it was a flop?

The lights dimmed, candles glowed, music started. The kids did what kids do—hit some lines, missed others, wandered around the stage—but they looked great! Several members are costume designers, and they'd worked hard.

The moment of the Annunciation arrived. A hush fell. There was no music, no irony, just a child in a white robe telling a teenage girl she would soon give birth to the Son of God. I felt a tingle down my back. It was as if we were all there in Nazareth, witnessing a miracle.

There was huge applause at the end; all on their feet. Kate got up to say a few words to the congregation, and the applause continued. I needn't have worried. This pageant was worth the wait. And, of course, it succeeded. We invited Someone Who makes every Christmas pageant everywhere a success.

This year I will pay special attention to Your Incarnation, Lord, every day as Christmas approaches.
—Jim Hinch

Digging Deeper: Isaiah 43:19

Christmas Eve, Monday, December 24

LIGHT IN OUR DARKNESS: God with Us

"Look, the virgin shall conceive and bear a son, and they shall name him Emmanuel," which means, "God is with us." —Matthew 1:23 (NRSV)

Every year we put up two Advent calendars. The old one was made by my aunt when I was a baby. It's a felt Christmas tree on felt backing, with tiny stuffed felt ornaments hanging from brass beads sewn into the tree. At the top goes an angel on December 24. Traditionally, the Santa Claus ornament gets hung second to last just below the angel.

As children, my brother and I fought over who got to hang Santa, which we considered more exciting than the angel. My kids get into the same argument, with each one gauging how to pace his or her turn hanging ornaments in order to end up with Santa.

The new calendar is sent each year by my mother-in-law. It's a thin cardboard Nativity scene with tiny cutout windows to be opened each day. Inside are pictures and a Bible quote.

I used to prefer the felt calendar because it was from my childhood. But now I like both because they disclose different gifts each day, slowly and deliberately, just like Advent.

The felt ornaments are ingenious—a toy soldier, an owl, some presents wrapped in glittery bows, a reindeer. I picture my aunt carefully stuffing and sewing each one. Her love and the combined love of our family linger on the tree.

But the cardboard calendar tells the story of Jesus. The Bible verses lead us ever closer to that moment when God's Son is born in a stable. The last window shows Him there, lit by a star, ready to begin His life that will change the world. It's the moment the kids and I have been waiting for.

> *Lord, I will consider each day its own facet of*
> *the gift of Your Incarnation.*
> —Jim Hinch

Digging Deeper: John 1:14; Hebrews 1:2–3

LIGHT IN OUR DARKNESS: The Savior Is Born!
The people who walked in darkness have seen a great light....
—Isaiah 9:2 (ESV)

It was a cool, fresh morning, still dark. I was outside running. My doctor had told me I was further along the road to healing and I could try running again. This was a gift beyond compare, as if Christmas had been restored to me.

Christmas is normally my favorite time of year. I love the solemnity of Advent, the cold weather, the wreath-making, the gift-giving, the carol-singing. This year, I had dreaded spending it in pain and debility. Now I could live once more in hope.

I drank in the quiet of the Central Park bridle trail, the soft scuff of my feet in the dirt, a gentle sighing through the trees. All of this was the voice of God, and once again I could hear it. I wanted to sing for joy!

Is that what the shepherds felt like when they reached the stable and peeked inside to see the Baby Whom the angel had told them about? Did the three kings cast aside their solemnity and sing hallelujah when their long journey ended and they bowed down before the King of the creation I now ran through? Did they shout thanks to the star that had guided them, just as I now glanced upward to see if any stars were visible, a rarity in New York City? (Yes, one or two!)

Christmas is a time for gifts. But, really, Christmas itself is the gift, the never-failing reminder that, no matter what, God is with us every step of our journey.

> *Lord, You are the great light shining in darkness.*
> *Today I will celebrate Your wondrous, abiding presence.*
> —Jim Hinch

Digging Deeper: Psalm 107:19–21; Isaiah 41:10; Philippians 4:19

Wednesday, December 26

Let the heavens rejoice, let the earth be glad; let the sea resound, and all that is in it. Let the fields be jubilant, and everything in them; let all the trees of the forest sing for joy. —Psalm 96:11–12 (NIV)

It wasn't the Christmas I was expecting. The sweet chaos of family I'd grown used to every year was now replaced with something quieter. Our parents had returned to Florida after a visit of many months, and every family member we were accustomed to spending the holidays with was either traveling or had other plans. My two boys, my sister, and I woke up on Christmas morning without the preparation of a big family gathering—no piles of presents for the boys under the tree, no giant feast to assemble.

I tried to make it happy for the boys. I put on Christmas music and danced around. I suggested we bake Christmas cookies together. They preferred to go downstairs and play video games.

The boys were content, but I wasn't. I wanted to cry. It was depressing and uneventful.

But there was something else unconventional about that day. The usual frigid weather around that time of year was surprisingly warm.

"Why don't we all get out of here," I suggested, "and go on a little nature walk?"

My sister knew the perfect spot.

The earthy fragrance of the forest filled my lungs and lifted my mood. We walked along the creek, walked over hills, and stopped to skip rocks. Suddenly, Christmas was amazing in a very different way. I was happy not to be cooped up in a house all day entertaining guests. Surrounded by beauty and the people I love, I no longer mourned over the loss of tradition but celebrated the act of creating a new one.

> *Lord, thank You for family and traditions,*
> *but help me to embrace change as well.*
> —Karen Valentin

Digging Deeper: Psalm 96:1

They asked, "Where is the newborn king of the Jews? We've seen his star in the east, and we've come to honor him." —Matthew 2:2 (CEB)

By some miracle almost all twenty-four of us were there. The only one we were missing was Tim (off doing mission work in Africa). Otherwise, all four generations were represented at Mom's house on Christmas Day: Mom, my brother, my two sisters, our spouses, our children, my sister's grandchildren. "Picture time!" someone shouted. "We've got to document this."

We trooped outside, gathering on Mom's front porch. The question was: Who would take this photo? We all needed to be in it. "Maybe one of the neighbors." My older sister, Gioia, dashed across the street and knocked on a door. Mom had only lived in this house for a little while so we didn't really know the neighbors, but I could imagine exactly what Gioia said: "I hate to interrupt your Christmas, but if one of you could spare a few moments, we need someone to take our picture...."

Next thing we knew, a fellow with just the right camera equipment was heading toward us. Carol took over for a moment as art director. "The kids in front, some of you should sit on the step, Peggy, you can stand...." No telling how long the patience of the under-four set would last.

"Smile," someone said. We smiled while Mom's neighbor clicked away. This was a moment to treasure. Then we broke up and went back inside for dinner. About an hour later there was a knock at the door. Mom's neighbor. Not only had he made a disc with all the good shots on it, but he'd also framed the best print.

"You know, I have the nicest neighbors," Mom said. A gift from a neighbor and a neighbor who was himself a gift.

As the wise ones from the East brought gifts to You,
we give thanks for the gifts we receive, every one of them a treasure.
—Rick Hamlin

Digging Deeper: Isaiah 9:6; Philippians 2:8–10

Friday, December 28

Share with the Lord's people who are in need. Practice hospitality.
—Romans 12:13 (NIV)

I knew what I should do. Invite the carful of my girlfriends to my home for a spur-of-the-moment lunch.

But that wasn't me. I planned luncheons for a long, thoughtful time, and when my guests arrived, everyone exclaimed, "Oh my!" I love to set tables with themes, display pretty bouquets of flowers, and serve food that's color-coordinated.

Several of us from my prayer group had been to visit Evelyn, who was temporarily a shut-in. We usually met across town at Freida's house. But now, leaving Evelyn's, we were only five minutes from my home. As we stopped for gas, I knew everyone was hungry. But my kitchen and my house weren't in shape for company.

Ask them anyway. The thought was gentle and real.

"Would y'all like to swing by my house and we can eat whatever we can find? I'm going to have to sit down when we get there. But you can raid the kitchen...."

They didn't even let me finish before I heard a chorus of yesses. I'd halfway hoped they wouldn't accept.

Inside, I instantly found my recliner in the living room and plopped down. I heard them exclaiming over what they'd found.

"Pimento cheese!" someone cheered.

"I'll get the pop," Missy said. "The sandwich meat is in the drawer."

"I have the pickles!" Jill exclaimed.

My cats joined in, meowing loudly. My friends sounded almost like my children had so long ago—laughing, asking, volunteering.

I shut my eyes, smiling at the spontaneous fun.

> *Oh, my Father, am I really practicing hospitality at last?*
> —Marion Bond West

Digging Deeper: Acts 2:44–45, 28:7; 1 Peter 4:9

Commit your work to the Lord, then it will succeed. —Proverbs 16:3 (TLB)

This morning I woke up early, even though it's a Saturday, anxious to hit the computer. I was feeling discouraged. The deadline of a big project had been moved up, and I was suddenly very behind schedule. To make things worse, my lower back was killing me from sitting at my desk.

Two hours in, I found myself feeling even more frustrated. The progress was slow. I got up to get another cup of coffee and thought that maybe I should dig out the heating pad from the bathroom closet, but the deadline loomed so I went right back to my oversize chair that is somewhat comfortable but dreadfully wrong to use in front of a computer.

Staring at the page that should have been full, I began to write. I was a few paragraphs in when I felt an incredible warmth on my aching back. For a second I thought it was the heating pad kicking in, but then I realized I hadn't got it.

I looked down at my back. The rising sun came through the window and shone on the exact place it hurt. The warmth was strong and radiant, and in an instant my aching pain was soothed. The light seemed to say, "Keep at it. I am with you. You do your part, and I'll do mine."

Heavenly Father, thank You for miraculous moments that
reveal Your presence and inspire me to keep going.
—Sabra Ciancanelli

Digging Deeper: Psalm 46:1; Colossians 3:23

Sunday, December 30

Speak the truth to each other.... —Zechariah 8:16 (NIV)

Kathy and I have been friends almost forever. I have a framed message she gave me as a gift years ago: "A friend is one who knows the song in my heart and sings it to me when my memory fails." We've pretty much lived that out in our relationship.

For the last eight years I've headed up a ministry at our church called Stories. As I neared the end of my leadership, I felt sad that Kathy had only attended a couple of times. She was a busy counselor and often had clients at that time. But I missed her being part of *this part* of my life. For me, presence is a gift of friendship, showing we care about what the other cares about.

I'd been thinking that over on the day I unexpectedly ran into her at church. We were making small talk when my heart started that pounding thing. The fear of sounding pathetic almost stopped me, but I forced out the first words.

"I wish you'd come to Stories this week, Kathy. It would mean lots to have you there on Thursday."

"I'm so sorry. I didn't know it mattered," she said with true compassion. "I have clients scheduled. I'm really sorry."

"I understand," I said. "I just wanted you to know you matter."

We talked on a bit, and I think we both walked away feeling more known and understood. Later that day, she texted a message that sounded like the song in my heart.

"I'm coming to Stories. I rescheduled my clients. Can't wait. You matter to me."

> *Thank You, Lord, for the love in relationships*
> *that embraces the truth.*
> —Carol Kuykendall

Digging Deeper: Proverbs 18:24; John 15:13; Ephesians 4:15

And the Lord... will be with thee, he will not fail thee, neither forsake thee: fear not, neither be dismayed. —Deuteronomy 31:8 (KJV)

A dear friend of mine tells me a story about being with his dad in his last hour. "We sat there holding hands. We hadn't held hands for fifty years. You stop holding your dad's hand when you are like six or seven years old, but now I think we should keep talking, hand in hand, you know?

"Anyway, he knew it was the end and so did I. But he says, 'I'll always be with you, Son. I'll always be nearby. God knows how that will be, but I am sure it will be. You just talk to me same as always, and I will do what I can.

"'It'll be easier for me to be around you because we won't have to use the phone or the airplane. We get a hint of this in this life, don't we? You know when your kids are in trouble. You can just feel it somehow. I'll be near your mother and sister also. But who knows? No one knows except the Knower.

"'Remember that time we tried to write down every possible name of God? We started with ninety-nine names, but we got up to about four hundred. Even death is a gift from God somehow. It's sad, but it's a condition of the gift. "No" is partners with "yes." That's just how it works.

"'I'll always be nearby. You remember that. Love doesn't die. How that works exactly, I am not sure and I don't care. But I know it's so.'"

Dear Knower, everything is Your fingerprint, everything is rife and stuffed and crammed with Your possibility. Isn't that so?
—Brian Doyle

Digging Deeper: Joshua 1:9; 1 Thessalonians 4:14

GOD'S UNFAILING LOVE

1 _____

2 _____

3 _____

4 _____

5 _____

6 _____

7 _____

8 _____

9 _____

10 _____

11 _____

12 _____

13 _____

14 _____

15 _____

16 _____

17 _____

18 _____

19 _____

20 _____

21 _____

22 _____

23 _____

24 _____

25 _____

26 _____

27 _____

28 _____

29 _____

30 _____

31 _____

Much that has happened in the past year has prompted **Marci Alborghetti** of New London, Connecticut, to think about the importance of compassion. Whether dealing with family, friends, or even her young godsons, Marci is trying to practice the discipline of compassion. "God has blessed me by giving me a great model of compassion in my husband," Marci notes. Charlie has a real gift for kindness, from how he treats his colleagues and church committee members to the way he acts with the hospitality workers in the various places Marci and Charlie have visited, including Concord, New Hampshire, and Portsmouth, Maine.

"It was a hard year. Just plain hard. No, it was pretty much like God was planning on writing 2 Job and had chosen my family as the main characters," writes **Julia Attaway** of New York City. On the other hand, it was the year Julia learned that unfailing love is what God was asking of *her* in the face of extreme difficulty. "It was when I had three kids in hospitals in three different states that I stopped asking God to do what I wanted," Julia said, "and I simply began to pray, 'Thy will be done.' So it was a good year too. For I learned to love the Lord better."

"So often God shows His unfailing love through the people He sets around us," says **Evelyn Bence**. "Though they live three or more states away from me, my siblings bolster me spiritually and emotionally. Closer to my home here in Arlington, Virginia, I value relationships with church and community friends, including a neighbor girl who sees me as an extra grandma. Professionally I continue to edit for various publications and write on the themes of relationships and hospitality. With each passing year, I see anew that God is great, God is good, God is love."

God's unfailing love has brought blessings of true healing to **Erika Bentsen** of Sprague River, Oregon. The second surgery to repair her ruptured disk was completely successful. "After four years of not being able to ride, I couldn't find Jack's bridle, but I couldn't wait any longer. I just threw a leg over and rode him bareback. God stuck with me and brought me through these long years of doubt and pain. His love never fails!" By the year's end, X-rays showed that her back had healed. "From this point forward, it's time to live life wholly and deliberately and thankfully."

"Life was both busy and unexciting this year," **Rhoda Blecker** says. "It feels as if much of my time is spent letting the dog out and letting the dog in again. The big news is that my therapist is retiring, which seems to be God's way of telling me to go it alone. I certainly intend to try! Living in a destination location (Bellingham, Washington) often brings guests, so I had welcome visitors much of the summer, and no one overstayed, which made me appreciate them even more."

"I'm drawing again!" writes **Lisa Bogart** of Scarsdale, New York. "I jumped on board the recent coloring-book craze and enjoyed creating three devotional coloring books in one year. It was so neat to illustrate favorite verses. I've kept on drawing since the books were published. Sitting at my art table is part of my quiet time now. It's a joy to create with our Creator. I often draw the verse for the day, and then it stays in my head all day. I've always wanted to be better at memorizing verses, and this is helping. I also like to send copies of my latest drawings to family and friends. It's a fun way to encourage them too. And who doesn't like some cheerful mail?"

Sabra Ciancanelli of Tivoli, New York, says, "This morning the sunlight stretched over the dark treetops in magnificent pink hues, and I felt blessed to stumble upon such breathtaking beauty. So often it's in the still moments where I connect most closely with God's love: mornings like these, when I look out of the window as my son Solomon waits for the high-school bus, his trumpet case in hand, unaware that I still keep watch from the curtain's edge. My youngest, Henry, doodles a silly character on his middle-school notebook and giggles at our dog, Soda, who snuggles beside him. All is well, and I'm grateful for this time, for these glorious moments that I etch deep in my heart."

"It's strange—the older I get, the more I tip," muses **Mark Collins** of Pittsburgh, Pennsylvania. "Can't say why—maybe I see some past version of myself in the young waiter at our table." These days, the folks around the table are fewer in number, he says. "Grace is away at school, Faith has moved out, and Hope is at home but usually working. Mostly it's just Sandee and me, talking about all the changes in our lives. So when I tell the waiter to 'keep the change,' I'm thinking to myself, *Yeah, right.* Change is many things, but it's never something you can keep...or manage, for that matter."

Pablo Diaz of Carmel, New York, says, "My wife, Elba, and I continue to see our family expand and grow in wonderful ways. I had the honor of officiating at the wedding of my daughter Christine and Taun in the beautiful Hudson Valley of New York. Paul, our son, relocated to Michigan for a new position. We miss him but trust that the Lord has ordered his steps. I also wrote a booklet for Guideposts, *Empowered by Faith.* This was a rewarding experience and a great learning opportunity. God's faithfulness and unfailing love hold our family together through the ever-changing seasons."

John Dilworth of North Canton, Ohio, tells us: "Pat and I are pleased to have our son, Johnny, living in Texas after being stationed in South Korea and Hawaii. Providing coaching during his first home purchase—Pat with the furnishing and me with the buying—gave us each a special week with him. A milestone event for us was a cruise with six other couples celebrating twenty years of friendship. We all moved into our neighborhood around the same time. Twenty years of dinners and weekend retreats, along with the joys and challenges of nine kids growing into adults, created a blessing of friendship we deeply treasure."

Brian Doyle lives with his family in Portland, Oregon, where he is the editor of *Portland Magazine* at the University of Portland. He's excited to announce two new books: a novel called *The Adventures of John Carson in Several Quarters of the World* and a new collection of poems, *The Kind of Brave You Wanted to Be*. His prayer for this year was, "Dear Lord, give me the strength to not be 'strong' but to be humble, simple, straight, honest, clean, alert to the shard of holy in every heart there is…"

Amy Eddings is a writer and journalist who spent twenty-eight years in New York City and had the privilege of working at WNYC, the biggest public radio station in the country. In 2015, she returned to her native state of Ohio, moving to the rural village of Ada. She and her husband, Mark, operate Easter House Bed & Breakfast in their Queen Anne Victorian home. Two Guideposts readers were their first guests.

Fellowship Corner

"It's been a year of change," says **Logan Eliasen** of Port Byron, Illinois. "I started the year as a brand-new college grad, bouncing between seasonal jobs. In the fall, I grappled with my first semester of law school. One thing I've learned is that moving forward often means letting go of what's safe and familiar. However, no matter what I've had to relinquish, God never released His hold on me. I experienced His presence while working in a fast-food restaurant and when learning in a lecture hall. God really does reach us, no matter where we are in our walks of life."

For **Shawnelle Eliasen** of Port Byron, Illinois, life has taken on a new form of fullness. "We're busier than ever," she says. "The boys have swim team. Soccer. Scouts. But as my five sons grow, I'm growing in new ways too." Shawnelle is delighted by an increasing awareness of how God uses His children to share His unfailing love. "One day my girlfriends surprise-filled the front tables when I spoke at a women's brunch. Another day a son left a note that promised coffee and conversation after school. God does this. Over and over! My normal pace is breathless, but I'll never outrun His love."

Since becoming part of the *Daily Guideposts* family over fifteen years ago, **Sharon Foster** of Durham, North Carolina, tells us that she's been the beneficiary of countless prayers and well wishes. "Each one touches me and reminds me of God's unfailing love and faithfulness. One of my ongoing prayers has been that the Lord would allow me to help feed hungry people. This year, I republished one of my novels, *Abraham's Well*, in partnership with an organization that enables me to donate proceeds to help those in need. It's amazing that the Lord hears prayers and makes our dreams come true! I'd love to connect with you; come visit me (Sharon Ewell Foster) on Facebook."

 **Julie Garmon** of Monroe, Georgia, says, "When I open my new prayer journal, I begin by writing the word *Dance.* Seeing my five-letter word for the year sends a happy jolt to my heart. It reminds me of God's unfailing love and the prayers He's answered, like bringing me out of the deep, dark hole of clinical depression. He healed my shame and even helped me to write about it. On December 9, 2018, my husband and I will celebrate forty years of marriage. We married so young. Some said we'd never make it. But you'd better believe I'll be dancing on our anniversary! I might even persuade him to dance with me."

 "The older my kids get, the faster time flies," notes **Bill Giovannetti.** "My daughter, Josie, and son, J.D., who were homeschooled through grade school, are thriving at our local public high school here in Santa Rosa, California. We couldn't be prouder. Margi, my wife, has joined the staff of our church, where she does an extraordinary job of organizing special events and decor. She continues to serve as adjunct professor of business law at Simpson University. I was honored to release my sixth book, a verse-by-verse commentary on Esther called *MindGames: Rising Above Other People's Craziness.* I love hearing from readers on Facebook and Twitter, so stop by and say hi."

 "Last year," says **Edward Grinnan** of New York City, *Guideposts* editor-in-chief and vice president, "I told you about how Julee and I were mourning the loss of our beloved golden retriever, Millie. Yet I was grateful to God for sending this beautiful being to me to teach me so many important lessons." The more Edward thought about it, the more he saw a plan: All the dogs in his life had come to him at just the right time to help him grow and learn. The result is a new book, *Always By My Side: Life Lessons from Millie and All the Dogs I've Loved,*

available from Guideposts.org or wherever books are sold. "It's a book about dogs, but really it's a book about love."

"We had an extraordinary trip to South Africa last year to visit our son Timothy, who was living in a monastery and working at a school that the brothers had started," says **Rick Hamlin** of New York City. "But now both Tim and his older brother, William, seem firmly established in California, a little closer than South Africa but not exactly a car ride away." Rick and his wife, Carol, continue to sing together in their church choir. His newest book is *Pray for Me* about the healing power of prayer.

Carla Hendricks continues to focus on the matters that she cares about deeply—family, adoption, and unity in Christ. Her husband, Anthony, and four passionate children give her intriguing writing material as well. Carla is communications director for a diverse Christian K–6 school whose mission is to serve the underresourced community of Franklin, Tennessee. An adoptive mom, she also serves foster and adoptive families and families in crisis through a ministry created by her local church to love and lend a hand to vulnerable children in the community and around the world.

Kim Henry of Elizabeth, Colorado, had another travel-filled year: "Trips to and visits from family and friends as well as eye-opening journeys to countries with cultures and beliefs very different from mine. On a sad note, we lost Sage, one of our Australian shepherds, who almost made it to age thirteen. It's part of what we sign up for when pets join our family, but still so difficult to say goodbye. On the very joyful side, we welcomed two new grandchildren, Hunter Kirk, born to our son Kirk and his wife, Courtney, and Harper Kennedy, our daughter Lauren and her husband Chris's first child. What a blessing and a delight they are!"

Jim Hinch, Kate, Frances, and Benjamin of New York City did a whole lot more this year than worry about Jim's health, thanks be to God. The kids started first and fourth grades at their wonderful Episcopal school, and Kate saw many of the programs she's put in place at St. Michael's Church bear fruit as new families joined the congregation and members grew in faith and commitment. Despite missing their beloved West Coast, the whole family managed some good outdoor time, with several trips to the Adirondack Mountains. After fearing he'd never hike again, Jim took Frances and Benjamin on separate father-daughter and father-son backpacking trips in a nearby state park. Thanks be to God, indeed!

For **Ashley Kappel** of Birmingham, Alabama, this has been a year of finding balance. Raising two toddlers, working full time, and trying to maintain a sense of sanity can be draining, but daily she's reminded by God that there is so much joy to be found in the small moments. Ashley's best moments are sunny days when everyone can head to the backyard, play for hours, and then grab a picnic on the deck. Ashley lives with her two kids, her husband, Brian, and their golden retriever, Colby.

"'I have always wanted a little brother,' was my son Harrison's reaction, and baby David's arrival didn't disappoint," relates **Brock Kidd** of Nashville, Tennessee. While Mary Katherine, 5, and Ella Grace, 4, now have their own real-life baby doll, 17-year-old Harrison may be little David's biggest fan. Brock writes, "Life is busy, but when we're all sitting together at the dinner table, God's unfailing love becomes crystal clear...our family is complete!" After almost twenty-five years, Brock is still passionate about his career in wealth management. When not working, he and his wife, Corinne, enjoy family time together at a little cabin on Lake Weiss in northern Alabama.

"David and I often wonder how life could be this good," says **Pam Kidd** of Nashville, Tennessee, "and then we look outside our window and see God waiting in the eyes of the poor, in the hopes of our Zimbabwe children, and in the dreams of the new Americans. And just when we feel so overwhelmed that our inclination is to pull the curtains, He sends a message of His unfailing love: a modest ankle bracelet from an Indian refugee, a paint-smudged letter from a Zimbabwe child, a hug from a homeless man. Often His work is hard and takes us far from our comfort zone, but, honestly, I wouldn't have it any other way!"

It's been a quiet year for **Patty Kirk**. With both girls decisively flown, and with little likelihood of their returning to Oklahoma, Patty and Kris follow a strict weekday routine: breakfast, work, dinner, an episode of *Madam Secretary*, and then bed. They spent Patty's fall break at Half Moon Bay in northern California, visiting with Charlotte and Lulu, birding the shoreline, eating too much (including an amazing Indian meal cooked by Charlotte's boyfriend, Reuben), and playing Pokémon Go. Over Christmas, parents and daughters joined forces to take over every Pokémon gym in northwest Arkansas and northeastern Oklahoma. Go, Family Kirk!

"What a year of travel!" reports **Carol Knapp** of Priest River, Idaho. "Family weddings in Washington, DC, and Carmel, California. Accompanying grandchildren from Minnesota on their first train ride to visit our home. Our twentieth grandchild arrived, rounding out the count to ten girls, ten boys. Terry had a second back surgery, and he's looking at another foot surgery. Not our retirement dream, but God's unfailing love is just that—unfailing. Nature on the mountain continues to delight. In winter there's a clearing where elk bed down. Summer brings a bald eagle nesting. And spring—my favorite—yields colorful woodland blossoms and the luscious aroma of pines waking up."

"I've taken many personality tests and always resisted my labels until I took one this year," **Carol Kuykendall** of Boulder, Colorado, reports. "My personality type came out similar to the others, but my reaction was different. Because I finally recognize that's who I am: a helper. When I spend time with cancer patients, I know I'm right where I'm supposed to be. At MOPS (Mothers of Preschoolers), where I'm a mentor, I encourage young moms. I now know God calls me to these places, and I'm thankful."

Vicki Kuyper has been a writer for over thirty years and has written more than fifty books, including *A Tale of Two Biddies: A New Wrinkle on Aging with Grace*. An avid photographer and world traveler, Vicki enjoys a trip to anywhere, the more remote the better. However, her favorite destination is visiting with her absolutely exceptional grandchildren. When Vicki's not on the road or busy writing at her desk in Phoenix, Arizona, chances are she's sharing a long conversation and decadent dessert with a good friend or at a Pilates class trying to work off the dessert she just ate.

Patricia Lorenz is loving life in sunny Largo, Florida, with Jack, her "hunka-hunka-burnin'-love." She tells us: "Every Monday through Saturday begins with an hour of water aerobics in the large pool across the street. Now that my double knee-replacement surgery has nearly healed (they say it takes two years!) I'm back on track for more travel to visit my four children and nine grandchildren. Many exciting trips and adventures come about because I still hold on to my life philosophy: *Never say no to an opportunity unless it's illegal or immoral.* God, in His unfailing love, continues to put opportunities and adventures in my path."

"This year I felt grateful for the shining beacon of God's Word, guiding me through life, one decision at a time," says **Debbie Macomber** of Port Orchard, Washington. Debbie and her husband, Wayne, have four children and ten grandchildren. A number one *New York Times* best-selling author, Debbie has written cookbooks, an adult coloring book, and two acclaimed children's books in addition to her beloved and widely read novels. Debbie serves on the Guideposts National Advisory Cabinet and is World Vision's international spokesperson for its Knit for Kids charity initiative.

"My love did fail at times this year," says **Erin MacPherson** of Austin, Texas. "From helping my mom care for my grandmother with Alzheimer's to keeping up with soccer practice and swim meets and school demands, my patience slipped and I found myself failing to love well again and again. But despite my failure, His love never failed, as evidenced by those glimmers of clear conversation with my grandma, drop-in barbecues with great friends, sunsets watched from the back patio, and—perhaps most of all—in those quiet moments when God seemed to whisper His peace into my soul."

The world can seem so very huge when you learn you have a tumor on your tongue as **Roberta Messner** of Huntington, West Virginia, found out this past year. But when a *Daily Guideposts* reader intervened, it became comfortingly small. Roberta was discouraged and afraid, and then she ordered something on eBay. She heard from that *DG*-devotee seller, who recognized her from our pages. When she reminded Roberta that she had been strong and courageous in the past, Roberta was tremendously encouraged and knew once again that God loved her as if she were His only child.

Rebecca Ondov's year brimmed with challenges that caused her to soul-search while seeking solutions. Every answer she found was rooted in His unfailing love. Rebecca says, "It's so much easier to face pressure when I remind myself that God loves me and wants the best for me. He always leads me to a place of peace." In the evenings and on weekends, Rebecca enjoys hiking and horseback riding in the mountains that rim her small valley of Hamilton, Montana. Of course, Sunrise, her golden retriever, faithfully trots by her side. She invites you to connect with her via her Web site, RebeccaOndov.com, and on Facebook.

Natalie Perkins hosts and produces a podcast called "Better Not Mention It" for the Westar Institute where she also serves on the board. She recently celebrated the launch of a new center in Boulder, Colorado, that she cofounded called the Tanho Center. She performed with the USO Show Troupe and played a singer turned nun (the role of Deloris) in the musical *Sister Act* in Hilton Head Island, South Carolina.

Back in New York City, Natalie thoroughly enjoyed her first year of chaplaincy at New York University and is looking forward to continued connection with students as they shape their spiritual lives.

Ginger Rue will celebrate five years of marriage to her husband, Dwight, in 2018. An avid skier, Dwight recently took Ginger for her first run. "It lasted about ten minutes," Ginger says. "I have a notoriously tricky lower back, and I was so afraid I'd move wrong and pull a muscle. Plus, it didn't help when I looked up to see that my brother-in-law was filming me the entire time! Luckily, I came out unscathed. That was probably my first and last try, but it was fun, and I'm glad I did it. Colorado was beautiful. Still, I was glad to get back home to hot, humid Tuscaloosa, Alabama!"

Daniel Schantz's mother, Virginia, was laid to rest on her 94th birthday. Dan was the second of her six children. Dan's granddaughter Hannah graduated from the University of Missouri and went to work for Senator Roy Blunt in Washington, DC. The Schantzes flew there to see where she lives and works. Hannah's younger sister, Rossetti, began her studies at the University of Missouri. Dan and Sharon continue their happy routines of retirement in Moberly, Missouri, with an occasional day trip to a quilt shop or some historic site.

"My cup runneth over with the unfailing love of family and friends," says **Gail Thorell Schilling** of Concord, New Hampshire, who rejoiced in the anticipation and arrival of not one but two grandbabies! Auntie Tess staged lavish baby showers, which drew dozens of well wishers. While wintering in Florida, Gail guided tours at Bok

Tower Gardens and learned to knit baby things with her sister-in-love, Dana. Tom and Canay received their doctorates from Massachusetts Institute of Technology just weeks before little Leo arrived. Steve and Trina greeted Julia Hope days before Thanksgiving. Meanwhile, Hannah earned her driver's license, and Greg, Nikki, and William adopted Opie, a kissy puppy. "We are richly blessed."

"Our year held both joy and sorrow," **Penney Schwab** of Copeland, Kansas, writes. "When granddaughter Olivia graduated from high school, her church held a service of gifts and blessings. We gathered again when my sister and her husband celebrated their fiftieth wedding anniversary. Our family is growing: grandson Caden's parents are in the process of adopting two sisters. David, a Marine, is flying helicopters. Caleb and Mark have taken their first career steps, and Ryan and his wife, Paige, are happily settled in Fort Worth. My husband, Don, and I lost a good friend. But I echo the words of a grieving spouse: 'Death is part of life, but God's love never fails.'"

This year **Elizabeth (Tib) Sherrill** and her husband, John, revisited favorite places in England and France. Not much closer to their home in Hingham, Massachusetts, is Portland, Oregon, where granddaughter Kerlin is rector of St. David of Wales Episcopal Church. Kerlin's son Adin turned 13 in March. "We wanted to see him one more time before he's taller than we are!" Adin was named for Tib's great-great-great-grandfather, Adin Briggs, who fought in Colonel Tupper's Massachusetts Regiment in the Revolutionary War. "Adin must add three more 'greats' to his namesake," says Tib. "It makes the passing of the generations seem very swift."

"I'm living in such gratitude these days," says **Melody Bonnette Swang** of Mandeville, Louisiana. Taking a moment to look around at her ever-increasing family that now includes thirteen grandchildren and seeing her four grown children thriving in their work and personal lives, Melody has many reasons to be thankful. In a beautiful evening ceremony surrounded by friends and family beneath the moss-covered Louisiana oaks, Melody married her longtime friend Cary Menard. "I stood alongside Cary and bowed my head as Pastor Randy prayed a blessing over our marriage. I felt so deeply God's unfailing love."

Jon Sweeney is a husband, father of three, and author of many books, including Book of the Month Club and Quality Paperback Book Club selections. His popular history, *The Pope Who Quit: A True Medieval Tale of Mystery, Death, and Salvation*, has been optioned by HBO. He loves to snowshoe in the mountains near where he lives in Montpelier, Vermont.

Stephanie Thompson and her husband, Michael, will be celebrating fifteen years of marriage in February. The couple live in a suburb of Oklahoma City with their middle-school-aged daughter, Micah, two dogs, and a cat. "We're a soccer family," admits Stephanie. "Most weekends are spent at the soccer fields." Despite Micah's competitive soccer schedule, the family found time to vacation in a mountainside retreat cabin in Colorado last summer. White-water rafting, visiting the Royal Gorge, horseback riding, sightseeing in quaint towns, and hiking natural springs brought them closer to each other and to God.

Marilyn Turk and her husband, Chuck, checked off some more "places to see" from their bucket list. "This time, we traveled from our home in Niceville, Florida, up the East Coast, trying to view as many lighthouses as possible along the way. Of course, our seven-year-old grandson Logan, who's lived with us for four years now, was with us. We also served as volunteer lighthouse keepers for a week at Little River Light in Maine, a first for Logan, for whom the island was a little boy's paradise. We see God's love protecting us on our journeys. And, just maybe, He wants us to view the world through the enthusiasm of a child."

Karen Valentin writes, "A year ago I didn't know how I would pay for my sons to train as gymnasts. It seemed impossible, considering my income at the time. But God's faithfulness and my life as a single mother in New York City trained me well in the art of tackling the impossible. Scholarships, fund-raisers, and sacrifices kept them in the gym month after month, and their phenomenal progress proved it was worth it. The boys run to me after each competition, adorned with clinking medals. Each one is a reminder that my God is the giver of my strength, and with Him anything is possible."

Scott Walker of Macon, Georgia, writes: "This past year has been enjoyable and rich for the Walker family. Our son Luke was recently married to Jessica, a wonderful young woman from Brazil, and they now live close to us in Atlanta. Our two preschool grandchildren, Andrew and Alice Rushton, have taken center stage in our lives. Our daughter, Jodi, moved from Manhattan to Brooklyn, where she is a freelance entertainment writer. It is meaningful for me to see her blossoming as a writer and journalist. We realize increasingly that God's love is truly unfailing from generation to generation. And we are grateful!"

"My sweet Gene hasn't fully recovered from a broken hip/leg," writes **Marion Bond West** of Watkinsville, Georgia. "Three autoimmune diseases often cause me extreme exhaustion and pain. We had become snappy with each other or grimly silent. Gene and I began to attend marital counseling. Our thirty-year marriage had been phenomenally marvelous. We couldn't allow it to disintegrate into bitterness and unforgivingness. A godly counselor gave us an assignment at the end of our first session: make a list of ten things each of you do that makes the other feel loved. We began laughing spontaneously again. I admire Gene openly. He winked at me today!"

SCRIPTURE REFERENCE INDEX

ACTS
14:23, 239

CHRONICLES 1
16:33, 291
28:9, 83

COLOSSIANS
1:9-10, 271
2:6-7, 356
3:12, 374
3:13, 27, 295
3:17, 265
4:17, 321

CORINTHIANS 1
1:30, 211
2:16, 211
5:6, 42
5:7, 49
6:19, 109
8:2, 194
8:3, 323
10:16, 52
12:20, 151
12:27, 208
13:1, 383
13:2, 385
13:4, 7, 202
13:4, 7-8, 133
13:11, 319
13:12, 269
16:14, 20

CORINTHIANS 2
4:1, 78
5:17, 283
9:8, 203
9:10, 42
9:15, 350
12:10, 148

DANIEL
2:20, 32

DEUTERONOMY
3:22, 286
6:6-7, 85
11:19, 13
29:9, 352
31:8, 107, 169, 399
32:18, 307

ECCLESIASTES
3:1, 338

3:11, 90, 380
3:13, 207
4:6, 23
4:9-10, 29
4:12, 214
4:17, 58
7:8, 248
9:9, 26

EPHESIANS
2:10, 321
3:16, 379
3:17-18, 30
3:17-19, 66
4:1, 12, 327
4:32, 122
5:2, 259
6:7, 152

EXODUS
4:11-12, 282
14:14, 229
15:2, 6
20:3, 290
20:12, 75

EZEKIEL
11:19, 178
14:23, 71
36:26, 47, 243
38:7, 344

GALATIANS
5:25, 135
6:2, 260
6:9, 56
6:10, 292

GENESIS
22:8, 163

HEBREWS
1:14, 22
4:9, 10, 277
6:19, 115
10:24, 14
10:24-25, 378
11:1, 3, 201
12:1, 224

HOSEA
2:1, 347
6:6, 345

ISAIAH
2:4, 364
9:2, 393

11:6, 217
14:3, 351
30:21, 73
35:1, 61
40:11, 31
40:31, 190
41:10, 119, 297
42:1, 176
43:2, 308
43:4-5, 182
45:5, 222
45:8, 242
55:1, 134
55:8, 38, 337
57:2, 112
60:1, 317
62:6, 117

JAMES
1:17, 309, 377
1:19, 315
1:19-20, 263
2:10, 130
4:6, 87
4:14, 181
4:17, 174

JEREMIAH
10:23, 40
15:16, 53
29:5, 127
29:11, 108
31:3, 48, 301
31:25, 51, 74

JOB
2:13, 171
8:21, 147
14:7, 349
14:16, 25
16:20-21, 252
30:31, 254
37:6, 77
38:32-33, 246

JOEL
2:13, 273

JOHN
1:5, 353
1:16, 45
4:10, 14, 134
8:12, 185
8:32, 280
10:10, 89, 141

11:25, 341
13:5, 81
13:34, 63
14:2, 124
14:13-14, 36
14:26, 285
14:27, 156
15:12, 324
15:13, 346
15:15, 293
15:17, 303

JOHN 1
3:1, 69, 200, 389
4:7, 268
4:8, 336
4:19, 68

JOSHUA
1:9, 7

KINGS 1
8:28, 9
15:5, 376
17:6, 157

KINGS 2
19:14, 358

LAMENTATIONS
3:22-23, 116, 149, 227
3:26, 120, 388

LEVITICUS
26:4, 106

LUKE
1:35, 391
1:48, 51-52, 371
2:7, 369
2:14, 373
2:19, 146
2:37, 302
6:13, 144
6:21, 332
9:23, 84
9:62, 253
12:15, 270
12:32, 239
15:9, 118
20:17, 250
21:4, 188
22:42-43, 92
23:26, 247
23:34, 226

Scripture Reference Index

MARK
1:17, 91, 275
4:30-32, 140
4:40, 342
9:23, 82
9:37, 159
9:41, 261
10:45, 173
14:37, 79

MATTHEW
1:23, 17, 392
2:2, 395
5:7, 262
5:8, 294
5:9, 76
5:16, 158, 279
5:44, 382
5:44-45, 306
5:48, 180
6:11, 143, 272
6:14, 245
6:19, 381
6:33, 153, 235
7:2, 311
7:7, 386
7:11, 189, 236
9:12, 205
10:29, 164
10:29-31, 223
10:31, 322
11:28, 15
12:36, 126
13:27, 237
14:29, 363
17:20, 3
18:3, 175
19:14, 258
19:26, 276
20:28, 50
21:16, 114
22:30, 296
23:12, 191
25:35, 221, 293
25:40, 387
25:43, 325
28:20, 94, 111

MICAH
6:8, 155
7:19, 67

NEHEMIAH
8:10, 172

PETER 1
2:23, 80
4:8, 234
4:10, 348
5:5, 362

PHILIPPIANS
1:6, 93
3:10-11, 96
3:12, 88, 192
4:7, 177, 241

PROVERBS
3:3, 304
3:5, 137
3:13, 160, 365
3:34, 340
4:18, 316
10:1, 2
12:10, 210
13:7, 57
13:22, 238
14:29, 274
15:1, 10
15:4, 126
16:3, 397
16:24, 126
17:17, 213
18:4, 184
18:22, 129
18:24, 219
19:22, 70
21:2, 24
25:8, 287, 355
27:1, 154
27:17, 339
28:20, 186
31:22, 225
31:25, 60, 95
31:25-28, 305
31:26, 128

PSALMS
3:3, 343
18:1-3, 62
19:14, 249
23:4, 11
25:4, 197
26:2, 218
27:5, 216
27:14, 5
30:9, 150
31:24, 318
32:8, 110
33:22, III

34:4, 264
34:18, 357
36:5, 1
37:7, 354
39:6, 288
39:12, 105
46:1-2, 240
46:10, 246, 313, 370
51:8, 125
51:10, 376
51:12, 376
51:17, 139, 376
52:8, 167
54:4, 326
61:2, 314
63:1, 39
63:3, 390
68:17, 46
86:5, 335
86:15, 284
90:10, 196
90:14, 329
91:9-10, 187
95:4-5, 215
96:1, 251
96:11-12, 209, 244, 394
98:4, 204
103:3, 281
104:24, 289
105:2, 179
105:5, 310
107:1, 257
107:29, 375
116:15, 97
118:17, 138
118:24, 123, 136, 162
119:18, 361
119:76, 102
119:105, 59
131:2, 255
138:3, 4
138:8, 183
139:5, 43
139:7, 312
139:9-10, 19, 331
139:12, 19
139:13-14, 28
139:14, 193
139:17-18, 168

139:23-24, 218
143:8, 18
147:4, 228
149:3, 8
150:3, 37

ROMANS
2:1, 360
5:3, 220
5:8, 35, 161
6:5, 101
6:13, 195
8:18, 72, 103
8:26, 372
8:35, 100
10:17, 142
12:1, 16
12:6, 170
12:9-10, 41
12:12, 298, 384
12:13, 121, 396
12:18, 328
15:33, 330

SAMUEL 1
13:14, 376
SAMUEL 2
11:1, 86
SONG OF SOLOMON
2:15, 320
4:1, 21
8:7, 145

THESSALONIANS 1
5:11, 12, 256
5:17, 359
5:18, 62, 231
TIMOTHY 1
2:1, 278
2:1-3, 54
4:4, 212
4:14, 104
TIMOTHY 2
2:4, 206
2:13, 44
2:24, 113, 230

ZECHARIAH
4:10, 55
8:16, 398
3:17, 368

AUTHORS, TITLES AND SUBJECTS INDEX

Acceptance: of God's plans, 175; of help, 140; of oneself, 193; of one's limits, 84

Advent calendars, 392

Adversity: that stretches us, 220; walking through, together, 308

Al-Anon, 222

Alborghetti, Marci, *Falling into Grace* series, 6, 40, 71, 105, 140, 205, 273, 306, 342

Alcoholic, 38, 379

Alligator shoes, 316

Aloneness: counteracting others', 311

American Cemetery (Normandy, France), 173

Anchor, 115

Anorexia, 52, 84, 185

Apologizing: need for, 24

Appreciation: expressing, 102; for one's blessings, 288; for our daily networks, 292; for our fallen soldiers, 161; for those who provide our food, 272; of friends, 118, 124; of other people's efforts, 113

April showers, 106

Asking for what one needs, 386

Atonement, 369

Attaway, Julia, *Confidence in Difficulty* series, 52, 84, 150, 185, 251, 285, 318, 353

Attitude of gratitude, 356

Authenticity, 317

Baby teeth, 319, 338

Backing off, 10

Back pain, 11, 59, 78, 397

Back surgery, 220

Bad turned into good, 248

Barista, 20

Bauby, Jean-Dominique, 188

Beauty: despite imperfection, 390; revealed, 218; unexpected, 77

The Beauty of Simplicity series, 18, 57, 88, 120, 155, 191, 222, 257, 290, 323, 359, 388

Becoming a better teacher, 339

Befriending someone in need, 118

Being oneself, 28, 191

Being prepared, 344

Being present: amid the needs of others, 308

Being spiritually fit, 25

Being teachable, 12

Being there, 2, 119, 171

Being together, 214

Belonging, 389

Bence, Evelyn, 23, 162, 183, 292, 330, 347, 373

Bentsen, Erika, 11, 59, 78, 86, 220, 288, 344

Best, the: assuming in others, 355

Be still, 370

Bible, the: as our treasure, 280; focused time with, 235; love letters in, 53; seeking God in, 85

Bible study class, 339

Birds, 86, 125, 142, 164, 190, 223, 343

Bird's nest, 110

Blecker, Rhoda, 9, 58, 125, 147, 219, 286, 352

Blessings: being ready to receive, 217; giving thanks for our, 350; honoring our, 63; mothers as, 60; our loved ones as, 341; unlikely, 71

Blindness, 303

Blizzard, 7

Bogart, Lisa, 54, 151, 174, 229, 260, 360

Bottle of sand, 168

Box turtle, 210

Brokenness, 139

Brothers and sisters in Christ, 46

Building relationships, 41

Bullying, 30

Bunk bed, 193

Busyness, 26

Cancer, 4, 36, 90-97, 119, 216, 231, 305

Cape Cod, 230

Carburetor, 194

Car crash, 62

Card sending, 151

Careless words, 126

Caring, 127

Carrot patch, 213

Carrying each other's burdens, 260

Cats, 354

Ceding control, 40

Celebration: of freedom, 204; of life, 112; of love and commitment, 121; of the unexpected, 123; of those around us, 146

Change: embracing, 239, 240, 394; season of, 309

Charade parade, 321

Chariot races, 46

Childcare, 43

Children of God, 194

Children's book writer, 130

Choosing: to surrender, 92; what is right, 42

Christmas, 393

Christmas pageant, 391

Christmas photo, 395

Church community, 139, 205, 208, 239, 349

Ciancanelli, Sabra, 3, 37, 77, 127, 137, 168, 230, 245, 274, 326, 348, 397

Close call, 187

Closeness to God, 49

Collecting, 212

Collins, Mark, 79, 113, 194, 254, 296, 325

Community: of faith, 205; our comfort in, 29; sharing, 214

Compassion: acting with, 261; for our elected officials, 54; for the poor, 143; seeds of, 306; showing, 283

Computer, 292

Concentrating on the needs of neighbors, 252

Authors, Titles, and Subjects Index

Confidence in Difficulty series, 52, 84, 150, 185, 251, 285, 318, 353
Connecting with grown-up children, 388
Consolations: unexpected, 71
Contributing, 188
Cookies, 270
Costume party, 332
Counting steps, 25
Courage: to be who we are, 28, 93; to overcome heartbreak, 16
Creating a new tradition, 394
Crisis, 375
Cuckoo clock, 274
Cutting hair, 216

Dance, 8
Daring the unfamiliar, 111
David (sculpture), 250
D-Day, 173
"Dear Ones," 347
Death: as an open window, 223
Depression, 191
Determination, 16
Diaz, Pablo, 24, 114, 152, 256, 309, 337
Dilworth, John, 56, 73, 190, 227, 346
Disappointment, 326
Discard-it state of mind, 23
Disconnection, 323
The Diving Bell and the Butterfly, 188
Dogs, 10, 27, 77, 122, 136, 171, 271, 287, 289, 355, 359
Doing the right thing, 155
Donating clothes, 225
Downtime, 29
Doyle, Brian, 32, 128, 145, 186, 202, 262, 305, 336, 399
Dragging and dropping, 241
Dreams, 58
Drive-in movie, 238
Driving lesson, 360
Driving under the influence, 61, 310

Eagles, 190
Easter, 101
Easter decorations, 68
Eddings, Amy, 38, 47, 163, 340
Eliasen, Logan, 45, 85, 265, 282, 313, 338
Eliasen, Shawnelle, 14, 69, 103, 161, 177, 218, 235, 280, 312, 389
Embracing life, 181
Empathy, 306
Emptiness, 39
Encouragement: of friends facing hard times, 151; of kids in trouble, 56; of one another, 256; of one's family, 347; of others' faith, 107; of our spiritual friends, 14; of those who have stumbled, 61
Engagement, 337
Estate planning, 156
Eternal life: our promise of, 101, 138
Evers, Medgar, 16
Ever true to God, 376
"Excepts," 376

Face painting, 158
Faith: and the possible, 82; as belief in what is unseen, 3; holding on to, 6; in all circumstances, 150; in healing, 259; lessons in, 59; shaken by death, 254; strengthening one's, 103; that shapes God's answers to our prayers, 385
Faithfulness, 186
Falling into Grace series, 6, 40, 71, 105, 140, 205, 273, 306, 342
"Family," 378
Family ties, 347, 358
Fathers, 184
Fear: conquering, 192, 286; defeated by the truth, 257; of inadequacy, 282; of what we don't understand, 137

Feeding the hungry, 221
Fellowship, 139, 144, 208
Final arrangements, 112
Fire, 349
The First Day of Creation (needlepoint), 219
"Fleas," 231
Florist, 283
Fly fishing, 160, 214
Focusing: on God, 88, 246; on the positive, 162
Following Jesus, 91
Foot surgery, 331
Forgiveness: and forgetting, 67; asking for, 24; choosing, 27; freeing nature of, 217; healing through, 245; our, 226; power of, 295; sharing, 80; without hesitation, 263
Foster, Sharon, 16, 143, 217, 243, 327
Freedom: celebrating, 204; found in obedience, 163
Friendliness, 20
Friendship: 80% of the time, 48; offering, 293; renewing, 229; restored, 295

Garden center, 265
Garmon, Julie, *The Beauty of Simplicity* series, 18, 57, 88, 120, 155, 191, 222, 257, 290, 323, 359, 388
Generosity, 9
Gentleness, 256
Getting right back up, 74
Gift-giving, 380
Gift(s): a neighbor as a, 395; caring as a, 127; cherishing our unique, 170; Christmas as a, 393; each day as a, 123, 149; everyday, of grace, 361; forgiveness as a, 80; from the heart, 22; grace as a, 76; Jesus's incarnation as a, 392; laughter as a, 147; music as a, 179; our friends

as, 219; peace as a, 156; play as a, 207; service as a, 155; sharing our, 104, 348; unexpected, 176

Giovannetti, Bill, 116, 192, 211, 255, 277, 324, 361, 383

Giving: confidence, 21; to the needy, 316

Giving thanks: despite setbacks, 342; for food, 143; for friends, 124; for God's provision, 196; for good health, 154; for medical professionals, 152; for mothers, 145; for our "fleas," 231; for our blessings, 350, 356; for spring, 86; for those who died on D-Day, 173; for veterans, 206

Giving up and turning to God, 153

Godly living, 70

God's all-knowingness, 323

God's beauty, 106

God's blessings, 277

God's bounty, 203

God's care, 31, 164

God's closeness, 32

God's creation, 215, 219, 244, 271, 314

God's encouragement, 286

God's faithfulness, 312

God's forgiveness, 263

God's generosity, 189

God's gifts, 209, 377

God's glory, 246

God's goodness, 78, 223

God's grace, 130, 281, 324

God's greatness, 158

God's guidance, 110, 153, 190, 227, 251, 309

God's handiwork, 291

God's hands, 40

God's light, 185, 353

God's love: cosmic ocean of, 336; despite our brokenness, 390; despite our flaws, 362,

371; even in our disbelief, 184; expressions of, 44; extravagance of, 69; healing through, 259; price of, 50; protective, 52; that saves, 379; that stretches our hearts, 382

God's mercy, 84, 116, 262

God's miracles, 327

God's path, 59

God's patience, 329

God's peace, 15, 177, 216, 328

God's plan, 55, 205, 273, 318, 326, 337, 342

God's presence, 4, 17, 94, 111, 169, 310, 351, 393, 397

God's promise, 282

God's protection, 182, 187

God's provision, 108, 297

God's reassurance, 243

God's sight, 211

God's steadfastness, 183

God's strength, 313

God's teaching, 285

God's timing, 7, 306, 338, 370, 380

God's unchangeableness, 240

God's voice, 142

God's ways, 38, 57

God's will, 36

God's wisdom, 340, 365

God's wonders, 125, 212, 289

God's Word, 134

God the Knower, 399

The Golden Rule (mosaic), 364

Good Friday, 96

Grace: everyday gifts of, 361; moving ahead with, 230

Graduate degree program, 163

"Grandma's House," 214

Grandmothering, 120, 362

Gratitude: attitude of, 356; showing, 102

Grief, 44, 97

Grinnan, Edward, 10, 60, 81, 109, 122, 187, 210, 249, 271, 328, 345, 379

Groceries, 272

Growing older, 109, 196, 302

Growing up, 271

Growing younger, 175

Growth, 103

Guardian angels, 22

Guggenheim Museum, 294

Gymnastics, 108

Hairspray, 195

Hamlin, Rick, 19, 46, 67, 129, 144, 179, 208, 241, 278, 315, 363, 395

"Handsome is as handsome does," 70

Happiness: catching, 160

Healing: having faith in, 259; invisible wounds and, 281; shared, 78; through forgiveness, 245; through kindness, 261

Heart-shaped mirror, 390

Help: asking for, 157, 247; with a gentle heart, 260

Helpers, 387

Henderson, Wesley, 179

Hendricks, Carla, 63, 89, 106, 258, 341

Henry, Kim, 30, 173, 184, 226, 289, 371

Hibiscus, 149

Hiking, 224

Hinch, Jim, 7, 176, 215, 240; *Light in Our Darkness* series, 370, 377, 384, 391, 392, 393

Holding grudges, 217

Holy Saturday, 97

Home purchase, 227

Homeless, the, 297, 304, 322

Honor flight, 346

Honoring veterans, 346

Hope, 101, 159, 318, 325

Horses, 27, 195

Hospitality: everyday, 88; practicing, 396

House for sale, 277

Humiliation, 340

Humility, 374

Authors, Titles, and Subjects Index

Hunger, 143
Husband and wife: and prayer together, 298, 359; communication between, 26; forgiveness between, 129; kindness between, 155; love between, 202

Identity, 73
Iguanas, 102
Inadequacy, 282
Inattentiveness, 79
Independence Day, 204
Inspiration, 250
"I want my face back," 269

Jamba Juice, 203
Job search, 74
Job skills program, 56
Journeying intentionally, 90
Joy, children's, 172
Judging: too quickly, 360; without knowing, 357
Jumper cables, 324
Jumping to conclusions, 287

Kappel, Ashley, 146, 169, 209, 242, 317
Keep calm and carry on, 375
Kidd, Brock, 26, 160, 214, 238, 304, 365
Kidd, Pam, 53, 87, 228, 248, 279, 316, 351
Kindness: healing through, 261; learning new ways of, 374; of a stranger, 330; receiving, 238
King, Jr., Dr. Martin Luther, 16
King David, 376
Kirk, Patty, 17, 43, 72, 142, 175, 180, 311, 343, 385
Knapp, Carol, 42, 107, 126, 134, 246, 293, 321, 358, 376
Knitting, 362
Knowing when to ask for help, 247
Knox, Henry, 82

Knox, John, 135
Kuykendall, Carol, 398; *Preparing for the Resurrection* series, 90-97, 101
Kuyper, Vicki, 31, 123, 157, 193, 224, 291

Late-night snack, 374
Laughter: as a gift, 147; practicing, 95; when faced by embarrassment, 332
Law school, 282, 313
Leaking plumbing, 116
Learning: from our children, 37; how to fall, 326
Lemonade, 159
Less unbelief, 278
Letters in a trunk, 358
Letting go: of earthly treasures, 225; of our children, 255, 319; of the past, 45; of worry, 228
Letting God be God, 222
Life: preciousness of, 62
Light in Our Darkness series, 370, 377, 384, 391, 392, 393
Listening, 119, 315
"Little foxes," 320
Little things, 81
Living in a construction zone, 284
Loneliness, 39, 94
Lorenz, Patricia, 22, 50, 102, 112, 252, 272, 332, 364, 374
Lost first tooth, 319
Love: a friend's, 213; as reason for our existence, 128; between husband and wife, 202; for one's neighbors, 364; for our children, 32; for the creatures of this earth, 210; for your neighbor, 325; from a child, 120; in relationships, 398; looking with, 303; not hate, 328; offered generously, 307; of

life, 188; practicing, 47, 75; reminders of, 381; ringing out, 383; shared by family, 68; showing, 122; undying, 399
Love letters, 53
Low-mileage car, 276
Lung infection, 19

Macomber, Debbie, 25, 135, 156, 331, 356, 369
MacPherson, Erin, 172, 263, 284, 355; *Relying on God's Unfailing Love* series, 4, 36, 119, 216, 231
Making a difference, 151
Marriage: as a foreign country, 296
Mattering, 279
Maundy Thursday, 95
Meaning well, 355
Mementos, 381
Memorable moments, 321
Memorial Day, 161
Men's breakfast, 144
Mentoring, 275
Mercy, 345
Messner, Roberta, 20, 48, 124, 141, 276, 307, 350, 357, 382
Middle school, 264
Mindfulness, 168
Minyan, 352
Miraculous moments, 397
Misperception, 269
Missing a loved one, 341
Monster truck cake, 201
Moose, 244
Morning routine, 329
Mother-love, 305
Mothers, 21, 60, 145
Mother's Day, 146
Mother Teresa, 273
Mountaintop getaways, 314
Mourner's kaddish, 352
Mourning, 58, 254
Moving ahead with grace, 230

Moving toward the light, 185
MRI, 384
Mustard seed, 3

Nails, 50
Nashville, 304
Nativity sets, 369
Neighbors: loving one's, 364;
 needs of, 252
New beginning, 55
Nose operation, 351
Nursery duty, 15

Ocean, 312
Ondov, Rebecca, 27, 117, 195,
 259, 287, 390
One Grain of Rice (book), 42
Opening ourselves to the new, 197
Opportunities: recognizing,
 5; seeing little, 81; to be
 a helper, 387; to build
 community, 174; to give
 back, 75; to let goodness
 shine through us, 265
Ornaments, 371
"Overtime," 302

Palm Sunday, 91
Paper cut, 9
Parenting: flawed, 362; good,
 13; worry in, 385
Participating, 141
Patience, 274, 284, 354, 384
Pausing to be with God, 51
Peace: as a gift, 156
Peacemaking, 76
Pecan pie, 357
Perkins, Natalie, 29, 41, 75,
 203, 294, 386
Perseid meteor shower, 246
Perseverance, 74, 89, 148, 224
Perspective, 242
Photography, 291
Pinata, 373
Pirates, 280
Pity party, 157

Pollination, 170
Pool, 169
Porcelain kitchen table, 307
Positive, the: finding, 162
Power outage, 235
Practicing mercy, 345
Prayer: and our "God to
 handle" file, 241; any way,
 105; being continually
 in, 135; children's, 114;
 dance as a, 8; feeling, 11;
 for elected officials, 54;
 for less unbelief, 278; for
 one another, 359; for one
 minute every morning, 236;
 for strength and patience,
 298; for those who hurt, 30;
 for wrongdoers, 80; healing
 through, 19; intercessory,
 372; a mother's, 264; secret,
 17
Prayer reminder, 83, 117
Praying Hands (Albrecht Durer),
 221
Pre-Cana classes, 296
Preoccupation, 79
Preparing for the Resurrection
 series, 90-97, 101
Present, the: living fully in, 58,
 136, 149
Procrastination, 154
Progress, 72
"Purpose in life," 311

Quietening one's mind, 384
Quiet moments, 195

Racial reconciliation, 243
Rain, 106, 242
Rainbows, 176
Ranch, 288
Reaching out, 122
Reading: joy of, 377
Receiving: as well as giving, 157;
 kindness, 238
Refueling, 344

Regrets, 93, 194
Relationships: fixing our, 320;
 love in, 398
Relying on God's Unfailing Love
 series, 4, 36, 119, 216, 231
Renewing one's commitment to
 God, 49
Re-seeing, 180
Resting, 313
Restoration: of friendship, 295
Retirement, 276
Revealing our hearts, 294
Revision, 180
Rhubarb, 162
Right to vote, 63
Rue, Ginger, 15, 80, 130, 189,
 269
Run for Hope (marathon), 89
Runner sled, 389
Running "right," 343

Salvation Army bell, 383
"Saturday Place," 107
Saying grace, 114
Schantz, Daniel, 13, 44, 70,
 159, 178, 204, 247, 281,
 320
Schilling, Gail Thorell, 2, 76,
 104, 138, 170, 213, 261,
 270, 314, 362, 381
School lunch program, 279
Schwab, Penney, 118, 164, 171,
 196, 225, 239, 298, 372
Second chances, 180
Secrets, 128
Seeing ourselves with God's
 sight, 211
Self-acceptance, 193
Self-confidence, 201
Self-discipline, 270
Self-image, 322
Self-improvement, 237
Self-righteousness, 360
Senior citizens, 196
Serving: at-risk children, 258
Setbacks, 342

Authors, Titles, and Subjects Index

Sharing: by listening, 315; more deeply, 47; our gifts, 104, 348

Sherrill, Elizabeth, 21, 82, 111, 148, 188, 221, 250, 303, 349, 375

Shetland Islands (Scotland), 123

Silence: embracing, 97; power of, 354

Silent Saturday, 97

Silver cross overlaying Star of David, 117

Simplicity, 57

Skunk, 361

Sleepaway camp, 240

Slowing down, 109, 142

Snakes, 137

Snow, 77

Soccer, 172

Social media, 290, 317

Socks, 363

Sonora Pass, 215

Soup kitchen, 221

"Spider!," 286

Spiritual renewal, 331

Spring, 86

Spring water, 134

Spur-of-the-moment lunch, 396

Sri Lanka, 87

Standing together, 352

Star Trek: The Next Generation (TV show), 325

State fair, 178

Stepping out in love and faith, 174

Stickers, 330

Stop, look, smell, listen, 136

Stretching beyond oneself, 220

Striving to be your best self, 275

Struggling, 72

Successful life, 365

Suffering: enduring, 96

Summer play, 207

Sunset, 209

"Sunset deck," 248

Support group, 310

Surrendering to God's will, 92

Surviving, 285

Swang, Melody Bonnette, 49, 74, 121, 153, 283, 387

Swearing, 249

Sweeney, Jon, 51, 62, 83, 136, 182, 244, 322, 378

Swimming, 148

Swing set, 182

Tablet, 12

Taking a break: from social media, 290; to pray, 51

Taking a chance, 87

Talent show, 348

"Teachable moment," 197

Teachable Moments (book), 327

ten Boom, Corrie, 231

Tending one's spirit, 23

Thanksgiving, 357

Thinking twice before reacting, 332

Thompson, Stephanie, 5, 55, 181, 207, 264, 302, 380

Time with friends, 229

Tomatoes, 127

Tournament of Roses Parade, 2

Trampoline, 177

Trumpet player, 37

Trust in God, 6, 18, 43, 115, 137, 163, 164, 175, 201, 228, 257

Trying new things, 178

Turk, Marilyn, 68, 154, 212, 237, 329, 339

Tutu Fantasy (watercolor), 31

Twenty-four-hour hold, 227

Unpredictability of life, 181

"Uptown Funk" (video), 141

Vacation Bible school, 183

Valentin, Karen, 8, 39, 108, 158, 201, 295, 319, 394

Valentines, 48

Veterans, 206

Veterans Day, 346

Vukovar, Croatia, 226

Vulnerability, 294

Waiting, 5, 370

Walk of the Patient One, 224

Walker, Scott, 28, 115, 149, 197, 223, 253, 275, 308

Walking, 154, 174;

Walking in Jesus's footsteps, 363

Weaning, 255

Wedding, 57

Wedding anniversary, 129

Wedding reception, 121

Weeds, 237

Welcoming God's son, 391

West, Marion Bond, 12, 61, 110, 139, 206, 236, 297, 310, 354, 396

What's really important, 242

Whittling, 218

Who you are vs. what you do, 73

Willing spirit, 79

Willow tree, 247

Work of our hands, 373

Working at love, 41

Worry: vs. trust, 18, 228

Yelling, 67

Zip-lining, 192

A NOTE FROM THE EDITORS

We hope you enjoyed *Daily Guideposts 2018*, published by the Books and Inspirational Media Division of Guideposts, a nonprofit organization that touches millions of lives every day through products and services that inspire, encourage, help you grow in your faith, and celebrate God's love.

Thank you for making a difference with your purchase of this book, which helps fund our many outreach programs to military personnel, prisons, hospitals, nursing homes, and educational institutions.

We also create many useful and uplifting online resources. Visit Guideposts.org to read true stories of hope and inspiration, access OurPrayer network, sign up for free newsletters, download free e-books, join our Facebook community, and follow our stimulating blogs. To delve more deeply into *Daily Guideposts*, visit DailyGuideposts.org.

You may purchase the 2019 edition of *Daily Guideposts* anytime after July 2018. To order, visit Guideposts.org/DG2019, call (800) 932-2145, or write to Guideposts, PO Box 5815, Harlan, Iowa 51593.